Experiential Exercises and Cases in
MANAGEMENT

McGraw-Hill Series in Management

KEITH DAVIS and FRED LUTHANS, CONSULTING EDITORS

ALLEN Management and Organization

ALLEN The Management Profession

ARGYRIS Management and Organizational Development: The Path from XA to YB

BECKETT Management Dynamics: The New Synthesis

BENTON Supervision and Management

BERGEN and HANEY Organizational Relations and Management Action

BLOUGH International Business: Environment and Adaptation

BOWMAN Management: Organization and Planning

BROWN Judgment in Administration

CAMPBELL, DUNNETTE, LAWLER, and WEICK Managerial Behavior, Performance and Effectiveness

CLELAND and KING Management: A Systems Approach

CLELAND and KING Systems Analysis and Project Management

CLELAND and KING Systems, Organizations, Analysis, Management: A Book of Readings

DALE Management: Theory and Practice

DALE Readings in Management: Landmarks and New Frontiers

DAVIS Human Behavior at Work: Human Relations and Organizational Behavior

DAVIS Organizational Behavior: A Book of Readings

DAVIS and BLOMSTROM Business and Society: Environment and Responsibility

DeGREENE Systems Psychology

DUNN and RACHEL Wage and Salary Administration: Total Compensation Systems

DUNN and STEPHENS Management of Personnel: Manpower Management and Organizational Behavior

EDMUNDS and LETEY Environmental Administration

FIEDLER A Theory of Leadership Effectiveness

FINCH, JONES, and LITTERER Managing for Organizational Effectiveness: An Experiential Approach

Experiential Exercises and Cases in
MANAGEMENT

Fremont E. Kast

James E. Rosenzweig

Graduate School of Business Administration
University of Washington

McGRAW-HILL BOOK COMPANY

New York   St. Louis   San Francisco   Auckland   Düsseldorf
Johannesburg   Kuala Lumpur   London   Mexico   Montreal   New Delhi
Panama   Paris   São Paulo   Singapore   Sydney   Tokyo   Toronto

**Experiential Exercises and Cases
in MANAGEMENT**

Copyright © 1976 by McGraw-Hill, Inc.
All rights reserved.
Printed in the United States of America.
No part of this publication may be reproduced, stored in a retrieval system,
or transmitted, in any form or by any means,
electronic, mechanical, photocopying, recording, or otherwise,
without the prior written permission of the publisher.

2 3 4 5 6 7 8 9 0 B A B A 7 8 3 2 1 0 9 8 7

This book was set in Press Roman by Creative Book Services,
subsidiary of McGregor & Werner, Inc.
The editors were William J. Kane and Edwin Hanson;
the cover was done by Nicholas Krenitsky;
the production supervisor was Angela Kardovich.
George Banta Company, Inc., was printer and binder.

Library of Congress Cataloging in Publication Data

Kast, Fremont Ellsworth, date
Experiential exercises and cases in management

(McGraw-Hill series in management).
1. Management. 2. Organization. I. Rosenzweig,
James Erwin, date joint author. II. Title.
HD31.K333   658.4   76-187
ISBN 0-07-033343-2

Contents

Preface

Organizations are not distant, impersonal phenomena detached from our daily lives. They are everywhere, and they affect all of us. The informal social group, the athletic team, the corner store, the Sierra Club, the National Organization of Women, the United Farm Workers, McGraw-Hill Book Company, General Motors, and the United Nations are all organizations. And they are all managed, some better than others.

However, it is apparent that many students view textbooks on organization and management as dealing with abstract issues, far removed from reality—from their own experiences. Many excellent textbooks help provide a body of knowledge about organizations and their management but frequently do not relate the concepts and ideas directly to everyday experience.

This book, *Experiential Exercises and Cases in Management*, is dedicated to the view that the study of organizations and their management can be interesting, exciting, and directly related to our observable world. The experiential exercises and cases are designed to facilitate a learning process in which the content of what is to be learned is experienced as directly as possible by the participant. This book is intended to serve as a complement to existing organization and management texts. It is hoped that students will utilize the concepts gained from studying the cognitive materials presented in texts as a knowledge base for experiencing and reflecting on reality-oriented classroom exercises, cases, and field observations.

In our efforts to facilitate the learning of undergraduates, graduate students, and practicing managers, we have seen the need to develop means whereby students can apply ideas and practice skills. The 25 exercise units in this book cover a wide variety of issues in organization and management. They utilize various approaches: cases, in-class exercises, field observations, survey instruments, discussion of current events, and comparative analysis. Obviously, they cannot begin to cover all the issues that could be regarded as relevant for organizations and their management. They do consider environmental, societal, economic, technological, and structural factors as well as behavioral and human relations issues. Management is not just "dealing with people" (although this is of major importance); it involves many other factors. This book is not limited to organizational behavior and human relations but tries to encompass the whole range of organizational issues and managerial activities.

We are aware of the changes taking place in regard to the roles and relationships of minorities and women in organizations and throughout our society. Although some of the issues and conflicts resulting from these changes may be "uncomfortable" at times, we have tried to deal with them directly in several exercises. We personally believe that the increased number of minorities and women moving into managerial positions in many of our organizations and institutions is a healthy trend; we hope it will accelerate.

The problem of sex bias is still evident in much of the management literature—assuming a male in the role of manager or executive and females in subordinate or helping positions. We have consciously tried to eliminate such bias in this book by using more current cases and exercises that illustrate women in managerial and professional positions. Any lapses from this endeavor are inadvertent.

We are indebted to many colleagues and students for helping in the development of this book. It is often difficult to acknowledge the original source of ideas for many of the exercises. Most are original, but several are adaptations of existing materials. Fortunately, there has developed a rather elaborate network for sharing ideas on cases, exercises, teaching approaches, and other materials in the field of organization and management. However, the exact origins of ideas often are not well documented. We have participated in various meetings, workshops, and informal sessions with colleagues and students where ideas and concepts were shared. Many of them have found their way into this book. Where possible, we have identified the original sources of the concepts for the various exercises, but we know that there are many unacknowledged contributors.

We have used these exercises in our classes and in executive training programs. The participants have contributed many ideas for refining the cases, exercises, and other materials after testing the various units. Their feedback has been very helpful. We have used a number of short readings within the exercises to provide additional information. We are grateful to the authors and publishers for letting us use this material. A number of ideas for exercises were inspired by articles in our local newspapers—the *Seattle Times*, the *Seattle Post-Intelligencer*, and the University of Washington *Daily*. Their editors have graciously permitted us to use these materials.

We appreciate the resources made available by the Graduate School of Business Administration, University of Washington. Special thanks are due Nancy Pearson, Sheryl Rosenzweig, and Sandra Goodman.

Fremont E. Kast
James E. Rosenzweig

Experiential Exercises and Cases in
MANAGEMENT

Introduction

Jack Andrews was looking out the window at the ship canal and Lake Washington. It was a gray, over-cast day; he was in University Hospital and his leg hurt like hell. He could see the cars and students arriving for the first day of classes of Winter Quarter. The clock indicated that it was only 7:20 a.m., but it already seemed to be one of the longest days of his life. Maybe it was time for a short nap—he hadn't slept much all night. As he began dozing off, he thought about the past few days. . . .

After his first quarter in the School of Business Administration, he was financially strapped; he had seriously underestimated the costs of attending the university. It had been a lot less expensive living at home and going to the local community college for his first two years. Anyhow, he had just barely made it through Autumn Quarter and final examinations week. Thank God he was able to get a short-term job before Christmas working at the post office sorting the Christmas mail. What an experience! He had no idea that a large city post office could be so busy and confusing. He had heard a lot about governmental inefficiencies, but all the old-timers certainly worked plenty hard, at least during the Christmas season. He was sure glad he didn't have to look forward to that type of work for the rest of his life. It was almost as bad as the summer he worked in the pea cannery in Walla Walla—but that's another story.

The post office job had given him a few bucks with enough surplus to go skiing for a few days in the Cascades. He had been skiing several times before, but it hadn't come naturally. He knew a little instruction might help, so he signed up with the Rainier Ski School for a series of lessons. It had been raining when he left for the pass, but the rain had turned to a light snow by the time he got to the top of the lift with the other 10 members of the class and the instructor. Things had gone OK at first—except that the instructor kept yelling at him to do the opposite of what came naturally. He had made a few half-way decent stem turns to the right, and was getting the feel. But, then it happened! He had finished his turn and had just climbed back up the hill to take his place in the line of students, when out of the snow came the hotdog, obviously out of control. He hit Jack, who in turn flew into the rest of the group—wiping out at least six or seven in one crash. Jack thought he had it made after he survived the first hit, but somehow his leg got twisted and he felt the sickening snap. He must have blacked out for a few moments because the next thing he remembered was the Ski Patrol setting up the crossed skis. Somebody was bringing up the basket and Jack finally realized it was for him. "My God, I've seen them take casualties off the hill in those things and hoped it would never happen to me." Fortunately, the two guys and the girl in the Mountain Ski Patrol seemed to know what to do, and the ride down the hill wasn't so bad. His leg hurt so much that he really didn't care what else happened; even the clods gawking at him from the chair lift didn't bother him.

Once in the ski hut someone gave him a shot which relieved the pain. Later he found out that it was a doctor who had been skiing and was on call with the Doctors Emergency Service. Someone called the Washington State Patrol, which arranged for an ambulance from North Bend and also somehow took care of getting his VW driven back to Seattle. The 60-mile ambulance ride was uneventful, but Jack kept thinking to himself, "Good God, all this when I was standing completely still minding my own business." He wondered if anyone else was hurt, but no one seemed to know.

By the time he arrived at the emergency entrance of University Hospital, it was after 9 p.m. on Sunday night. He didn't feel too bad but he couldn't help wondering whether there would be anyone there to take care of him. He had heard of the doctor shortage and problems of getting adequate emergency treatment. Although he had to wait about 45 minutes in the emergency room because there perhaps were others more seriously injured than he, it wasn't too bad. Several people in white suits came by (interns, he assumed) to look at him, but they didn't do much. They didn't seem to be much concerned. "Wonder what it would take to get them excited?" By then he was pretty doped up but he did remember seeing the doctor come in, getting x-rayed, and learning that he had a spiral break of the left tibia. Guess they must have set it OK because the next thing he remembered was being awakened by the usual hospital sounds at 6 a.m., with his leg in a cast and feeling sick all over.

The nurse brought him back to reality by taking his pulse and temperature. "Wow—I have a broken leg; what are they doing this for?" She seemed much too cheerful and soon left. Jack had some uneasy feelings that he might need the john. "Wonder how we deal with that?" He had thought he could wait awhile, so he hadn't mentioned it.

"How could this happen to me? It couldn't come at a worse time. I signed up for 18 credits (knowing I wouldn't get them all), and the computer printout came back indicating that I would have only 9 hours of classes because the rest were filled or had been canceled." He had planned to contact the advisor early this morning and go sit on the doorsteps of several professors, hoping to get two additional classes. He had to complete 135 hours by the end of his junior year so that he would have a chance for one of the few accounting internships which were coming up for next summer. If he were really lucky, he might get some good experience which would help him land a permanent job with Arthur Andersen or one of the other big CPA firms after he graduated. But now everyone else was getting the only open classes, and he was lying here, SOL. But, at least he would have a visible cast so that professors might let him in their classes and go easy on him for awhile. A better reason for being late than those guys who go to Hawaii for the vacation and come back a week late with telltale tans.

"Let's see. Out of the 9 hours which I am scheduled for, I have a 3-credit class in intermediate accounting, 3 hours of business economics, and a course in organization and management. I can understand what accounting and economics are all about and can see their relevance. But what about this course in organization and management? It's required, so I might as well get it over with so I can concentrate on my major. I guess that management is pretty important, but it really won't be for me when I first graduate, and I can learn enough about it when the time comes. And organizations? Who needs them that much, and especially who needs to study them for a whole quarter?"

Wait a minute, Jack! Think back on your reflections this morning and the number of organizations that you came into contact with over the past several days, or those that you are concerned with for the future. Let's see now; here are just a few of them:

The hospital
The U.S. Post Office

The Quality Pea Cannery
The Rainier Ski School
The Mountain Ski Patrol
The Doctors Emergency Service
The Washington State Highway Patrol
The North Bend Ambulance Service
The Emergency Center
The university
The local community college
The summer internship program
Your future work organization(s)

Jack's relationships had been better with some of these organizations than with others, and maybe they all weren't the model of efficiency. But many of them were vital to his current and future well-being. They all had to operate with a certain level of effectiveness in order to accomplish their objectives. And, in many cases, the performance of their functions was really important to him. Although Jack had come in contact with or thought about each of these organizations, he had personally experienced only a small part of their total functions. On reflection, he would admit that these organizations and their activities did not occur by chance. A large number of people were involved in carrying out the various tasks and in planning and coordinating the activities. Somehow, these organizations were managed; somehow, they performed a variety of functions.

But, this is all too much for Jack to worry about now. Besides, his leg hurts and his bladder is bulging and he wonders how he is going to cope with that problem. Come to think about it, in every organization he has joined, it has taken him some time to learn how he should behave and how things were done. Let's see, there must be a button here to get that nurse—maybe it will be a male nurse and then it should be easier.

WHAT THIS BOOK IS ABOUT

This book is concerned with organizations and their management. Although they are not so traumatic as Jack's experiences, we all have many contacts with organizations, and they have a tremendous impact on our society.

Hundreds of thousands of business enterprises provide goods and services. Millions of students spend a great deal of time in schools. Governments at all levels contain many agencies that perform a wide variety of functions and activities. Hospitals, unions, churches, prisons, bowling teams, Disneyland, and the Rose Bowl Committee are part of the vast array of organizations which exist in our society. The study of these organizations and their management is important, if for no other reason than they are so much a part of our lives.

A significant body of knowledge has been developed to help us understand organizations and to help people become more effective managers. Much of this knowledge has been contributed by practitioners—past and current managers/administrators of many different types of organizations. Knowledge has also come from the more academic, theoretical side through empirical research and conceptualization. This accumulated knowledge about organizations and their management is available to students in many existing textbooks, tradebooks, magazines, and newspapers. Students, such as Jack, can learn a great deal from studying these knowledge-oriented sources.

EXPERIENTIAL LEARNING

However, "book learning," although valuable in many respects, cannot totally replace learning which comes from experience and the application of knowledge. *Experiential learning* is an essential complement to conceptual or knowledge-oriented learning. For example, Jack can learn a substantial amount about hospitals in the next few days if he really observes what is happening around him. In fact, he would have a fairly good course in organization and management if he could spend a few weeks observing each of the 12 or 13 organizations he was thinking about earlier. He would certainly know even more about the subject if he were to be employed in each of these organizations for a longer period. Practical experience in organizations does help us learn a good deal about their operations and management.

Unfortunately, personal experiences take considerable time, and we could spend a lifetime understanding only one or a very few organizations. Besides, doesn't it seem a waste of time requiring each student of organizations to reinvent the wheel? There are many knowledge-based concepts about organizations and their management which we can learn about without first-hand experience. We do have substantial knowledge about leadership styles, motivation, organization structure, group dynamics, and planning and control processes, for example, which can be learned "from the book." However, for more effective learning, this knowledge should be complemented with more direct involvement and personal experience. But, how do we get this personal involvement for students in a classroom situation?

This book is focused toward that objective—that of trying to help bridge the gap between knowledge-based learning and learning based on practical experience. Experiential learning is designed to provide a classroom climate in which students can experience relevant situations and participate in the application of the concepts which comprise the body of knowledge.

The contrast between the conceptual approach (knowledge-oriented learning) and the experiential approach is fundamental in the training of professionals in many fields. Medical students must learn a great deal of the existing knowledge in their specific fields of specialization. However, this knowledge is complemented by active experiential learning in a clinical environment. During internship, the student is observing real medical patients and applying knowledge. The law student learns concepts and facts from books, but also experiences actual or simulated situations. A significant part of the training involves observing the courtroom and other legal processes and helping work up "real" cases. The education of practicing professionals in every field should provide an effective integration of conceptual and experiential learning.

More specifically, the question in the study of organizations and their management relates to the issue of whether management is a science or an art. The view that management is a science suggests that emphasis should be placed on understanding all the currently available knowledge about it (through textbooks and lecture-discussion). The view that management is an art suggests that the only way to learn is through actual experience, application, and practice. It is our view that management is both a science *and* an art. (There is nothing as practical as a theory that works!) The growing body of knowledge about organizations and their management can be transmitted through study by oneself or in a group. It is neither necessary nor advisable for students of management to rely on personal experiences alone. Such learning would be time-consuming and limited. At the same time, it is questionable that all knowledge about management can be learned by reading text materials. While a text can provide conceptual and background knowledge, the real world of the manager is often more complex, confusing, and uncertain than can be covered via typical texts and lecture-discussion methods. Just as medical students can learn through taking their body of knowledge into the clinical environment, so can students of management enhance their learning by application in real or simulated situations.

Ideally, experiential learning should occur in the actual setting of the practicing manager. Certainly we know that managers in business and other types of organization are continually learning through experience. However, it is difficult to integrate this type of experiential learning into the classroom. Continuing education is a rapidly growing endeavor in our society, and an important segment of this education is executive development and training programs that bring practicing managers back into a university environment where they can relate their experience to conceptual knowledge. However, this process is more difficult to achieve for undergraduate and graduate students in management.

The alternative, which we have used in this book, is to attempt to bring experiential learning into the classroom. The primary emphasis is on learning from the student's own experiences and observations. The exercises provide situations in which students can become directly involved. They are generally action-oriented in that individuals or groups of students make decisions, develop action plans, and then implement them during the exercise.

The exercises are different from a more traditional case approach in which the instructor leads the discussion and remains the center of the communication process. We have stressed student involvement, with the instructor playing a facilitating role rather than being a focal point. We anticipate that this workbook will be used in conjunction with a text in organization and management which will provide the basic conceptual knowledge. Therefore, we have included a minimum amount of such material. In some of the exercises and cases, we have included short excerpts or readings. These readings stress application of knowledge and relate to the specific learning objectives of the exercises. They emphasize the relevance of the learning experience to actual situations.

OUR KNOWLEDGE ABOUT ORGANIZATIONS AND THEIR MANAGEMENT

In the development of this book, we have assumed that students will have a foundation of conceptual knowledge about organizations and their management that is obtained from textbooks and lectures. Most texts typically trace the evolution and changes in organization and management theory. Figure 1 presents one view of the evolution of this theory and serves as a framework for a brief historical review.

Traditional theory	Modifications	Emerging view—systems approach
Scientific management (Efficient task performance)		Views an organization as:
Bureaucratic model (Authority and structure)	Behavioral sciences (Psychological, sociological, cultural issues)	(1) a subsystem of its broader environment, and
Administrative management theory (Universal management principles)	Management sciences (Economic-technical rationality)	(2) goal-oriented; including (3) a technical subsystem, (4) a structural subsystem, (5) a psychosocial subsystem; and coordinated by (6) a managerial subsystem.
1900	1930s	1960s 1970s

FIGURE 1 Evolution of organization and management theory.

A systematic body of knowledge on the subject is relatively new. It is closely associated with the industrial revolution and the rise of large-scale enterprises that required the development of new organizational forms and management practices. Traditional theory is based on contributions from a number of sources, including scientific management, administrative management theory, and the bureaucratic model.

The primary emphasis of scientific management was on planning, standardizing, and improving the efficiency of human work. It viewed management as a science rather than an individualistic approach based on rule of thumb.

During the first half of the twentieth century, a body of knowledge termed "administrative management theory" was developed. Henri Fayol was one of the earliest exponents of a general theory of administration. Other writers, primarily those actively engaged in management or consulting practices, developed their views according to the pattern established by him. The pyramidal form, scalar principle, unity of command, exception principle, authority delegation, span of control, and departmentalization concepts were set forth by this group.

Another thread in classical organization theory was provided by Max Weber and his bureaucratic model. He viewed bureaucracy as the most efficient form for complex organizations. His model included such dimensions as well-defined hierarchy of authority, division of labor based upon functional specialization, a system of rules, impersonality of interpersonal relationships, a system of work procedures, and placement based upon technical competence.

Traditional management theory included certain assumptions about the nature of organizations and the people in them. Management should plan, direct, and control the activities of the work group. Authority had its source at the top of a hierarchy and was delegated downward. Principles were established to guide managerial practices. Basically, managers planned the activities and organized, directed, and controlled their subordinates. Employees were expected to be relatively passive, to accept the manager's authority, and to follow orders.

Traditional theory has been criticized for employing closed-system assumptions about the organization which are unrealistic. It fails to consider many of the environmental and internal influences. It makes unrealistic assumptions about human behavior. The classical principles of management have been described as too vague and contradictory.

In spite of these criticisms, the classical concepts represent an important, although limited, part of organization and management theory. Many of them are still utilized in organizations and can serve as an initial step or first approximation. They serve as the foundation for more modern views of organization theory and management practice. Many forces have modified the traditional theory. The two broad strands of change are the *behavioral sciences*, which emphasize the psychosocial system and the human aspects of administration, and the *management sciences*, which emphasize the economic-technical system and quantification, mathematical models, and the application of computer technology.

The behavioral sciences use an open-system approach and consider many variables which were excluded from the traditional models. The behavioral approach has been developed primarily by psychologists, sociologists, and anthropologists who are interested in empirical investigation to verify their concepts. They have a humanistic orientation which differs from the traditional school and also from the management science approach.

Management science can be considered as a basic extension of scientific management, with modifications. It is concerned with the organization as primarily an economic-technical system. This movement has flourished since the end of World War II, with major contributions from economics, engineering, mathematics, and statistics. The increasing sophistication of quantitative techniques, together with developing computer technology, provides the basic tools for this approach.

The newer approaches have utilized knowledge from a wide variety of disciplines and have provided new informational inputs for organization theory and management practice. The behavioral scientists and the management scientists have frequently become change agents in organizations by advocating approaches and practices which differ from traditional ways of operating. Conflicts and a "communications gap" frequently develop among these scientists and managers.

A fully integrated body of knowledge representing organization and management theory has not emerged. With the great diversity of disciplinary inputs, the theory has tended toward divergence rather than convergence. Each school of thought has emphasized the aspects of the organization which it considers most important. This tendency to view organization and management from a subsystem standpoint is reinforced by the type of academic training of the various theorists.

This diversity should not be considered undesirable. Rather, it is an indication of the active intellectual interest in the study of organizations and their management. Students should welcome these diverse contributions. Organizations are complex systems made up of psychological, sociological, technical, and economic elements which require intensive investigation. The view which is emerging as a basis for modern theory is the systems approach.

THE SYSTEMS APPROACH

The systems view of organizations and their management serves as the basic conceptual framework for the exercises and cases presented in this book. *A system is an organized, unitary whole composed of two or more interdependent parts, components, or subsystems and delineated by identifiable boundaries from its environmental suprasystem.*

Systems of various types are all around us. For example, we have mountain systems, river systems, and the solar system as part of our physical surroundings. The body itself is a complex organism including the skeletal system, the circulatory system, and the nervous system. We come into daily contact with such phenomena as transportation systems, communication systems (telephone, telegraph, etc.), and economic systems. We obviously can't consider all these systems—their study would involve most of the total subject matter of a major university, and even more. We will concentrate our attention on a narrower subset of systems—social organizations.

We need a general definition and a conceptual model of organizations which are appropriate for all types: small and large, informal and formal, simple and complex, and those engaged in a very wide variety of activities and functions. In this context, we define an organization as

1. A subsystem of its broader environment, consisting of
2. Goal-oriented people with a purpose
3. A technical subsystem—people using knowledge, techniques, equipment, and facilities
4. A structural subsystem—people working together on integrated activities
5. A psychosocial subsystem—people in social relationships
6. A managerial subsystem—which coordinates the subsystems, and plans and/controls the overall endeavor.

As illustrated by Figure 2, a basic premise is that the organization, as a *subsystem of the society*, must accomplish its goals within constraints which are an integral part of the environmental suprasystem. The organization performs a function for society; if it is to be successful in receiving inputs, it must conform to social constraints and requirements. Conversely, the organization influences its environmental suprasystem. For example, automobile companies perform a transformation function in turning raw materials, energy, information, and financial resources into cars. The output is accepted because it meets a societal need to which the companies have responded. However, the production, distribution, and utilization of cars have had a tremendous effect on the environment. The auto industry has led to the development of complex highways, altered living patterns, and affected the very air we breathe. Certainly, there has been a major interactive effect—the society influences the organization, but the organization also influences the society.

The internal organization can be viewed as composed of several major subsystems. Organizational *goals and values* represent one of the more important subsystems. Each of the organizations that Jack Andrews came into contact with had different and diverse goals and values. While the organization takes many of its values from its broader sociocultural environment, it also influences societal values.

The *technical subsystem* refers to the knowledge required for the performance of tasks. By organizational technology we mean the techniques, equipment, processes, and facilities used in the transformation of inputs into outputs. The technical subsystem is determined by the purposes of the organization and will vary according to the task requirements. The technology frequently prescribes the type of organization structure and affects the psychosocial system.

For example, Jack had plenty of time to observe the technical subsystem of the hospital. He saw how many of the professionals were applying highly specialized technology—the doctors, x-ray technicians,

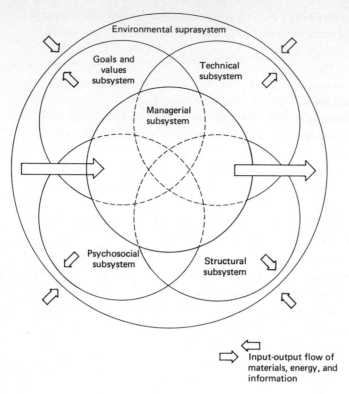

FIGURE 2 The organization system.

nurses, and others. And he also observed how they were aided by sophisticated machinery and equipment—the physical manifestations of technology.

Every organization has a *psychosocial subsystem* which consists of individual behavior and motivation, status and role relationships, group dynamics, and influence networks. This subsystem is, of course, affected by external environmental forces as well as by the technology, tasks, and structure of the internal organization.

Jack had observed how important the "people side" was while he was working in the pea cannery and the post office. He had wondered why some people seemed to work hard and were highly motivated, while others tried to do as little as possible. There were major differences in leadership styles—some bosses gave very detailed directions and seemed to be watching every action, while others let the people below them "do their own thing." At the time, he wondered which style was best for the productivity of the organization. He had also seen how strong group relationships were. It had taken him about a month during the summer before he felt he was really a part of the work group in the cannery. In the post office, he never really got to be "one of the gang." He didn't understand all about group relationships, but he did know that, for him, it was a lot better to be one of the insiders than to be left out.

Intermeshed with the technical and the psychosocial subsystems is the organization *structure*. Structure is concerned with the ways in which the tasks of the organization are divided (differentiation) and with the coordination of these activities (integration). In a formal sense, structure can be set forth by organization charts, job descriptions, and rules and procedures. It is concerned with patterns of authority, communication, and work flow. The organization's structure provides for formalization of relationships among the technical and psychosocial subsystems. However, it should be emphasized that the linkage between these subsystems is by no means complete; many interactions and relationships occur which bypass the formal structure.

Structure was more abstract and difficult for Jack to observe and understand. He had seen an organization chart on the wall showing the formal structure of the United States Postal Service from the Postmaster General down to the local substation. In the hospital, he recognized that there were many separate departments: the emergency room, the x-ray department, and various medical departments, such as orthopedics. But the organization seemed much more complicated. He wondered how the nurses, interns, residents, dieticians, outside medical practitioners, professors from the medical school, and many others whom he had observed running around fit in. With all this diversity of people and functions, he was surprised that things seemed to work out pretty well most of the time. He continued to wonder what really held everything together.

The *managerial subsystem* plays a central role in goal setting, planning, organizing, and controlling activities, as well as in relating the organization to its environment. Managerial functions and practices are vital to the integration of activities in all the other subsystems.

Maybe this is at least a partial answer to Jack's questions about how things worked together. Most of his contacts with organizations had been at the lower, or operating, levels where people were performing various tasks. He did recognize that there were people above these levels who were not directly engaged in specific task performance but who were managing those who did. It hadn't been by chance that the Washington State Highway Patrol was on the scene shortly after his skiing accident. Someone, perhaps a sergeant in the patrol, had planned and scheduled the activities of the patrol cars so they would have adequate coverage of their assigned areas. In the hospital, he had heard frequent references to the hospital administrator and his staff. While he was working in the cannery, he knew that there were a fairly large number of management and staff personnel performing a wide variety of functions, even though he had little direct contact with them. Most of the time, he and the other workers on the canning line had thought that those guys in the ties and suits were excess baggage to the organization. They drove big, new cars and seemed to come and go as they pleased. But they must have been doing something for the organization that related to putting peas in cans. He wished he knew more about their activities.

OUTLINE OF THE BOOK
The concept of the organization as a system in interaction with its environment and as composed of subsystems serves as the basic framework for the exercises and cases presented in this book. The rest of the book is divided into the following sections:

Part 1 Conceptual Foundation of Organization and Management
Part 2 Evolution of Organization and Management Theory
Part 3 Environment, Boundaries, and Goals of Organizations
Part 4 Technology and Organization Structure
Part 5 The Psychosocial System in Organizations
Part 6 The Managerial System in Organizations
Part 7 Comparative Analysis and Contingency Views
Part 8 Organizational Change and the Future

Although the exercises and cases are presented under particular parts and the learning experiences relate primarily to that area of knowledge, it should be emphasized that we cannot force an absolute compartmentalization. The systems approach and experiential learning both suggest that we cannot segment knowledge and/or experience into neat packages. The world of organizations and the critical issues of management are not separable into distinct areas. Organizations do not have separate value issues or technological, structural, people, or managerial problems. They have all these, usually combined in complex and interrelated ways. In fact, many of the exercises are geared to providing a learning situation in which students can experience these complexities and interrelationships.

Therefore, the conceptual model and order of presentation of the exercises and cases should by no means provide constraints to the learning experiences. These experiential exercises and cases are intended to capture some of the complexity, uncertainty, and excitement of actual situations, and lead to better understanding of organizations and their management.

By the third day in the hospital, Jack was feeling much better. His brief hospitalization had given him new understanding about that organization. He was getting out tomorrow and could face up to getting his classes scheduled. Maybe there was a course in health care administration that he could get into? He knew the accounting and finance course would be OK, and maybe there was something for him to learn in the organization and management course. After all, he had seen a number of organizations in action over the past few days. And someday he did expect to have a management position. He only hoped that the course was not just textbook reading and theory, and that he could relate the ideas to his experiences. He had a lot of good questions and wanted to find some answers.

(By the way, Jack did get registered; he did get into the summer internship and did learn a lot about one CPA firm; and he did graduate with a degree in accounting. However, he didn't go to work for a large CPA firm—he was employed by the accounting and systems department of a large metropolitan hospital.)

PART 1
CONCEPTUAL FOUNDATIONS OF ORGANIZATION AND MANAGEMENT

How do we begin the study of organizations and their management? We might start with a long review of the historical development of social organizations—from the family, to the clan, to the village, to the nation-state, and then to the myriad of large, complex organizations which make up a modern society. The history of the human race could be appropriately studied from the viewpoint of the evolution of social organizations. In fact, the nature and form of human organizations are key reference points for the cultural anthropologist. But, such a historical discussion would obviously take a great deal of time. Even more serious, such an approach would depart from the basic concept of this book—using our own experiences and observations as a basis for learning.

We can't go back to study organizations of the past. Fortunately, however, many of the organizational forms which used to exist have modern counterparts; for example, the family and many types of informal groups. Also, we can observe changes in the same organization over time. New organizations are created continually in our society. Some of them survive and grow; many don't. We can observe changes in the internal operations of organizations. What happens when we have a major change in technology—for example, when a new computerized information system is introduced? What are the consequences when a business organization modifies its structure through decentralization? What are the outcomes (intended and unintended) when a school system tries to respond to environmental pressures for racial integration? What are the results in terms of student satisfaction and motivation when the college grading system is changed from letter grades to a pass/fail system? In short, there are organizations all around us that provide considerable food for thought.

We will start our study of organizations and their management by using our existing knowledge and experiences enhanced by observation and reflection. We can further our understanding if we share our ideas and experiences with other members of the class. We will use two exercises to help us with this process.

Our Organizational Society: Your Association with Organizations is an exercise which asks you (1) to identify those organizations in which you are involved or with which you have contact, and (2) to reflect on their key characteristics.

In the exercise Informal and Formal Organizations: Sandlot and Little League Baseball, you will be comparing two organizational forms in detail. Specifically, we will be interested in reflecting on the similarities and differences between a personal, informal group and a more formal, structured organization.

Exercise 1
Our Organizational Society: Your Association with Organizations

LEARNING OBJECTIVES

1. To identify some of the important organizations in your life.
2. To determine relevant, specific characteristics of organizations.
3. To describe some of the important functions of management in organizations.

ADVANCE PREPARATION

Read the Overview and Procedure Sections. Complete the form "Profile of Organizations" on page 15.

OVERVIEW

Jack Andrews had personal experiences with a number of organizations. Undoubtedly, you also have had recent experiences with numerous organizations. Use the definition of organizations provided on page 7 as a starting place. Ten to fifteen minutes of reflective thinking should result in a fairly large list of organizations. Don't be misled by thinking that only large organizations, such as your college or General Motors, are relevant for consideration. How about the clinic with the doctor(s), nurse(s), and secretary/bookkeeper? Or the corner garage or service station? The local tavern, McDonald's Golden Arches, and the neighborhood theater are all organizations. You should not have any difficulty in listing a number of organizations with which you have had recent contact.

The second part of the exercise, however, gets tougher. You are asked to describe several of the key characteristics of the organizations that you have listed. One of the major issues in studying and describing organizations is deciding *what* characteristics or factors are important. Some of the more common characteristics considered in the analysis of organizations are:

1. Size (small to very large)
2. Degree of formality (informal to highly structured)

3. Degree of complexity (simple to complex)
4. Nature of goals (what the organization is trying to accomplish)
5. Major activities (what tasks are performed)
6. Types of people involved (age, skills, educational background, etc.)
7. Location of activities (number of units and their geographic location)

You should be able to develop a list of characteristics that you think are relevant for each of your organizations.

Now, to the third, final, and most difficult task. Think about what is involved in the *management* of these organizations. For example, what kinds of functions do their managers perform? How does one learn the skills necessary to be an effective manager? Would you want to be a manager in any of these organizations?

In effect, in this exercise we are asking you to do what Jack Andrews did—think specifically about organizations you have been associated with recently, develop your own conceptual model for looking at their characteristics, and think more specifically about the managerial functions in each of these organizations. You probably already know a great deal more about organizations and their management than you think. This exercise should be useful in getting your thoughts together.

PROCEDURE

STEP 1

Prior to class, list up to 10 organizations (e.g., work, living group, club) in which you have been involved or with which you have had recent contact.

STEP 2

Enter five organizations from your list in the form on page 15, Profile of Organizations.

   a. List the organization.
   b. Briefly outline the characteristics that you consider most significant.
   c. Describe the managerial functions in each of these organizations.

STEP 3

During the class period, meet in groups of five or six to discuss your list of organizations, the characteristics you consider important, and your descriptions of their management. Look for significant similarities and differences across organizations.

STEP 4

Basing your selections on this group discussion, develop a list entitled (see page 16):

What We Would Like to Know about Organizations
and Their Management

Be prepared to write this list on the blackboard or on newsprint and to share your list with other groups in the class.

Profile of Organizations

Organization	*Key characteristics*	*Managerial functions*
1. _____		
2. _____		
3. _____		
4. _____		
5. _____		

SUMMARY AND CONCEPTUALIZATION

Your individual, group, and total class lists of organizations and their key characteristics reflect a wide diversity of experience and knowledge. And they involve only organizations with which you have had some contact! Think of the many types of organizations which exist in our society but are not included in your lists. How can we possibly learn very much about all these organizations and their management? Obviously, learning in depth about each of these organizations would take many lifetimes. Fortunately, however, organizations and management practices have some common characteristics that can serve as a starting point. In your group discussions, you probably noted significant similarities in key characteristics and management functions even though you were describing different organizations.

This exercise has been the starting point for our study of organizations and their management. Its primary purpose was to help you recognize that you already have considerable experience with organizations and do have some knowledge about their operations. You probably have more limited knowledge about the management of these organizations, but—hopefully—this exercise has caused you to think more critically about these functions.

In this exercise you have generated a wide diversity of ideas and information. You have also generated a number of questions concerning what you want to know about organizations and their management. In order to facilitate our experiential learning process, we will need to develop some conceptual models to help us integrate our knowledge. In the next exercise we will look at one of the key ingredients in this conceptual model the similarities and differences between informal and formal organizations.

Exercise 2
Informal and Formal Organizations: Sandlot and Little League Baseball

LEARNING OBJECTIVES

1. To compare two different organization types—the informal and the formal.
2. To identify changes which occur in organizations and their management as they evolve from informal to more formal.
3. To increase our understanding of managerial roles and processes in different situations.

ADVANCE PREPARATION

Read the Overview and the Procedure. Complete the form, Individual Comparative Analysis of Sandlot and Little League Baseball, on page 21.

OVERVIEW

One of the major characteristics of a modern society is the development of numerous and more complex organizations. Through nearly all of history, our social institutions have been primarily on an informal, face-to-face basis. Up through medieval times, the feudal system provided the primary large-scale system to which the individual belonged. Within the past several centuries, the growing importance of large groups or organizations has been a pervasive phenomenon. The industrial revolution, with its demand for concentration of resources and its greater scale, fostered large economic organizations. Modern governments are typically massive organizations. Schools, unions, universities and colleges, correctional institutions, hospitals, and the military all have grown in size and complexity.

We can make a distinction between informal organizations, such as the family, social group, or informal work group, and formal organizations, such as General Motors, the Teamsters, the City Hospital, or the State University. In many ways the informal and formal organizations are similar; however, there are also many differences.

One of the major consequences of the rise of larger, more complex organizations is the evolution of a more distinct *managerial* role. In the small, informal group, management is often performed by several members in the group. (Who is the real manager in a family or a social group?) However, as the organization becomes more formal, there is a tendency to develop more specialized managerial functions. Briefly, we can say that management involves the coordination of human and material resources toward objective accomplishment. Typical definitions suggest that management is a process of planning, organizing, and controlling activities.

We have all had association with many informal and formal organizations. For example, you have had some direct experience in recreational endeavors. Several decades ago it was most common for youths to engage in various informal athletic activities—sandlot baseball, backyard basketball, the old swimming hole, touch football, etc. Increasingly, particularly in metropolitan areas, more formal organizations have developed, such as Little League baseball and football, community swim meets. etc. Obviously, these more formal athletic programs have not completely displaced informal, pickup, or spontaneous games, but they have become ever more important.

In this exercise, you are asked to draw upon your individual and shared experiences to look at the similarities and differences between these two forms of athletic organizations—sandlot baseball and Little League baseball.

The comparative analysis forms suggest several dimensions which you may use to compare the two types of organization. You may develop any additional dimensions that you consider relevant.

PROCEDURE

STEP 1
Before class, prepare the Individual Comparative Analysis of Sandlot and Little League Baseball, page 21.

STEP 2
Meet in groups of five or six and develop a group composite of your comparative analysis on the form on page 23.

STEP 3
Select one group to report to the entire class on its composite analysis.

STEP 4
Engage in total class discussion.

Individual Comparative Analysis of Sandlot and Little League Baseball

	Sandlot baseball (Informal organization)	Little League baseball (Formal organization)
1. Who are the participants? How are members of these organizations identified?		
2. What are the goals of these organizations? Who determines the goals?		
3. What are the rules that govern these organizations? Who makes the rules?		
4. How structured are these organizations?		
5. Who performs the managerial functions of planning, decision making, and control in these organizations?		
6. How would you describe the relationships among the people in these organizations?		

Individual Comparative Analysis of Sandlot and Little League Baseball

	Sandlot baseball (Informal organization)	Little League baseball (Formal organization)
7. What motivates people in these organizations?		
8. What are the leadership and influence patterns in these organizations?		
9. How do these organizations relate to their environments—such as other groups, competitors, etc.?		
10. How long-lived are these organizations? How are they perpetuated?		
11. What is the nature of the technology used; i.e., equipment, knowledge, strategy, etc.?		
12. What other similarities and differences are there?		

Group Composite of Comparative Analysis of Sandlot and Little League Baseball

	Sandlot baseball (Informal organization)	Little League baseball (Formal organization)
1. Who are the participants? How are members of these organizations identified?		
2. What are the goals of these organizations? Who determines the goals?		
3. What are the rules that govern these organizations? Who makes the rules?		
4. How structured are these organizations?		
5. Who performs the managerial functions of planning, decision making, and control in these organizations?		
6. How would you describe the relationships among the people in these organizations?		

Group Composite of Comparative Analysis of Sandlot and Little League Baseball

	Sandlot baseball (Informal organization)	Little League baseball (Formal organization)
7. What motivates people in these organizations?		
8. What are the leadership and influence patterns in these organizations?		
9. How do these organizations relate to their environments—such as other groups, competitors, etc.?		
10. How long-lived are these organizations? How are they perpetuated?		
11. What is the nature of the technology used; i.e., equipment, knowledge, strategy, etc.?		
12. What other similarities and differences are there?		

SUMMARY AND CONCEPTUALIZATION

In this exercise, most groups' composites of the comparative analysis of sandlot and Little League baseball are similar. Typically, groups use some of the following characteristics to describe sandlot baseball: nonspecific membership, personal goal of having fun, loose structure, integration of managing and doing, short life, rudimentary technology, flexible rules, and changing patterns of influence. In contrast, Little League baseball is described as having specific membership, multiple goals which emphasize competition, tight structure, separation of managing and doing (coaches and players), permanency, more refined technology, rigid rules and policies, and hierarchical patterns of influence. There are usually variations based on the experiences of individual class members with these two types of organization.

If we extend our analysis to other types of organization, we find many of the same trends as they move from the small, informal group to the more formal, complex organization. For example, the same pattern was true as unions moved from informal worker associations to large-scale, international unions. The movement from the small, one-room schoolhouse to the large, unified school district is another example. Even consumer and environmental groups that were created originally to "fight the establishment" have themselves become more formal and structured—much like the establishment's organizations.

We do have a term for this process of moving from informal to more formal organizations: bureaucratization. The term *bureaucracy* as developed by Max Weber and his followers is not used in the popularized, emotionally charged sense of red tape and inefficiency. The bureaucratic model possesses certain structural characteristics and norms which are used in every complex organization.

Max Weber, looking from the perspectives of the early twentieth century and the growing industrial development, viewed bureaucracy as the most effective and efficient form for complex organizations—business, government, military, for example—arising out of the needs of modern society.

Several of the key concepts of bureaucracy are:

1. Division of labor based upon functional specialization
2. A well-defined hierarchy of authority
3. A system of rules covering the rights and duties of positional incumbents
4. A system of procedures for dealing with work situations
5. Impersonality of interpersonal relations
6. Promotion and selection based upon technical competence

Do these dimensions of bureaucracy best fit sandlot or Little League baseball? Most people would agree that, in this theoretical model, *Little League baseball is an emerging bureaucracy*.

Perhaps some of your values and feelings reflected in the discussion of this exercise are typical of your reactions to other organizations. We do tend to have negative views about large-scale, complex organizations. The popular connotation of bureaucracy is big, inefficient, slow-moving, and stifling to the human spirit. On the other hand, we recognize that large organizations are essential to our society and lives. We do seem to have respect for, and even take pride in, such organizations as the National Aeronautics and Space Administration when it accomplishes space missions. If we can afford it, we want to go to the best, most sophisticated treatment center for medical attention (such as the Mayo Clinic or Bethesda Naval Hospital). In short, when the chips are down, we know that *many* large-scale organizations can do certain things much better and more efficiently than any small, informal group. How do we explain these schizophrenic feelings about large organizations? This question may be an interesting one for additional observation and reflection.

PART 2
EVOLUTION OF
ORGANIZATION AND
MANAGEMENT THEORY

Organizations have changed significantly over the past decades. As suggested in the previous exercises, there has been a general trend from small, informal to larger, more complex organizations. In the small, informal organization there was not much need for management theories. Typically, the managerial functions were performed by the participants directly involved in the operations. For example, in sandlot baseball the planning and organizing functions were performed directly by the players themselves. However, in more complex organizations, more explicit concepts about management are needed.

A systematic body of knowledge concerning organization and management is a product of the late nineteenth and the twentieth centuries. It is closely associated with the industrial revolution and the rise of large-scale enterprises which required the development of new organizational forms and management practices. We have briefly traced the evolution of organization and management theory in the Introduction (pages 5–9) and have provided an overall summary of this development in Figure 1 on page 5. Most management texts will provide you with a more extensive view of this evolution. You will find it helpful to review this literature in preparation for the following exercises.

In understanding how organization and management theory has evolved, it is desirable for you to develop a better "feel" for the setting of organizations, their climate, and the overall management concepts at different stages in history. It is also useful to understand how various ideas stemming from the different strands of organization and management theory may be applied in a specific situation. Our concepts about organizations and their management are not codified into any single, well-defined set of principles. Rather, we have many viewpoints about what is appropriate and many prescriptions about how to improve an organization's performance. Traditional management theory (including scientific management, the bureaucratic model, and administrative management theory), behavioral science approaches, and management science techniques have different views that typically lead to different prescriptions for solving the same problem. The following exercises should help you understand these differences.

Historical Comparisons of Organizations: Profiles of the Past and Present provides short excerpts about organizations of the past and present. It helps provide a perspective on the changes in organizational climates and managerial practices over time.

Different Management Theories and Perspectives: Acme Aircraft Corporation provides an opportunity to look at the problems in a particular organizational situation and to develop solutions based on different management theories. It should help you understand how there may be differential emphasis in problem identification, diagnosis, and solution, depending on which segment of organization and management theory is utilized.

Exercise 3
Historical Comparisons
of Organizations:
Profiles of the Past and Present

LEARNING OBJECTIVES

1. To compare and contrast organizational climates in several specific examples.
2. To understand how social values affect organizational climates.
3. To identify changing views concerning the role and responsibilities of management.

ADVANCE PREPARATION
Read the Overview and the four profiles.

OVERVIEW
It is obvious that there have been substantial technological and economic advancements over the past century. One of the more important trends has been the development of larger, more complex organizations to accomplish our purposes more effectively and efficiently.

Many subtle, evolutionary changes are not readily apparent on a day-to-day basis, however. They include the general requirements and demands which the organization makes upon the individual— essentially, the organizational climate in which people work.

> Organizational climate . . . refers to the perceived, subjective effects of the formal system, the informal "style" of managers, and other important environmental factors on the attitudes, beliefs, values, and motivations of people who work in a particular organization.[1]

[1]George H. Litwin and Robert A. Stringer, Jr., *Motivation and Organizational Climate*, Harvard University Graduate School of Business Administration, Boston, 1968, p. 5.

In many ways the organizational climate reflects broader sociocultural values concerning the importance of the individual, the constraints imposed upon behavior, and views as to the nature of people.

From the present viewpoint, it is difficult for us fully to understand what working in organizations was like in the "good old days." We can have work experiences in existing organizations, but we cannot go back in time to experience the organizational life of the past. However, we can get some glimpses of bygone periods by talking to old-timers, reading the literature of past eras, seeing old movies, and looking at old newspaper and periodical files.

In this exercise we will compare the organizational climates of the past and present. To do this, we have selected two profiles of the past and two profiles of the present. They are taken from two organizational types: (1) school systems, and (2) business organizations. Obviously, these profiles cannot be completely representative of organizations of their time. What is a "representative" organization, anyhow? There is undoubtedly a spectrum of organizational climates now, as there was at any moment in time past. However, these profiles present views which were generally typical of their time.

PROCEDURE

STEP 1
Read the four profiles:

  a. When Teaching Rules Were a Sentence
  b. Criteria for Evaluation of Teachers
  c. Boston Office, 1872
  d. Polaroid: An Award for Developing Human Resources

STEP 2
The class should be divided into four groups. Each group will analyze one of the four profiles in detail. Try to imagine how you would feel as an employee in this situation. You may want to relate the profile to your own work experiences. A representative should be selected to describe the highlights of your analysis to the total class.

STEP 3
The entire class engages in discussion. Have a representative describe the analysis of the profile from each group. The class should then compare the similarities and differences in organizational climates as indicated by the four profiles.

SCHOOL SYSTEM: PROFILE FROM THE PAST

WHEN TEACHING RULES WERE A SENTENCE*
Male teachers could go courting one night a week if they attended church regularly, but women teachers were not to keep company with men at all.

These were two of the regulations in Samuel M. Barbiero's contract when he began teaching school in 1927 in the now-vanished community of Mount Harris near Steamboat Springs in the Colorado Rockies.

Barbiero, who recently retired as supervisor of the pupil personnel department of the Jefferson County Public Schools, found a copy of his first contract while sorting mementos of his 47 years in teaching.

Here are some of the contract's provisions:

Seattle Post-Intelligencer, July 4, 1973.

"Women teachers are not to keep company with men and agree to be at home between the hours of 8 p.m. and 6 a.m. unless attending a school function.

"Women teachers agree not to get married. This contract becomes null and void immediately if a woman teacher marries.

"All school employes are not to leave town at any time without the permission of the chairman of the school board.

"The teacher agrees not to smoke cigarettes.

"This contract becomes null and void immediately if the employe is found drinking alcoholic beverages.

"Women teachers are to dress and conduct themselves in a puritanical manner as follows: not to dress in bright colors; not to dye her hair; to wear at least two petticoats; not to wear dresses more than two inches above the ankle; not to use face powder, mascara or paint the lips.

"Men teachers may take one evening a week for courting purposes, provided they attend church regularly or teach a Sunday school class.

"The teacher agrees to keep the classroom clean, to sweep the classroom floor at least once daily, to scrub the classroom floor once a week with hot water and soap, to clean the blackboards at least once daily and to start the fire at 7 a.m. so the room will be warm at 8 a.m. when the patrons arrive; to carry out the ashes at least once daily and shall perform other duties as prescribed by the board of education.

"Each teacher should lay aside from each pay a good sum of his earnings so he will not become a burden to society."

SCHOOL SYSTEM: PROFILE FROM THE PRESENT

CRITERIA FOR EVALUATION OF TEACHERS

Many school districts have developed comprehensive programs for the evaluation of teachers in order to improve the teaching process and to aid in career planning. The following is taken from *A Manual on Observation for Improving the Teaching Process*, prepared by the Seattle Public Schools. It should be noted that this process involves actual observation of the teacher in the classroom. The observation and evaluation are followed by conferences with the teacher to discuss special strengths and weaknesses and to develop an individualized program for improving teaching effectiveness and for long-range career planning.

GENERAL DESCRIPTIVE EXAMPLES OF ITEMS INCLUDED IN THE OBSERVATION FOR IMPROVING THE TEACHING PROCESS

The lists of teaching characteristics which follow are intended to be useful in formulating comments and suggestions during the processes of observation and formal appraisal. It is not possible for all teachers to maintain excellence in each area. This is not expected. It is desired that teachers understand the teaching process and try to improve instruction.

I. THE TEACHING PROCESS
   A. PREPARATION (to Be Discussed in Conference with the Teacher)
      1. Objectives
         a. Are clear, specific, measurable and evident to the students
         b. Have meaning for students and are realistic
         c. Encourage personal goals while serving department and building objectives
         d. Are appropriately organized and thoughtfully structured in proper sequence as to what precedes and what follows in the development of the subject
      2. Learning Experiences
         a. Serve objectives and achieve learning, while being cognizant of the varying skills and abilities of each student
         b. Consider available resources and are worth time spent
         c. Are organized, carefully structured, flexible and imaginative
         d. Encourage student planning, effort and the desire to learn more

3. Content
   a. Stimulates inquiry and the development of intellectual curiosity
   b. Is appropriate and important; fulfills objectives; and is based on the current scholarship in the field
   c. Is organized, carefully selected, sequentially valid and based on breadth of general information
4. Evaluation
   a. Is related to objectives and serves as a learning experience
   b. Uses formal and informal techniques to assess achievement, costs and content and to improve instruction
   c. Teaches self-evaluation and does not stress conformity when the teaching emphasizes creativity
   d. Provides for diagnosis of teaching and learning as a continuous and integral part of instruction

B. ACTION (to Be Observed in the Classroom)
1. Atmosphere for Learning
   a. Considers physical factors in providing the framework for learning
   b. Considers personal needs, morale, self-respect, self-discipline and individual responsibility of both students and teacher
   c. Understands student behavior; is equitable and consistent; and shows tolerance for sincere student error
   d. Provides support and encouragement; is conducive to learning; stimulates thinking; provokes inquiry and curiosity; and leads to respect for knowledge
   e. Maintains reasonable control with a minimum of tension and strain; anticipates difficulties; and encourages creativity and enthusiasm while providing balance between freedom and control
2. Instructional Methods
   a. Excite, intrigue, and stimulate students to develop intellectual curiosity and the ability for critical and creative thinking
   b. Provide appropriate introductions, demonstrations and illustrations, clear and concise lessons and assignments, positive incentives and economical use of class time
   c. Develop summaries and reinforcements which support learning, provoke thought; and stimulate independent, critical and creative thinking
   d. Determine pace through student progress, making use of differentiated assignments and flexible grouping to meet the interests, abilities and needs of individual students
   e. Permit deviation from established routine when it will encourage learning and feature appropriate balance of classroom activities to develop the ability of the students to think critically, analyze objectively and generalize effectively
   f. Provide data for evaluation
3. Teaching Materials
   a. Are current, appropriate, well-organized, authoritative and artistically compiled
   b. Are put to careful and effective use, are not contrived, are used imaginatively, and encourage questions and critical examination
   c. Are utilized by students who have been trained in their use, and the maintenance of their orderly arrangement
4. Student Participation
   a. Is balanced with teacher direction; employs student planning; and uses students' talents and interest so each student becomes an active and valued member of the class
   b. Encourages inquiry and the exchange of ideas, which are supported by the teacher, so that sincere questions at however fundamental a level are respected
   c. Initiates questions, doubt and wonder, encouraging self-respect, confidence and the development of intellectual curiosity
   d. Encourages independence; stimulates enthusiasm; and leads to the development of communicative skills
   e. Helps students to direct their own learning and assume responsibility

C. EVALUATION (to Be Discussed in Conference with the Teacher)
1. Interpretation of
    a. Progress toward objectives and possible hypotheses regarding remedial action
    b. Problems in procedure and the ways these could be solved
    c. Costs to teachers and students, and methods to ameliorate these
    d. Costs in time and materials, and possible action which could be taken to use these more efficiently
    e. Students' self-evaluation and achievement, and the techniques which could be used to increase attainment in these areas
2. Translation into
    a. Improvement in preparation to perfect teaching
    b. Improvement in teaching to insure learning
    c. Improvement in evaluation to interpret student needs and abilities
    d. Improvement in student understanding and in attitude toward students
    e. Improvement in grade level or departmental planning which will insure curricular development

II. FACTORS OUTSIDE THE TEACHER'S CONTROL WHICH INFLUENCE THE TEACHING PROCESS
A. PHYSICAL FACTORS
    1. Is there appropriate light in the room?
    2. Is there sufficient ventilation?
    3. Does the temperature in the room vary widely?
    4. Is there enough room?
    5. Are there display areas?
    6. Is there adequate storage?
    7. Is there appropriate seating for students?
    8. Is the room noisy:
        a. because of construction nearby?
        b. because of location near the gym, playfield, lunchroom, or music room?
        c. because of noisy lights and ventilation equipment?
        d. because of lack of acoustical protection?
    9. Is equipment necessary to the subject available in the room?
    10. Is resource equipment readily available?
    11. Is there an adequate amount of teaching materials and supplies available?
    12. Are resource materials readily obtained?

B. SCHEDULING
    1. Is it difficult for students to elect courses?
    2. Is the teacher a floating teacher? How often?
    3. Is student composition in the class unusual because of scheduling problems?
    4. Does the teacher have a large percentage of unique student problems?
    5. Is there an awkward lunch break?
    6. Is the classroom dual purpose, with loss of class time because of other necessary activities held in the room?
    7. Is there a wide variety of numbers in each of the classes the teacher has? What is the daily pupil load?
    8. How many preparations does the teacher have daily? Is the teacher teaching in his major or minor field?
    9. Does the teacher have adequate time and a place in the building to prepare for teaching?

C. EXTRA-CURRICULAR ACTIVITIES AND RESPONSIBILITIES WHICH REQUIRE TIME AND ENERGY OUTSIDE OF TEACHING
    1. Is the teacher assigned to more than his share of supervision, coverage, extra-curricular activities, and meetings?
    2. Is the teacher attending school with a heavy credit load for purposes of improvement and salary credits?
    3. Does the teacher have excessive demands from the community on his time?

III. SPECIAL STRENGTHS

The major emphasis in this evaluation procedure is on recognizing and developing competence in the areas mentioned in the section on the teaching process. The following personal and professional characteristics could appear as part of the teaching process and be mentioned in the notes taken during the observation, or comments during formal appraisal. However, these strengths appear here and on the forms as a means of stressing the adequacy of the teacher, to be sure potentiality for great teaching is recognized, and as a means of mentioning strengths other than those appearing on the form.

A. PERSONAL CHARACTERISTICS

1. In relationships with students and colleagues, the teacher
   a. Respects the opinions of others while holding to personal convictions
   b. Has breadth of interest, knowledge and appreciation
   c. Is self-confident, practices self-control and is self-reliant
   d. Has a good sense of humor and is adaptable
   e. Is friendly, cheerful, warm, and shows consideration for others
   f. Has dignity and poise
   g. Is sympathetic, patient, courteous and tactful
   h. Shows good judgment and sincerity, as well as freedom from prejudice
   i. Is conscientious, and demonstrates initiative and perseverance
   j. Is efficient and organized, and has the ability to analyze
   k. Is prompt, responsible, and gives attention to detail
   l. Is original, creative, versatile, imaginative and resourceful
2. In respect to personal appearance, the teacher
   a. Practices good grooming
   b. Dresses appropriately
3. Physical fitness is evidenced by
   a. Adequate health and vitality
   b. Regularity in attendance
4. The teacher demonstrates emotional fitness, and
   a. Is emotionally stable and mature
   b. Is free from excessive worry
   c. Has adequate self-control

B. PROFESSIONAL CHARACTERISTICS

1. Teaching Skills
   a. Is able to plan and organize and has good work habits
   b. Has ability to achieve objectives
   c. Has competence in self-evaluation
   d. Desires to improve and has the ability to seek help
   e. Practices effective and clear written expression
   f. Uses correct English and converses readily
   g. Enunciates and has a pleasant voice
   h. Has knowledge of subject matter
   i. Is widely read and has breadth of general information
   j. Has knowledge of current affairs
   k. Shows interest in other subjects
   l. Has an appreciation of fine arts
   m. Is creative and stimulates enthusiasm
   n. Fosters critical thinking
   o. Has concern for students and respect for the subject area being taught
2. Attitude
   a. Recognizes that the primary responsibility is the education and training of students
   b. Accepts a reasonable and fair share of work with extra-curricular activities
   c. Meets his responsibility for the equipment and materials assigned to him
   d. Supports the total school program
   e. Is cooperative with colleagues, parents and administration
   f. Assumes responsibility for his own words and actions
   g. Respects personal relationships and the confidences of others

3. Preparation and Growth
   a. Has the necessary background and subject preparation for the area or grade level taught
   b. Is familiar with current trends in subject area and is willing to try new methods in teaching
   c. Continues professional training
   d. Utilizes the services of consultants, helping teachers, department heads and other professional personnel
   e. Supports professional organizations
4. Community Relations
   a. Has an understanding of the social, cultural and intellectual needs of the community
   b. Is able to work with members of the community
   c. Recognizes the responsibility to inform parents of each child's progress in school
   d. Conducts parent conferences with proper preparation and understanding
   e. Makes parents feel welcome when they seek understanding of the school program and its relationship to their children
   f. Represents the school to visitors and in the community

BUSINESS ORGANIZATION: PROFILE FROM THE PAST

BOSTON OFFICE, 1872*

8 RULES FOR OFFICE WORKER IN 1872 REVEALED

A Boston office manager, cleaning out a file in preparation for his firm's move to a new location, came across the office rules for 1872.

He wanted to read them to his office force, but all the members were out on one of the day's several coffee breaks. They were:

1. Office employees each day will fill lamps, clean chimneys and trim wicks. Wash windows once a week.

2. Each clerk will bring in a bucket of water and a scuttle of coal for the day's business.

3. Make your pens carefully. You may whittle nibs to your individual taste.

4. Men employees will be given an evening off each week for courting purposes, or two evenings a week if they go regularly to church.

5. After 13 hours of labor in the office, the employee should spend the remaining time reading the Bible and other good books.

6. Every employee should lay aside from each pay day a goodly sum of his earnings for his benefit during his declining years so that he will not become a burden on society.

7. Any employee who smokes Spanish cigars, uses liquor in any form, or frequents pool and public halls or gets shaved in a barber shop, will give good reason to suspect his worth, intentions, integrity and honesty.

8. The employee who has performed his labor faithfully and without fault for five years, will be given an increase of five cents per day in his pay, providing profits from business permit it.

BUSINESS ORGANIZATION: PROFILE FROM THE PRESENT

POLAROID: AN AWARD FOR DEVELOPING HUMAN RESOURCES†

When it comes to innovative, costly, continuing, and unconventional involvement in social action and community affairs, Polaroid Corp. of Cambridge, Mass., towers as high over most U.S. companies as its price-earnings ratio, which reared to a lofty 98 at midweek.

*The Boston Sunday Herald, October 5, 1958, p. 50.
†Business Week, June 30, 1973, pp. 74–75.

This should come as no surprise to anyone familiar with Dr. Edwin H. Land, the 63-year-old founder, president, and company research genius who likes to talk of his camera and film company as "... not just a place to make a product but a place in which people can join with other people to say, 'What's worth doing? How do you have a rich experience all day long?' " Adds Peter Wensberg, senior vice-president: "Land has always felt that your job and your company should be things you can take pride in. He has always encouraged employees here to do things on their own. People know this and they realize Polaroid has a tradition of being concerned with more than the balance sheet."

Just how thoroughly Land's philosophy has shoved Polaroid beyond social tokenism shows up in statistics.

Some 12% of the company's nearly 10,000 U.S. employees are black, with 6.4% in salaried jobs. Another 3% are disadvantaged in other ways: physically or mentally handicapped, or with a poor grasp of English.

More than 150 ex-convicts have been hired during the past several years, and only two have gone back to prison.

A five-year-old Polaroid subsidiary in Boston's black ghetto of Roxbury continues to expand. There, 243 "unemployable" workers have learned enough skills to graduate to regular jobs at Polaroid and elsewhere.

Polaroid is involved with 143 community projects in Greater Boston and New Bedford, Mass., ranging from camera loans to family planning services.

While the figures suggest the company's broad commitment, they do not adequately reflect such factors as courage. Land uses that word to describe Polaroid's decision in 1971 to stay in South Africa rather than pull out as demanded by anti-apartheid forces within the company and around the world. It would have been far less costly, both financially and in terms of public image, if the company had simply abandoned its tiny, $1.5-million yearly volume. But Land and such top executives as Thomas H. Wyman, now general manager, dropped everything at the height of the buildup for the new SX-70 camera and launched into marathon meetings with militant civil rights representatives.

Higher wages. Land's decision to keep the company in South Africa was strongly influenced by a group of Polaroid employees he sent there to find out what the blacks wanted. The answer: stay and work for better wages and conditions. Some church groups and others continue to castigate Polaroid's presence, but Robert M. Palmer, director of community relations, points to the record: The company's distributor is paying his black employees twice as much as in 1970, though still far below white levels. Insofar as possible under apartheid rules, it has increased supervisory jobs for blacks. On balance, Polaroid has gotten considerable mileage out of its South African experiment.

In the U.S., Polaroid is deeply involved in the politically dangerous area of prison reform. Palmer is president of a statewide movement that last year helped rewrite archaic corrections laws and push them through the Massachusetts legislature. This year he has been struggling to implement such reforms as furloughs for prisoners. He has drafted at least two dozen Polaroid people for projects behind prison walls. One personnel man was dispatched to Norfolk Prison for 90 days, at the request of inmates who wanted help in listing grievances.

Since the riots and killing at Walpole Prison, reform is something of a dirty word. But Palmer is fighting to keep it alive: "I don't have to check with anybody around here on what I'm going to say."

Offbeat rules. Palmer and other Polaroid officials, including Wyman, are trying to persuade other Massachusetts companies to hire former inmates. They cite low training costs, low absenteeism, and almost no turnover. They tell skeptical executives how Polaroid trains offenders while they are still in prison, and carefully follows through when they get out. "Massachusetts will release 1,000 men this year," says Palmer. "If bigger companies would hire only a couple each, it would provide jobs for most parolees and go a long way toward solving one of the worst failures of our society." He points out that 98% of Polaroid's former inmates have stayed out of jail, compared with only 30% of total inmates released. In part, of course, that is because Polaroid is fairly careful in its screening.

A broad involvement in community affairs is a hallmark of Polaroid policy and the company's rules on contributions is typically offbeat. It starts with the premise that the company will respond to community needs on the community's terms. The company reviews priorities each year. Palmer adds that an employee committee sifts through the proposals—5,000 last year—and decides how to disburse money without interference or suggestions from Land or top management.

The company's most conspicuous internal program is in education. Classes are conducted, often on company time, in everything from basic English to advanced chemistry. There is generous financial support to employees seeking doctoral degrees. An astounding 20% of Polaroid's employees are in the educational curriculum, which probably qualifies Polaroid, or "Land University," as the third biggest school in Cambridge, after Harvard and MIT.

SUMMARY AND CONCEPTUALIZATION

One of the main purposes of this exercise was to help you understand some of the differences in the climate for employees in organizations of the past and present. We hope you were able to empathize in this exercise. How would you *feel* as an employee in these four organizations? Obviously, you could have looked at them from a purely logical/rational view and explained the differences in climates from a detached viewpoint. However, we hope you also were able to relate at the level of feelings, attitudes, and values. These profiles help us understand some of the important changes in our views related to work, being an employee, and being a manager.

One of the more obvious differences relates to the size of the organizations. But, this is not too unrealistic. Most business organizations of 100 years ago were small and similar to the Boston Office. Even 50 years ago, most school systems were very small. For example, in the school year 1931–1932 there were nearly 130,000 individual school districts in the United States, whereas by 1975 there were less than 16,000. Small-sized organizations were characteristic of the past, and larger, more complex organizations are typical of the present.

In both profiles of the past, there is evidence of the strong Protestant ethic of the time which stressed hard work, sobriety, thrift, strict religious beliefs, and self-denial. The regulations were strict, to ensure that the employees conformed to this view there was little room for individualism or variation on the employee's part. (But they could whittle nibs to their individual taste!) The regulations had strong authoritarian tones. The school board and the proprietor set forth definite rules to control any possible deviant behavior.

There was an assumption that engaging the individual for work also gave the employer the right to regulate outside-of-work activities. The discrimination against women teachers is obvious (frequently they were paid less than one-half as much as men teachers for the same job). The "good old days" most often provided an organizational climate which most of us would find extremely distasteful by today's standards.

Implicit in these profiles of the past is a view of the management role. Management assumed the inherent right to determine the conditions of work and to prescribe employee behavior—both on the job and off. Social Darwinism (survival of the fittest) was strong and workers were regarded as inferior.

One senses a different view in the profiles of the present. There is much less emphasis on controlling the total lives of employees and more emphasis upon individual self-respect, growth, and satisfaction. The evaluation process in the Seattle School System seems far removed from the emphasis on a puritanical life style of the earlier profile. It stresses the continuous evaluation and improvement of the teaching process. The underlying assumption is that teachers are professionals who should participate, rather than workers who should be totally controlled. Reading of this profile suggests the emphasis that is placed upon individualized learning and considerate treatment of students. It is apparent that the organizational climate generated in the schools would also have a major impact upon the teacher-student relationship. Given the constraints placed upon the teacher in the community of Mount Harris, the restrictions very likely reflected directly on the classroom. "Spare the rod and spoil the child" was apt to have been the dominant view.

Perhaps the profile of Polaroid is a bit too rosy. There still are many situations in industry where companies do place "profits above people." Perhaps you have experienced such situations yourself. Yet, there is a substantial difference in tone from the earlier profile. The large business of today has come to recognize that it does have responsibilities to society more than just making a short-term profit. The profile of Polaroid suggests the trend away from the rigid Protestant ethic toward a broader view of social responsibility.

These brief profiles concerning the climates of four organizations do reflect certain broad changes in values in our society. These organizations mirror the culture of their times. All organizations are part of a broader environmental system and are greatly affected by the values and ethics which exist within the society.

Exercise 4
Different Management Theories and Perspectives:
Acme Aircraft Corporation

LEARNING OBJECTIVES

1. To improve our skills in analyzing complex organizational problems.
2. To understand and compare several theoretical views and approaches for dealing with management problems.
3. To recognize the interrelationships among different prescriptions for solving organizational problems.

ADVANCE PREPARATION

Read the Overview, the Acme Aircraft Corporation case, and the Procedure. You should also analyze the case independently prior to class and be prepared to participate in one of four class groups in the role-playing exercise.

OVERVIEW

We have suggested that an organization can be viewed as a system composed of a subsystem of goals and values, a technical subsystem, a structural subsystem, a psychosocial subsystem, and a managerial subsystem. (See pages 7–9 and Figure 2.) Most real problems in organizations are not confined to just one of these subsystems but most frequently are related to the other subsystems as well. Also, solutions to organizational problems are likely to have interactive effects on several of the subsystems. For example, the introduction of a new technology, such as a computerized information system, will often require a restructuring of activities and procedures, will oblige people to learn new tasks and roles and to develop new group relationships, and will cause changes in managerial planning and control processes. A change in goals and strategies toward diversification will have implications throughout the organization. For example, an aerospace firm moving from aircraft production into mass surface-transportation systems may require major structural changes as well as adaptations in the other subsystems.

We have also suggested that there are several strands of management and organization theory with different perspectives and emphasis on certain types of solutions for organizational problems. For example, traditional management theory tends to emphasize structural solutions to problems. Proponents of this view stress the development of organization charts, more clearly defined authority and responsibility relationships, and well-defined rules and procedures. They also emphasize the development of more effective planning and control systems.

The management scientists tend to emphasize improvements in the technical system. They advocate technical solutions to problems; for example, a new computer system or a more effective plant layout. Their prescriptions for changing the managerial system stress the development of more sophisticated management tools, such as systems analysis, operations research, and mathematical modeling.

The behavioral scientists tend to emphasize improvements in the psychosocial system. They stress motivation and satisfaction of participants, emphasize interaction and communication among people and groups, and improvements in leadership. They will generally advocate changes in the managerial system toward more democratic, participative styles and emphasize the role of the manager in coaching, leading, and developing individuals and teams.

The systems approach suggests that each of these strands of management and organization theory has concepts, knowledge, and prescriptions for problem solving and improvement that are appropriate in dealing with some problems. We cannot reject any of these approaches but should seek to integrate them into a more comprehensive and situational view.

In this exercise, the management of Acme Aircraft Corporation is seeking the advice of three management consulting groups to help the firm develop a program for dealing with the problems raised in the case. The management executives have asked the consulting groups to make a preliminary investigation of the situation and to lay out a program of action which the consultant would help implement. They have contracted to pay each consulting group $1,000 for the time spent in this preliminary investigation. After they have heard the preliminary analyses and proposals for implementation from the three consulting groups, they will choose one of the consultants to carry out the program including the suggested changes. They have budgeted a maximum of $50,000 for services rendered in this second phase.

Acme Aircraft Corporation*

George Bruster took an engineering job with the Acme Aircraft Corporation soon after his graduation from State Engineering College in June, 1961. He was initially assigned the responsibility of supervising a group of engineers and engineering aides involved in conducting experimental test programs on various models of airplanes and airplane components.

Prior to his graduation, Bruster had spent several summers working for Acme Aircraft and had worked part-time for this organization for a period while attending school. At the time of his permanent employment he had held every position in the testing group other than that of crew chief. Because of his previous experience he was assigned the position of crew chief—an unusual assignment for a "new" engineer.

The average size of a testing crew was seven to ten individuals, of whom five were usually graduate engineers and the remainder engineering aides and technical assistants. The responsibilities of the crew chief included the over-all planning and coordinating of the test programs with which his group was involved. Approximately half of the crew chief's responsibilities were administrative rather than technical; and because of the nature of his responsibilities, the crew chief often was not the engineer on the crew who had the most experience or the greatest technical knowledge. Often older engineers, specialists in electronics or design, for example, would be working

---

*From *Human Elements of Administration: Cases, Readings, Simulation Exercises* by Harry R. Knudson, Jr. Copyright © 1963 by Holt, Rinehart and Winston, Inc. Reprinted by permission of Holt, Rinehart and Winston, Inc.

on crews headed by younger, less experienced engineers. This type of arrangement had rarely created friction in the past—especially as the older specialists were usually not interested in accepting responsibility for anything but their particular part of a testing series. In addition, crew membership was constantly changing as crews were disbanded and reformed as tests were completed and new tests undertaken.

Exhibit 4-1 is an example of the organization of a typical testing unit.

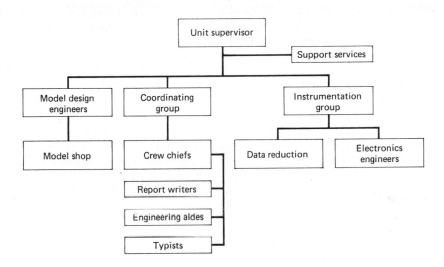

EXHIBIT 4-1 Organization chart of a testing unit.

On November 1, 1961, George Bruster's group was assigned the project of testing a new model component for an experimental aircraft which Acme was developing. It was only the second major assignment that George's group had had since he took over as crew chief in June. This particular test series was of prime importance, for the results of the tests would be instrumental in providing data upon which Acme would base its design proposal to government representatives. If the company could provide an acceptable design, it would be in a favorable position eventually to gain a large—and profitable—production contract.

The unit supervisor stressed the importance of this particular series of tests to George and informed him that the entire testing group was under considerable pressure from top management to get quick and accurate results. Top men from the model design and instrumentation groups had been assigned to the tests, as well as one of the best report writers in the coordinating group.

Because of scheduling problems regarding the test facilities available at the Bristol plant of Acme—the "home" office of the test group headed by Bruster—arrangements were made for the current series of tests to be conducted at the Culver City facilities of Acme. Culver City was located approximately 900 miles from Bristol; and while the Culver City operations were organized in the same manner as those at Bristol, the operations were run autonomously because of the physical distance between the two facilities. Thus, while Bruster and his crew would actually conduct the tests, they would be using the equipment and facilities of the Culver City operation.

George Bruster arrived at the Culver City test facility on November 7 to coordinate with the people there and make final test arrangements. After determining that the test was scheduled for December 1 and that his crew would receive the full cooperation of the local facility, he went to the data reduction group to arrange for the computer processing of data that would result from the test. The head of the data reduction unit, Gil Harmon, introduced George to the chief programmer, Dick Jones, with whom he was to work throughout the data reduction process.

George explained the importance of the test and showed Dick the type of information that would be required as final data from the digital computers.

After studying the information for a few minutes, Dick said, "I'll have to write a new program in order to give you the information you want. None of our present standard programs are capable of handling this job."

"How long will it take to write a new program?" George asked.

"Oh, I could probably have it finished by the fifth of December. That's the last day of your test, so it will be done in time to reduce your data."

"That won't do!" George exclaimed. "We must have data from day to day all during the test. This proposal is red hot, and we must analyze our data on a day-by-day basis. That's the only way we can be sure we are taking the right approach in our test program. Each day's testing will be dependent on the data from the day before."

"So, what do you think? Can you have your program finished by the first?"

"Well, I dunno," mumbled Dick. "I might be able to finish by the first if there are no hitches in the program, but things seldom go that smoothly."

"But it is possible to finish by the first?" insisted George.

"It's possible, but I have other important programs to work on. Everything would have to work properly the first time."

"This project is so important it just has to be done on time. We don't have any choice but to plan it for the first of the month."

"Okay, I'll give it all the effort I can. With a little luck it will probably be ready for the first."

"Swell," concluded George. "I'll count on it."

After concluding all pretest arrangements, George returned to Bristol. During the remainder of November he was in frequent telephone communication with Culver City. All preparations were progressing satisfactorily and Dick Jones assured George that the program would be finished by the last day of November.

On November 30 George and his crew arrived at Culver City. The test was to begin the next day.

George found everything in readiness for his test, except that the data program was not quite finished. He went to Dick Jones and asked what the holdup was.

"No holdup," Dick replied. "The program will be completed by the end of the day, and we can check it out on the computer first thing in the morning. If everything checks out okay, we will be able to run your data from the first day's testing sometime tomorrow night. So you'll have your data the next day, just as you requested."

"What happens if everything doesn't check out?" asked George.

"It'll take a little while to iron out any bugs that may show up. But it shouldn't hold us up much; a few hours maybe."

"Will you be able to work overtime on this if it becomes necessary?"

"I think so. We should be able to get your data for you one way or another, so don't worry. We'll let you know if we run into any major problems."

George was reassured and returned to his hotel satisfied that all was in readiness for the start of his test the following day.

The testing groups existed as staff units. As such, they conducted tests at the request of line and project groups who were in need of the particular information. It was the usual practice for the group requesting a test to send along a representative to make whatever decisions regarding the test program that might come under the jurisdiction of the line organization.

The requesting group for this test had sent along their senior project engineer, Richard Wallen, because of the importance of the test. Wallen was a fairly new supervisor but was well qualified technically. He was a "driver," worked his subordinates hard during rush programs such as this, and had a reputation of sometimes "rubbing people the wrong way" in order to achieve an immediate goal.

Wallen was directly responsible to the division general manager for the success of the program. One of his major concerns was whether or not the final data would be ready on a day-to-day basis. He asked George about it the night before the test.

George replied, "Dick Jones told me everything would be ready on time. The odds are real slim that anything would go wrong; and if something went wrong, it would only slow us down a couple of hours."

The following day the data from the first shift of testing was turned over to Jones for processing. However, the program did not check out properly and Jones was unable to give George his data the following day.

The same situation occurred the next two days of testing, with Jones unable to make his program work despite working several hours overtime each day.

On the fourth day the results were no better. Three hours after the testing shift was completed Wallen and Bruster went to see Jones. When they found that Jones had gone home, Wallen "blew his top" and told George Bruster to telephone Jones at his home and demand to know why he wasn't at the office working on the programing problem.

A few minutes later Gil Harmon, head of the data reduction unit, received a worried phone call from Jones, who quoted George as saying, "If you don't get down here and start working on this program, it may cost you your job!"

Harmon passed on this information to Conners Simpson, who was instrumentation supervisor at Culver City. Simpson was shocked and angered at the attitude the visiting group was taking toward one of his men. He immediately phoned Wallen and demanded an explanation. He told him in no uncertain terms to "lay off" his men and also told Wallen to follow the proper chain of command and notify him first next time there was a problem. In addition, Simpson stated that he "had no intention of letting Jones come down and work on your damn program. Jones has been working twelve hours a day for the past week and has several other problems to deal with also. Besides, it's too late to salvage much of the data."

Before he hung up the phone, Simpson told Wallen, "This thing has gone too far. I'm going to take it to the boss and get it ironed out first thing in the morning. I want you and your crew chief to meet me, Jones, and Harmon in the boss's office at eight o'clock tomorrow morning."

The meeting was held, but the test series was considered unsatisfactory by all involved. The group had failed to get the desired information, and additional tests would have to be rescheduled at considerable cost in time and money.

The meeting proved to be a unique experience for George Bruster. Wallen denied outright that he had told George to use the strong language in speaking to Jones that had upset everyone so badly.

George could only reply that he thought that such language was Wallen's intent. George subsequently left the meeting, shaking his head unhappily and trying to understand how the whole affair had deteriorated into such a mess.

PROCEDURE[1]

STEP 1
Before class, read the Overview and analyze the Acme Aircraft Corporation case.

STEP 2
Divide the class into four groups and randomly assign the four roles listed below. Each group should meet together, read its specified role, and evaluate the case from its particular frame of reference.

Group 1: Prestige Consultants—traditional management theory
Group 2: Modern Systems, Inc.—management sciences
Group 3: Human Resources Associated—behavioral sciences
Group 4: Management of Acme Aircraft Corporation

A brief description of the four groups is provided to help you get started.

STEP 3
Each of the three consulting groups should select a representative to make a presentation to Acme management, giving its analysis and suggestions. *Remember*, this is your preliminary report, and if you are successful in impressing management with your approach, you will be awarded the $50,000 contract to help with the implementation of the suggestions.

[1] The initial idea for this exercise came from reading Harold J. Leavitt, *Managerial Psychology*, 3d ed., Chicago, The University of Chicago Press, 1972, chap. 24, "The Volatile Organization: Everything Triggers Everything Else," pp. 259–265.

STEP 4

After hearing from representatives of the three consulting groups, management will confer to reach a consensus as to which consulting group it will hire. This will be done openly, in full view of the entire class. You must select one of the consultants.

STEP 5

After management has reached its decision, the entire class will discuss the exercise. The class may want to hear from the losers and/or take a vote on which of the three consultants management should retain. The result can then be compared with management's decision.

STEP 6

Read the Summary and Conceptualization and the excerpt "The Volatile Organization: Everything Triggers Everything Else."

ROLE FOR GROUP 1: PRESTIGE CONSULTANTS—TRADITIONAL MANAGEMENT THEORY

You are the local branch manager of this very reputable, older consulting firm. It is one of the largest consulting firms in the community and has been in business for many years. Your staff is composed primarily of people who have had substantial experience in business and know the ins and outs of many business firms. They have a thorough background and understanding of scientific management, the bureaucratic model, and administrative management theory. They generally look at management as a process of planning, organizing, staffing, directing, and controlling. You have generally emphasized the development of effective organizational structures and the clear delineation of authority and responsibility relationships. In past consulting assignments, you have designed new organizational structures (charts), developed procedure manuals, and written position descriptions. You have been active in the American Management Association, the Society for the Advancement of Management, and other long-established professional management associations. Your people make a point of dressing well and knowing the right people in the business community. You can really talk the language of the manager because you have been there yourself.

ROLE FOR GROUP 2: MODERN SYSTEMS, INC.—MANAGEMENT SCIENCES

You are a young consulting organization, having been in business for only 5 years. Generally, your personnel are also fairly young and have not had experience as practicing managers. But most of your people have advanced university degrees in such areas as computer sciences, systems analysis, engineering, etc. In past consulting assignments, you have generally not been concerned with the structure of the organization but have made recommendations to improve the *technical* and *analytical* processes of the company. You have substantial skills in statistics, computers, systems analysis, network planning methods such as PERT and CPM, and all types of operations research techniques. Your members are actively involved with the Operations Research Society, the Institute of Management Sciences, and the American Institute of Decision Sciences. You like to work with facts and figures but do not have much patience with all the frailties of human beings which seem to get in the way of technical rationality. You are comfortable with mathematical models and computers but a bit uneasy with people.

ROLE FOR GROUP 3: HUMAN RESOURCES ASSOCIATES—BEHAVIORAL SCIENCES

You are a relatively young consulting organization. Several of your top people are ex-university professors. They all have advanced degrees in clinical psychology, social psychology, sociology or the other behavioral sciences. You view the world from the humanist perspective. Although you do recognize the importance of structure and technology, your primary concern is to improve the organizational climate for more effective human accomplishments. In past consulting assignments, you have used laboratory training (T-groups), management grid seminars, organization development, attitude surveys, management-by-objective programs, and leadership training programs. You believe in maximum participation and power equalization within organizations. Your people are members of the American Psychological Association, the OD Network of the National Training Laboratories, and the Organizational Behavior Division of the Academy of Management. You sincerely like to work with and through people and do not feel very comfortable in dealing with the more technical aspects of business. You don't know much about accounting, finance, and other functional areas of business and try to stay away from these issues. You view your role as "change agent" in helping the people in the organization to improve their performance and to increase their satisfaction in their work.

ROLE FOR GROUP 4: MANAGEMENT OF ACME CORPORATION
You have had a number of problems in your organization similar to those of George Bruster and his testing group at Acme Aircraft. You have decided to get ideas from three consulting firms before you take any action. You will listen to their recommendations and then select one consultant to help you implement an improvement program.

You should select several members of your management group to listen to the presentations and to formulate your plans. The following four people should be involved (you may select others):

The Division General Manager of the Bristol plant
The Division General Manager of the Culver City facilities
The Supervisor of the testing unit at Bristol (George Bruster's superior)
A representative from the project managers

SUMMARY AND CONCEPTUALIZATIONS
This was not an easy exercise. Applying theoretical concepts to real-world problems is never easy. Likely, many different viewpoints were expressed and substantial conflict appeared both within your group and among groups. Poor management—it was placed in the difficult position of choosing among three alternatives and had to use judgmental decision making in deciding the direction in which to go.

You probably had difficulties in fulfilling your roles as different types of consultants. You may have lacked knowledge as to just what alternatives to advocate. We hope that you were able to utilize some of your knowledge gained in other courses in analyzing the situation and making recommendations. Perhaps you were even stimulated to find out a little more on your own about some of the approaches that might be utilized. That's good; at the current stage in your educational process you can't be expected to know all about these various techniques. However, most of you will have the opportunity to learn more about them in this and other courses.

You also probably had difficulty in sticking within your defined roles. It is likely that your recommendations moved you into one of the other consulting groups areas. However, you should recognize that different management consulting groups do have particular views of organizations and their management and have developed special skills and techniques. Like the handyman with a new set of power tools, they frequently are looking for places where their skills and techniques can be applied. They may have "solutions seeking problems which fit." And in complex organizational situations, there are usually places where their solutions are appropriate.

Which of the proposals is best? Our experience with this exercise suggests that there is not a consensus as to which consulting group is retained. Management groups have selected different consultants. In a number of cases, the management group refuses to accept any of the consultants' proposals but decides to seek a solution on its own (even though this was not suggested). But, they could all be right. A good case can be made for selecting any one of the proposals. For example:

More clearly defined authority and responsibility relationships and better planning as advocated by the traditional management consultants could help improve the situation.

A systems analysis of the computer facilities and development of network planning as advocated by the management scientists might help.

More effective interpersonal relationships, better communication, and participation as advocated by the behavioral scientists should lead to improvement.

The alternate possibilities suggest that each of the consulting groups may well have advocated a program which could lead to some improvement in the situation. There is "more than one way to skin a cat," and there are frequently alternative ways to approach an organizational problem and to obtain some improvement. This emphasizes the concept of *equifinality* as applied to systems. In open systems such as organizations, there are alternative means for achieving goals.

The management group had the problem of deciding which of the feasible approaches it should take. Supposedly, the executives also had a systems perspective in which they recognized that any proposed changes in one subsystem would have implications for the other subsystems. For example, what would be the effect of tighter structure on the motivation and performance of the human participants in the situation? Would the attempt to create a more fully defined pattern of authority and responsibility relationships create inflexibilities on future projects? What would be the implication of a program to improve communication and resolve interpersonal conflicts?

Management must deal with the complex interaction of technical, structural, and human variables. It cannot concentrate on any one to the total exclusion of the others. It should think in systems terms about all these relationships and should be prepared to use its best judgment as to appropriate courses of action for improvement. It is highly unlikely that it will be able to arrive at the optimal solution to every problem. It is hoped that it will have a good batting average (probability) of achieving a satisfactory solution to most critical problems. The following excerpt, "The Volatile Organization: Everything Triggers Everything Else," provides a good summary for this exercise and more ideas for reflective thinking.

The Volatile Organization: Everything Triggers Everything Else*

In this first chapter in part 4, we have just one purpose—to encourage the reader to think about organizations not just as simple, static charts or as milling collections of people or as smoothly oiled man-machine systems but as rich, volatile, complicated but understandable systems of *tasks, structures, tools,* and *people* in states of continuous change.

Toward that purpose, consider the following example:

> If, as a manager, you have a rather complicated problem, you may want to call in a consultant for help. Suppose the problem is a typically hard one: One of your larger field units is turning in much poorer results than all your forecasts had predicted. It isn't performing the assigned tasks up to standard.

*Harold J. Leavitt, *Managerial Psychology,* 3d ed., Chicago, The University of Chicago Press, 1972, pp. 259–265. © 1972 by The University of Chicago. All rights reserved.

So you call in the partner in charge of the local office of one of the reputable older consulting firms—the largest in town. They contract to take on the problem and send some people out to the unit to collect information.

When they finally come in with a report, you scan it and then turn to the recommendations. They recommend the following: (1) You need tighter controls. (2) Job relationships need to be reorganized and redefined; job descriptions need to be rewritten with greater precision (to get rid of squabbles about overlapping authority). (3) The functional form of organization they now have down there ought to be switched over to a product form. (4) In fact, that unit has grown so big that it ought to go through a partial decentralization itself, with a lot more authority given to the product managers. (5) You need a thorough methods analysis. The number of reports that are being generated now is excessive. There is wasteful duplication of effort and communication. You ought to streamline the organization's procedures. (6) And you may have to move a few people out, too. There is too much fat in the organization, and so on.

If you are a manager with an experimental turn of mind and a pocket full of money, you will decide not to act on this consultant's report yet. You decide, instead, to knock on the door of another consultant and get a second independent assessment.

You had gotten to know the first firm by now. You had found that the people in it were active in the Society for the Advancement of Management, and highly experienced in business organization. You note, with some discomfort, that this second firm professes different allegiances and displays other pedigrees. This second group is active in the Operations Research Society, and the Institute of Management Sciences. Its experiences in industry really are not as extensive as those of number-one firm, but it has done a lot of recent military work, and its senior people all have Ph.D's. It looks like a group of whiz kids. But they have cut their hair and they sound reasonable, so you hire them to look into the same problems.

They send their people out to the unit, and they, too, come up with a report. But their conclusions are different. Instead of recommending modifications in the *structure* of the organization, they recommend modifications in the *technical* and *analytic* methods being used. They are technologists who think technological improvement is the means to the best of all possible worlds. They want to linear program the inventory control methods being used in that division, and to automate the purchasing operation. They want to modify the information flows, so that decisions can be made at different points in the organization, and faster. And instead of job descriptions and organization charts as their tools, their pockets are full of computers and long equations. You will have to hire some hot-shot college boys if you want to carry out their recommendations, because neither you nor any of your top people can fully understand them.

But if you are really an experimental manager, and if your pockets are really full of gold, and if you don't satisfy easily, you call in the only other consulting firm in town. Its members are Ph.D. types, too. Their offices aren't very elaborate, either. Their affiliations are different, again. They are members of the American Psychological Association, and/or members of the consultant network of the National Training Laboratories. They are clinical or social psychological types. And they view the world from the human side. They don't carry computers in their back pockets, or write job descriptions, or draw organization charts. Their favorite tools are the meeting, the discussion, the face-to-face group, and the open-ended interview.

So you hire them and let them take a look at your difficult unit. And they too come up with a report. But their report is different again. It argues that the solution to unit X's problem lies in changing the attitudes and interrelations of the people in that unit. Morale is low, they say. Apathy is high. People are constricted and anxious, afraid to speak up or take risks. What your organization needs is more openness, more participation, more involvement, more creativity.

So their recommendation is that you work on the people end of the problem. They want you to set up an organizational development program, in which you take groups of your people from division X out to a country club for a week at a time to talk things over, to open up valid communication among themselves, to express what they really feel, and to develop much more mutual trust and confidence. Then you go on to a continuous O.D. program of team-building and problem-solving back inside the organization.

Probably you could go on experimenting, but the board members are giving you strange looks by now, and the people in unit X are really up in the air. So you decide to stop there and take a look at what you have. Which of the three firms' recommendations should you follow up? Since you are the manager, we'll leave it to you to answer that question.

But though we can't answer it, let's not leave it quite there. As of right now we have a situation that looks like this:

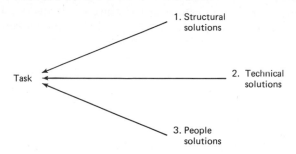

We have one group that wants to handle the task of unit X by working on structure, by changing the organization chart and the locations of authority and responsibility. We have another group that's going to solve the same problems technologically, by improving the analytic quality of decisions and applying new techniques for controlling and processing information. And we have a third group that's going to solve the very same problems humanly, by working on persons and interpersonal relations. But there is one more important point that needs to be made here, before you decide which one of these to use. They aren't mutually exclusive. The point is that the diagram above is incomplete. Because no one of these actions will affect the way the task of division X gets done without also involving each of the other points on that chart. Structure and technology and people are not separable phenomena in organizations. If we hire the structurally oriented firm, and if we decentralize the unit, or if we change the present allocation of responsibilities, it will not only affect the task but will also affect (perhaps adversely) people's attitudes and interpersonal relations. We will have to draw an arrow like this:

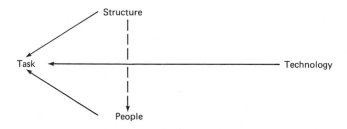

If you tighten controls, for example, some people may get angry or uncomfortable. If you switch from a functional to a product organization form, there will be new problems of interpersonal relations.

And if we play with the organization structure we will also get some effects on technology. The kinds of techniques that are now appropriate in a highly decentralized scheme—the accounting techniques for example—may have to be very different than those appropriate for highly centralized organizations.

And similarly, if we hire the technically oriented consulting firm, and go on to introduce the computer and new information flows, then we can darn well expect effects not only on the way the job gets done but also on structure and on people. If we can centralize information in locations where we couldn't centralize before, we will find decisions being made and responsibilities being taken in different places than they were being taken before. And while we may be talking about *de*centralization, that new information system may be pushing us toward centralization. We may also find that the kinds and numbers of people we need in our new, technically sophisticated organization may be quite different from the kind and number of members we needed before. Moreover some things that were done judgmentally and thoughtfully are now pretty well programed, so that essentially they can be done by the machine—with some consequent effects on the attitudes and feelings of persons.

Finally, if we move in on the people side, hiring the human relations firm, we will encourage people to be more open and more valid in their communication, encourage people to take more responsibility, and encourage people to interact more with other members of the organization. If we do these things, let us not for a moment think that we can do them without exerting great pressure on our existing organizational structure. The authority system will change and so will the status system. And we will exert pressure on technology too. The newly freed people may want new tools or the abolition of old ones that have been technically useful but are psychologically frustrating.

And so we move toward a diagram that looks like this:

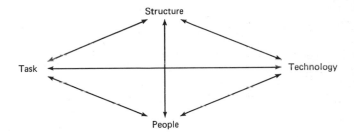

In this one everything feeds back on everything else, so that although we started out to worry only about the relationship between structure and task, or technology and task, or people and task, we must end up worrying about the effects of changes in any one on all of the others. Some of those changes may be very helpful, but some may be negative. And the manager has to somehow diagnose the secondary and tertiary effects of action in any one of these areas.

For organizations do not stand still. If we inject something into one part of the system, bells begin to ring and lights begin to go on all over the system, often in places we hadn't counted on and at times we hadn't expected.

We must take at least one more step before we rest. This model we have just drawn is still incomplete. It is a picture of an organization in an empty world. Certainly if there is anything U.S. organizations learned in the last half of the sixties, it is that their environments are anything but empty. The organization is very much shaped by its social life, by the pressures that are exerted on it by government, by consumers, by ethnic groups, and by hosts of other organizations. The modern organization is a city dweller. It lives in a pressing, crowded world. And it presses back. So let's enclose our model in a world.

This is not to say that the complexity of the organization is so great that we can never tell what will happen when we do something. It is only to say that an organization is complex

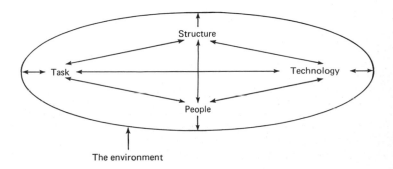

The environment

enough to make any simple structural or technical or human model inadequate. But we have made a lot of progress in understanding the complexities in the last few decades. We now know a good deal more about ways of acting on structure or people or technology; and we know somewhat more about how they are wired to one another. There is real progress in the organizational world. The three classes of consulting firms in our example should not be taken as an indication that things have gone to pot. On the contrary they are an indication of how much we have learned about organizations. And about how much we now know of ways to change or modify them.

The practitioner in each of these three realms may be oversold on his own product. He may be overly enthusiastic about all that can be done by changing structure, or technology, or people. Each may be partially and understandably blind to the perspectives of the others. But the manager need not be blind. He has lots more to work from than he did in the days when we so naively believed that the simple line drawing on the organization chart actually did capture the essence of our vital, volatile organization.

IN SUMMARY

Organizations can be thought of as lively sets of interrelated systems designed to perform complicated tasks. We can try to manipulate at least three dimensions of those systems in order to get the performance of tasks changed or improved. We can manipulate the organization structure—which means we can manipulate the communication system or the authority system or the system of work flows and processes. We can manipulate the tools and techniques used in the system—which means we can provide new and better hammers or new and better information-processing devices. And we can enter from the people side, to change bodies or attitudes or interpersonal relations—which means we can change the training and skills of our people or the numbers of people involved or the kinds of people we hire.

But we must never for a moment forget that when we tamper with any one of these three variables, structure or technology or people, we are likely to cause significant effects on the others, as well as on the task.

And we must never forget either that the organization operates in a world of other organizations and institutions, changing that world, but also being changed by it.

PART 3
ENVIRONMENT, BOUNDARIES, AND GOALS OF ORGANIZATIONS

You have looked at typical organizations in previous exercises. Although they may be distinct entities, they are also components of a larger system—the society in which they exist. As we saw in the exercise on Historical Comparisons of Organizations, significant changes in general societal values and goals impact all organizations to some extent. It is obvious that sandlot and Little League baseball foster different types of organizations and that the variations stem from their specific environments and goals. In the Acme Aircraft Corporation case, one of the most important forces was outside the organization—the necessity to meet the government's design requirements for an experimental aircraft.

Every organization is a subsystem of an environment that provides resource inputs and utilizes the organization's outputs. Each society has certain fundamental characteristics—people, values, technology, resources, etc.—that affect the nature of its organizations and their management. The social organization has a loosely defined boundary that separates it from its environmental suprasystem. However, organizations are open systems and this boundary is permeable to a variety of inputs and outputs.

The environment in modern societies is becoming increasingly turbulent, causing organizations to adapt continually. As society becomes more complex and dynamic, managers must devote increasing attention to external forces. In recent years we have seen increased activism on the part of groups stressing issues such as ecology, consumer protection, civil rights, and women's liberation—all pressuring organizations to respond to their needs.

Formal organizations involve people working together to accomplish specific goals. The basic values which underlie goal setting and decision making are a fundamental part of the organizational system. Values are normative views held by individuals of what is good and desirable. Social values reflect a system of shared beliefs which serve as norms for human behavior. For its very existence, the organization depends on a minimum level of values shared with internal participants and with the external society.

Goals can be considered from three primary perspectives: (1) the environmental level—the constraints imposed on the organization by society; (2) the organizational level—the goals of the organization as a system; and (3) the individual level—the goals of organizational participants. The general and task environments both have an impact upon organizational goals. Responding to environmental forces leads to continual modification and/or elaboration in the goals of the organization.

Organization goals pertain to the purposes and desired conditions which the organization seeks in the future. Continuing existence, growth, profitability, and stability are examples of such goals. There is a trend toward more explicit definition of the multiple goals necessary for effective and efficient long-term endeavors. Moving from the strategic through the coordinative to the operating level, goals and the means for their accomplishment typically become more specific, short-range, and measurable.

Goals of individual participants often are both compatible with and in conflict with organizational goals. It is necessary to satisfy a certain level of participants' needs in order to induce them to remain in the organization. However, it is unrealistic to expect perfect compatibility and complete satisfaction of all individual and organizational goals. Some conflict is inevitable.

Management has a major role in setting operational goals and in coordinating the implementation of action programs. Many approaches have been utilized to integrate individual and group goals with overall organization goals. One of the most comprehensive is "management by objectives and results" (MBO&R). We will use a version of this approach in one of the following exercises.

Many difficulties are evident in measuring and evaluating the performance of individuals and organizations. Both have a variety of goals and typically use multiple criteria in measuring performance. Regardless of the complexity, it is essential to establish means of evaluating performance (both quantitative and qualitative) in all areas that are important in determining organizational success.

The exercises in this section provide an opportunity to look at the impact of changing societal values on organizations. They also provide a means for setting your own goals and those of a specific organization.

Society's Views of Business: Survey of Attitudes toward Business and Other Institutions gives you the opportunity to assess your personal attitudes toward a variety of organizations and to compare your views with others in the class and with a nationwide cross section of society.

Social Responsibilities of Business: Scientists and Professionals Pension and Insurance Association asks you (1) to make specific decisions that reflect your views on a number of social responsibility issues, and (2) to articulate the rationale for your decisions in a letter to the management of the companies involved.

Goal Setting: Personal and Organizational requires you to think explicitly about your own long-range goals, to set specific short-range objectives, and to establish measures by which to evaluate your performance. The same process is followed in order to provide you with an opportunity to experience goal setting for an organization of your choosing.

Exercise 5
Society's Views of Business:
Survey of Attitudes Toward
Business and Other Institutions

LEARNING OBJECTIVES

1. To identify our attitudes toward business and other institutions and to understand the values underlying these attitudes.

2. To compare and contrast our individual views regarding business and other institutions and their social responsibilities with the views of other class members and a broader cross section of American public opinion.

3. To understand more fully the role of business in our society and the changing public expectations of business.

ADVANCE PREPARATION

Read the Overview and the Procedure. Complete the form entitled Individual Survey of Attitudes Toward Business and Other Institutions. Do not read the Results from National Surveys of Attitudes Toward Business and Other Institutions section until after your group discussion.

OVERVIEW

The organization can be thought of as a subsystem of the broader sociocultural environment in which it operates. The ideologies of the business enterprise are therefore strongly influenced by the values and norms of the broader society. In a sense, the values of the organization legitimitize its existence and activities in the broader social system.

We have seen the evolution of business ideologies and values over time. It is impossible to define a single current, dominant business ideology. Ours is a society of ethical pluralism, and the business manager, as an element of this society, is often caught in the middle of conflicting values. Pluralism has been a dominant characteristic of the American social scene.

Although there are many threads to this ethical pluralism, the major conflict appears to be between the Calvinistic or Protestant ethic and the Judeo-Christian or social ethic. The Calvinistic ethic supports the view that laissez faire and the profit maximization ideology are the basis upon which business should operate. It places primary emphasis on production efficiency and the role of the business organization as a creator of goods and services. The Judeo-Christian ethic, on the other hand, suggests that the business enterprise has a broader social responsibility and should not be concerned solely with profit maximization. These ideologies are often in conflict and present many dilemmas for managerial decision making. However, there is increasing evidence of the business community's willingness to recognize the social consequences of its actions and to participate in finding means for moderating any adverse effects. Furthermore, it has shown a greater tolerance for accepting the role of other institutions, such as the government and unions, in dealing with social problems.

Society's views of business have undergone significant fluctuations. In the medieval period commercial activities were viewed as a necessary evil. This view was gradually transformed so that business leaders were held in high regard, particularly during the second half of the nineteenth century. During the twentieth century there have been significant variations. The regard for business reached a zenith during the 1920s but declined to a very low ebb during the Depression of the 1930s.

Public opinion surveys taken during the 1950s and 1960s suggested a high degree of public acceptance. People regarded business favorably for its accomplishments in providing goods and services, for building up the economy, and for providing jobs and good wages. However, there were indications of some misgivings. People were satisfied with the economic output and functioning of the business system, but there was a growing concern about the social consequences of business activities. Recent public opinion surveys indicate more societal disenchantment with the performance of business.

In this exercise you are asked to respond to questions similar to those in a number of public opinion surveys taken by Louis Harris and Associates, Opinion Research Corporation, and Gallup Opinion Surveys. After you have completed the opinion survey individually, you will discuss your responses in small groups and then compare your results with those from national surveys. The process, if successful, will provide you with more factual information concerning public attitudes toward business and other institutions and will help you assess changing social expectations.

PROCEDURE

STEP 1
Before class, complete the form: Individual Survey of Attitudes toward Business and Other Institutions (pages 56–61).

STEP 2
Meet in groups of five or six to compare your individual responses.

STEP 3
Compare your individual and group responses with the published results from the national opinion surveys (pages 62–71).

STEP 4

Write out (on a blackboard or newsprint) one or two questions concerning issues you would like the total class to discuss.

STEP 5

Engage in total class discussion.

INDIVIDUAL SURVEY OF ATTITUDES TOWARD BUSINESS AND OTHER INSTITUTIONS

1. *Public Regard for Institutional Leadership.*

   As far as the people running our institutions are concerned, would you say you have a great deal of confidence, only some confidence, or hardly any confidence at all in them? Check your response for the following institutional types:

Institutional leadership	A great deal of confidence	Only some confidence	Hardly any confidence
Advertising leaders	_____	_____	_____
Congressmen and U.S. senators	_____	_____	_____
Doctors	_____	_____	_____
Educators	_____	_____	_____
Executive branch, federal govt.	_____	_____	_____
Financial leaders	_____	_____	_____
Labor leaders	_____	_____	_____
Military leaders	_____	_____	_____
Press leaders	_____	_____	_____
Psychiatrists	_____	_____	_____
Religious leaders	_____	_____	_____
Retailers	_____	_____	_____
Scientists	_____	_____	_____
Top business leaders	_____	_____	_____
TV leaders	_____	_____	_____
U.S. Supreme Court	_____	_____	_____

2. *The Job That Business Is Doing in Running Its Business.*

In your opinion, how effective a job is American business doing in each of the following 18 areas of business activity?

Activity	Positive	Negative	Not sure
Allowing people to use their full creative abilities	———	———	———
Bringing better quality products to the American people	———	———	———
Building new plants to make the economy grow	———	———	———
Contributing to the national defense	———	———	———
Dealing fairly with labor unions	———	———	———
Developing new products through research	———	———	———
Expanding new markets and growth opportunities	———	———	———
Helping take care of workers displaced by automation	———	———	———
Keeping profits at reasonable levels	———	———	———
Keeping the cost of living down	———	———	———
Offering young people a chance to get ahead	———	———	———
Paying good wages and salaries	———	———	———
Paying out adequate dividends to stockholders	———	———	———
Providing enough steady jobs for people	———	———	———
Providing job openings for blacks and other minorities	———	———	———
Providing stockholders with sound investment opportunities	———	———	———
Putting in latest improvements in machinery	———	———	———
Really caring about the individual	———	———	———

3. *Rating Business Help in the Community.*

In your opinion, have most business leaders been a real help or not much help in each of the following 12 civic activities in which they are active in most communities?

Activity	Real help	Not much help	Not sure
Backing scientific progress	_____	_____	_____
Building up the community	_____	_____	_____
Controlling air pollution	_____	_____	_____
Controlling water pollution	_____	_____	_____
Helping minority groups	_____	_____	_____
Helping the needy	_____	_____	_____
Setting an example of good citizenship for the young	_____	_____	_____
Supporting colleges and universities	_____	_____	_____
Supporting cultural activities	_____	_____	_____
Supporting education	_____	_____	_____
Supporting hospitals	_____	_____	_____
Working for good government	_____	_____	_____

4. *Has Business Been Taking Leadership in Key Social and Economic Areas? Should It?*

In your opinion, has business been taking leadership in the following key social and economic areas? Should it take leadership in these areas?

Key areas	Has been taking leadership		Should be taking leadership	
	Yes	No	Yes	No
Controlling air and water pollution	——	——	——	——
Controlling crime	——	——	——	——
Controlling too rapid population growth	——	——	——	——
Cutting down accidents on highways	——	——	——	——
Cutting out government red tape	——	——	——	——
Eliminating economic depressions	——	——	——	——
Eliminating racial discrimination	——	——	——	——
Eliminating religious prejudice	——	——	——	——
Enabling people to use their talents creatively	——	——	——	——
Finding cures for disease	——	——	——	——
Giving a college education to all qualified	——	——	——	——
Raising living standards around the world	——	——	——	——
Raising moral standards	——	——	——	——
Rebuilding our cities	——	——	——	——
Reducing the threat of war	——	——	——	——
Wiping out poverty	——	——	——	——

5. *What is your overall attitude toward business?*

Little approval _____
Moderate approval _____
High approval _____

6. *Just as a rough guess, what percent profit on each dollar of sales do you think the average manufacturer makes, after taxes?*

_____	0- 5%	_____	26-30%
_____	6-10%	_____	31-35%
_____	11-15%	_____	36-40%
_____	16-20%	_____	above 40%
_____	21-25%		

7. *Do you think business as a whole is making too much profit, a reasonable profit, or not enough profit?*

_____ Too much profit
_____ Reasonable profit
_____ Not enough profit

8. *In industries where there is competition, do you think companies should be allowed to make all they can, or should the government put a limit on the profits companies can make?*

_____ Allow companies to make all they can
_____ Government should limit profits

9. *Do you agree or disagree with the following statements?*

	Agree	*Disagree*	*No opinion*
a. Large companies are essential for the nation's growth and expansion.	_____	_____	_____
b. The profits of large companies make things better for everyone who buys their products or services.	_____	_____	_____
c. In many of our largest industries, one or two companies have too much control of the industry.	_____	_____	_____
d. There's too much power concentrated in the hands of a few large companies for the good of the nation.	_____	_____	_____
e. For the good of the country, many of our largest companies ought to be broken up into smaller companies.	_____	_____	_____
f. As they grow bigger, companies usually get cold and impersonal in their relations with people.	_____	_____	_____

10. *Do you think it is necessary for the federal government to pass new laws to help consumers get full value for their money, or are existing laws enough?*

Favor new laws _____

Oppose new laws _____

11. *What is the most practical way for workers to increase their standard of living?*

Produce more _____

Get more of what companies make _____

12. *How favorable or unfavorable are your opinions or impressions of the following industries?*

Industry	Very favorable	Mostly favorable	Moderately favorable	Unfavorable
Aerospace	_____	_____	_____	_____
Aluminum	_____	_____	_____	_____
Automobile	_____	_____	_____	_____
Banking	_____	_____	_____	_____
Book and magazine publishing	_____	_____	_____	_____
Chemical	_____	_____	_____	_____
Computer	_____	_____	_____	_____
Electric light and power	_____	_____	_____	_____
Electrical equipment, appliances	_____	_____	_____	_____
Electronics	_____	_____	_____	_____
Food	_____	_____	_____	_____
Insurance	_____	_____	_____	_____
Oil and gasoline	_____	_____	_____	_____
Packaging, containers	_____	_____	_____	_____
Photographic equipment	_____	_____	_____	_____
Prescription drugs	_____	_____	_____	_____
Steel	_____	_____	_____	_____
Telephone, communications	_____	_____	_____	_____
Tire and rubber	_____	_____	_____	_____
Tobacco	_____	_____	_____	_____

RESULTS FROM NATIONAL SURVEYS OF ATTITUDES TOWARD BUSINESS AND OTHER INSTITUTIONS

The national survey results for the first four questions were reported in Louis Harris, "The Public Credibility of American Business," *The Conference Board Record,* March 1973, pp. 33-38.

1. "As far as the people running our institutions are concerned, would you say you have a great deal of confidence, only some confidence, or hardly any confidence at all in them?"

Public Regard for Institutional Leadership

	"Great deal of confidence"			Change from 1966
	1973	1971	1966	
	%	%	%	%
Doctors	48	61	72	−24
Financial leaders	39	36	67	−28
Scientists	37	32	56	−19
Military leaders	35	27	62	−27
Educators	33	37	61	−28
Psychiatrists	31	35	51	−20
Religious leaders	30	27	41	−11
Retailers	28	24	48	−20
U.S. Supreme Court	28	23	51	−23
Executive branch, federal government	27	23	41	−14
Top business leaders	27	27	55	−28
Congressmen and U.S. senators	21	19	42	−21
Press leaders	18	18	29	−11
TV leaders	17	22	25	−8
Labor leaders	15	14	22	−7
Advertising leaders	12	13	21	−9

Source: Louis Harris and Associates, Inc. Reprinted by permission of *The Chicago Tribune.* All rights reserved.

2. The cross section of the public was asked to give its impression of the job that American business is doing in each of 18 areas of business activity.

The Job Business Is Doing in Running Its Business

	1973			1971			1966			Change from 1966
	Positive	Negative	Not sure	Positive	Negative	Not sure	Positive	Negative	Not sure	
	%	%	%	%	%	%	%	%	%	%
Developing new products through research	69	19	12	73	17	10	92	5	3	−23
Putting in latest improvements in machinery	59	26	15	60	26	14	89	6	5	−30
Building new plants to make the economy grow	55	35	10	51	39	10	78	12	10	−23
Expanding new markets and growth opportunities	54	30	16	53	30	17	X	X	X	X
Providing enough steady jobs for people	48	45	7	43	51	6	76	21	3	−28
Providing job openings for blacks and other minorities	49	39	12	47	42	11	57	33	10	−8
Paying good wages and salaries	48	45	7	52	41	7	72	25	3	−24
Contributing to the national defense	46	31	23	43	32	25	66	9	25	−20
Paying out adequate dividends to stockholders	42	22	36	43	23	34	56	12	32	−14
Providing stockholders with sound investment opportunities	42	20	38	42	24	34	56	12	32	−14
Bringing better quality products to the American people	42	52	6	47	46	7	75	10	6	−33
Offering young people a chance to get ahead	41	58	1	40	50	10	73	22	5	−32
Dealing fairly with labor unions	41	39	20	42	38	20	56	27	17	−15
Allowing people to use their full creative abilities	34	48	18	36	46	18	62	25	12	—
Really caring about the individual	22	66	12	20	65	15	39	51	10	−17
Helping take care of workers displaced by automation	19	61	20	22	60	18	40	18	42	−21
Keeping profits at reasonable levels	19	69	12	22	64	14	16	40	14	−27
Keeping the cost of living down	10	84	6	11	81	8	21	74	5	−11

3. In the social area, we asked if most business leaders have been a real help, or not much help, in each of 12 civic activities in which they are active in most communities.

Rating Business Help in the Community

	Change from 1971	1973			1971			1966			Change from 1966
		Real help	Not much	Not sure	Real help	Not much	Not sure	Real help	Not much	Not sure	
	%	%	%	%	%	%	%	%	%	%	%
Building up the community	−3	59	26	15	62	23	15	80	14	6	−21
Backing scientific progress	−7	53	22	25	60	19	21	64	15	21	−11
Supporting colleges and universities	−3	51	26	23	54	26	20	68	15	17	−17
Supporting education	−1	48	34	18	49	32	19	73	16	11	−25
Supporting cultural activities	−8	45	30	25	53	25	22	62	19	19	−17
Supporting hospitals	−1	43	33	24	44	33	23	64	17	19	−21
Working for good government	−2	42	35	23	44	34	22	70	17	13	−28
Setting an example of good citizenship for the young	−	42	36	22	42	37	21	66	21	13	−24
Helping the needy	+1	39	44	17	38	45	17	61	28	11	−22
Helping minority groups	−3	37	41	22	40	38	22	43	33	24	−6
Controlling air pollution	+6	25	56	19	19	63	18	26	42	32	−1
Controlling water pollution	+5	24	57	19	19	63	18	26	42	32	−2

4. Has business been taking leadership in key social and economic areas? Should it take leadership in these areas?

Has Business Been Taking Leadership in Key Social and Economic Areas . . . Should It?

	1973					Change in gap from 1966
	Has been	Should be	Gap	1971 gap	1966 gap	
	%	%	%	%	%	%
Rebuilding our cities	60	92	−32	−27	+7	−39
Raising living standards around the world	52	80	−28	−20	+18	−46
Eliminating racial discrimination	50	84	−34	−32	−11	−23
Finding cures for disease	47	76	−29	−27	+8	−37
Enabling people to use their talents creatively	41	85	−44	−41	−8	−36
Eliminating economic depressions	41	88	−47	−47	+2	−49
Giving a college education to all qualified	40	75	−35	−32	−6	−29
Controlling air and water pollution	36	92	−56	−61	−34	−22
Wiping out poverty	35	83	−48	−42	−6	−42
Cutting down accidents on highways	29	72	−43	−41	−21	−22
Eliminating religious prejudice	28	63	−35	−28	−3	−32
Controlling crime	23	73	−50	−40	−12	−38
Raising moral standards	21	70	−49	−41	−10	−39
Controlling too rapid population growth	21	44	−23	−24	+6	−29
Reducing the threat of war	18	68	−50	−43	−32	−18
Cutting out government red tape	11	57	−46	−38	−15	−31

The national survey results for the following questions were compiled by Opinion Research Corporation, Princeton, New Jersey.

5. Overall attitude toward business. (The findings shown below are based upon a modified Scalogram analysis of individual responses to six agree/disagree statements shown on pages 67–69.)

Overall Attitude toward Business (Total Public)

	1959	1961	1963	1965	1967	1969	1971	Latest
Little approval	52%	55%	52%	47%	46%	56%	60%	67%
Moderate approval	28	27	27	31	32	26	27	25
High approval	16	15	18	20	20	15	11	8
Unclassifiable	4	3	3	2	2	3	2	0

6. Just as a rough guess, what percent profit on each dollar of sales do you think the average manufacturer makes, after taxes?

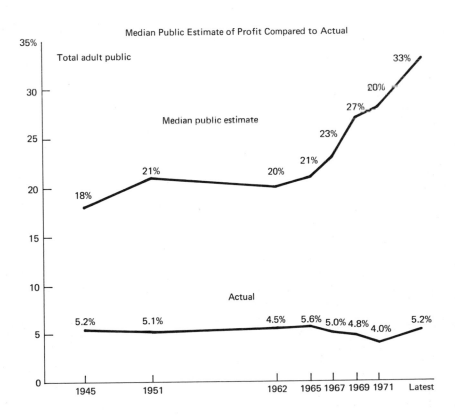

Median Public Estimate of Profit Compared to Actual

7. *Attitudes toward Profits of Business as a Whole.*
   "Do you think business as a whole is making too much profit, a reasonable profit, or not enough profit?"

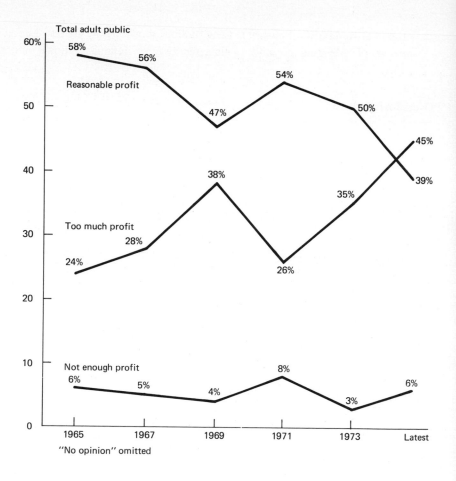

Total adult public

- Reasonable profit: 58% (1965), 56% (1967), 47% (1969), 54% (1971), 50% (1973), 39% (Latest)
- Too much profit: 24% (1965), 28% (1967), 38% (1969), 26% (1971), 35% (1973), 45% (Latest)
- Not enough profit: 6% (1965), 5% (1967), 4% (1969), 8% (1971), 3% (1973), 6% (Latest)

"No opinion" omitted

8. *Attitudes toward Government Control of Profits.*

"In industries where there is competition, do you think companies should be allowed to make all they can, or should the government put a limit on the profits companies can make?"

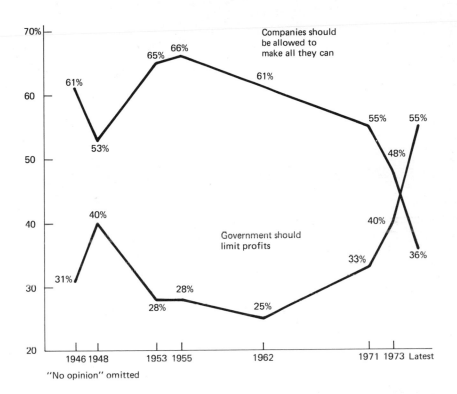

"No opinion" omitted

9. *a.* "Large companies are essential for the nation's growth and expansion."

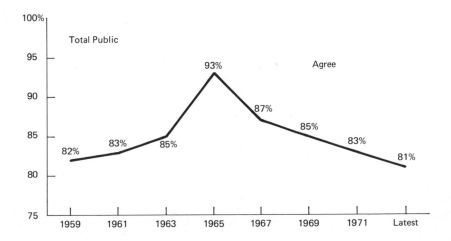

b. "The profits of large companies help make things better for everyone who buys their products or services."

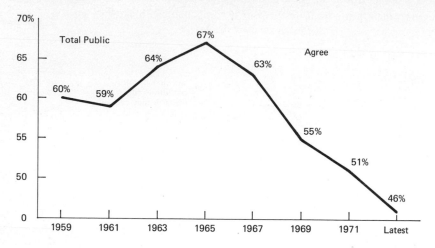

c. "In many of our largest industries, one or two companies have too much control of the industry."

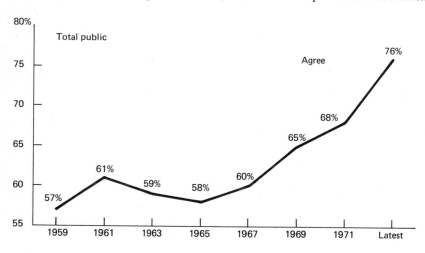

d. "There's too much power concentrated in the hands of a few large companies for the good of the nation."

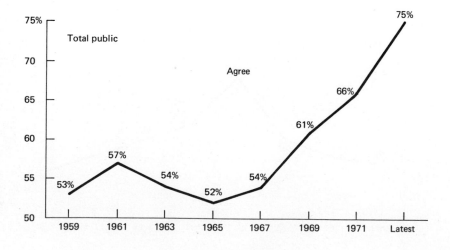

e. "For the good of the country, many of our largest companies ought to be broken up into smaller companies."

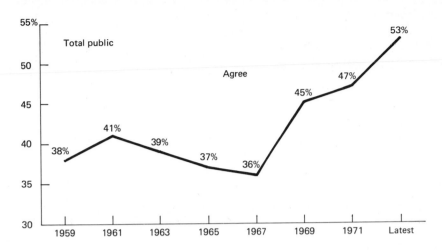

f. "As they grow bigger, companies usually get cold and impersonal in their relations with people."

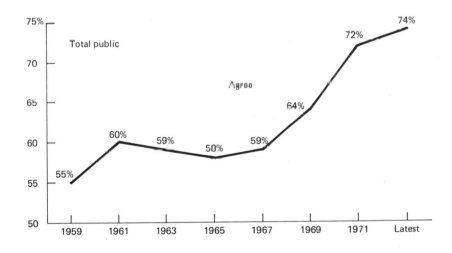

10. Do you think it is necessary for the federal government to pass new laws to help consumers get full value for their money, or are existing laws enough?

Percentage of Respondents Who Favor New Federal Laws as Necessary to Help Consumers Get Full Value for Their Money

1967	1968	1969	1971	Latest
55%	58%	68%	66%	66%

11. **Most Practical Way for Workers to Increase Their Standard of Living.**
"Which do you think is the most practical way for workers to increase their standard of living—by all workers producing more, or by all workers getting more of the money companies are already making?"

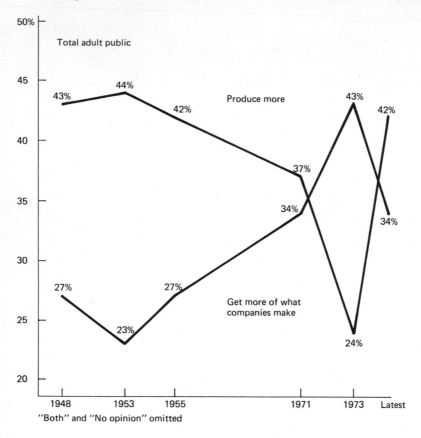

"Both" and "No opinion" omitted

12. How favorable or unfavorable are your opinions or impressions of the following industries?

Industry Favorability Trends (Very or Mostly Favorable)

	1965	1967	1969	1971	Latest
Banking	--	--	65%	58%	58%
Electric light and power	--	--	77%	58%	58%
Telephone, communications	--	--	77%	64%	57%
Electrical equipment, appliances	73%	68%	69%	57%	55%
Electronics	--	--	58%	46%	47%
Tire and rubber	70%	62%	63%	45%	47%
Automobile	75%	67%	63%	43%	45%
Computer	--	--	47%	43%	45%
Food	--	72%	64%	54%	45%
Prescription drugs	--	--	51%	37%	44%
Insurance	--	--	57%	34%	42%
Steel	64%	56%	47%	43%	42%
Photographic equipment	--	--	--	--	40%
Aluminum	69%	60%	60%	47%	39%
Book and magazine publishing	--	--	38%	36%	39%
Packaging, containers	--	--	--	43%	39%
Aerospace	--	--	--	--	34%
Chemical	55%	49%	43%	32%	34%
Oil and gasoline	73%	65%	65%	45%	34%
Tobacco	--	--	24%	22%	23%

SUMMARY AND CONCEPTUALIZATION

How were your attitudes concerning business and other institutions similar to, or different from, others in your group, and how did they compare with the responses in the national opinion polls? It is likely that there were varying opinions because of differences in your basic values and your own experiences with organizations. A variety of backgrounds usually leads to ethical pluralism—different views of what is good and desirable.

However, a common theme seems to exist in the various opinion polls. There are a growing disenchantment and a lowering of public esteem for business and other institutions. Did your group reflect this view? This rising skepticism is not directed exclusively at business organizations. There is evidence of a loss of public confidence in the performance of most institutions: business, government, education, courts, labor unions, religion, and the scientific community. One of the key issues is whether (1) our institutions are performing less well in meeting society's needs, or (2) there is a rising social expectation for improved performance which is not being met. We tend to favor the latter interpretation.

During periods of major economic, social, and technological change, it is difficult for established organizations to respond and adapt. Organizations, by their very nature, routinize and standardize their operations and screen environmental inputs in order to operate effectively. In a sense, they are "conservative" and resistors of change. These characteristics also represent a source of strength because they provide stability.

Organizations have great difficulty in responding to all society's demands, many of which are not well articulated and are often in conflict with one another. Frequently, social demands outrun the ability of organizations to respond. In many cases, we view social progress as too slow, not because improvements are not being made, but because aspirations outrun our ability to perform.

The survey results indicate that society appears to be changing the "rules of the game" for business organizations. No longer will effectiveness be measured exclusively in terms of economic performance. The public has increasing expectations for the performance of business in many social areas.

The survey results suggest a decline in the pure capitalistic ethic and a move toward a more complex social ethic. The public does not appear willing to accept the traditional competitive model as the gospel. In fact, many people do not feel that true competition is present in many industries. They seem to be suggesting a move toward modified competition in which society establishes certain rules of the game rather than let them be determined only in the marketplace.

How do we explain this rising level of expectations for business and other institutions? Certainly increasing education and knowledge of our population have been factors. Evidence suggests that the more highly educated and professional groups are among the strongest critics. Furthermore, social awareness of issues and problems in our society is rising because of extensive coverage by a variety of media—books, periodicals, newspapers, radio, television, and public hearings ("town meetings"). However, this awareness appears to be accompanied by a growing sense of helplessness concerning what to do about the problems.

On the positive side, we do see evidence that business leaders and other institutional executives are responding to social pressures. We may be discouraged that changes are not more rapid, but they are occurring. Our problem seems to be to develop more responsive organizations and leadership and not to let the gap between expectations and performance become too large.

While the survey results do indicate a decline in public confidence in business and other institutions, they do not reveal a "revolutionary" movement to destroy the system and start all over. The results suggest that changes should be made within the current institutional framework. Our society has become more educated, informed, sophisticated, and skeptical, and we have higher personal aspirations for the good life. This change has been translated into higher aspirations for our total society. We know we can be economically productive and produce many goods and services—history has shown this. We think we can be productive and *also* meet other social needs. This challenge is the key issue for the future.

One last thought. The very fact that we do have such public opinion surveys is a reflection of growing public awareness and the desire to communicate our views. Business and other institutions also need the type of feedback which these surveys provide. Although we may be frustrated at times and feel that we are not listened to, there is evidence that organizations do respond to such feedback. At least, these surveys are one way in which society can express both positive and negative views. In the long run, we are optimistic in believing that society's views really do count.

Exercise 6
Social Responsibilities of Business: Scientists and Professionals Pension and Insurance Association

LEARNING OBJECTIVES

1. To increase our understanding of some of the social responsibility issues facing organizations.
2. To identify the role of institutional investors and appreciate their potential impact.
3. To consider specific issues of social responsibility and to make decisions which reflect our views.
4. To be able to articulate and communicate our views concerning social responsibility more precisely.

ADVANCE PREPARATION

Read the Overview, the articles "Institutions That Balk at Antisocial Management" and "The Power of Institutions" and the excerpt "Social Issues Raised at This Year's Annual Meetings." Read the Procedure and all the issues before class.

OVERVIEW

In the preceding exercise, Survey of Attitudes toward Business and Other Institutions, you compared your attitudes toward business and other institutions with those of your peers in the class and with a broader cross section of American public opinion. In this exercise you will translate these attitudes and opinions into specific decisions concerning issues of social responsibility.

*All names of persons, companies, and associations have been disguised in this exercise. However, the issues are taken from real situations. The names of the institutional investors and companies involved were changed because it is not possible to present all the relevant information available on these issues; in fairness to the various parties, they should not be identified without full disclosure of all information.

The modern business corporation has developed into a major source of power and influence on the American scene. Over the past 100 years, the corporation has become not only our most important economic institution but also a major force for social change. Furthermore, the public at large and many business leaders have adopted the position that business has the clear-cut basic responsibility for efficient execution of the economic function—producing goods and services, providing employment opportunities, and stimulating economic growth. There is also an emerging view that business should exercise this economic function with a sensitive awareness of changing social values and priorities; for example, in hiring and employee relations, respect for environmental conservation, and meeting customers' expectations of complete information, fair treatment, and protection. Certain segments of the public are exerting growing pressures, and at least part of the business community is accepting the view that corporations should be more broadly involved in actively improving the social environment and in dealing with major social problems, such as poverty, urban blight, and the quality of life.

One of the current issues in the arena of the social responsibility of business is reflected in the role of large institutional investors—insurance companies, pension funds, bank trust funds, college endowment funds, etc. It is estimated that they control 40 to 50 percent of the stock in major American corporations. Traditionally, institutional investors took a passive role and guarded against interference with the management of the corporation in which they held stock. The basic consideration was profitability over the short run, and the institutions exercised their influences primarily through buying or selling stocks of individual companies. However, as indicated in the following articles, institutional investors have shown a trend to exercise their power to influence management.

Scientists and Professionals Pension and Insurance Association (SPPIA) is a nonprofit association which provides pension and insurance plans for scientists and professional workers. It has a wide variety of pension plans for both individuals and groups. It also has a number of group and individual insurance programs. As a result of rapid growth in these programs, SPPIA currently holds $1.8 billion in common stock in nearly 200 American corporations. These investments tend to be in the largest corporations.

The Association has become increasingly concerned about utilizing its influence to promote greater social responsibility in business. Obviously, profitability of its investments is of major importance. However, the Board of Trustees of the Association subscribes to the view that the long-term profitability of the corporations in which it invests will be improved if the firm is more aware of, and gives significant attention to, social issues. Therefore, the Association has established the Advisory Investments Subcommittee, which advises the Board of Trustees on how to vote its stock proxies at the annual stockholders meeting for each corporation in which the Association has holdings.

In addition to using the proxy votes, the Board has a policy of communicating its position on these issues in letter form directly to the corporate management.

In this exercise you are asked to take the role of the Advisory Investments Subcommittee and to make recommendations to the Board of Trustees of the Association concerning six separate issues with different corporations. In each case a group of minority stockholders has proposed certain changes which will be presented at the annual stockholders meeting. In every case the existing management of each corporation has argued against the proposed change. Your committee can recommend three possible actions on the proposals.

Accept—which is a vote for the proposal and against the current management position
Reject—which is a vote against the proposal and for the current management position
Abstain—which, in effect, says you think it is inappropriate to use your influence on this issue and/or you do not want to take sides

In addition, in each case you will draft a letter to the corporate management explaining the Association's position.

PROCEDURE

STEP 1

Before class, read the Overview, the Procedure, the articles, and the six proxy issues for consideration.

STEP 2

Divide the class into six groups (Advisory Investments Subcommittees) and randomly assign one of the issues to each of the groups.

STEP 3

Each Advisory Subcommittee should meet to make a decision on its recommendation for voting the Association's proxies and to write the letter to management explaining its position.

STEP 4

The entire class will convene to hear the recommendations and letters prepared by each of the Advisory Investments Subcommittees. After hearing each recommendation and letter, the entire class (acting as the Board of Trustees) will vote on whether to accept the Subcommittee's recommendation and letter. Keep a tally of the recommendations of each Advisory Subcommittee and the vote of the entire class on the Summary Tabulation, page 97.

STEP 5

The total class discusses the results.

THE POWER OF INSTITUTIONS*

THEY CAN INFLUENCE CORPORATE ROLE IN SOCIETY
by WILLIAM C. GREENOUGH†

Just a year ago, General Motors stated that "a corporation can only discharge its obligation to society if it continues to be a profitable investment for its stockholders." But it is time to rearrange these priorities: A corporation can only continue to be a profitable investment for its stockholders if it discharges its obligations to society.

In theory, stockholders can utilize their votes on the proxy to insure that corporations meet these obligations. However, in an increasing number of cases, some form of financial institution stands between the individual and the corporation. In fact, New York Stock Exchange statisticians estimate institutional holdings at over 40 per cent of all holdings. Thus, institutional managers have achieved a position of great potential power—and responsibility.

My position with one of the larger institutions has led me to consider the responsibilities of the institutional investor. Should he permit any short-run earnings reduction to improve the probable long-term economic gain of his institution and of society?

What guidelines can the institutional investor use, especially when he considers substituting his judgment for management's when voting against a management recommendation?

Is maximizing investment return a fiduciary responsibility that is absolute and unqualified? There is a vast amount of trust law relating to this subject, but a good many of the questions involved are primarily economic and social.

A major, perhaps the major, unanswered question is the time span over which maximization should be judged. To be sure, the name of the game is profits, but the game is a long one.

*The New York Times, May 2, 1971. © 1971 by The New York Times Company. Reprinted by permission.
†Chairman of the Teachers Insurance and Annuity Association and the College Retirement Equities Fund, which have assets totaling $3.8 billion.

Fortunately, most institutional investors are interested in long-term investments and long-term trends. This is true of university endowments, pension funds, insurance companies and bank trust funds.

They are interested in tying into the development of the American economy itself in its broad economic and social trends. If this is done, then the institutional investor can support and nudge corporate managements in their efforts to solve ecological and social problems, efforts that may cause additional expenditures in the short run, but gain effective new sources of wealth and income for many companies in the long run, and make government mandates and requirements with rigid specifications unnecessary.

Of course, this long-term orientation is not unanimously held. As with corporations, some institutional investors are, or have been, excessively oriented toward the short term.

For example, during 1967, 1968 and 1969 there was a high performance fad in the investment world. In 1970, high performance turned into low or even disastrous performance. The investment gunslingers should be unhorsed by now, but they will probably ride again one of these days as if nothing had happened.

There is another problem with the short-term investment approach. Assume that it were possible to choose which corporations were going to do a good long-term job, but only by reducing short-term profits. The short-term-oriented investment manager might shift away from them to other corporations showing a better short-term opportunity cost. Then, at an opportune time, he would shift back again.

This process would have to be timed well, but it clearly would be an obligation of the institutional investor if one accepts on its face value the possibility of maximizing profits in each time unit, and if one believes that prices of corporate shares actually respond that way to such forces.

There is considerable reason to believe that most institutional investors do have a longer time horizon and that therefore stock market pricing does not work as indicated above.

But if the short-termers were to have their way, where will the company or industry trying to solve its pollution-control problems get the necessary capital? Corporate efforts to solve problems are not going to be encouraged by institutional investors who jump in and out.

From a socially responsible point of view, undue emphasis on short-run so-called high performance is certainly not a desirable goal. Rather it is the long-term-oriented investor who will help solve the problems.

In the same manner, broadside demands are made that institutional investors should not finance public utilities or paper companies because they are air and water polluters. Such lack of financing would tend to remove capital from those industries just when they need it to solve the problems of air and water pollution.

In its supporting and nudging role, the institutional investor has access to a potent power lever available to move the American corporation—the voting of corporate shares. The coming decade will, without doubt, be one of increased activity in the area of voting corporate shares, both by institutional and individual investors. It is time we give careful analysis to this process.

It seems to me that there are seven options available to the institutional investor who must decide how the shares he holds are to be voted.

He may decide to not vote the shares. This may have been a viable approach once; certainly it is an easy way of handling things. But it is no longer acceptable. What it means, when shares of a corporation are 30, 50 or even 70 percent institutionally owned, is a vacuum in the responsible exercise of a corporate power.

He may follow the common practice and always vote for management-sponsored propositions. Advocates of such a policy claim that institutional owners should either have enough faith in management to vote for all of management's propositions or should sell the stock.

Such a policy implies that if the investor wants to vote for one opposition proposal and vote for six management proposals, he should sell the stock because of his one negative vote. This is an extreme and unhelpful approach, which does nothing to benefit the corporation, its stockholders or the public.

Institutions can vote selectively on the propositions. It is unwise for management to promote the idea that you're either voting for or against management. This makes everything a sort of parliamentary question, in which a single vote against a management position should result in resignation of the top management of the corporation. Most corporate managements really do not take that view of the matter. It is equally certain they would not resign unless the unfavorable vote was on their own continuance in office.

I hope in the future that voting will be considered a matter of individual balloting on specific propositions. Such balloting should take place under a process insuring adequate consideration of the issues involved. It should be the result of responsible and informed judgments.

Institutional management may decide to abstain actively. Some will always view such abstention as a "cop-out," but that is not necessarily the case. A pointed comment can be made by abstaining. The causes for abstention can be presented to management and, if desired, to a larger public.

Some have suggested that institutions might pass voting rights through to their clientele. I suspect that in most cases the expense to the institution would be prohibitive. However, there might be methods available to institutional investors short of pass-through that could be effective. Arrangements are so varied that particular recommendations are impossible. The question, however, should be examined by institutional investors.

Institutions might initiate propositions. This is an option rarely used except in a take-over bid. Its potentials for good are great, but so also are its dangers of misuse. Clearly institutional investors should not be trying to manage American business, nor to give specific directives through frequent sponsorship of propositions. But there are occasions when such initiative would be both practical and helpful.

An institutional investor may use any of the options discussed and add a letter to management. Such letters explain the votes of the institutional investor on either controversial or non-controversial items, and bring out the thoughts of the investor and his clientele.

While some letters in the past have been ritualistic, face-saving, public relations orations, the useful ones have been thoughtful and frank. Careful use of such a letter can be an effective way for an investor to try to change prevailing management attitudes even where the total of all votes on a proposition may be overwhelmingly in favor of management's recommendations.

In short, I think that the institutional investor should realize that his responsibility can best be met by considering the long-term future of his actual and potential holdings and by realizing that the environment, broadly defined, is an important contributor to this future. In the processes of achieving the maximum gain over this long term, he should carefully consider the options through which he can influence certain decisions of managements of those companies in which his institution has a position.

INSTITUTIONS THAT BALK AT ANTISOCIAL MANAGEMENT*

THEY ARE USING THEIR PROXIES TO DEMAND SOCIAL RESPONSIBILITY

Aetna Life and Casualty, a proper old insurance company with $1.5-billion in common stocks and no known radicals on its board, cast its proxies four times last year against the managements of companies in which it holds stock. Aetna supported stockholder resolutions that called for disclosing business activities in South Africa, ending investment in the South African territory of Namibia, publicizing political contributions and lobbying, and hiring an outside auditor. It will vote against management again this year whenever companies in its portfolio fail to live up to their social responsibilities, Aetna spokesmen say calmly.

Aetna is not the only corporation or institution currently gearing up for the annual attempt to use proxy power at spring stockholder meetings. Other commercial institutional investors that have either voted proxies against management for social ends or have established high-level committees empowered to recommend such votes include Bank of America, First National City Bank, Morgan Guaranty Trust, Northwestern National Bank of Minneapolis, Prudential Insurance, Travelers Insurance, Equitable Life Assurance, Teachers Insurance & Annuity Assn. (TIAA), Massachusetts Financial Services, Scudder, Stevens & Clark, and Phillips-Van Heusen (whose committee on corporate accountability makes decisions for stocks held by the company's pension fund).

*Business Week, Jan. 19, 1974.

A small but growing group, these companies explain their new activism in terms made familiar by the churches and foundations that preceded them.

"Our primary investment purpose is financial return," says Robert B. Nicholas, Aetna's vice-president for corporate planning. "But once you have bought a company's stock, you assume the responsibility of a shareholder." Adds William C. Greenough, chairman of nonprofit TIAA: "In its supporting and nudging role, the institutional investor has access to a potent lever to move the American corporation—the voting of corporate shares." Failure to use this lever leaves "a vacuum in the responsible exercise of corporate power," he says.

The issues. This year the companies will have plenty to exercise their power about, warns Elliot J. Weiss, whose Investor Responsibility Research Center, Inc. (IRRC), a research group formed by universities and foundations to analyze corporate-responsibility issues, includes most of the activist institutions among its subscribers. Weiss expects the heaviest volume of social-responsibility proposals to date, especially stockholder demands that companies publicize the minority hiring and promotion data they give the Equal Employment Opportunities Commission. The Glide Foundation, which supports San Francisco's Glide Memorial Church, has already voted to file such resolutions with American Home Products, Celanese, Schering-Plough, Southern California Edison, Southern Co., and Transamerica.

Other topics coming up at 1974 annual meetings, Weiss notes, are strip mining, political contributions, production of atrocious military weapons (with Honeywell, General Electric, and Rockwell International the prime targets), business activities in Latin America, Ireland, and the Middle East, environmental and energy policies, and disclosure of investments in South Africa and Rhodesia.

Most institutional investors, of course, will leave these hot issues strictly alone. They agree with former Securities & Exchange Commission Chairman William J. Casey, who maintains: "I doubt very much that money managers have the right to use funds committed to their trust to impose their social or political objectives on other shareholders."

The Investment Company Institute quotes Casey in its guidelines to members on how to deal with social responsibility criteria. It adds, however, that corporate responsibility issues should be considered investment matters when they involve management's responsiveness to change.

Indeed, even those companies committed to proxy action move with conspicuous care, emphasizing that they plan no wholesale assault against management on all social responsibility issues. Aetna, for instance, supported management last year against two other stockholder resolutions dealing with South African investments because it felt the two companies were handling the problems intelligently. And it abstained on a proposal demanding the appointment of outside directors after the company president assured Aetna Chairman John H. Filer that outsiders would be appointed voluntarily.

In this way, this assurance itself dramatizes the institutional investors' clout. It is rare for a stockholder proposal to pass, or even to get 10% of the vote, but most managements take notice when a substantial group of stockholders object to their policies—and doubly so when the objectors wield power in the financial community.

Scudder, Stevens & Clark, which supported a few social issues resolutions for the first time last year, abstained on others they felt were badly drawn, even though they favored them. In such cases, the investment firm speaks informally to management, says John L. Casey, a senior vice-president.

Most of the newly activist corporations agree with Casey that the 1973 proxy season was the "getting-to-know-you year, when we repeatedly found issues a lot more complicated than they first appeared." They agree also with Scudder Senior Vice-President W. Russell Peabody that this year they know more and expect to function more effectively.

"We've identified nine sensitive issues likely to come up in stockholder resolutions and have told our analysts to buck them automatically to our top committee," Casey says. The sensitive nine: disclosure, political and charitable contributions, fair employment and employee safety, restrictions on investment powers, environment, military contracts, director qualifications, shareholder voting procedures, and charter amendments.

Other subjects may emerge this month and next as stockholders file proposals under the SEC rule requiring filing at least 70 days before the issue date of the previous year's proxy.

The motives. The decision to vote for or against these proposals will involve corporate self-interest as well as morality, the activist investors concede freely. Lawsuits and bad publicity damage profits, they note, and the management that ignores this effect raises questions about its competence.

"If a company has a 'public be damned' attitude in this day and age, one could infer that the management is not too sharp," says Philip R. Reynolds, senior vice-president for finance at Travelers Insurance Co., whose portfolio holds more than $1-billion in common stocks. Other officials cite the EEOC settlement that cost American Telephone & Telegraph Co. $38-million, the EEOC suits against General Motors, Ford, General Electric, and Sears, Roebuck, and the less publicized EEOC complaints against 160 other companies.

Says Robert Heisterberg, trust department vice-president of the Bank of America, which manages stocks worth some $6-billion: "We have a high level of awareness about issues and how they will affect corporate performance. I tend to look at the implicit social contract of the corporate form of organization as a permanent part of the investment environment."

The decisions. Whether undertaken for moral or financial reasons, weighing the social merits of a stockholder's proposal requires hard work. "Several hundred employee hours were spent reviewing the question, mailing documents to owners, tabulating results, and voting the proxies," says Peter A. Heegaard, vice-president of Northwestern National Bank of Minneapolis, of its 1973 decision to oppose the appointment of a public director to the board of a public utility. "It would be only honest to say that the trust investment committee experienced new pressures and anxieties in dealing with the question." The bank polled the owners, Heegaard says, because "the presence of an interlocking director relationship made it especially important that the issue be debated fully."

Among corporate institutional investors, the pioneer activist was probably TIAA which began voting its proxies on a social-responsibility basis three years ago. Last year TIAA and its affiliated College Retirement Equities Fund backed shareholder proposals calling on Caterpillar Tractor, General Electric, and IBM to disclose their South African employment practices, on Eastman Kodak and ITT to disclose political contributions, and on Ford to disclose efforts to promote auto safety.

No other company has taken action on so many major fronts—in fact, no other company will even identify the managements it has opposed—but the trend is moving in TIAA's direction.

The Institute of Life Insurance, which omits proxy voting from the list of social-responsibility areas on which its members report, is considering including the subject on its next list, says Stanley Karson, director of ILI's Clearinghouse on Corporate Social Responsibility. The American Bankers Assn. has already come out for an activist position. "If controversial items are on the agenda and the trust institution has a majority or large minority interest, the shares should be voted in person," it instructs.

And here and there some institutional investors go so far as to quote Yale law professor John G. Simon, whose 1972 book, *The Ethical Investor,* laid down guidelines for Yale's own investment policies. "If the power of institutional investors is strong enough to control the outcome of corporate policy disputes," he wrote, "it underlines the extent to which investors, by failing to oppose socially injurious practices, may be said to cause them."

Social Issues Raised At This Year's Annual Meetings

Corporation	Subject	Corporation	Subject
American Metal Climax	Strip mining in Northern Plains	General Electric (Cont.)	South Africa review committee
C. R. Bard	Political nonpartisanship		B-1 Bomber/Product evaluation
Bethlehem Steel	Strip mining		Energy crisis impact report
	Withdraw from Mozambique	General Motors	Political nonpartisanship
Celanese	Equal employment		Facilities impact statements
	Women on board	Getty	Withdraw from Namibia
Chase Manhattan	Political nonpartisanship	Gulf	Political contributions
			Equal employment committee
Continental Oil	Strip mining in Appalachia		Equal employment disclosure
	Strip mining in Northern Plains		No sex discrimination on directors
	Withdraw from Namibia		One woman director
Du Pont	Political contributions report		Proportionate women directors
Eastman Kodak	Political contributions ban		Report on Cabinda operations
			Energy crisis information
Engelhard	South Africa disclosure	Honeywell	Military production— WIMMIX
Exxon	Strip mining in Northern Plains		Military production— antipersonnel
	Withdraw from Guinea Bissau		
	Energy crisis information	IBM	Equal employment disclosure
First National City	Political nonpartisanship		South Africa review committee
	Corporate information committee	ITT	Political contributions ban
			Political contributions report
Foote Mineral	South Africa border areas	Kennecott	Strip mining in Appalachia
Ford	Political contributions report		
	Equal employment disclosure	Manufacturers Hanover	Political nonpartisanship
	Operations in the Philippines		
General Electric	Political contributions report	Marathon	Political nonpartisanship
	Equal employment report		Political contributions report

Social Issues Raised At This Year's Annual Meetings—(Cont.)

Corporation	Subject	Corporation	Subject
3M	Illegal contributions "deplored"	Standard Oil of Calif.	Political nonpartisanship Board approval of statements Withdraw from Namibia
Newmont	Equal employment worldwide	Union Carbide	South Africa disclosure
J. C. Penney	Political nonpartisanship	Union Oil of Calif.	Political contributions ban
Phillips	Illegal contributions "deplored" Political contributions ban Withdraw from Namibia	U.S. Steel	Political nonpartisanship Strip mining in Appalachia
Pittston	Strip mining in Appalachia Mining activities report	Warner Lambert	Political contributions ban
RCA	Political nonpartisanship	Westmoreland Coal	Strip mining in Appalachia
Southern Calif. Edison	Equal employment disclosure	Xerox	Political nonpartisanship Woman as director
Southern Co.	Equal employment disclosure		

Source: Elliott Weiss, "Proxy Voting on Social Issues: A Growth Industry," *Business and Society Review,* Autumn 1974, p. 19.

ISSUE #1: EQUAL EMPLOYMENT WORLDWIDE

SPPIA owns 150,000 shares in Continental Equipment Corporation. This holding represents 0.6 percent of the total common stock of this corporation. The current market value of each share is $65 for a total value of $9,750,000.

The following proposal was submitted by a group of church-affiliated stockholders who own shares in Continental. This proposal will be introduced on the floor at the annual meeting of the company.

STOCKHOLDER'S PROPOSAL

Certain church-affiliated stockholders have given notice that they intend to present for action at the annual meeting the following resolution:

> Be it RESOLVED that in its operations abroad the Corporation will adhere to principles of fair employment, including equal pay for comparable work, equal employee benefit plans, equal treatment in hiring, training and promotion, and equal eligibility to supervisory and management positions, without regard to race, sex or religion. In any country where local laws or customs involve discrimination in employment on grounds of race, sex or religion, the Corporation will request its affiliates to initiate affirmative action programs to achieve meaningful equality of job opportunity.

They submitted the following statement in support of this resolution:

> The employment policies and practices of business corporations in the United States are subject to all pertinent provisions of the Constitution of the United States and the laws of Congress. The Civil Rights Acts of the 1960s have outlawed racial discrimination in hiring, compensation, training and promotion in business operations in the United States. When U.S. corporations, their subsidiaries and affiliates employ personnel in other countries, they are morally obligated to practice the same principles of fair employment there as at home. The proposed resolution requires the Corporation to be inventive in finding legal ways to move toward effectively equal opportunity for employee groups oppressed by local discrimination, such as Asians, Coloureds and Blacks in South Africa. It encourages management to use all proper means to develop fairer laws, regulations and customs. It sets a direction by which management's performance in a difficult domain can be periodically evaluated.

MANAGEMENT'S RECOMMENDATION

The Board of Directors of Continental recommends a vote AGAINST the adoption of this stockholder proposal. Unless the stockholder otherwise specifies in the accompanying proxy, it will be voted AGAINST such proposal.

The portion of the foregoing resolution calling upon the Corporation to adhere to the principles of fair employment is unnecessary because that has been the policy of the Corporation for many years and has been reiterated in our recent Annual Reports.

The portion of the foregoing resolution which calls upon the Corporation to direct its affiliates operating abroad to initiate programs of a political nature to bring about changes in the laws in other countries bearing upon employment conditions would require action contrary to the successful and time-tested foreign business policy of the Corporation. It would, therefore, not be in the best interests of the stockholders.

Continental Equipment Corporation has business interests in about 90 countries or territories. In the more than 95 years of its existence, it has learned that it can hope to continue the stable performance of its important function of supplying industrial equipment only by operating as a commercial entity, not as an instrument for political change. Wherever a Continental affiliate operates, it must not only comply with the laws of the host country, but it must avoid trying to force the social and economic customs of the United States upon other countries which have embodied different social and economic customs in their laws and regulations. To behave otherwise will jeopardize our continued existence there.

For those concerned about South Africa such a policy would be particularly counterproductive. Continental, working within the framework of existing South African law, has established a good record in providing wages and benefits to non-whites. Improvement has been appreciable in recent years. Thoughtful, nonwhite South Africans believe the continued presence of companies like Continental with their quietly progressive employment policies within the law represent their best hope for continued economic progress. For these reasons the Board recommends a vote AGAINST the proposal.

Issue #1: Recommendation of the Advisory Subcommittee on Proposal for Equal Employment Worldwide

For _____

Against _____

Abstain _____

Letter to Continental Management

President
Continental Equipment Corporation

Dear Sir:

SPPIA has decided to vote _____.

Our reasons for this vote are:

Sincerely yours,

SPPIA Board of Trustees

ISSUE #2: DISCLOSURE OF INFORMATION ON AIR POLLUTION CONTROL, AUTO SAFETY, AND MINORITY-HIRING AND FRANCHISING PRACTICES

SPPIA owns 400,000 shares in Universal Automobile Corporation which represent 0.9 percent of the total common stock of this corporation. The current market value of each share is $78 for a total value of $31,200,000.

The following proposal was submitted by the Stockholders Concerned with Corporate Responsibility who own a small number of shares in Universal. This proposal will be introduced on the floor at the annual meeting of the Corporation.

STOCKHOLDER'S PROPOSAL

PURPOSE: To require the Corporation to disclose in the Annual Report data in three areas: air pollution control, auto safety, and minority-hiring and franchising practices. REASONS: Shareholders have both the right and the responsibility to be concerned about the policies of the Corporation which affect the community. Shareholders require information about the Corporation's activities and its policies in order to assess their adequacy. The proposal would require management to furnish to the shareholders in the Annual Report the minimum information needed in three key areas of concern to the Corporation and its shareholders: minority-hiring and franchising, pollution, and safety. Unless this information is furnished, the shareholders would be prevented from carrying out their proper role as owners.

MANAGEMENT'S RECOMMENDATION

Universal in its Annual Report, its quarterly reports, its special mailings to stockholders and its numerous formal statements to the press has an enviable record of open disclosure to its stockholders and the public generally. Detailed information is also filed with city, state, and federal agencies. These filings are available to those having a legitimate interest in them. The final decisions as to matters to be included in stockholder reports, the degree of detail and the timing of the information included should be determined by those charged with the successful operation of the company. The degree of success they have achieved over the years is evidenced by the many awards Universal has won for the excellence of its reporting.

The Board of Directors of Universal Automobile Corporation recommends AGAINST the proposal.

Issue #2: **Recommendation of the Advisory Subcommittee on Disclosure of Information on Air Pollution Control, Auto Safety, and Minority-Hiring and Franchising Practices**

For _____

Against _____

Abstain _____

Letter to Universal Management

President
Universal Automobile Corporation

Dear Sir:

SPPIA has decided to vote _____ .

Our reasons for this vote are:

Sincerely yours,

SPPIA Board of Trustees

ISSUE #3: PROPOSAL ON OFFICERS, DIRECTORS, AND EMPLOYEES FOUND GUILTY OF ANTITRUST VIOLATIONS

SPPIA owns 300,000 shares in Progressive Company which represent 1.2 percent of the total common stock of this corporation. The current market value of each share is $101 for a total value of $30,300,000.

The following proposal was submitted by a group of minority stockholders and will be introduced on the floor at the annual meeting of the Company.

STOCKHOLDER'S PROPOSAL

RESOLVED: That the share owners recommend that no person, including present officers and employees of the Company, who has pleaded guilty, been found guilty, or entered a nolo contendere plea to an indictment for violation of any antitrust laws, shall be permitted to serve the Company as an officer, director or employee.

REASONS: Violation of antitrust laws by directors, officers and employees of the Company is a betrayal of responsibility to the Company. The Company occupies a position of such great importance in the business life of this nation that it carries a special responsibility to make its operations conform to its oft proclaimed support of the free enterprise system. Employment of such antitrust law violators constitutes in effect a repudiation of the basic principles of the free enterprise system.

Defendents' pleas of guilt, or failure to deny the criminal charges, destroys the usefulness of persons whose integrity must be above suspicion.

MANAGEMENT'S RECOMMENDATION

The Board of Directors recommends a vote AGAINST this proposal for the following reasons, among others.

This proposal recommends that no person be permitted to serve the Company as an officer, director, or employee who has at any time (regardless of how long ago), anywhere, whether acting for the Company or for someone else, ever pleaded guilty, or entered a nolo contendere plea to any antitrust indictment, regardless of the circumstances pertaining to the individual's involvement in the particular antitrust proceedings and regardless of whether or not, all things considered, including antitrust involvement, it might still be in the Company's best interests to employ the individual or to retain the services of any such individual. It is pertinent in this connection to note that, as the complexity of business and particularly of the law and administrative rules and regulations affecting business have increased, the possibility of being charged with a technical violation of these rules and regulations has become increasingly greater for corporate employees. This is true even though the violation may have been wholly unintentional or the result of action taken in good faith. In such circumstances to summarily fire all such employees, as this proposal provides, would be manifestly unsound, unfair, and contrary to the best interests of the Company.

The question of what action to take with respect to individuals involved in antitrust cases is one of great difficulty and complexity. There are many elements to be considered that bear on what course of conduct would best serve the interests of the Company, many matters of degree to be evaluated, many distinctions to be made. In deciding what action to take (whether to fire, to demote, etc.), many factors should be considered such as the following: There is the need to be fair to each individual, to take account of what each individual's behavior has been, the attending circumstances, whether his violation related only to the past and whether his current behavior has been in accord with the Company's Directive Policy, the extent of his involvement, his personal litigation expenses, the criminal penalties, etc. It is also important that action be directed to deterring future violations without at the same time being unduly punitive and vindictive. The individual's future usefulness to the Company is a further relevant factor. It may well be that a person who was once involved in an antitrust case can later loyally and effectively serve the Company in a position of responsibility.

These many and complex considerations, varying from case to case, demonstrate why the sweeping action recommended—fire everybody, sight unseen—would be indefensibly reckless and clearly not in the Company's interest. In fact, the obvious blunderbuss character of this proposal itself suggests to your Directors that the proposal is not really trying to make practical and constructive suggestions to help the Company in the midst of a difficult situation, but instead is simply trying to embarrass the Company and its management.

The Board of Directors recommends AGAINST the proposal.

Issue #3: Recommendation of the Advisory Subcommittee on Proposal on Officers, Directors, and Employees Found Guilty of Antitrust Violations

For _____

Against _____

Abstain _____

Letter to Progressive Management

President
Progressive Company

Dear Sir:

SPPIA has decided to vote _____ .

Our reasons for this vote are:

Sincerely yours,

SPPIA Board of Trustees

ISSUE #4: DISCLOSURE OF POLITICAL CONTRIBUTIONS AND CORPORATE LOBBYING

SPPIA owns 200,000 shares in International Corporation which represent 0.4 percent of the common stock of this corporation. The current market value of each share is $98 for a total value of $19,600,000.

The following two proposals were submitted by New Directions, Inc., which owns a small number of shares in International. These proposals will be introduced on the floor at the annual meeting of the Corporation.

PROPOSAL #1: DISCLOSURE OF POLITICAL CONTRIBUTIONS

New Directions, Inc., has stated that they will introduce the following resolution:

RESOLVED: That the by-laws of the Corporation be amended to require an annual written report to shareholders listing all contributions by the Corporation to federal, state and local election or referendum campaigns, and the following information with regard to any separate, segregated fund utilized by the Corporation or its subsidiaries.

a. The names of each fund's principal officers and their positions, if any, with the Corporation.

b. The names and principal occupations of any persons outside the Corporation who participated in the establishment of each fund.

c. An account of each fund's method of operation and the total contributions to each fund.

d. An accounting of the contributions, expenditures or other transfers of funds made by each fund.

e. The contributions to funds by officers of the Corporation.

REASONS: When a corporation commits its name and/or resources to the expression of a political preference, the shareholders have the right to be informed. This information is of vital importance for shareholders to make knowledgeable judgments on the performance of management. There is a growing public suspicion about business exercising undue influence on government, and unless corporations counter these suspicions with greater openness about their political activities, demands for greater governmental restriction and regulation of corporations may result.

MANAGEMENT'S RECOMMENDATION

Your management opposes the adoption of the resolution at this time. The proposal is ill-conceived, impractical, and unnecessarily burdensome. There already exist sufficient federal and state laws to regulate or prohibit political contributions by corporations. Adoption of this resolution may well lead to difficulties because it may be at variance with present or future laws on the subject. Management has always attempted to abide by these laws and the current resolution would increase cost and provide little additional benefit.

We recommend a vote *AGAINST* this resolution.

PROPOSAL #2: DISCLOSURE OF CORPORATE LOBBYING

New Directions, Inc., has stated that they will introduce the following resolution:

RESOLVED: That the by-laws of the Corporation be amended to require an annual written report to shareholders containing:

a. Brief descriptions of positions communicated to the federal government concerning any matter of unusual significance to the Corporation.

b. Information concerning all trade associations or ad hoc committees to which the Corporation belongs, amounts paid to them, and corporate officers or employees who held any position in the associations or committees. An accounting of how these funds were used.

REASONS: Under this proposal, the Corporation would inform shareholders about positions it has taken and communications it has made to influence policies and actions by the White House, Congress, and federal departments and agencies. Shareholders must know more about these relations in order to adequately evaluate management's performance. Shareholders should at least be told about positions the Corporation has taken on government matters that are of unusual significance. The disclosures called for in this proposal concern corporate lobbying activities that are generally not matters of public record. Shareholders know far too little about the Corporation's on-the-record political life; they know nothing about its off-the-record affairs. Recent experience has shown that the excessive zeal corporations sometimes demonstrate and the secret muscle they sometimes exert in attempting to influence the government can result in damage to the company's reputation and economic interests. The best safeguard against impropriety is full disclosure.

MANAGEMENT'S RECOMMENDATION

Your management recommends a vote against this resolution. We have always supported the view of full disclosure of corporate activities except in those cases where there would be a distinct competitive disadvantage. There already exists substantial legislation concerning the lobbying activities of corporations, and we will continue to abide by these laws. The resolution is vaguely written and the costs of complying for the Corporation would be substantial. Furthermore, we consider that it is not only a constitutional right but a duty for corporate officers to express their views involving national policy issues. This resolution would severely restrict this right. In a corporation as large and diversified as International, it is obvious that management and employees will have many and varied contacts with federal officials. To attempt to disclose all positions communicated on these issues would be impossible. Furthermore, the Corporation and its subsidiaries belong to a significant number of trade organizations over which we have very little influence as to the manner in which they conduct their business.

Your management is dedicated to the full disclosure of corporate activities whenever feasible but considers this resolution to be burdensome and unworkable and recommends a vote *AGAINST*.

Issue #4: Recommendations of the Advisory Subcommittee on Proposals for Disclosure of Political Contributions and Corporate Lobbying

Proposal #1   For _____   Proposal #2   For _____

                     Against _____   Against _____

                     Abstain _____   Abstain _____

Letter to International Management

President
International Corporation

Dear Sir:

SPPIA has decided to vote _____ .

Our reasons for this vote are:

Sincerely yours,

SPPIA Board of Trustees

Issue #5: NOMINATION AND ELECTION OF MEMBERS OF BOARD OF DIRECTORS

SPPIA owns 200,000 shares in Pacific Corporation which represent 0.9 percent of the total common stock of this corporation. The current market value of each share is $78 for a total value of $15,600,000.

The following two proposals were submitted by the Stockholders Concerned with Corporate Responsibility who own a small number of shares in Pacific. These proposals will be introduced on the floor at the annual meeting of the Corporation.

PROPOSAL #1

RESOLVED: That the shareholders recommend that the Board of Directors amend the by-laws of the Corporation relating to the nomination and election of Directors to establish a procedure whereby the Corporation's shareholders may submit nominees for the Board of Directors to be included on the Corporation's proxy statement.

REASONS: Under the current practices, the only candidates listed on the Corporation's proxy statement, which is furnished to all shareholders, are those intended to be nominated by management at the annual meeting. Shareholders may make nominations only at the annual meeting, after virtually all of the votes for Directors have been cast on the Corporation's proxy. This proposal would permit candidates nominated by shareholders to be listed together with management's nominees on the Corporation's proxy, thus permitting all shareholders to consider candidates in addition to those proposed by management. Shareholders would still be permitted to nominate candidates at the annual meeting.

MANAGEMENT'S RECOMMENDATION

Your management opposes the adoption of the resolution at this time in the belief that implementation of the proposal has not yet been demonstrated to be in the best interests of our shareholders or the Company.

Your management has stated repeatedly that the Board of Directors should represent all shareholders equally and not any special interest group. A person nominated by one shareholder or a small group of shareholders might feel obligated to represent and act only for the special interest group which brought about this election.

We believe that the present system of nomination has worked well, as evidenced by the caliber of your Directors and the performance of the Company over the years. Therefore, we see no real reason for change.

The Board of Directors recommends a vote AGAINST this proposal.

PROPOSAL #2

Shareholders Concerned with Corporate Responsibility will offer the following resolution from the floor of the annual meeting.

RESOLVED: Regardless of the size of the Board of Directors, three of the Directors would be nominated by groups of employees, dealers, and consumers.

REASONS: This amendment recognizes the need to broaden the decision-making base of the Corporation by adding to the Board persons chosen by groups who have a vital interest in the Corporation's affairs. Employees, dealers, and consumers are unable at present to influence significantly the policies of the Corporation. The Corporation will better serve the interests of the larger community if these groups can participate intimately in decision making. At the same time, the shareholders' ultimate ownership right to choose Directors is maintained since they can veto absolutely any candidate.

MANAGEMENT'S RECOMMENDATION

The proposal would require Pacific to poll the members of each of these three groups to determine their nominees. How the poll would be conducted is not specified, except to require that it would be done "in a manner reasonably calculated to reach each member of the constituency." With respect to consumers, the proposal states that a poll conducted through Pacific dealers would be "reasonable." This proposal is hopelessly impractical. No reliable poll of these groups could be conducted without setting up voting procedures as elaborate as the election processes of some of our states. Under the proposal, the expense of conducting such polls would be borne by all the stockholders. The proposal ignores the fact that each member of the Board of Directors is charged by law with representing *all* the stockholders. It seems inevitable that Directors elected under this proposal would soon find themselves in a conflict of interest. They would be divided between their allegiance to the group which nominated them—the dealers, employees, or consumers—and the entire body of stockholders, to whom each Director has a legal responsibility.

The Board of Directors recommends AGAINST this proposal.

Issue #5: Recommendations of the Advisory Subcommittee on the Nomination and Election of Members of the Board of Directors

Proposal #1   For _____   Proposal #2   For _____

                        Against _____   Against _____

                        Abstain _____   Abstain _____

Letter to Pacific Management

President
Pacific Corporation

Dear Sir:

SPPIA has decided to vote _____.

Our reasons for this vote are:

Sincerely yours,

SPPIA Board of Trustees

ISSUE #6: PORTRAYAL OF WOMEN IN ADVERTISEMENTS

SPPIA owns 60,000 shares in Gladex Household Products. This holding represents 0.8 percent of the total common stock of this corporation. The current market value of each share is $25 for a total value of $1,500,000.

The following proposal was submitted by a group of church-affiliated stockholders who own shares in Gladex. This proposal will be introduced on the floor at the annual meeting of the Company.

STOCKHOLDER'S PROPOSAL

RESOLVED: That the Corporation provide a special annual report concerning portrayals of women in its commercials and advertisements. This report should provide a summary of the various roles in which women are commonly depicted in the firm's most frequently used television commercials and most widely printed magazine ads. The description should include, but not be limited to, specific categories such as: housekeeper, mother, sex object, secretary, nurse, or social worker.

The report should also include an explanation of the specific methods and criteria used to pretest the ads prior to their public release. The explanation should also indicate the composition of pretest audiences by occupational categories and sex.

The report should include a statement of corporate guidelines for advertising agencies on the portrayal and utilization of women in our Company's advertising.

REASONS: Commercial advertising tends to reflect and reinforce existing stereotypes of women. They are generally depicted as "housekeepers, mothers, and sex objects," even though they make up nearly 40 percent of the nation's work force. Shareholders have both the right and the responsibility to be concerned about advertising policies which may depict adversely a major consumer segment of Gladex products. This proposal would require management to report annually on the ways that women are depicted in the firm's 100 most frequently used television commercials and the 50 most widely printed magazine ads. Shareholders have the right to this information and the responsibility to the Corporation to ensure that the advertising policies are in conformity with emerging social views concerning women and their roles. This annual report will help stockholders in carrying out their proper role as owners, concerned with the best long-term interests of the Corporation.

MANAGEMENT'S RECOMMENDATIONS

Your management recommends a vote *AGAINST* this proposal. We are well aware that in the past some commercials and advertisements have depicted stereotyped views of women. However, we have continually modified our advertising formats to meet changing social views concerning the roles of women. Throughout our organization we are dedicated to programs which eliminate discrimination, both overtly and covertly, in relationship to race, sex, or religion. We have made major strides in increasing the number of women and minorities in our professional and managerial ranks. We are obviously vitally concerned to ensure that our advertising policies and programs do not antagonize an important segment of our consumers.

However, this proposal is so vague and general as to provide major difficulties in compliance. Our research suggests that individual people react very differently to our various commercials and advertisements. Who will determine what role a specific commercial depicts? In issues of perception we have found that there are extreme individual differences. Furthermore, while we recognize that in the past there may have been an overemphasis upon women as housekeepers and mothers, we see dangers for the success of the Company in overzealously eliminating our commercial appeals to these groups.

The purpose of all advertising is to interest people in the purchase of products. Since over 85 percent of the purchases of our products are by homemakers, our advertising naturally presents women in the role of homemaker. Gladex Household Products disagrees with those who believe that the role of homemaker is in any way demeaning. We do not portray homemakers, or anyone else, in a demeaning fashion in our advertising.

We will strive to provide a balance in depicting modern women in their various and diverse roles, but passage of this resolution would be a hindrance rather than a help in this direction.

The Board of Directors recommends a vote AGAINST this proposal.

Issue #6: Recommendation of the Advisory Subcommittee on Portrayal of Women in Advertisements

For _____

Against _____

Abstain _____

Letter to Gladex Management

President
Gladex Household Products

Dear Sir:

SPPIA has decided to vote _____.

Our reasons for this vote are:

Sincerely yours,

SPPIA Board of Trustees

Summary Tabulation of Vote by SPPIA on Issues of Corporate Social Responsibility

	Advisory Investments Subcommittee Recommendation			SPPIA Board of Trustees Decision		

Issue #1
Equal Employment
Worldwide — For___ Against___ Abstain___ For___ Against___ Abstain___

Issue #2
Disclosure of Information
on Air Pollution Control,
Auto Safety, and Minority-
Hiring and Franchising
Practices — For___ Against___ Abstain___ For___ Against___ Abstain___

Issue #3
Officers, Directors, and
Employees Found Guilty
of Antitrust Violations — For___ Against___ Abstain___ For___ Against___ Abstain___

Issue #4
Disclosure of Political
Contributions and
Corporate Lobbying

Proposal #1 (Contributions) For___ Against___ Abstain___ For___ Against___ Abstain___

Proposal #2 (Lobbying) For___ Against___ Abstain___ For___ Against___ Abstain___

Issue #5
Nomination and
Election of Members of
the Board of Directors

Proposal #1 (Timing) For___ Against___ Abstain___ For___ Against___ Abstain___

Proposal #2 (Representation) For___ Against___ Abstain___ For___ Against___ Abstain___

Issue #6
Portrayal of Women in
Advertisements — For___ Against___ Abstain___ For___ Against___ Abstain___

SUMMARY AND CONCEPTUALIZATION

You likely found that opinions differed widely concerning these six issues. Questions involving social responsibilities of corporations are rarely clear-cut and one-sided. Conflicts often result because of differences in values and goals, and there frequently are logical reasons supporting either side on a given question.

We hope that your groups and the class were able to reach some consensus and did not take the compromise of abstaining on the issues. Even though you reached agreement, you probably had some difficulties in articulating your views to management in your letters. Many people are *for* greater social responsibility of business in general but have a difficult time translating this attitude into explicit action on specific issues. In our view, it is not the attitude (which may be expressed eloquently through public relations speeches) but the action that counts.

The voting of proxies on social issues by institutional investors is also a dilemma. Perhaps some of you felt that this entire approach was not appropriate and that institutional investors should stick to the traditional "Wall Street Rule" of vote with management or sell. With the growing importance of institutional investors, continued adherence to this concept would negate an important source of stockholder influence. "Corporate social responsibility" is not something to be left to "others" but, rather, is an area in which many participants in organizational activities should exert influence.

You may also have considered the question of how much influence such actions by institutional investors have on management. Some of you may have felt that the effort was futile—"They won't listen anyhow." We are more optimistic. We think that corporation managers do listen and can be influenced. In fact, we see many examples of how various groups have affected corporate decision making. Environmental and consumer groups have become a growing source of influence on corporate decision making.

Obviously, groups seeking to move corporations toward greater social responsibility don't win all the battles. It is likely that in most of these six issues, management's view would prevail. This outcome, however, does not mean that management has not been influenced. In many cases the people and/or groups interested in affecting the organization's decisions on issues such as these have been able to negotiate with management to reach some compromise. In many instances these compromises are satisfactory to both sides and the resolution to stockholders has been withdrawn. Influence has been used.

It is our view that all people, including managers, respond to the influence of others in the performance of their roles. These various "role senders" help the individual determine those attitudes and behaviors which are appropriate for a given position. The "role" of the teacher has been modified substantially because of influence from students. The role of the managers of our corporations as defined by society has changed substantially over the past several decades. The earlier socially defined role emphasized pure profit maximization and self-interest. The new socially defined managerial role places a much stronger emphasis upon social responsibilities. In this view, it is important for various groups in our society continually to send "role messages" to managers. In the past, the role senders for managers were likely to be close associates and colleagues who had very similar values and attitudes. The board room and the prestigious business club were the primary settings for influence attempts. Currently, there are many more role senders who are attempting to influence managerial decision making. This fact creates substantially more role conflicts for the manager and frequently makes decision making more difficult. These attempts to influence have at least been partially successful, and we certainly hope they continue. Scientists and Professionals Pension and Insurance Association is performing a valuable social function in helping to redefine the roles of managers and the social responsibilities of corporations.

Exercise 7
Goal Setting:
Personal and Organizational

LEARNING OBJECTIVES

1. To increase our understanding of the nature and role of goals in personal and organizational endeavor.
2. To experience an explicit goal-setting process, both personally and organizationally.
3. To determine the factors that are most relevant in making the goal-setting process effective.

ADVANCE PREPARATION

Read the Overview. Complete Part A of the Procedure, Personal Goals, before class. Be prepared to share your draft with two colleagues and to use them as a sounding board to help you refine your goals.

OVERVIEW

Goal setting is a pervasive phenomenon; in fact, all behavior is goal-oriented. Remember how Jack Andrews was concerned about his long-range career goals (a job with a large CPA firm), his medium-range goals (a summer internship), and his short-range goals (an appropriate schedule of classes for Winter Quarter). All of us have similar sets of goals with differing degrees of specificity and importance. Individuals, groups, and organizations plan and act (consciously or subconsciously) in order to achieve desired results. The question is not "if," but "how," goals are set. They are always set, at least implicitly. The real question is how goal setting can be made more explicit in order to facilitate improved effectiveness, efficiency, and participant satisfaction.

Value systems provide an overall frame of reference for goal setting; they are normative views held by individuals (consciously or subconsciously) of what is good and desirable. They supply standards by which people are influenced in their choice of actions. When we use the words "should" or "ought," we are making value statements. The Ten Commandments are value statements about desirable human behavior. The laws of a nation, state, or municipality are codified, formal value systems governing both personal and organizational behavior. The Bill of Rights is a reflection of our society's emphasis on individual freedom.

Organizations appear to hold certain values, but defining them precisely and showing how they influence goal setting and decision making are difficult. The difficulty stems from potentially conflicting values—for example, individualism versus cooperation. By definition, organizations (two or more people jointly pursuing a common goal) require cooperation and hence preclude completely individualistic purposes and actions.

Every human participant brings a certain set of values to the organization. Value inputs also come from a variety of external sources—customers, competitors, suppliers, and other elements of the organization's task environment. Therefore, in dealing with value issues, we should consider at least five levels:

Individual values: Those values held by individuals that affect their actions.

Group values: Those values held by small, informal, and formal groups (a consensus of the members) that affect the behavior of individuals and also the actions of the organization.

Organizational values: Those values held by the organization as a whole—a composite of individual, group, total organizational, and cultural inputs.

Values of constituents of the task environment: Values held by those in direct contact with the organization—customers, suppliers, competitors, governmental agencies, etc.

Cultural values: Values held by the entire society.

This ever-present value system provides a framework for goal setting. It provides the means of determining (1) which goals are legitimate or illegitimate; (2) relative merit among several goals; and (3) the legitimacy and/or merit of potential means of achieving goals.

Emphasis on long-range planning, management by objectives, or other programmatic methods are efforts toward explicit goal setting. They provide a means of emphasizing desired future conditions which the organization strives to achieve. They include consideration of a hierarchy of goals which includes missions, purposes, objectives, targets, quotas, and deadlines. As we move down the hierarchy, the goals become more definitive, quantifiable, and measurable. Filing your income tax return by April 15 is a specific goal with measurable results—you either get it in the mail by midnight on April 15 or you don't. A sales quota of 10 automobiles per week is definite and measurable. A quota of 10 new customer contacts for life insurance seems definite, but measurability may be a problem unless "contact" is spelled out in more detail. The desired results are completed sales, premium income, and longevity (continued premium payment).

The term *objective* is often used as synonymous with goal, an approach that is quite appropriate as long as there is a recognition of a variety of objectives differentiated on the basis of time, specificity, and measurability. We prefer the use of the term *goal* to cover the entire spectrum and to refer to objectives as operational goals that are attainable, although not always quantifiable. "To improve customer service" is a legitimate objective that may be difficult to measure. Our own perceptions of customer satisfaction might be a first approximation to evaluation; a random sample of customer opinion might be used; or a comparison of the number of customer complaints from one time period to the next might be used. Other typical objectives include profitability (return on sales, assets, or net worth), market share, total sales, efficiency (cost per unit or output per man-hour), and new services or products introduced.

At the top of the goal hierarchy, statements of mission or purpose are usually so comprehensive and/or long-range that they defy measurement. For any organization, a basic purpose is to provide goods or service and to survive (through profits or budgetary allocations) long enough to do so. The time frame may be fixed or open-ended. For example, consider the following statement of the mission or purpose of a typical university.

> The university is a base for the free generation and exploration of ideas and for the preservation of the intellectual and cultural heritage of mankind. It is a resource provided by society for use by individuals in pursuit of the highest scholarly, esthetic and humane goals to which mankind can aspire. As such, it must both attract and cultivate men and women of high capability and must develop their potentialities as human beings. In turn, society can expect to gain from its

universities both increasing knowledge and informed, sensitive, vigorous persons prepared to work toward the improvement of man's condition.

To fulfill these purposes, universities typically engage in teaching, research, and service. Thus, it would be necessary to establish goals in each of these areas. Moreover, we would want to subdivide the areas in an attempt to establish meaningful operational objectives. Teaching might be subdivided into undergraduate, graduate, professional, and non-degree programs. If the educational program were to be measured on the basis of number of graduates per year, we would have a definite, measurable goal. However, if the goal is "amount of learning per year," measurement is much more difficult, if not impossible.

Over the past several decades, programmatic efforts to increase effectiveness, efficiency, and participant satisfaction via explicit goal setting have received considerable attention. Two examples are *life and career planning* for individuals and *management by objectives and results* for organizations. This exercise provides an opportunity to experience both these processes. However, because the elements or steps are quite similar, we will discuss the general framework within an organizational setting.

One of the first steps is a personal and/or organizational commitment (value judgment or norm) that emphasis will be placed on results. Obviously, however, means of achievement should be considered, and they must be legitimate, wholesome, and appropriate over the long run. The second step is to identify key areas of concern. Objectives are needed in every area where results affect the survival and performance of the organization. What specific objectives must be accomplished in order to achieve overall, long-range purposes? Within the total list we need to assign priorities in order that efforts can be focused most appropriately. The next step is to make specific objectives operational by ensuring that they are clear, challenging, measurable (quantitatively and/or qualitatively), and integrated (e.g., among individuals and/or organizational subunits that are interdependent). Figure 7-1 provides some guidelines for checking to see that objectives have been constructed appropriately.

---

1. Is the objective statement constructed properly?
   a. Does it start with the word "To," followed by an action verb?
   b. Does it specify a single key result to be accomplished?
   c. Does it specify a target date for its accomplishment?
2. Is it measurable and verifiable?
3. Does it relate directly to the manager's role and mission and to higher-level roles, missions, and objectives?
4. Can it be readily understood by those who must implement it?
5. Is the objective a realistic and attainable one that still represents a significant challenge to the manager and the organization?
6. Will the result, when achieved, justify the expenditure of time and resources required to achieve it?
7. Is the objective consistent with basic company and organizational policies and practices?
8. Can the accountability for final results be clearly established?

FIGURE 7-1 Key questions for evaluating objectives.

Source: Adapted from George L. Morrisey, *Management by Objectives and Results,* Reading, Mass., Addison-Wesley, 1970, p. 63.

PROCEDURE

This exercise provides an opportunity to practice goal setting in two different situations: (A) your personal life and career goals, and (B) the goals of either an actual or a hypothetical organization.

Part A should be completed individually before class and the results shared by trios of students during the first phase of the session.

Use the same or different trios for Part B. Either of two options might be selected at this point: (1) an actual organization which is familiar to at least one person in the group, or (2) a hypothetical organization (a new venture, such as a tavern or hobby shop) for which the group would serve as founding partners, officers, or directors. In either case, each trio should have a reasonable degree of expertise with regard to the specific type of organization selected, so that the goal-setting process can be realistic.

A: PERSONAL GOALS

STEP 1
Write a description of a successful "you." Jot down the first thoughts that come to mind; use descriptive phrases or adjectives; don't worry about complete sentences or polished prose. Brainstorm some ideas without evaluating them at this stage. Think in terms of outcomes or results—not activities (e.g., a bowling average of 180, a golf handicap of 10 or less, ownership of a specific business, or an income of $?????). Push yourself to be long-range and comprehensive (a variety of dimensions). Ten years from now, how would a close friend or a colleague describe you in an ideal letter of recommendation?

STEP 2
Refine the ideas expressed in Step 1 by listing the important areas of concern or key dimensions (e.g., family, career, vocational, and personal skills), that will be important for you in determining success.

STEP 3

Determine priorities for the above items by identifying the most important as 1, the second most important as 2, and so forth throughout the list. Write the five most important dimensions in the spaces below and describe how you will measure performance and/or judge results. Be as specific as possible while recognizing that not all indicators can be quantified.

Key areas of concern   *Measures of performance*

1. _____   _____
                                   _____
                                   _____

2. _____   _____
                                   _____
                                   _____

3. _____   _____
                                   _____
                                   _____

4. _____   _____
                                   _____
                                   _____

5. _____   _____
                                   _____
                                   _____

STEP 4

For each of the key areas of concern that you have identified in Step 3, write several specific objectives for a relatively short time period—one year or less. Refer to Figure 7-1 for guidelines.

Key areas of concern   *Specific short-term objectives*

STEP 4 *Specific objectives* (continued)

Key areas of concern   *Specific short-term objectives*

STEP 5

Review Steps 1 through 4. Check to see if the several phases are consistent. Do the key areas of concern "fit" your overall goals? Do the specific objectives "fit" the key areas? Are the various elements interdependent? If so, are they supportive or potentially conflictive? Note any problems that suggest adjustments at this stage or that you should at least be aware of in the future.

STEP 6

Reflect on your statement of objectives and make some preliminary estimates of the actions that will be required to achieve them. How much control do you have? Are there any major contingencies that could affect your results? What resources are required? Are you dependent on other people? To what extent? Should you engage in joint goal setting and planning with key people? Make notes concerning these and other considerations for future reference in a later exercise on action planning.

STEP 7

Take a few minutes to think about how you will follow up and evaluate progress toward your goals. How will you initiate the evaluation? How much will you rely on your own interpretation of the results? On others' interpretations or generally recognized standards? How will you learn from your experience in order to become more effective in future goal-setting efforts?

STEP 8

Share the results of your goal-setting efforts with two colleagues. Use the guidelines in Figure 7-1 to facilitate the evaluation process. Note similarities and differences. Refine your statements on the basis of feedback from this discussion.

B: ORGANIZATION GOALS

STEP 1

Work in groups of three—the same trio you used in Part A or a different trio based on common interest in a specific actual or hypothetical (new venture) organization (see page 101). Write a description of a successful organization. Jot down the first thoughts that come to mind concerning organizations in general and the specific one that you are using for this part of the exercise; use descriptive phrases or adjectives; don't worry about complete sentences or polished prose. Brainstorm some ideas without evaluating them at this stage. Think in terms of outcomes or results—not activities (e.g., sales, return on investment, client/customer satisfaction, or innovations in products/services). Push yourselves to be long-range and comprehensive (a variety of dimensions). From management's point of view, what would an ideal organization be like?

Name of organization: _____

STEP 2

Refine the ideas expressed in Step 1 by listing the important areas of concern or key dimensions (e.g., size, profitability, customer relations, employee relations) that will be important to you as managers in determining success.

STEP 3

Rank the above items by priority, identifying the most important as 1, the second most important as 2, and so forth throughout the list. Write the five most important dimensions in the spaces below and describe how you will measure performance and/or judge results. Be as specific as possible while recognizing that not all indicators can be quantified.

Key areas of concern   *Measures of performance*

1. _____   _____

   _____

   _____

2. _____   _____

   _____

   _____

3. _____   _____

   _____

   _____

4. _____   _____

   _____

   _____

5. _____   _____

   _____

   _____

STEP 4

For each of the key areas of concern that you have identified in Step 3, write several specific objectives for a relatively short time period—one year or less. Refer to Figure 7-1 for guidelines.

Key areas of concern   *Specific short-term objectives*

STEP 4 *Specific objectives* (continued)

Key areas of concern   *Specific short-term objectives*

STEP 5

Review Steps 1 through 4. Check to see if the several phases are consistent. Do the key areas of concern "fit" the overall goals? Do the specific objectives "fit" the key areas? Are the various elements interdependent? If so, are they supportive or potentially conflictive? Note any problems that suggest adjustments at this stage or that you should at least be aware of in the future.

STEP 6

Reflect on your statement of objectives and make some preliminary estimates of the actions that will be required to achieve them. How much control do you have? Are there any major contingencies that could affect the results? What resources are required? Are you dependent on "outside" individuals or organizations (banks, suppliers, government agencies, etc.)? To what extent? Should you engage in joint goal setting and planning with key outside people or organizations? Make notes concerning these and other considerations for future reference in a later exercise on action planning.

STEP 7

Take a few minutes to think about how you will follow up and evaluate progress toward your goals. How will you initiate the evaluation? How much will you rely on your own interpretation of the results? On others' interpretations or generally recognized standards? How will you learn from your experience in order to become more effective in future goal-setting efforts?

STEP 8

Share the results of your goal-setting efforts with another trio. Use the guidelines in Figure 7-1 to facilitate the evaluation process. Note similarities and differences across types of organizations (public–private, large–small, new–old, etc.). What conclusions emerge?

SUMMARY AND CONCEPTUALIZATION

Goal setting is a pervasive human activity; in fact, all behavior is goal-oriented. Individual and organizational activity is directed toward goals that are set implicitly, if not explicitly. Goals can be identified along a spectrum of varying specificity from vague, general descriptions of mission or purpose to more definite, measurable objectives (including targets, quotas, and deadlines). The goal-setting process is the first step in developing long-range, comprehensive plans that in turn facilitate managerial direction and control of organizational endeavor. Explicit objectives encourage achievement, and if good performance is recognized and rewarded, the performer gains a sense of accomplishment, satisfaction, and increased motivation.

You have gained experience in setting goals for yourself and for an actual or a hypothetical organization. Goal setting is a complex process and not easy the first time. However, it is a skill that can be developed with practice. The second time should be easier. Most managers who have introduced management by objectives and results (MBO&R) as an overall program find the experience frustrating in the beginning. However, about the third time around they begin to "swing with it" and would not manage without it.

Several key factors should be considered in establishing a program of management by objectives and results. First, it must be emphasized that MBO&R is a *means* to achieve effectiveness, efficiency, and participant satisfaction rather than an end in itself. It must be seen as a natural way of managing rather than as an added burden of filling out forms periodically. Objectives should be developed in a variety of categories; for example, the basic task for the individual or group, innovation, problem-solving capability, and personal growth. Organizations get what they measure. Therefore, it is important to stress those dimensions which spell success or failure for a particular endeavor. Dimensions should not be included just because they're easy to measure, nor should they be excluded because they are difficult to measure. The MBO&R process should transcend written documents and include extensive discussions of mutual expectations—both vertically and horizontally. This approach identifies overlaps, gaps, and interdependence. It facilitates collaboration and team building—important considerations in most organizations.

The general approach should be both "top down" and "bottom up" simultaneously in order to be effective. Top down ensures consistency in the means-end chain. The objectives at a subordinate level fit the more general goals at a superordinate level. However, within general guidelines, subordinates must be encouraged to develop objectives as they see fit. In order to ensure commitment, delegation in the goal-setting process should be based on genuine respect for the ability of each individual or group to develop consistent, realistic, and challenging objectives.

Appropriate measures of performance should be agreed on ahead of time in order to facilitate review and follow-up. The review process should begin with the subordinate evaluating his or her performance, followed by comments from the superior. Because individuals will probably be more critical of their own results than the boss, this approach allows the boss to be supportive and to avoid having to overemphasize the negative aspects. Adjustments stemming from the review process may be in either the ends (objectives) or the means used in attaining them. We might need more effort or new and different activities. Or, we might need an increase or a decrease in the objective or a change in the kinds of objectives included.

Your experience in this exercise provides an overview of the various elements, key considerations, and potential pitfalls of formalized goal setting. Before attempting an organizationwide, programmatic MBO&R process, you would be well advised to consult any one of a number of detailed books on the subject. They provide an extensive discussion of what is involved and exactly how to proceed step by step. In this exercise, we have dealt with the initial phase only—goal setting. However, it is the most critical phase because without appropriate objectives, a managerial process based on MBO&R would be meaningless.

The message here is to keep working at it. Obviously, it will be easier to do so with regard to personal goals because you have more control over the way you manage your own endeavors. On the other hand, you may find it feasible to use a more explicit goal-setting and action-planning process in your work organization even though it does not have a formalized approach. With a little tailoring, you can fit your own version of MBO&R to any work situation. We think you will find it a worthwhile endeavor.

PART 4
TECHNOLOGY AND ORGANIZATIONAL STRUCTURE

Technical and structural subsystems are major elements in any organization. The *technical subsystem* refers to the knowledge, equipment, and techniques used in task accomplishment. In the narrowest view, the term *technology* is associated with machinery, the mechanical means for the production of goods and services (the replacement or extension of human effort). This mechanistic view emphasizes such visible manifestations of technology as the automated production line, television transmission and receiving equipment, electronic computers, and the complex system of boosters, capsules, launchpads, and monitoring equipment necessary for a spaceflight. But physical manifestations are just one aspect of technology—they are the top of the iceberg. In a more general sense, technology refers to the application of knowledge to accomplish tasks in the most efficient way. It includes all the techniques used in the transformation of inputs into outputs. For example, the industrial concern utilizes both machinery and specialized methods of production planning and control in order to transform raw materials into finished products. Accountants may use the computer in performing their tasks, but they also utilize techniques based on a knowledge of accepted accounting procedures. A market research department utilizes a specialized technology in conducting consumer surveys. A doctor utilizes a knowledge-based procedure in accomplishing a heart transplant with, of course, the support of an imposing array of vital machinery and equipment—the physical manifestations of technology.

The nature of the technical system has a significant impact on other organizational subsystems. For example, in organizations where the technology is stable, the structure tends to be rather fixed: people are assigned to perform well-defined, routine tasks, and the planning and control processes are specific and detailed. The technical system also prescribes many of the interpersonal relationships. For example, working on a production assembly line usually restricts the individual's activities and also determines the extent of social interactions.

On the other hand, organizations with a dynamic and complex technology tend to have more flexible and changing structures. People do not have a high degree of task specialization, but contribute their knowledge in more general ways. Interpersonal relationships are more varied and complex than under a stable, routine technology. Examples might be a research and development laboratory, a complex diagnostic and treatment process for a medical patient, or a precision machine shop with a variety of small jobs.

The nature of the technical system is one of the most important factors influencing the entire organization—its structure, managerial system, leadership styles, group dynamics, motivation of employees, and many other facets.

Organization structure is the established pattern of relationships among the components or parts of the organization. It is concerned with the ways in which the tasks of the organization are divided (differentiation) and with the coordination of these activities (integration). In a formal sense, structure can be set forth by organization charts, job descriptions, procedures, and rules. It is concerned with patterns of authority, communication, and work flow.

For our purposes we will consider three of the most important aspects of structure:

1. The way in which the various activities or tasks are broken down and assigned to different departments and/or people in the organization (differentiation).
2. The way in which these separated activities or tasks are coordinated (integration).
3. The authority relationships within the organization.

Obviously, the structure of an organization is difficult to investigate. It cannot be "seen," but must be inferred from observations. For example, we would infer a highly structured organization if it had a large number of departments or work units, if the tasks were specialized and prescribed by detailed methods, if there were many well-established procedures for how people and functions were to be interrelated, and if the authority relationships were clearly defined and stable. High structure would be typical for a standardized production line or a basic training camp in the military.

We would infer a loosely structured organization if we found flexible departmental functions, generally defined tasks, few rules and procedures, and authority patterns that varied depending on the particular tasks or problems facing the organization. This loose structure is typical for a university academic department or a professional organization such as a law office, CPA firm, or nonprofit research and development laboratory.

The structure has an impact on other organizational subsystems. For example, managerial processes and leadership styles are affected by the degree of structure. The nature of the work people perform, their interactions with other people and groups, and even their motivation and degree of satisfaction are influenced by the structure. Some people have personality characteristics which are suitable for membership in highly structured organizations. They may prefer this to the uncertainties and ambiguities which exist in less structured situations. Other people resist highly structured situations.

The three exercises in this section are specifically designed to investigate the technical and structural subsystems within organizations and to observe their impact on other subsystems. In the first exercise, *The Impact of Technology and Structure: Speedy Delight and Shady Corners Café*, you are asked to observe and analyze the interrelationships among the technical system, organization structure, psychosocial system, and managerial systems in two familiar organizations.

The second exercise, *Organization Structure and Process: Mellow Motors, Inc.,* also provides an opportunity to engage in field observation of a familiar organization. It focuses on the way the activities are departmentalized and coordinated. It also asks you to consider the technology used in various parts of the organization.

The third exercise, *Organization Design: Atlas Electronics Corporation (A) and (B),* is a comprehensive case; you are asked to look at alternative structural arrangements and to choose the one which is most appropriate for the specific situation.

Exercise 8
The Impact of Technology
and Structure:
Speedy Delight
and Shady Corners Café

LEARNING OBJECTIVES

1. To understand the concepts of task, technology, and structure through personal observation and analysis of real organizations.
2. To identify the relationships among technology, structure, and other organizational subsystems.
3. To compare and contrast two familiar organizations in terms of relevant characteristics or variables.

ADVANCE PREPARATION

Read the Overview and the Procedure. Complete Step 1 before class.

This exercise requires that each of you, independently or in small groups, go out to the "real world" to observe the operation of two organizations. Spend 15 to 30 minutes observing (1) an independent, locally owned restaurant or café (we will call it the Shady Corners Café), and (2) a fast-food service operation such as McDonald's, Kentucky Fried Chicken, Pizza Pete, Burger King, Taco Time, or any similar owner-operated or franchised operation (we will call this Speedy Delight).

You have probably already patronized these two types of away-from-home food-service operations and have noted both similarities and differences. In this exercise, you are asked to observe these operations more explicitly, not only as a patron, but from the viewpoint of a student of organizations. Undoubtedly some members of the class will have worked in different types of food-service operations and their experiences can be shared.

You may make your observations individually or in small groups (two to four people). Perhaps the best way to begin is simply to go in as a patron, buy a cup of coffee, a hamburger, or a meal, and observe what happens. Ideally, you will be able to obtain additional information from the employees through informal discussion and interviews. This technique should not be too much of an imposition—after all, we are throwing business their way.

We don't want to structure your observations too much. You should be flexible in making up your own lists of similarities and differences for the two organizations. However, the Individual Observations form on pages 121–123 provides you with some possible areas for consideration.

OVERVIEW

In the United States, total away-from-home food sales in 1974 were approximately $40 billion. This market has expanded significantly over the past several decades with many more people eating out. There are over 300,000 eating and drinking places in the United States, and the organizations in this industry cover a wide range, including small, locally owned cafés and doughnut shops, fancy hotel and nightclub restaurants, many national and regional chains such as Denny's, Howard Johnson, and International Pancake House, and fast-food service operations such as McDonald's and Kentucky Fried Chicken.

This latter group of fast-food service operations represents the most rapidly growing segment of the away-from-home market, with sales estimated at approximately $10 billion annually.[1] The number of establishments expanded from 16,000 in 1960 to over 50,000 currently. While some of them are part of large corporate chains, many are franchised. The franchise concept has made possible rapid economic and geographic expansion by utilizing local capital, entrepreneurial skills, and personnel. Although agreements vary widely in their nature and scope, the franchise is basically a contract under which a fast-food service chain lends its name and services to an individual entrepreneur in return for a fee and other considerations.

Although all the away-from-home food-service organizations provide a similar social function—food for hungry people—there are major differences in their technologies, structures, psychosocial and managerial systems, and relationships with their environments and customers. In this exercise we will observe some of these differences in two types of operations: Shady Corners Café, a small, locally owned café, and Speedy Delight, a unit of a fast-food service chain.

PROCEDURE

STEP 1

Observe (individually or in small groups) a Shady Corners Café and a Speedy Delight in action. Pick any representative franchised fast-food operation for Speedy Delight and any locally owned and operated café or restaurant for Shady Corners Café. Fill in the form entitled Individual Observations on pages 121–123.

STEP 2

Meet in groups of five or six to compare your observations. The form, Group Composite Analysis, on page 124, provides a listing of areas for your consideration.

STEP 3

Each group will be assigned (randomly) one of the seven areas for more intensive analysis (technical system, structure, etc.). Using newsprint or the blackboard, a representative from each group should compare and contrast (noting similarities and differences between) Shady Corners Café and Speedy Delight for their assigned area of analysis (Group In-Depth Analysis, page 125). Explain your results to the total class.

STEP 4

The entire class discusses all the findings.

---

[1] For a discussion of the growth of McDonald's, see "The Burger that Conquered the Country," *Time*, Sept. 17, 1973, pp. 84–92.

	Shady Corners Café	Speedy Delight

Technical System
Nature of equipment, degree of mechanization, etc. (Include both cooking and service equipment.)

How was the technical knowledge required to perform tasks developed in these two organizations?

Products—Inputs and Outputs
Standardization of product. How much variation is provided for customers?

The degree of standardization or uniformity of raw material inputs.

What are the outputs for customer satisfaction?
What do customers seek in types of food and/or service?

Structure
How are tasks divided? Degree of task specialization.

How are tasks integrated?

What are authority patterns?

Draw a simple chart of superior-subordinate relationships for each organization.

Psychosocial System
The age, background experience, and general characteristics of workers.

Your impression of their motivation and satisfaction with job. Why are they working there?

Observations on the informal organization; group relationships, etc.

	Shady Corners Café	Speedy Delight

Psychosocial System (continued)
How does the technology and structure affect the human relationships?

Customer and Environmental Relationships
Who are the customers of these organizations?

Have customers and employees established interpersonal relationships?

How long—in minutes—are the customers in interaction with the organization?

In the future, under what circumstances will *you* patronize the two establishments?

Total Organizational System
Is there a pattern of relationships among the above factors?

How easy would it be to duplicate each organization at another location?

Are the factors which contribute to success or failure the same for each of the two organizations?

Individual Observations (Continued)

	Shady Corners Café	Speedy Delight
Other comparisons		

GROUP COMPOSITE ANALYSIS

Share your observations and analysis with other members of your group. It is likely that each of you will have looked at a number of different organizations and therefore can extend your comparative analysis.

Use the following framework for your group comparisons. Jot down key words or phrases for each area of analysis.

	Shady Corners Café	*Speedy Delight*
Technical systems		
Products—inputs and outputs		
Structure		
Psychosocial system		
Customer and environmental relationships		
Total organization system		
Other comparisons		

GROUP IN-DEPTH ANALYSIS

Each group should prepare an in-depth analysis of the major similarities and differences in these two types of organizations for a specific area (assigned randomly). Your analysis should be placed on the blackboard or newsprint and explained to other class members. These analyses will serve as the basis for a full class discussion.

Area:

Shady Corners Café:

Speedy Delight:

SUMMARY AND CONCEPTUALIZATION

Although we may classify organizations as being in the same industry or as performing a similar social function, their operations may show significant differences. For example, even though we may initially think of them as the same, there are differences among correctional institutions. Institutions that have *confinement* and *punishment* of inmates as their goals, such as maximum security prisons, tend to be very closed and highly structured, and to exercise tight control over inmates. Institutions which emphasize the *rehabilitation* of participants usually are more open to society (for example, work or educational release programs), have a more flexible structure, and try to develop each person's self-control.

Within the military, differences exist depending upon the nature of the specific activities. The organization utilized for basic military training displays characteristics of the highly structured, bureaucratic system. However, in the design, development, and procurement of advanced weapon systems, the military organization is typically more flexible and adaptive.

Your observations in the away-from-home food industry have provided you a basis of comparison in two relatively simple, but contrasting, organizations. Although there may have been variations within organization types, Speedy Delight quite likely had a more specialized technology, with equipment geared to standardized production of a narrow line of products. Tasks were more specialized, the structure was more rigid and prescribed, and there were many specific procedures for doing the work. In many ways, Speedy Delight was similar to a production-line operation. In contrast, Shady Corners Café tended to have a flexible technology with general-purpose equipment. Tasks were not as specialized. Procedures were apt to be less precise and more informal. The human systems in the two organizations very likely were quite different. The managerial skills required for success were also somewhat different. You probably found a great many more similarities among the Speedy Delights than among the Shady Corners cafés. You could walk into a McDonald's anywhere in the country (or even Japan) and see an operation almost identical to the one around the corner.

In this exercise you have actually been engaged in *comparative organizational analysis* using a systems approach. Researchers who are trying to understand the similarities and differences among organizations and then to translate their findings into more effective managerial practices typically follow a similar approach. You might be interested in using this comparative approach to contrast other types of organizations, such as retail stores, educational institutions, and unions. It is often surprising to find that an in-depth analysis of apparently similar organizations will uncover significant differences.

Exercise 9
Organization Structure
and Process:
Mellow Motors, Inc.

LEARNING OBJECTIVES

1. To increase our understanding of structure and process by designing a specific organization.
2. To increase our understanding of differentiation and integration of organizational activities by writing job descriptions and specifying various means of integration.
3. To identify examples of technology used in carrying out organizational activities.
4. To identify examples of several types of decisions necessary for planning and controlling organizational activities.

ADVANCE PREPARATION

Read the Overview and the Procedure for the exercise. Visit an automobile dealership and familiarize yourself with the activities involved. If possible, interview the owner/manager (or other key employees) with the objective of understanding something about how the business is organized and managed.

OVERVIEW

An organization, by definition, involves two or more people working toward a common goal. This requirement implies a division of labor and a means of integrating activities and results into a composite whole. When Abe Schwartz takes on a part-time employee in his delicatessen (a sole proprietorship), the work of the organization is then divided between two people. Abe will probably continue to do the buying and selling with Charlie Jones stocking shelves, running errands, and making deliveries. If Charlie is a good employee and stays with the organization long enough, he may become a partner. This step would involve a redefinition of duties and responsibilities, with both partners sharing the planning and doing functions. With two or more people involved, the activities can be coordinated rather informally via face-to-face communication and mutual understanding. As organizations become larger and more complex, the process of differentiating and integrating activities grows both more important and more difficult.

However, the same basic considerations are involved. For a football team, we see a basic division between linemen and backs. Within each of these categories are specific positions or roles—ends, tackles, guards, center, quarterback, and running backs. Each position has a general description of duties and responsibilities plus specific assignments on each play. The sum of the general position descriptions provides a composite picture of the total capability of the team. The specific assignments on a particular play must be coordinated in order to achieve success. A running back must follow the blockers; and the quarterback must throw the ball where the receiver is. During a game we can see examples of perfect execution that result in a touchdown, as well as missed assignments that result in failure.

All organizations, however large or small, have some means of differentiating and integrating activities. Two elements are involved: structure and process. Each one has both formal and informal aspects. The formal structure is the result of explicit decision making concerning organizational patterns and is typically expressed in charts, manuals, and position descriptions. Organization charts are usually highly simplified, abstract models of the structure, and they deal with a limited number of relationships—particularly horizontal division of work among functional units and vertical division among levels. The formal organization chart shows superior-subordinate relationships (who reports to whom) and indicates the authority structure. An organization chart, coupled with detailed descriptions of the duties and responsibilities of each position, provides a comprehensive picture or model of the organization. However, it is a static picture and must be augmented with descriptions of organizational processes in order to describe the way the organization functions. By tracing the flow of materials, energy, and information in an organization, we can get a better picture of how the organization works. How do materials flow through the system from raw materials to finished products? What techniques or procedures are used to apply energy (physical and human) at specific stages? What decisions have to be made at various stages, and what information is required in making those decisions?

Organizations also have informal structures and processes that can be either functional or dysfunctional in achieving goals. Informal adjustments are often necessary in order to accomplish a task effectively and efficiently. Some people in the organization acquire more authority than is spelled out in their position description because of their experience, knowledge, or persuasive ability. Differential influence can't be diagrammed; it is just "understood" in the system by the people involved.

Formal policies and procedures are sometimes adjusted because they "just don't fit the situation." These adjustments may be functional and result in improved performance. On the other hand, informal adjustments are sometimes made toward longer coffee breaks, less output, etc. Such behavior becomes the established norm based on precedent and lack of any repercussion. The formal flow of information may follow established channels as depicted in the organization chart. However, the organizational grapevine seems to be an ever-present phenomenon. It may be functional if it increases the amount of information flow, particularly if the messages are accurate. However, it can be quite dysfunctional if messages are distorted either through embellishment or filtering.

The coordination and integration of organizational activity can be accomplished in multiple ways, and the complexity involved is directly correlated with the degree of differentiation. The more the work is subdivided and specialized either horizontally or vertically, the more sophisticated the means of integration must be. One obvious means of integration is through the formal hierarchy. The president integrates the producing and selling functions. The vice president of marketing integrates the advertising and selling functions. The advertising director integrates the direct mail, newspaper, magazine, radio, and television advertising.

Formal policies, procedures, and rules are also means of integrating activities—making behavior reasonably consistent throughout the organization. Long-range, comprehensive plans provide a means of integrating activities over time and among subunits in the organization. Strategic plans are translated into medium-range tactics and short-range operational steps. The technology—e.g., automation and/or detailed procedures and specifications—often provides the means of integrating the many steps in a manufacturing process.

General rules, such as a 9-to-6 workday, are also a means of integration. The rule on working hours provides that the employees of a department store are available at the same time as the customers and that cross-departmental coordination can occur during a particular time frame. Formal committees, ad hoc committees, and task forces are other means of integrating activity in complex organizations. As suggested earlier, informal voluntary coordination often takes place in organizations. When the situation is dynamic and changing, it is often necessary to make "spur of the moment" decisions that affect several individuals or departments. Coordination is often achieved via an informal discussion over coffee or lunch.

The managerial task involves designing organization structures and processes most appropriate to a given situation. Differentiation and integration are the fundamental building blocks for effective organizational endeavor. Once an appropriate organization design has been achieved, the task becomes one of planning and controlling activities via information-decision systems. We find it useful to identify strategic, coordinative, and operating decisions as well as the kinds of information used in each case. For a proprietorship, all the decisions are made by one individual. For larger, more complex organizations, decision-making responsibility is differentiated both horizontally and vertically. For controlling the operating system, the relevant information is primarily internally generated—amount of stock on hand, number of rejects per hour, etc. Information for strategic decisions often comes from outside the organization—market opportunities, economic and political conditions, competitor actions, etc. Information for coordinative decisions is typically a combination of strategic and operating aspects. The introduction of a new product or service must be correlated with consumer demand (market research) and production capabilities. The timing of implementation should be correlated with the demand rate and the amount of old stock on hand. These examples merely illustrate the kinds of decisions made in various subsystems of any organization. A much longer list could be developed for organizations in general, and they can be specified for particular organizations, such as taverns, flower shops, police departments, paint manufacturers, and airlines.

The focal point in this exercise is an automobile dealership. We have chosen this organization because it is quite pervasive and should be familiar to almost everyone. However, the exercise could be carried out with regard to any organization of interest to you or a subgroup of the class.

PROCEDURE

STEP 1

Meet in a group of three to six. Assume you are going to own and operate a full-service automobile agency. You are incorporated as Mellow Motors, Inc., and according to state law you must have a board of directors with at least three members.

Describe the purpose or mission of your organization and list the *functions* that must be performed in order for you to achieve your goal(s).

STEP 2

Draw an *organization chart* that indicates the *formal division of work*, both horizontally (departments, e.g.) and vertically (superior-subordinate relationships).

STEP 3

Write a *job description* for each of the *key roles* in your organization. Have each person in your group write one or more descriptions, then share the results and develop a complete set that has been refined (adjusted for gaps, overlaps, etc.) by the group. The description should include:

1. Functions and responsibilities (work activities)
2. Authority relationships (reports to . . . , supervises . . . , interacts with . . .)

The results of this step should be a set of differentiated jobs or roles that represents the total activity required for the organization to accomplish its goals.

STEP 4

How will you ensure integration and coordination of activities? List as many means as you can think of. Be specific.

STEP 5

List several examples of the technical subsystem (knowledge, equipment, and techniques) to be used in carrying out your organizational task.

STEP 6

What kinds of decisions will be necessary in planning and controlling your organizational activity? List as many as you can in each of the three categories.

Strategic:

Coordinative:

Operating:

STEP 7

General discussion of organization structure and process. Have one subgroup put its organization chart on the blackboard or newsprint. Have the members read their position descriptions for key roles in the organization. Solicit comments from other class members. Consider the following questions:

a. Is their model representative of those developed by other subgroups?

b. What adjustments are suggested by other subgroups?

c. How useful are the organization chart and position descriptions for understanding the functioning of any organization?

d. What else would you want to know in order to develop a more complete understanding of an organization?

e. How often should charts and position descriptions be adjusted in order to keep a reasonably accurate picture of the organization?

SUMMARY AND CONCEPTUALIZATION

To manage effectively, one must understand as much as possible about organizations. Two important dimensions are structure and process. You have experienced an exercise in designing a specific organization by developing an organization chart or model of differentiated roles. The position descriptions you have developed provide additional "flavor" for organizational activities. Taken together, the organization chart and position descriptions provide a model of activities and relationships. You have identified some of the technology used and several means of coordinating and integrating individuals and subunits. Specific approaches to differentiation and integration will vary with the organization and the particular situation.

It is important to recognize that both formal and informal structure and process exist simultaneously in organizations. In designing organizations, managers should keep this fact in mind by facilitating the development of informal structures and processes that are complementary and functional.

You have identified typical decisions made in carrying out organizational endeavor. Carrying this approach a step further would require identifying the information required in the decision-making process. Focusing on the information-decision system is another way of understanding organizations. The system cannot be drawn as simply or explicitly as an organization chart; however, it does provide a realistic picture of what goes on in organizations. This model allows us to trace the flow of material, energy, and information through the transformation process, a fundamental aspect of all organizations. It provides another view of the relationships among organizational members, their tasks, and the attendant technology.

Exercise 10
Organization Design:
Atlas Electronics
Corporation (A) and (B)

LEARNING OBJECTIVES

1. To increase our understanding of organization design by considering the advantages and disadvantages of functional and project structures.
2. To develop a specific organization design and convince top management of its merits.
3. To consider a specific organizational conflict and to reach an agreement concerning its resolution.

ADVANCE PREPARATION

Read the Overview, the case of Atlas Electronics Corporation (A), and the Procedure for Part A.

Read Atlas Electronics Corporation (B) only after the class discussion of Part A has been completed. This exercise will probably extend over two class periods. Therefore, Atlas Electronics Corporation (B) should be read between the two sessions.

OVERVIEW

Organizations traditionally have been departmentalized into functional departments—such as sales, finance, production, and personnel. One of the major advantages of this structural form is to ensure the integration of activities within the specialized departments.

The project or program management form is an attempt to overcome some of the difficulties of functional specialization. It has been used increasingly in organizations that deal with advanced technology and complicated new processes and products. Project management involves the appointment of one individual, the project manager, who has the responsibility for the overall planning, coordination, control, and ultimate results of the project. This manager usually is superimposed on the functional organization, and the imposition of this integrating agency tends to create new and more complex organizational relationships. In some ways, authority and responsibility for the performance of certain tasks are not as clear-cut as under the functional structure.

Any major change in organization structure requires adaptations in the psychosocial and managerial systems. People have to learn new and different tasks and roles. Interpersonal relationships are frequently modified. A new structure requires changes in managerial information systems and in the processes of planning and control. New authority and responsibility relationships have to be worked out. In effect, any new structural arrangement cannot be superimposed on the organization with instant understanding and acceptance. There is usually an uncertain period of learning-adapting in which organization members are required to learn new roles, relationships, and authority patterns.

This case situation allows us to look at the dynamic process of designing an appropriate structure and simulates the process of implementing it within the organization.

PROCEDURE FOR ATLAS ELECTRONICS (A)

STEP 1
Read the Atlas Electronics Corporation (A) case thoroughly before class.

STEP 2
The class divides into three groups which are randomly assigned to represent the following people in the case:

a. Howard Datson, head of the Receiver Department and an advocate of assigning the Spyeye project to his department.

b. Burt Saunderson, manager for previous projects and an advocate of assigning Spyeye as a special project.

c. President Homer Skillton and Executive Vice President John Doan, who have to make the decision on the organization design.

The three groups should meet separately and prepare a rationale for their points of view. Empathize with the assigned individual(s) and develop a proposal for organizing the Spyeye project. Each group should select members to take the role(s) of their assigned executive(s) and help them develop their arguments.

STEP 3
President Skillton conducts a meeting of the key people in front of the entire class. He should allow Howard Datson and Burt Saunderson each 10 minutes to present their views. Then he and Executive Vice President Doan should confer (again in front of the class) to consider the arguments and render a decision as to which alternative is to be implemented. Or, they may come up with a third alternative. In any event, they must make an explicit decision.

STEP 4
The entire class should discuss the executive meeting and evaluate the process and the final decision.

Atlas Electronics Corporation (A)*

SPYEYE PROJECT—ORGANIZATION

COMPANY HISTORY

Atlas Electronics Corporation was organized by a group of engineers and scientists who pioneered electronic research and development for the Office of Scientific Research and Development during World War II. After the war, members of this group joined together to form a private company to continue their efforts.

From the start, Atlas earned a reputation among government and corporate customers as a leader in advanced electronic techniques and systems. Its present capabilities cover a wide spectrum of electronic applications and skills, including aviation systems, radar, space payloads, communications, and electronic warfare (reconnaissance and countermeasures). Atlas had continued to distinguish itself for advances in the state-of-the-art and for superior quality on numerous prototype and initial operational equipments developed for U.S. government agencies. Full 95% of its business is on government R & D contracts, whether directly or for prime government contractors.

Atlas' success is largely due to the competence, dedication, and stability of its staff. Of its 3,000 employees, over half have engineering or scientific degrees. Approximately 15% of these have advanced technical or MBA degrees or are working toward them. The primary resource of management is the brainpower of these men, who are professional specialists in diverse fields.

COMPANY ORGANIZATION

Atlas Electronics Corporation is a typical engineering company organized along functional lines. Its functional engineering departments are oriented to various technical disciplines and are staffed with engineers, scientists, and technicians who work on developing advanced techniques and in the support of projects.

The departmental organization structure starts with the department head and goes down the line through the section heads, group leaders and supervisory engineers, to the scientists, engineers and technicians who are doing the detail work. The department heads report to John Doan, Executive Vice President. Communications, approvals, and directions flow through this organization in an orderly manner. Each level is under the supervision of the level above it and normally will not operate without higher level approval and direction.

Atlas has three engineering functional departments: an Antenna Department, a Receiver Department, and a Data Systems Department. Each of these is responsible for developing advanced techniques, performing engineering, and for giving support to R & D projects in its technical area. The organization of each of these departments is shown in Exhibits 10-1 to 10-3.

In addition, Atlas has a Manufacturing Department (Exhibit 10-4), which does fabrication, assembly and testing of production units. This Department also reports to John Doan. Purchasing, accounting, personnel administration, and other services are performed by various company staff departments not shown in the Exhibits.

From time to time, Atlas sets up an ad hoc Project Management to handle a large R & D contract. This is a semiautonomous group consisting of a project manager and other personnel drawn from the functional organizations in the company. It has complete responsibility for meeting all of the requirements of the contract, but it gets the work done in the functional departments. At the end of the project it is dissolved.

The Project Management assigns technical tasks to each supporting department to perform. To a limited extent, it is permitted to cut across organizational lines so that it can deal with the people doing the work without having to go through the whole hierarchy of their functional

*This case was developed and prepared by Dr. William R. Lockridge, Associate Professor, Graduate School of Business Administration, C. W. Post Center of Long Island University. Reprinted by permission. All names have been disguised.

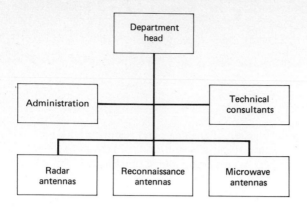

EXHIBIT 10-1 Atlas Electronics Corporation (A), Antenna Department.

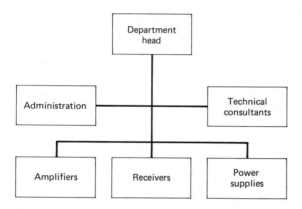

EXHIBIT 10-2 Atlas Electronics Corporation (A), Receiver Department.

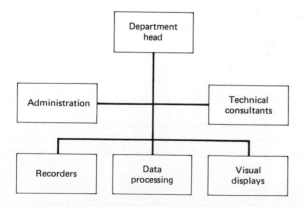

EXHIBIT 10-3 Atlas Electronics Corporation (A), Data Systems Department.

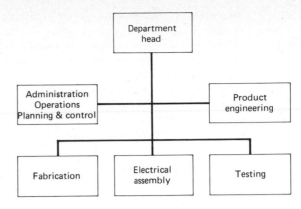

EXHIBIT 10-4 Atlas Electronics Corporation (A), Manufacturing Department.

organizations. It handles scheduling and overall cost control; it deals with subcontractors and maintains liaison with customers; and it coordinates all of the technical inputs and "hardware" from the supporting organizations into the overall system which is delivered to the customer.

The people who are literally transferred to the Project Management are mostly of a supervisory or senior category and report directly to the project manager. Their function is to advise him in their respective technical disciplines, to cooperate with him in managing the project, and to give "work direction"[1] to the personnel in the functional departments who are doing the work. The Project Management staff cannot directly supervise the work of the department personnel because these workers report in line to their department head. The department head may be on the same level or a higher level than the project manager. Consequently, the project manager has the problem of getting the utmost in effort from people who are responsible to someone else for pay raises, promotion, performance, and other aspects of line relationship.

SPYEYE PROJECT

As the result of a successful competitive proposal, the government has awarded Atlas an R & D contract for an airborne reconnaissance system called "Spyeye." The system consists of an antenna, a receiver, an amplifier, and visual read-out equipment. This is an advanced system requiring the development of specific equipment whose performance characteristics are beyond the existing state-of-the-art. Atlas agrees to produce a prototype model in 9 months. Following acceptance by the government, it agrees to produce 5 operational systems within another 6 months.

The contract is for a firm fixed price of $6 million, of which $5.6 million is the estimated target cost and $400,000 is Atlas' fee. The contract has a profit-sharing incentive whereby the government and the contractor share any cost-saving below the $5.6 million on a 90/10 percent basis. It also provides penalties on the contractor for overrunning the cost, for late delivery, and for failure to meet performance specifications. The government will debit Atlas dollar for dollar against its fee for any cost overrun, and will assess it $200 for every day of late delivery. Various penalties, up to 20% of the fee, are provided for failure to meet technical performance specifications.

PROJECT SUPPORT

The Spyeye project requires support from many functional areas throughout the company. It needs technical advice, engineering and "hardware" from the reconnaissance section of the Antenna Department, the amplifier and receiver sections of the Receiver Department, the visual displays section of the Data Systems Department, and the fabrication, assembly, and testing facilities of the Manufacturing Department. (See Exhibits 10-1 to 10-4.)

---

[1] "Work direction"—definition of the goals, specifications, and constraints (budget, schedule, etc.) for a technical task, as distinguished from detailed supervision of the work to perform it; the "what" to do, not the "how" to do it.

ALTERNATIVES FOR PROJECT ORGANIZATION

Company management has to decide whether to organize Spyeye as an ad hoc Project Management, or to handle it through one of its functional departments. Two men are available to lead the project, but the one selected will depend on the choice of organization. These men are Howard Datson and Burt Saunderson.

Howard Datson, 55, is head of the Receiver Department. He has been with the company since its inception and has built his department to the largest in the company. Datson and his group were responsible for numerous innovations in the receiver line and have kept the company ahead of most of its competition in that field.

Datson put in a strong plea to the President, Homer Skillton, to let the Receiver Department manage Spyeye as a project within its functional organization. "My department has been in existence since this company started," he said. "We've a well-trained staff with a lot of managerial and technical know-how. We'll have to do the bulk of the development anyhow. And I'm sure we can handle the interfaces with the other departments without any trouble."

Datson went on to express some of his personal feelings about the alternative of setting up a Project Management. "You must recognize that we've built the reputation of this company on the technical capability and quality performance of its functional departments. I personally dislike becoming a 'service' organization to a group who will be here today and gone tomorrow. Also, it'll probably be managed by someone who is not as technically oriented as any of our department heads.

"One thing I want to make particularly clear," he continued, "nobody's going to come into my department and tell my men how they must do their work. They report to me and my supervisors and we're the ones who call the shots."

Burt Saunderson, 45, is a section head in the Antenna Department and has held that position for six years. He started as a project engineer twelve years ago and worked up through the group leader level to section head. A year ago he was relieved of his functional assignment and was appointed Project Manager in an ad hoc Project Management for an R & D project called "Moonglow." Moonglow was much smaller than Spyeye, but it had many of the same characteristics, such as the support from several different functional departments, a fixed-price, and penalties for failure to meet cost, schedule, and performance specifications.

Saunderson and his Project Management group had successfully completed the Moonglow project. They had delivered the system on time, and the performance was satisfactory to the customer, although the equipment deviated slightly from the specification. They also had been able to increase the company's fee 1½% by bettering the target cost. But Moonglow was now over and the people on it had to be reassigned.

While waiting for a new assignment, Saunderson served as bid manager on the Spyeye proposal to the government and was responsible for having come up with the reconnaissance system which the government finally bought. He felt he was the logical one to head up the Spyeye Project, if President Skillton decided to organize it as a Project Management. Accordingly, Saunderson sent a memorandum to Skillton outlining his reasons for this type of organization, which were, in essence as follows:

1. The project involves four of the company's operating organizations. If management is established in any one of these, the company would have the awkward situation of one functional department directing the activities of others who are on a parallel with itself in the company organization structure.

2. The project involves more than mere technical development. Cost, schedule, and technical performance all must be evaluated and balanced to produce the optimum overall result. A functional department, steeped in its own technology and hampered by its organizational structure, would lack the objectivity to view the overall project problem in perspective and to meet the ever-changing operational crises which arise from day to day.

3. The project does not involve pure research. It requires some innovation in the techniques area which can be done by the supporting functional departments. But someone will have to develop the overall system and that can best be done by a Project Management.

4. The project will add little to the long range technical capability of the company. What it needs is an organization to "get the job done,"—an organization which can use the

technical support of the functional organizations without causing any permanent disruption in the company's organization structure.

President Skillton recognized that both men had good arguments.

PROCEDURE FOR ATLAS ELECTRONICS (B)

STEP 1
Read the Atlas Electronics Corporation (B) case thoroughly before class.

STEP 2
The entire class should discuss some of the specific issues such as *(a)* the personal qualifications required of a good project manager and how they might differ from those needed in a functional manager, *(b)* how to give the Spyeye project manager sufficient authority to get the job done without usurping the authority of the supporting department heads, and *(c)* the reactions of Jack Davis and Abe Marks and their misgivings concerning the program.

STEP 3
Three groups (from Part A) should meet separately to develop their position on the performance problem at the end of the case. Again, assign roles to be taken in the follow-up meeting to resolve the problem.

STEP 4
Meeting of Datson, Saunderson, Doan, and Skillton to resolve the problem. An explicit decision must be made during the meeting and made clear to the entire class.

STEP 5
The entire class discusses the meeting and the entire exercise.

Atlas Electronics Corporation (B)*

SPYEYE PROJECT—OPERATIONAL PROBLEMS

SPYEYE PROJECT MANAGEMENT
President Skillton met with executive Vice President John Doan to discuss the Spyeye Project. "John, I've decided to organize Spyeye as a Project Management instead of assigning it to any of the functional departments. It's too big and too complex and it'll be in trouble from the start. I don't want to upset the stability of any department by temporarily expanding its personnel and giving it a coordinating job to handle." (See Exhibits 10-5 and 10-6.)

PROJECT MANAGER
"But this creates some problems on which I'll need your help," he continued. 'The first is the selection of a Project Manager. He's got to be at home in the front office talking about budgets, time schedules and corporate policies and also at home in the laboratory talking about technical research and development problems. Of course, we can't expect him to double as a member of

*This case was developed and prepared by Dr. William R. Lockridge, Associate Professor, Graduate School of Business Administration, C. W. Post Center of Long Island University. Reprinted by permission. All names have been disguised.

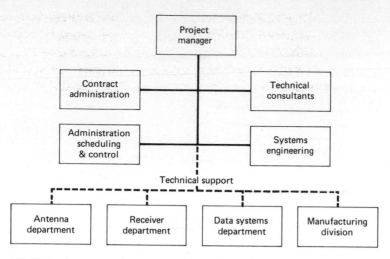

EXHIBIT 10-5 Atlas Electronics Corporation (B), Spyeye Project Management.

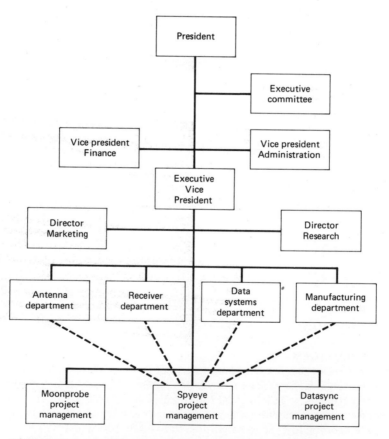

EXHIBIT 10-6 Atlas Electronics Corporation (B), Spyeye Project.

top management and a scientist equally well, but he's got to know what can be done technically and be enough of a business man to get it done within the contract."

"I'm thinking of Burt Saunderson for the job. But I'd like your opinion of him. Burt's a graduate engineer with a BS and MS in electrical engineering. From his earliest training, he's dealt with scientific analysis. He's accustomed to working objectively with tangible things. But as a Project Manager, he'll have to marshal pieces of preliminary or tentative information, juggle several problems at once, compromise one requirement for the benefit of another, and make decisions that are often based on experience and judgment rather than on specific knowledge.

"Another thing," Skillton continued, "as a section head, Burt's accustomed to having direct-line authority over the people in his department doing the work. They do as he says. But as a Project Manager, he'll have to win the cooperation of the supporting department heads and their staffs to get things done. This kind of management means dealing with human nature, and Burt will have to put a lot of emphasis on human factors to succeed."

"Well, I feel his performance on the Moonglow Project shows he can do the job," Doan replied. "I'd rather have him than one of our department heads. Each of them is a professionally dedicated individual, highly skilled in the techniques of his field. What we need here is a different breed of cat—a manager who can run a business, rather than a professional who is endeavoring to optimize a technical advance."

PROJECT MANAGER AUTHORITY

President Skillton then raised another point. "No matter who we appoint, we've got to give him sufficient authority to get the job done. But we've a delicate situation here. We can't permit him to step in and tell a department head how to run his department. Yet we must give him sufficient status to compel their respect and cooperation. I'll have him report to you. This will place him on the same organizational level as the department heads who are supporting the project."

"That's OK with me," Doan replied. "After all, I've other project managers reporting to me and I try to treat them and the department heads alike."

"Of course, Burt will have overall management of Spyeye and will assign technical tasks to each supporting department," Skillton continued. "But these will be in the nature of subcontracts with budgets and schedules which he'll have to negotiate with each department head and on which he'll obtain their commitment. He can tell them what to do, but not *how* to do it. This will keep design development in the functional departments where it belongs.

"But I'm not too happy about this arrangement," Skillton reflected, "because it gives the Project Manager little control. So when Burt meets with a problem that requires some pressure on a supporting department, he'll have to come to you, if he can't reach an agreement with the department head."

"Well, I'll have to assume that as my responsibility," Doan replied. "All the operations report to me and it's my job to see that any conflicts are resolved in the best interest of the company."

PROJECT STAFF

"Another problem we have to consider," Skillton continued, "is how we'll staff the Spyeye Project Management. Obviously, it should be with supervisory or senior technical people from the departments skilled in the project techniques. But each of these departments needs these people in its own operations. I don't want to step in and direct any department head to transfer people to the Project Management. Burt will have to convince each department head that it's in the best interest of the company and the individual concerned to transfer him. Personally, I feel that it broadens a man's experience and capability to be assigned to a project for a while."

PROJECT SUPPORT

President Skillton meditated for a moment and then continued, "In mulling over the problem, John, it appears to me that if we could induce each department head to set up a Spyeye support group as a sub-project within his own department, responsible solely for support to the Spyeye Project Management, it would overcome some of the weakness of the ad hoc organization concept.

"This would, in effect, create a 'project within a project,' headed by a project leader who would take his 'work direction' from the Project Management staff rather than from his own departmental supervision. I think this would cut across the organizational lines to implement the interfaces between the Project Management and the supporting groups, and I feel it would inspire a team spirit on the project. At the same time, it would preserve the status of the functional department supervision, because detailed supervision of the work would remain with them. I want you to see if the Spyeye support can be organized in this manner," he concluded. (See Exhibit 10-7.)

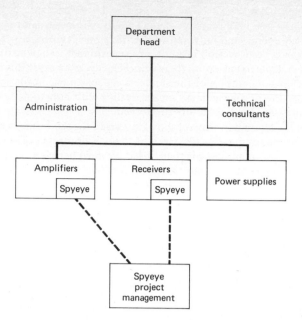

EXHIBIT 10-7 Atlas Electronics Corporation (B), Receiver Department, Spyeye Project support.

EMPLOYEE MORALE

Skillton and Doan had another problem which neither of them had discussed. That was, how to maintain employee morale under the structure of "two bosses" which the Spyeye Project Management created.

Jack Davis was a group leader in the Data Systems Department before he was transferred to the Spyeye Project Management. His new assignment required that he be the operational communications link between the project and his "home" department. He gave "work direction" to Abe Marks who was the project leader heading up the Spyeye Project group in the Data Systems Department.

Jack and Abe were having lunch together in the company cafeteria. "I can't keep from wondering what'll happen to me when the project's over," Jack remarked. "Will I be transferred back to the Data Systems Department? If so, will I have lost ground by my temporary absence? Or will they assign me to another project? I don't see anything new coming in and I don't like it. Believe me, I keep looking around."

"I've my problems, too," Abe replied. "While I'm still in the department and report to Joe (his section head), I'm working exclusively on the Spyeye Project. I like the assignment. I feel I'm part of the project team, and when that equipment starts flying out there, I'm sure they'll give me credit for my part. But how does this affect my status and salary?

"When it comes time for rate review," he continued, "will Joe know how I'm doing? Burt knows more about my work than Joe does. Will they talk to each other, or will I be dropped in the crack?"

"I'm in another bind," Abe continued. "Often I have to decide what's best for the project as against what's best for the department. Should I do what the project needs to meet its contract or be loyal to the department's policies and standards? If I 'bite the hand that feeds me' where'll I wind up?"

"I guess these are some of the risks we have to take," Jack philosophized. "Some guys prefer the challenge of strict technical development. Others want the action of a project. Personally, I feel that this project assignment will broaden my experience, or I wouldn't have taken it. But I can't help but worry about what it'll do to my future."

Burt Saunderson didn't hear this conversation, but he knew that these feelings persisted with personnel working on the project, either on his staff or in the supporting departments. He wondered how he could induce these men to keep their "eye on the ball" and devote their full effort to the project when they were worrying about their personal futures.

PERFORMANCE PROBLEM

Seven months after the project started, Saunderson noted from his progress reports that the Receiver Department still failed to meet the technical performance specification on the receiver. The specification required a band spread from 1000–10,000 mc. The breadboard model would only operate at 1050–9200 mc.

Time was getting short and he had to take prompt action. Investigation disclosed that it was doubtful if the circuit, as designed by the Receiver Department, would ever meet the specification. Consequently, it did not appear advisable to spend more time on it. Saunderson's technical staff advised him that the addition of another transistor on the lower end and the substitution of a 2QXR tube for a transistor at the upper end would cure the situation. Both of these would increase the cost and the tube would change the configuration of the "black box." His project administrator advised him that the project could absorb the cost and the customer said that the slight change in the configuration was not important. But here an obstacle arose. The Receiver Department was not satisfied with the quality of the 2QXR tube and refused to use it.

Saunderson met with Datson to discuss the problem. "Howard, we've got to do something to get that receiver up to spec. Time's getting short. We'll get socked $200 a day for late delivery and they'll take a slice of our fee for failure to perform. Now, I know you hate to use the 2QXR, but it'll do the job long enough to meet the life requirements and will satisfy the customer. We've got to give somewhere or we'll be in serious trouble."

"Yeah, I know how you feel," Datson replied, "but I've got to preserve the quality reputation of the company. After all, we obtained Spyeye because of our reputation for quality as much as for our technical competence and favorable price. If I do anything to impair that image it'll only hurt us in the long run."

SUMMARY AND CONCEPTUALIZATION

You have experienced the problems involved in designing an appropriate structure for a specific organization. Obviously, there were several alternatives, each with advantages and disadvantages. Reaching a decision and obtaining agreement from all managers were difficult, and the implementation of the new design created unanticipated problems. It was evident that there were strong personal and group feelings about the structure. It was difficult for everyone to be organizationally rational. The personalities of Datson, Saunderson, Skillton, and Doan (as depicted in your role playing) had a major impact on the way in which the organization was designed and on the implementation process. Structure is not something which is set apart; it is closely related to the tasks, technologies, psychosocial relationships, and managerial processes.

You probably felt uncomfortable because you could not reach a "perfect" solution to the structuring of this organization. *But that's the way real organizations and real managerial problems are.* You also recognized that any decision which President Skillton reached was not really final. Rather, making the new structure operate effectively was a continuing process.

PART 5
THE PSYCHOSOCIAL SYSTEM IN ORGANIZATIONS

Individuals and social relationships constitute the psychosocial system in organizations. The individual is the fundamental unit of analysis in organization theory. Your previous study of the behavioral sciences—anthropology, psychology, and sociology—provides a foundation for understanding individual behavior in organizations. Several of the exercises in Part 5 will give you an opportunity to build on that foundation by experiencing individual and group behavior and reflecting on that experience. You will have an opportunity to increase your self-awareness through feedback on questionnaires and through the observation of your behavior by others in the class.

Our study of the psychosocial system will focus on motivation and behavior occurring in an organizational context which includes status and role systems, group dynamics, influence systems, and leadership. The exercises will highlight specific aspects of these concepts. At this point, it may also be helpful to reflect on the class as a learning organization and to think about our own psychosocial system. We can illustrate this approach by referring to each of the mentioned concepts in turn.

Status systems structure social relationships and provide a framework within which group endeavor can be coordinated toward objectives. Role systems are integrally related with status systems. Status concerns the relative perceived prestige of a position in a structural relationship within organizations; role relates to the behavior patterns identified or expected for a given position. Is there an identifiable status system for the class? What factors are involved? Is there a formal designation such as professor, teaching assistant, and student? There are also informal status systems that develop according to factors such as age, experience, and knowledge. What roles are being played? Have we developed expectations about how people in different roles should behave?

Small groups typically provide a mediating mechanism among individuals and organizations. Group dynamics—activities, interactions, and sentiments—play an important part in organizational behavior. An individual's higher-level needs (social esteem, self-esteem, and self-actualization) are often satisfied via his or her position in a small group or large organization. So far in this class you have been involved in a number of small groups—some temporary, and some over the entire period. What have you felt and observed so far? Are some groups more effective than others? Is a certain group more effective for some activities than for others?

Status and role systems, along with group dynamics, provide the setting within which motivation operates to affect individual behavior. Recognizing the complexity of the psychosocial system, managers are interested in effecting ways to influence behavior, i.e., to provide leadership to the organization. Leadership styles are related to influence systems; they should reflect the situation, the leader, and the led. The determination of an appropriate leadership style involves consideration of all elements in the psychosocial system of organizations and an appraisal of the most effective ways to influence behavior. Again, in the various activities of this learning organization (often in subgroups), you have been in a number of situations with various people. Some people have readily assumed the leadership function; others have shunned it completely. Have you been effective in influencing others? If so, how? What approaches have worked well? Not so well? Why?

In summary, many aspects of the psychosocial system have been evident in our own learning organization. Therefore, we should be able to draw on that experience to augment and strengthen the knowledge we have gleaned from the behavioral sciences. To further this process, we will engage in a series of exercises that call attention to specific aspects of the psychosocial system.

Value Systems: Managerial Attitudes and Behavior allows us to compare our actual behavior in specific situations with our professed attitudes concerning management.

Motivation and Behavior: Incidents in Organizations illustrates behavior in a variety of situations. The cases can also facilitate reflection on our own experience in organizations—what caused us to act the way we did.

Influence Systems in Organizations: Leadership Styles involves a questionnaire that provides feedback on each individual's probable leadership behavior. The results provide the basis for group and class discussions of alternative leadership styles and of the situations where they are most appropriate.

Individual and Group Decision Making: The Mountain Survival Problem provides a means to compare individual and group decisions. It also offers an opportunity to observe and reflect on the process and dynamics of group decision making.

Evaluating Performance: State University Grading System reviews some of the factors involved in making major modifications in a university grading system. It considers problems of evaluating individual performance in a complex organization. Another major issue is how to obtain effective participation from diverse groups—students, faculty, and staff.

Exercise 11
Value Systems:
Managerial Attitudes
and Behavior

LEARNING OBJECTIVES

1. To identify various factors affecting attitudes and behavior.
2. To increase our understanding of the relationship between attitudes and behavior.
3. To become more aware of our own attitudes and behavior in supervisory/managerial situations.

ADVANCE PREPARATION

Read the Overview. Do not read further until the class session on this exercise. It is important that all participants complete the exercise simultaneously.

OVERVIEW

Managerial behavior is affected by general value systems and specific attitudes in organizations. This exercise is designed to provide a better understanding of the relationship between attitudes and behavior.*

Behavior refers to "the way one acts," especially to actions that can be observed. For example, we could observe the way a manager behaves in conducting a staff meeting. Similarly, we can observe the way a professor teaches a class or the way a basketball coach acts on the bench during a game.

Values and attitudes are more difficult concepts because we can't see them; they must be inferred from actual behavior, verbal descriptions, and/or written statements. An individual's total past experience provides a value framework (a propensity to think or act) by which the person evaluates the relative merit, usefulness, or importance of things, ideas, or alternative courses of action. Value systems (for groups and

*Adapted from Patrick Suessmuth and Marit Stengels, "Attitudes vs. Behavior," *Training*, March 1973, pp. 38–39.

individuals) represent a general view of what is desirable or undesirable. Attitudes are more specific; they refer to a person's disposition, opinion, or mental set concerning objects such as things, people, ideas, or policies. Free enterprise might be considered generally desirable or undesirable by someone who has a specific opinion about farm subsidies or import tariffs on electronic equipment.

In this exercise we will look at both attitudes and behavior as well as the relationship between them. For maximum learning, it is best not to read further until the class meets and everyone proceeds simultaneously.

PROCEDURE

STEP 1
In class, complete the Behavior Check Questionnaire (page 155).

STEP 2
Complete the Attitude Check Questionnaire (page 156) by estimating where your attitude is on the continuum. Write A (for Attitude) at the appropriate point on the continuum.

STEP 3
Place an S on the Theory X–Theory Y continuum (Attitude Check form, page 156) at a point representing where you would like your supervisor's attitude to be.

Behavior Check Questionnaire

Instructions: For each question, check the choice that most accurately describes your behavior. Be sure to check one box for each question. Work quickly; do not ponder.

	Usually	Often	Sometimes	Seldom
1. I would supervise my subordinates closely in order to get better work from them.	☐	☐	☐	☐
2. I would inform my subordinates about my goals and objectives and sell them on the merit of my plans.	☐	☐	☐	☐
3. I would set up controls to assure that my subordinates are getting the job done.	☐	☐	☐	☐
4. I believe that, since I would carry the responsibility, my subordinates should accept my decisions.	☐	☐	☐	☐
5. I would make sure that my subordinates' major workload is planned for them.	☐	☐	☐	☐
6. I would check with my subordinates daily to see if they need any help.	☐	☐	☐	☐
7. I would step in as soon as reports indicate that the job is slipping.	☐	☐	☐	☐
8. I would have frequent meetings to monitor what is going on.	☐	☐	☐	☐
9. I would rescind unauthorized decisions made by my employees.	☐	☐	☐	☐
10. I would push my people to meet schedules if necessary.	☐	☐	☐	☐

Attitude Check Questionnaire

Instructions: Read the definitions of Theory X and Theory Y and then, on the scale below, estimate where your attitude lies. Write A (for Attitude) at that point.

Theory X	Neutral	Theory Y
10	25	40

Theory X

* The average human being has an inherent dislike of work and will avoid it if possible.

* Because of this human characteristic of dislike of work, most people must be coerced, controlled, directed, or threatened with punishment to get them to put forth adequate effort toward the achievement of organizational objectives.

* The average human being prefers to be directed, wishes to avoid responsibility, has relatively little ambition, and wants security above all.

Theory Y

* The expenditure of physical and mental effort in work is as natural as play or rest.

* External control and the threat of punishment are not the only means of inducing effort toward organizational objectives. People will exercise self-direction and self-control in the service of objectives to which they are committed.

* Commitment to objectives is a function of the rewards associated with their achievement.

* The average human being learns, under proper conditions, not only to accept but to seek responsibility.

* The capacity to exercise a high degree of imagination, ingenuity, and creativity in the solution of organizational problems is widely, not narrowly, distributed in the population.

* Under the conditions of modern industrial life, the intellectual potentialities of the average human being are only partially utilized.

STEP 4

Score the Behavior Check Questionnaire (page 155) as follows:

1 for Usually
2 for Often
3 for Sometimes
4 for Seldom

Write B (for Behavior) at the point on the continuum (page 156) represented by your total score.

STEP 5

Compare A (Attitude), B (Behavior), and S (Supervisor's attitude). Discuss the results in subgroups of five or six and/or the total class.

a. Identify specific personal experiences (your association with organizations) that may have influenced your B, A, and S scores.

b. Is there a general pattern for the group as a whole? For example, is the Behavior score (B) typically to the left of A and S?

c. What factors might account for the results?

d. Discuss specific examples of situations that you have observed where expressed attitudes seemed to differ from actual behavior. To what do you attribute the differences?

e. List the forces in an organization (e.g., this class) that may make it difficult for us to translate our professed attitudes into actual behavior.

SUMMARY AND CONCEPTUALIZATION

Did your results on the two questionnaires fit the general pattern as indicated below?

	Own behavior B		Own attitude A	Supervisor's attitude S
Theory X 10		Neutral 25		Theory Y 40

What factors might account for such results? Several problems are apparent in responding to questionnaires of this sort. We are trying to ascertain as accurately as possible both attitudes and behavior. Some people are able to define them better than others. In some cases, people respond in terms of how they "wish" they behaved as managers or of what they think is the "correct" behavior according to the current popular theory. The same problem exists with regard to attitudes: Do we respond in terms of our actual attitude or in terms of the correct attitude for this course or this occasion?

For example, one participant in a management development program for the U.S. Navy suggested, after the session in which we used this exercise, that his responses were biased somewhat because this was the third day in a 5-day program and he felt that there must be some implied best answers. Even though we continually profess that there is no "one best way," much of the current literature does seem to suggest moving toward a Theory Y approach in attitude and behavior.[1] Alternative views have been expressed, but they seem to appear less frequently.[2]

Do you see any discrepancies in professed attitudes and actual behavior in the world around you—among parents, friends, business executives, politicians, etc.? Why do such discrepancies exist? One overriding issue is the difference between theorizing and practicing. It is easy to espouse the Golden Rule; it is more difficult to live by it. Or, as Mark Twain put it, "To be good is noble. To tell people how to be good is even nobler, and much less trouble." We judge ourselves according to our intentions; we judge others according to their actions. Theory Y is essentially an optimistic view of the nature of human beings. It assumes that people are basically good, industrious, intelligent, and responsible—as opposed to bad, lazy, dumb, and irresponsible. Most of us would like to believe the optimistic view, and yet we know individuals who are indeed lazy and irresponsible; thus we have a difficult time implementing a Theory Y approach to management.

A typical explanation of why behavior seems to support Theory X more than attitude goes as follows:

> I am good, industrious, intelligent, and responsible. Thus, I know that at least some people can be trusted and therefore I would like to maintain an optimistic view of the nature of human beings. This pushes my attitude toward the Theory Y end of the spectrum. And, it explains why my supervisor should have an optimistic view. Obviously, my boss can trust me.

> On the other hand, I am not so sure about the people that work for me. Can they be trusted? Shouldn't I check up on them to make sure they are doing OK?

We have found that this explanation is offered by managers at all levels. In essence, it says that those above me should have an optimistic Theory Y attitude but that I can't afford to because I am not sure about the people below me.

Other explanations for the difference in behavior and attitude revolve around built-in organizational constraints. Traditional organizational processes (e.g., rules and regulations) may favor Theory X and preclude Theory Y managerial behavior. Long-standing union versus management antagonisms and contract provisions may also get in the way of an approach more supportive of Theory Y.

[1] Douglas McGregor, *The Human Side of Enterprise*, New York, McGraw-Hill, 1960. His Theory X—Theory Y conceptual model has been used extensively in research and training over the past 15 years.
[2] See, for example, "McClelland: An Advocate of Power," *International Management*, July 1975, pp. 27—29; and Robert N. McMurray, "Power and the Ambitious Executive," *Harvard Business Review*, November—December 1973, pp. 140—145.

These factors are all reasonable explanations for significant differences between professed attitudes and actual managerial behavior. Behaving in a particular way—e.g., choosing a leadership style—is affected by forces in the leader, in the followers, and in the situation. A change cannot be accomplished by merely vowing to change one's attitude. Ingrained personal habits must be unfrozen, changed, and refrozen. This change usually cannot be accomplished unilaterally. It is much easier if the total organizational climate is changed, including the attitudes and behaviors of superiors, peers, and subordinates.

In deciding on a particular managerial style, individuals must include enough flexibility so that they can behave appropriately in a variety of situations. Managers would be well advised to adopt a contingency view that calls for a situational diagnosis as the basis for managerial behavior. A crisis situation, such as mechanical failure on an assembly line, calls for a different approach from day-to-day clerical operations in the finance department. Different tasks (production, sales, research, etc.) call for different approaches; one's own basic personality cannot be modified too greatly, and subordinates vary on a wide range of dimensions (age, education, temperament, etc.). As an example, in one of our workshops a vice president for a large industrial firm seemed to take forever to complete the Behavior Check Questionnaire—in spite of our suggestions to work quickly without pondering each response. Later, he told us that he had to fill out the questionnaire four times, a different response for each of his division managers. He rationalized that his behavior was significantly different toward each person because of their individual differences in personality and experience. This latter factor was particularly important—one person had been with the company 25 years, whereas another had been there only 4 months. We suggested that his approach was realistic and appropriate (even if it did hold up the completion of the exercise).

Are there any guidelines that might be suggested in terms of Theory X and Theory Y? Our answer is yes. Our bias leans toward an optimistic view of people, and we suggest that managers should behave in a way that reflects that optimism as much as possible. The phrase "as much as possible" allows situational analysis and a realistic approach that recognizes variations in goodness, industriousness, intelligence, and responsibleness. One important reason for being as optimistic as possible is that pessimism can be a self-fulfilling prophecy.

> It makes a great deal of difference in systems of social control whether those involved tend to view man, in general, as good or evil. If we assume that man is good, we can believe that misbehavior is a reactive response rather than a manifestation of character. This will lead to a search for causes in his experience rather than in his nature. If we are to find a cause for behavioral failure, we are more apt to look outside the offender than inside and thus consider a whole new range of variables as contributory circumstances.
>
> If, on the other hand, we assume that man himself is bad, a priori, then we are prone to assume that misbehavior is caused by something within him which we cannot alter directly. Accordingly, our attention will focus on limiting his freedom to choose and to act through external curbs or controls. In limiting the causes of behavior, we exclude ourselves from powerful internal sources of control.[3]

These summary statements reflect polar positions which, admittedly, are unrealistic. People are neither completely good nor completely evil. There are obvious spectra for behavior in terms of cooperation—competition, love—hate, friendship—enmity, or harmony—discord. Given a particular issue, an individual's behavior will reflect a position on one or more of these continua. However, the basic assumption one makes can have a significant impact on organization and management. Relationships are structured in certain ways; compensation systems are designed; communication patterns are established; authority-responsibility relationships are identified; planning and control processes are established; and many other pertinent organizational considerations are affected by management's basic assumption with regard to the nature of human beings.

---

[3] Henry P. Knowles and Borje O. Saxberg, "Human Relations and the Nature of Man," *Harvard Business Review,* March–April 1967, p. 178.

McGregor saw Theory X and Theory Y as more than polar extremes of human nature. He considered those who held a Theory X view as relatively closed-minded and less able to cope with dynamic situations and complex problem solving. He saw the advocates of Theory Y as more open-minded, flexible, and dynamic. Theory Y fosters situational diagnosis and problem solving while recognizing variations in task, technology, and human resources. Rather than being a utopian view, it tempers optimism with pragmatism.

Exercise 12
Motivation and Behavior:
Incidents in Organizations

LEARNING OBJECTIVES

1. To identify factors that affect behavior, particularly performance in work organizations.
2. To increase our skills in diagnosing behavior in specific situations—in understanding why people act the way they do.
3. To develop a managerial approach for motivating people that recognizes individual and situational differences.

ADVANCE PREPARATION

Read the Overview and the cases.

OVERVIEW

How many times have we heard the comment, "I don't understand why he would do such a thing." Why do some people devote 10 years of their life for the very slim chance of making the Olympic team? What causes people in Northern Ireland to kill one another? Why do some people work harder than other people? Why do some people strive for promotions and others shun them? For example, the president of a multibranch organization was bewildered by the following episode. When he approached his best branch manager with an opportunity to come into the home office for additional experience in preparation for moving up the hierarchy, the individual declined and stated that he would rather remain in his current position. The president's reaction was the question, typical of all of us on almost a daily basis, "Why do people behave the way they do?!"

Behavior is caused, motivated, and goal-directed. In this unit we are concerned with motivation in general and particularly in work organizations. No one has ever seen or touched a motive. Thus, our study of this phenomenon must rely on our ability to infer motivation from actual behavior. If we can increase our understanding of what motivation is and how it operates, we can become more skillful in predicting human behavior. The complexity of our task is illustrated in Figure 12-1, which shows some of the influences on behavior in a work situation.

In our example of the branch manager who decided not to accept an assignment to the home office, a number of factors probably influenced his behavior. His personal value system included attitudes about what is good and desirable in terms of both goals and the means of achieving them. Apparently, staying in his current position would facilitate achievement of an important goal or goals. On the basis of one of the norms of Western culture, it is likely, but by no means certain, that he did value a promotion or "getting ahead." But his current personal situation may have influenced the decision significantly. Perhaps family considerations precluded moving to a new location. A promotion and an increase in salary probably pushed for accepting the new job. However, he may have been aware of predecessors who were "tested" in the same way and were no longer with the company. Or, he may have concluded that the increased responsibility, longer hours, and general hassle at headquarters were not worth the reward. He might have figured that the work situation would be challenging and exciting. Or, he may have decided that the new job was unpalatable or that he didn't have the necessary skills. He may have treasured the formal and informal relationships of the group in his branch and perceived significantly less rewarding personal relationships in the new situation.

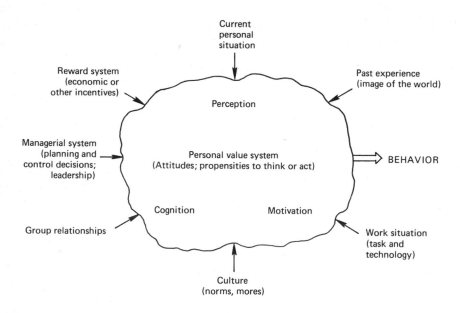

FIGURE 12-1 Some influences on behavior in a work situation.

Thus we see that there is a complex system of situational factors or forces that influence behavior in particular situations. Some of these are external to the individual and some are internal. Note how the interpretation and analysis of a particular behavioral act are based on assumptions and inferences that in turn are influenced by our own past experience and values. It is likely that two people would view the situation and attribute the resulting behavior to different cause-effect relationships.

A more direct approach to understanding motivation would be to ask a little girl, say, why she behaved in a certain way. "Why did you hit your brother?" "Because he hit me first!" This approach to understanding and predicting may be better, but not necessarily. Sometimes people either cannot, or are unwilling to, disclose their motives in detail.

One approach to understanding motivation emphasizes internal drives. People behave in certain ways because of physical, psychological, and social needs. The need-hierarchy concept was developed by

Abraham Maslow as an alternative to viewing motivation in terms of a series of relatively separate and distinct drives. His concept stressed a hierarchy, with certain "higher" needs becoming activated to the extent that certain "lower" needs become satisfied. For example, a man or woman who has adequate means for satisfaction of basic physiological and security needs will seek greater satisfaction of social, status, and self-actualization needs.

Five basic needs are identified as physiological, security, social, esteem, and self-actualization in Figure 12-2.

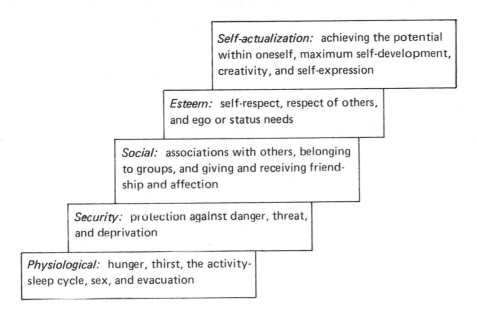

FIGURE 12-2   Hierarchy of needs.

This view is directly relevant to people working in organizations. It suggests that most working people have basic satisfaction of lower-level needs and, therefore, the most appropriate means of motivation is through satisfaction of higher-level needs.

Another view emphasizes the importance of expectations in motivation and behavior. People expend effort or behave in certain ways because they expect some results that will be recognized and rewarded. The following simplified model illustrates the concept:

Of course, other factors, such as knowledge and skill, also affect performance and should be considered in trying to understand behavior.

Internal drives and external expectations are not unrelated; they may differ only in degree of emphasis. We might take, as an example, the development of personal relationships. The *internal drive* view suggests that there are needs for satisfactory associations with others and for giving and receiving friendship and affection. The *external expectations* approach suggests that there is a conscious thought process that friendly behavior toward others will result in rewarding relationships.

Another view of behavior is that it is modified or shaped according to positive and negative reinforcement from the environment, including other individuals and organizations. This *operant-conditioning* view suggests that there is no need to consider complex psychological or thinking processes in order to understand behavior. Motives are unnecessary to understanding and predicting behavior. All that is necessary is to determine what actions have been positively reinforced and are likely to be repeated in the future. If performance is recognized and rewarded, it leads to satisfaction and development of consistent behavior patterns or habits.

The three views of motivation can be illustrated by referring to alternative prescriptions for changing behavior. If the desired behavior is abstention from alcohol, then drive theory would suggest emphasizing the social group of Alcoholics Anonymous; expectancy theory would suggest emphasizing the benefits of abstinence; and operant-conditioning theory would suggest emphasis on aversion therapy.

With this brief glance at some of the views of motivation, we turn now to some cases or incidents that will allow you to practice analyzing why people behave the way they do. The first step is identifying as many possible causes as you can and then determining the most likely explanation. Other concerns include predicting future behavior and/or designing a managerial approach that would motivate or cause people to behave in ways that are functional for themselves and the organization.

PROCEDURE

STEP 1
Divide the class into groups of three and randomly assign two trios to each case to be analyzed in depth.

STEP 2
Each trio should discuss its case in detail and prepare to share its analysis with another trio. In trying to understand the situation, list (on the form, Analyzing Motivation and Behavior, page 165) as many factors as possible that could be affecting the behavior of key individuals and/or groups. Brainstorm; don't worry about degrees of influence and importance. Then go back over the list and check (√) those factors that seem to you to be most important in this situation.

STEP 3
Share your analysis and recommendations with another trio. Note similarities and differences in perception and interpretation of various aspects of the case—facts, opinions, etc.

STEP 4
Briefly share your two trios' analysis and recommendations with the entire class. Invite comments.

STEP 5
Total class discussion.

   a. General comments about the incidents and/or similar personal experiences.
   b. Possible guidelines for managerial actions "most likely to succeed" in motivating people in work organizations. If no guidelines, why not? If guidelines exist, what are they?

John Cleveland:
Superior Tire and Brake Shop

John Cleveland was new at the Superior Tire and Brake Shop. He had worked for 10 years in a unit of a larger chain company in a similar job. However, that company had closed its service store in Des Moines. John had the opportunity to transfer to another service store in Omaha, but he had not wanted to move and uproot his family. He had previously met several of the

Analyzing Motivation and Behavior

Incident: _____

Individual(s) or groups   *Factors affecting behavior*

_____

_____

_____

_____

_____

_____

fellows working at Superior and they recommended him to the owner. He was pleased to be hired where he could continue his trade with a slight increase in wages.

John was a good worker. He prided himself on his fast, high-quality work. He specialized in brake repair jobs, but he could also handle most of the other work in the shop, such as front wheel alignments, muffler replacements, and shock absorber installations. Fortunately, the company needed a good brake man, so he spent most of his time at that job.

In his previous company, he had been paid a basic wage plus a small incentive for the number of brake jobs completed. This typically represented about 10 percent of his salary as a bonus. But, he was responsible for doing the job well. If there were any justified customer complaints, he made the corrections on his own time. There were few complaints.

At Superior Tire and Brake, all the workers were paid a straight hourly rate. At the end of the year, there was a small Christmas bonus roughly determined by how good business had been during the year.

The first day on the job, things were new and John couldn't work up to his usual standards. The equipment and working procedures were different enough to slow him down. However, by the end of the week he was back to normal and was able to complete four or five brake jobs each day. He saw that the other two brake men were doing somewhat less.

He continued the same work during the second week, but he noticed that the other workers were looking at him oddly and were not quite so friendly as they had been the first day. On Friday of his second week, Joe Rubinstein, one of the other brake men, approached him. "You are setting a pretty fast pace here. Why work so hard? We have always turned out three to four jobs a day. The boss is happy and is making plenty of money. Let's knock off for a while and have some coffee." John explained that he really wasn't straining and that he had always turned out four or five jobs a day during his 10 years in the business. Joe Rubinstein responded, "Yeah, but that's a cheap outfit; they don't do quality work like we do." John was a bit miffed, but he didn't say anything and kept working.

The third week things began happening. Nothing serious, just little things. John's tools seemed to disappear and he found them in odd places. He seemed to be getting the tougher jobs, particularly the foreign cars. One day someone spilled old crankcase oil on his lunch bucket. The other guys were noticeably less talkative; even the owner seemed less friendly. It was customary to go to the tavern after work on Friday, but John was no longer invited. He and his wife were excluded from the Sunday picnics of the workers' families.

This general climate continued for several weeks, and John's productivity began to suffer. Because of the distractions and small harassments, it was hard to keep up with his standard output of four to five brake jobs a day. His output was gradually reduced to no more than four, and frequently less. After 2 months he was producing only slightly more than the other two brake men. Things began to ease off for him. The other fellows invited him out for coffee and doughnuts, and he responded by staying 20 or 25 minutes instead of the prescribed 15-minute break. After finishing four jobs, he began helping other brake men complete their jobs and even pitched in to help with other repair work.

After 3 months on the job, John was one of the most popular workers in the shop. He turned out three to four brake jobs a day and had plenty of time to chat with customers and fellow workers and to give them a hand from time to time. His boss told him how pleased he was and suggested that his Christmas bonus would be good. John was a happy worker and "one of the boys."

Chester Marco:
Supreme Canning Company

Chester Marco was very happy when he was selected to be the laboratory technician at the Supreme Canning Company in Modesto, California. He had worked during summers for the past 4 years (while attending Fresno State College) in a variety of jobs, mostly bad. The Supreme Canning Company produced several products, including canned apricots, peaches, pears, and fruit cocktail under the company brand and for private labels. Chester had dumped fruit, unloaded cans, and worked on the labeling and boxing line. The work generally was difficult and boring and required long hours, but the pay was good. During the height of the canning season, he worked 12 hours a day, 6 days a week, and 8 hours on Sunday on the clean-up crew. Eighty hours a week was tough, but there was a lot of overtime and he made good money. This summer he was particularly interested in making a killing because he had been accepted for the MBA program at Stanford Graduate School of Business.

The job of laboratory technician was a plum. It wasn't hard work and he could move around the plant. No one was breathing down his neck for production and he could work at his own pace. Also, the pay was somewhat higher than for his previous jobs.

Chester was enthusiastic about his job and tried to be conscientious. His work entailed a variety of activities, mainly tests for the quality control of the products. An hourly schedule had been established that specified the testing procedures. He was required to record the results from the various tests for permanent quality-control records. Most of the tests involved a sampling procedure whereby he would take the product off the production line and analyze it. The tests were all very simple. For example, every hour he would take several cans off each fruit cocktail line and test them to see if they contained the appropriate amounts of cherries, pineapple, peaches, pears, and grapes, and if the sugar content was within the correct range. He also checked for foreign materials in the product. This was one of his easier jobs.

There were several tasks which Chester disliked. Every 2 hours he had to take the temperature of the gallon cans of apricot and peach pie mix coming out of the cookers. The cans were hot and Chester had to wear long gloves and use an instrument with a long glass thermometer to determine the temperature, which was supposed to be at least 180°. Taking the temperature was not easy. The instrument punched a hole in the can; the hot juices often squirted out all over him; and if he wasn't careful, the escaping juices would blow out the glass thermometer. It would usually sail through the air, crash to the floor, and break. This happened several times during the first week, and it wasn't long before his boss reminded him that the thermometers cost $9.50 each and he would have to be more careful. The second week, Chester broke one the first day and was very embarrassed to ask his boss for another. Then he developed his own system of inspection. Instead of every 2 hours, he took the sample only once in the morning and once in the afternoon, and he took only one can instead of the three required. Of course he had to have a full set of records, so he made estimates and faked the data. Rather than using the thermometer, he became fairly proficient in just touching the cans and estimating the temperatures. His record on thermometer breakage improved substantially and the work was a lot easier.

Another problem area was the testing of the full cans of fruit as they came off the vacuum seamer where the excess air was drawn out, the lids were put on, and the cans sealed. Every hour Chester was supposed to take a sample of six cans from each of the seven seamers to ensure that there was sufficient vacuum in the cans. Chester came to know each of the seven seamers personally. Some of them ran perfectly all the time, others were unpredictable, and several never seemed to run right. Chester varied his testing procedure accordingly. For the very good seamers, he took only occasional tests; he tested the poor performers more frequently. But there were problems when he found bad cans with insufficient vacuum. The machine had to be stopped, the maintenance men had to tear it down, and the entire line was delayed. Everybody was unhappy and seemed to resent Chester and his damn tests. So he began to fudge a bit and to give the benefit of the doubt to the machine. He reported only serious defects which were obvious and over which there would be no argument. Everyone seemed much happier and he was able to doctor his testing records so that things looked good.

These are just two examples of where Chester made his own adjustments in the sampling and testing procedure. His methods saved him time and made everyone else happier. At first, Chester felt some guilt in not taking all the tests required and in doctoring his records. He rationalized his actions by thinking that the sampling and testing procedures were not very scientific anyway. He had taken courses in statistics and sampling, and it appeared to him that the cannery's testing procedures were based on historical practices rather than on any scientific evaluation. Besides, he did not know of any adverse results from his testing procedures. He had heard rumors that some of the cases of fruit had "blown" when they were shipped east over the Sierra Mountains because of insufficient vacuum in the rarefied atmosphere, but no one mentioned this to him directly. By mid-summer, Chester was no longer concerned about the short-cuts he was taking. His job was easier, everyone was happier, and he hadn't received any complaints. He really didn't think of himself as being dishonest, but as just doing a job. He continued to work for the next two summers in the same job while he completed his MBA degree at Stanford. One of his favorite subject areas was ethics and social responsibilities of business.

Lucille Erickson:
Administrative Assistant

Lucille Erickson is an administrative assistant in the zoology department of a large university. She is white, approximately 55 years old, and a widow. She was thinking about seeking early retirement because of the increasing complexity of the job. In discussing her dilemma with her brother-in-law, she related the following incident:

"In the fall of each year, we usually hire two part-time clerical assistants to work in the department. These jobs are for students only. We find it works out well to have one student working in the morning and another in the afternoon. So we try to find people who can arrange their class schedules to suit our needs.

"In late September I placed an ad with the Student Employment Department for one part-time clerical assistant because we had already hired one. Seven students applied for the job, and each one took our 40-minute typing test. This consists of typing a table of numbers in good format and typing a letter in the proper form—no misspelled words, no incorrect grammar, and no visible typing errors.

"Out of the seven tests, I selected two good ones. In fact, they both looked beautiful! Since both tests were equally good, it was hard to make a decision on that basis alone. So how should I make the decision?

"One test belonged to Judy Barnes, who is white and 46 years old. The other test belonged to Beckie Smith, a black woman, 23 years old. So I had to decide between a white, older woman and a young black woman.

"In January the university had established an Office of Equal Employment Programs. All the departments were supposed to increase their number of minority persons employed at all levels.

"In May we all got a memo from the Office of Equal Employment Programs entitled 'Goal Charts for Minority Employment.' This memo suggested that each department set its own goals—realistic yet not conservative ones. In our particular department, we had three minority people on our teaching staff, but we had no minority member in our office services.

"I decided that it was part of my responsibility to assist in a small way in increasing our minority employment, if the minority person was reasonably well qualified. In this particular case, both applicants were equally well qualified. Moreover, the minority person was a black, and since our society has discriminated against blacks unusually severely, I decided to hire Beckie Smith.

"I called and offered her the job and she accepted. Then I called each of the other applicants and told them I had hired someone else for the job. When I called Judy and told her this, she was very indignant. She said, 'I was sure I would get the job because I am very well qualified, and there isn't any reason for rejecting me.' She pressed me to explain why I hadn't hired her, and I finally told her I had hired a black woman.

"The tone of her voice changed and she sounded very angry. She went into a review of all the jobs she had applied for and subsequently been turned down for because a black or some other minority person had been given preference. She accused me of wasting her time and my own time and the state's time by interviewing when I had no intention of hiring a white, older person. She claimed that she had applied for a large number of civil service jobs but had been turned down each time in favor of a minority person. She said that civil service ads had been a farce—advertising for help but not really wanting anyone other than minorities.

"She then asked me who gave me the orders to hire a black. I said that I had not been *ordered* to hire blacks but, through the university's Affirmative Action Program, it had been *suggested* that we give minority persons an opportunity if possible. She just kept on talking and yelling at me. Then she concluded by saying, 'Thanks a lot!' and hung up.

"About a-half-hour later, the Personnel Department called and asked to talk with me. It had just had a call from Judy. She had called to let Personnel know that I had hired a black in place of her. She told them the same story of her difficulty in finding work. She claimed that I had discriminated against her because she was white and because she was 46 years old. She said that I was using reverse discrimination in helping a minority person obtain a job more easily than a white."

Gregory Sorenson:
Assistant Pastor

Gregory Sorenson was one of two assistant pastors in a large suburban church located near Minneapolis. He had been assigned to the church 2 years earlier to work under Daniel Hargroves who, at 67 years of age, had been the pastor for 20 years.

Pastor Hargroves had been instrumental in initiating and carrying out a substantial building fund drive 12 years ago that had resulted in a large, modern facility. Membership had grown substantially during the earlier stages of his pastorship. The church was located in a growing suburban area which had a large population influx. However, over the past 5 years, church membership had not grown, and the average age of the membership had tended to become older. This, however, was not unique to this church and seemed to be happening throughout the country.

Gregory Sorenson had taken the assignment as assistant pastor with the expectation that it would be an excellent learning experience. He anticipated that Pastor Hargroves would retire soon and that he would be given substantial responsibilities in the interim while Hargroves took life more easily. He did not expect to succeed Hargroves in this church, but thought that the training would prepare him for eventually having a smaller church of his own.

Anthony Wolski was the other assistant pastor. He had been with the church for 3 years and had similar expectations.

Gregory soon found that his expectations were not met. Pastor Hargroves kept tight rein over all activities. For example, during the time that he was on his 1-month vacation, assistant pastors Sorenson and Wolski installed a telephone-answering service. Thus, calls could be received and returned when the pastors came back to the office. The cost was minimal and the benefits seemed great to Gregory. However, when Pastor Hargroves returned, he had it disconnected. He was of the old school who thought the people wanted one of their clergymen always to be available when they called. In his view, the duty of assistant pastors was to stay in the office to care for the needs of people who came in, rather than to visit homes or organize meetings that would take them out of the office. He saw no need for the answering service because he personally was there most of the time and always took the calls himself.

He had other views which ran counter to Gregory's. He felt that the primary duties of the pastors were to build the church and save the souls of the members. He was against the social activism in which many churches engaged and viewed it as outside the boundaries of church responsibilities. In his sermons, he preached the traditional faith and did not deal with broad social issues.

Assistant pastor Sorenson made many suggestions for change and for relating more closely to the real-world needs of the membership, particularly the younger people. It was an uphill struggle. It appeared to him that Hargroves's major criterion was, "Will it increase church attendance?" meaning the collection plate, rather than whether it would enrich people's lives. He was very conservative on expenditures and maintained a tight control on the budget. It was his philosophy that "This church exists to receive charity, not to give it." His criterion for a "good" church member was a "giving" member. He paid close attention to those members who were large contributors to the church.

Gregory became increasingly frustrated with his work. His only outlet was through being in charge of the Sunday school department, where he could take some limited initiative. He thoroughly enjoyed working with the young people of the church. Then, assistant pastor Anthony Wolski, who had continually asked for reassignment to another church for the past 2 years, was reassigned. When the new assistant pastor arrived, Pastor Hargroves turned over the Sunday school department to him and assigned Gregory new duties.

Even before this event, Gregory had been pressing for reassignment to another church. However, his efforts were fruitless. The senior administrators of the church felt that making a complete changeover of assistant pastors would look bad. Gregory also felt that they generally agreed ideologically with Pastor Hargroves and were not sympathetic to his views.

Three months after he had made the formal request for reassignment (which had not been acted upon by the senior administrators), assistant pastor Gregory Sorenson resigned from the church and returned to the university to work for a graduate degree in its School of Social Work.

Charles Robinson:
Moorfield Microscopes*

Charles Robinson turns impatiently away from his office window. The sight of earth-moving equipment clearing the ground for a new plant extension is an unpleasant reminder that he must soon make the most difficult decision he has faced as managing director of Moorfield Microscopes.

Last year the company decided to expand its only factory by 100% to meet rising demand. As plans to build the extension were proceeding, personnel director Peter Brown decided that before devising a recruiting campaign for new workers he should analyse the present workforce.

Until recently most employees were older married women who had joined the company 25 to 30 years ago. As they retired, their places were being taken by young girls just out of school. The girls learned the semi-skilled assembly work quickly. Each girl would repetitively perform one operation. The assemblies would pile up in an out-bin, to be gathered and carried to the worker who performed the next step.

After a month or two on the job, the young girls' performance began to drop. Nearly half the girls were quitting during their first year.

Brown brought these facts to Robinson's attention. The personnel director maintained productivity was low because the workers lacked proper motivation; they were bored by the limited scope of the repetitive work. Brown suggested using behavioural science consultants to find ways of making the work more satisfying to the firm's employees.

Robinson agreed and immediately went to production director Alan Smith to explain the situation. He stressed that the experiment, if successful, would benefit the production department and Smith himself. Smith listened stoically. He then told Robinson that he had grave personal doubts that "a couple of outsiders can come in and solve our problems in a few days."

However, when the consultants arrived Smith was friendly and cooperative. After three weeks' study the consultants suggested breaking up the production line arrangement and assigning teams of seven women to build the complete microscope from the components. Each member of the team would be trained to do a variety of tasks, and the team would be responsible for the finished product, which would then be inspected and packed.

When he heard the proposals, Smith stormed: "You don't really expect to increase productivity by increasing the complexity of the tasks to be performed!" He then produced his own plan. The jobs should be simpler, not more difficult, he contended. The new building should incorporate more automated equipment, such as a conveyor belt on the assembly line. Total employment could be reduced, and the $1-million additional investment required would be recovered within two years.

He said Brown had performed a real service in identifying the change in the workforce. Youngsters lacked the solid responsibility of the older generation. For this reason, more supervision, rather than less, was needed. Two new quality inspectors should be hired and a record kept of the individuals responsible for rejected units.

*Reprinted by special permission from the August 1972 issue of *International Management*. Copyright © McGraw-Hill International Publications Limited. All rights reserved.

Robinson decided to experiment with the work team scheme for three months on one of the main product lines. After a drop in the first month, output per employee rose. The incidence of faults dropped. Employees were enthusiastic.

Robinson announced the entire factory would be converted immediately to the new concept and the extension designed to accommodate it. Smith insisted that the girls' performance improved only because everyone was watching the experiment so closely. He asked Robinson to delay construction until further results were in. Robinson replied: "We have to get that plant started. But we don't have to finalize the interior design for another three months. We can change things right up to the time the foundation is laid, if necessary."

Now just as the foundations were to be laid the second three months' figures came in. The productivity gains on the original line had been wiped out, although quality remained up. The second product line showed slight improvements in output per employee, with lower fault rate and less labour turnover. But the product line accounting for the biggest-selling microscope showed a worrying 20% drop in output from the previous quarter. There was no change in the percentage of faults.

Smith was urging an emergency session with the contractors to change the plans. The automated production line would cost 50% less if it were put in as the building goes up. Brown insists the hitches are temporary and urges Robinson to stick to the original plan.

Brenda O'Brien:
Hurley's Hut

Brenda O'Brien, a university student, started working part-time as a waitress at Hurley's Hut Restaurant in mid-June, 1972. The Hut is what is commonly called a steak house, serving entrées such as steak (New York, top sirloin, rib, etc.), seafood (lobster, prawns, etc.), and a few specialty items.

As a waitress, her closest contacts were with other waitresses and busboys. The busboys were usually young men about 18 to 20 years old, working part-time. One busboy was assigned to work with two waitresses. Everyone was paid an hourly wage, but waitresses depended mainly on tips for income. It was the house policy that the waitresses give the busboys 20 percent and the hostesses 10 percent of their tips. Therefore, Brenda left the restaurant each day with approximately 70 percent of her tips—usually about $7. During a break in classes one day, Brenda described the following situation to several friends and asked for their advice on what to do.

"In October a new busboy, Tony, started working at the Hut. He had a hard time learning his job responsibilities, but he was amiable and we all were more than patient with him. But, as time went on, Tony was definitely not catching on as he should have so all the waitresses' tips were dropping considerably, because a good percentage of our tips depend on how well a busboy works with us in serving our tables.

"A few of us spoke to the manager about Tony and asked if he could do anything. He explained that Tony was a special education student (slow learner) and that he was getting high school credit for working. The manager benefited by having Tony work for him because he could pay him less than the minimum wage (approximately one-half), and Tony benefited by getting work experience, pay, and credit. He said that if he fired Tony, he would feel a lot of guilt, and he asked us to please try our best to work with Tony and help him out until his class was over.

"I can honestly say that we all tried our best to help him along (we felt sorry for Tony) after we understood the problem. But our tips just went on dropping.

"One day, I saw Tony actually taking the tip from one of my tables and putting it in his pocket. When I asked him for the money, he said that there wasn't any. I didn't say anything to Tony then, but I told another waitress about the incident. Then we all started watching our tables more closely. Several other times, we saw him pocketing tips. One waitress, Gretchen, actually told him she had seen him stealing, but he denied it.

"Gretchen and I went to the manager and told him the story. I told him that unless he did something soon about Tony, I would have to quit because I couldn't afford to work with him anymore. He asked me not to quit and said that he would take care of Tony. Two weeks passed and Tony was still there. Then I accidentally heard of another job opening. I didn't really want to quit at the Hut, but I wasn't making any money working with Tony, both because he stole tips and because he was a terrible busboy."

Gladys Chin: Head Nurse

Gladys Chin had received her diploma as a registered nurse in 1956 and had worked in various capacities as a private nurse and in several hospitals. For the past 7 years she had been employed at Metropolitan Hospital, 4 of these years in the orthopedics department. She had been appointed head nurse of the department 1 year ago.

There were 15 registered nurses in her unit, 12 with university degrees. Most of them were young and relatively new to the profession, having graduated within the past few years. There were also 5 licensed practical nurses and 10 nurse's aides.

Gladys Chin was a dedicated nurse who thoroughly enjoyed her work with patients. She was a great believer in TLC (tender loving care) for the patients and tried to establish this norm for her unit. She also had a definite view of the role of nurses. They should be dedicated to serving both the patients' needs and the doctors in the hospital. Her work experiences and training had indoctrinated her with the view that doctors' orders should not be questioned.

But things had changed for nurse Chin over the past several years. She had become a nursing supervisor with additional responsibilities that took her away from the thing she liked best, bedside nursing. Even more important, she was aware of increasing conflict with the younger nurses. They had different ideas about their role. Many of the newer nurses, particularly the degree nurses, viewed the nurse as a professional who should be substantially independent from the authority of the doctors. They felt that they had specialized training and were educated for more than "serving." They were aware of the many new challenging concepts in nursing and were continually urging nurse Chin to press their demands for an extended professional role. She found herself in the middle of many conflicts among the nurses, doctors, and other administrative staff. The younger nurses accused her of being too traditional and of considering nurses to be only hand-maidens of the doctors. The doctors, in turn, felt that changes were being made too rapidly and that the younger nurses were not willing to follow orders and to recognize authority. Nurse Chin was becoming increasingly frustrated.

In addition, there was a strong movement toward unionization of the nursing staff. There had been various meetings of the nurses to discuss collective action in terms of pay, benefits, and working conditions. Nurse Chin felt strongly that unionization was not appropriate for nurses, but she had not expressed these views openly. She was under pressure from many of the younger nurses to take an active role in support of unionization.

This general climate of conflict and disagreement created many problems for Ms. Chin. Whereas she had once looked forward to coming to work, now she was very apprehensive at the start of each day. One particular day had been most frustrating. All the beds in the orthopedics ward were filled and she had several patients scattered in other units. Two nurses were ill (as many nurses seemed to be, lately) and she was severely understaffed.

She made reassignments of personnel to take care of the patients as best she could and pitched in to help with the bedside duties. By 8:30 she had already tended to several patients and was working with Mr. Franklin. He had had a hip-joint operation several days earlier and was in considerable pain. He was the typical complainer. Everything was wrong—the food, the nurses, the doctors, the treatment, etc. And he needed the bedpan immediately. Nurse Chin met his needs cheerfully. She had learned to handle difficult patients with tact. She prided herself in never becoming irritated.

She was finally getting around to taking Mr. Franklin's temperature when Dr. Percy Roundtree, the physician in charge of the case, came by. Dr. Roundtree was known for his abrasive personality. Nerves of steel and a heart to match—at least around the hospital staff. He frequently shouted at the nurses and demanded complete obedience to his orders. Most of the nurses avoided him as much as possible. He checked the patient's hip and looked at the record, whereupon he exploded, "What's the matter with the nursing staff? They were 45 minutes late in getting medication to this patient, and these records are a mess!" Nurse Chin turned red but kept her cool and said nothing. Dr. Roundtree continued, "The nursing service on this floor is atrocious. Get that damned thermometer out of his mouth so I can examine him."

Nurse Chin removed the thermometer, shook it at him, and said, "Dr. *Sir,* you can take this damned thermometer and shove it in your *ear!*"

Ensign Lopez:
U.S.S. Toronto

Ensign Lopez was assigned as the Supply and Disbursing Officer aboard the U.S.S. *Toronto* immediately after completing Supply Officer's Midshipman School. His first experiences on board ship were confusing. He reported the night before the ship was to sail for the Pacific. He was a replacement for Supply Officer Darrington, who was being discharged from the Navy; Lt. Darrington was very anxious *not* to sail with the ship, so his staff worked all night transferring records and taking inventory. Ensign Lopez signed for everything with very little confidence and a lot of trust.

The next day he really felt like a Navy man as they sailed under the Golden Gate Bridge. Unfortunately, that didn't last long and the heavy swells began to get to him; he turned green with sickness. He spent the next 5 days in his bunk, caring very little about his duties as Supply and Disbursing Officer. He gradually got his sea legs and ventured down to the Supply Office to get acquainted with his duties and the personnel. He was in charge of acquiring and inventorying the provisions and stores, commissary activities, and the disbursement of funds for payroll and special purchases. He was also in charge of the ship's laundry and barbershop. He had 25 men reporting to him and was quite uneasy about his own knowledge of the various tasks and about his leadership ability.

Fortunately, he had several very good chief petty officers and storekeepers working with him, and he soon learned that they had a great deal more knowledge about the various activities than he did. Anyhow, things seemed to have run smoothly while he had been in the sack recuperating. He decided that a fairly easygoing, participative leadership style worked best. This may have been blind luck because he didn't know enough to be autocratic. His approach appeared to work well with the crew; his major difficulties seemed to be with the senior officers who felt that he should exert stronger leadership. But they didn't know even as much about the technical aspects of the supply and disbursing functions as he did, and, therefore, they left him alone until something went wrong. Furthermore, the captain and the executive officer were pretty reasonable and were concerned more with overall results than with strict adherence to Navy rules.

After several months, things were running fairly evenly and Ensign Lopez had settled down to a smooth routine. Three months after he first came on board ship, the executive officer was replaced by Commander Nelson. Nelson was traditional Navy and a stickler for rules and procedures. He frequently called Ensign Lopez to his cabin to make inquiries about the supply and disbursing activities and to ensure that Navy regulations were being followed. He felt that Lopez was too easy with his crew and was not always following the right procedures. He insisted that the men be properly attired and be present at all musters. Ensign Lopez's men had had substantial freedom because they performed more specialized functions and were not required to share in some of the more onerous duties, such as K.P. and night watches. Commander Nelson changed all this.

One day while Commander Nelson was getting a haircut, he noticed that several of the men were tipping the barbers. Although haircuts were free and the tips were always small, 25 to 50 cents, tipping was against Navy regulations. Commander Nelson called Ensign Lopez in and ordered him to talk to the three barbers about taking tips. Lopez spoke to the men and things went smoothly for several weeks. However, the old tipping habit was hard to break and Commander Nelson again called in Ensign Lopez to insist that it be stopped. He ordered Lopez to post a large sign in the barbershop, "No Tipping Allowed, U.S. Navy Regulations." No more was said and life was fairly calm.

About 2 weeks after the signs had been posted, Ensign Lopez went to the barbershop to get a haircut. Relationships still seemed to be friendly and he chatted with the barbers as he was having his haircut. As he got out of the chair, he reached into his pocket and handed barber Woodward 25 cents. Woodward looked surprised and embarrassed and backed away. Ensign Lopez seemed to insist, thrusting the coin on him. Finally, he said, "I can't take that, SIR, it's against Navy regulations," and pointed to the large sign which Lopez had posted. Lopez turned red, then white, and muttered something like "Good man" and left the barbershop fast.

That night Ensign Lopez lay in his bunk, still embarrassed from the incident in the barbershop. "What an ass! I had talked to the barbers about tipping and posted the sign. Then I tried to give one of them a tip. The guys must think that I was trying to trap them or that I am crazy." He was at a total loss to explain his own behavior.

John Terrell:
Nautilus Minerals, Inc.*

John J. Terrell was driving rather faster than usual as he made his way home from the airport. He was only too aware of what was disturbing his normally even temperament. His mind kept going over the most awkward decision he had had to face in his managerial career with Nautilus Minerals, Inc.

The crisis had appeared three weeks earlier, on the first anniversary of his appointment as general manager of Nautilus' lead smelting subsidiary, at its large, newly opened plant. The plant manager, Richard Everitt, came to see him. He brought along Dr. David Cohen, the part-time plant physician.

Cohen did most of the speaking. Three men had gone sick in the ore handling department in the past week, all suffering from serious lead poisoning. "They are now in hospital. I want to carry out screening tests immediately throughout the works to find out how widespread it is."

Terrell was concerned about the problem, but not too worried. He consented to sample screening of operators throughout the works to find the lead content in blood samples. He imagined the results would show the problem to be confined to one department, caused by operators not wearing masks or faulty ventilation, "But keep the reason for the tests quiet," he urged them.

The four men met a week later, when Cohen presented his report. The lead content in operators' blood throughout the site was dangerously high, and three more cases of poisoning had been found. "The source of the pollution is affecting the whole site," he emphasized, "and that means it is probably reaching the housing areas within a kilometre of here. We must stop it immediately."

Terrell authorized a study by outside consulting engineers to find the source and report on how it could be checked. Ten days later, the report bleakly confirmed his worst fears. The high blood lead levels were being caused by operators breathing fine lead dust which covered the whole site. It came from the high volume overhead conveyor which carried incoming ore from the unloading quays, 400 metres to the smelting sheds.

The consultants' report outlined the fabrications that would be needed to put a dust-tight cover along the length of this open conveyor. With strengthening of the structure, the cost of the work would amount to $500,000. It would need a complete plant shut-down for about three months to carry it out. This would cost the company almost $8 million in lost production.

Terrell questioned his colleagues on some of the assumptions and details of the report, but in the end he was faced with the stark fact that the pollution was serious.

Terrell decided that immediate action was necessary and called Harold Cort, Nautilus' managing director. Cort was stunned by the news. He asked for an immediate written report and recommendation and a meeting with Terrell three days later, when he had time to consider the implications. Terrell sent the report with a recommendation that the danger to the public and employees left the company with no choice but an immediate shut-down.

At the meeting later that week, Cort and the other executive directors listened quietly while Terrell gave a personal explanation of his recommendation. Then Cort rocked him with his verdict. "I agree with your recommendation, but it cannot be implemented for another six months. Our results are not going to be good this year and we couldn't carry another bad knock like this. Our share price must be maintained for the next few months, because we are going to the stock market with a new issue to raise the cash for our new Canadian mine."

Terrell protested about the risks the company would be running by deferring action. His protest about the public being harmed by the delay was met by a stony scepticism that the extra six months could make things seriously worse. The directors felt that Cohen was overstating the urgency of the problem.

Terrell left two hours later, exhausted and bitterly disappointed. As he drove home from the airport, he wondered what to do now. He could accept the decision as a regrettable necessity and wait six months before acting to solve the problem.

But how could he square this with his conscience, believing that delay was harmful to employees and nearby residents? He could quietly resign and wash his hands of the affair.

Alternatively, he saw a more positive course. He could resign in a blaze of publicity, sacrificing his chances of getting another good job in the smelting industry, but forcing the company to attend to the problem immediately. Suddenly, he had another idea. He could discreetly leak the story to a friend who edited the local newspaper. It may be underhand and unethical, he mused, but perhaps it is justified now.

Clifton Webber:
Advanced Aerospace Corporation

Clifton Webber had worked as an engineer for the Advanced Aerospace Corporation for 18 years. He had joined the company immediately after receiving his B.S. degree in aeronautical engineering from Pacific University. In his early career, he had held a wide variety of jobs with the company, but after a few years he became more specialized in working on the control components of hydraulic landing systems. He developed substantial technical expertise in this field and enjoyed working on different projects. Over the past 10 years, he had worked on a dozen or more aircraft and space vehicle projects. He was usually assigned to work on the research and developmental phase of the projects.

Ten years ago he had the opportunity to move into a supervisory position. However, he thoroughly enjoyed the technical aspects of his work and decided that he perferred to work where he had specialized expertise rather than move into management. The company had a dual ladder whereby technical specialists could advance in the organization at a rate equal to those who chose to move onto the supervisory ladder. He didn't regret the choice. He had continually advanced in the company and at this time had a very good salary which enabled him to meet living expenses and even to save enough to cover some of the planned expenses for his three teenage children, who would be attending the university within the next several years.

The Advanced Aerospace Corporation was engaged in research, development, and production of commercial aircraft and space vehicles. It had contracts with the major airlines, the U.S. Department of Defense, and the National Aeronautics and Space Administration. The company was organized on a project basis. That is, facilities and personnel were allocated to work on specific projects.

During his career, Cliff had been fortunate in being assigned to a new project whenever his job was phased out. On one occasion he had to move from the main headquarters in Southern California to Texas to work on a NASA project for 3 years. But, upon its completion, he had been able to negotiate for a new assignment back at headquarters.

Because of the nature of the industry and the high dependence on government contracts and the airlines, there were wide fluctuations in the level of activities. Cliff had seen the company's total employment move from 25,000 to a peak of 80,000 over a short span. But then the bottom fell out, and major cutbacks in government contracts and reductions in airline expenditures caused a reduction in force to 30,000 over a 4-year period. Cliff had survived, but many of his engineering associates, even some who had more seniority, had been on projects that were canceled, and they were laid off. Although still working, he was well aware of the general climate of gloom which these cancellations and layoffs created.

For the past year he had been assigned to the X-99 project, an advanced aircraft being developed to replace the current fleet in the airlines. From the start the project was shaky. Although the proposed aircraft did have superior performance and cost/benefit analysis indicated that it would be more economical to operate for the airlines, there were difficulties. Many airlines were in financial trouble because of the worldwide recession of 1975-1976, and they were having trouble in raising capital for new equipment purchases. The company had had to stretch out the program and substantially reduce the number of personnel assigned to it. Each day brought apprehension for Cliff. Would the project be terminated and would he be laid off next? Although he had been through project terminations before, this one was different. In the past, he had always been able to negotiate an assignment to another project. He was known to be highly qualified and personable. And he knew many of the key top managers. However, now there were no other projects on the horizon which looked as though they would need his skills.

Cliff thought of some of the ironies in the situation. During the earlier cutback, the company had first laid off some of the less effective personnel. Many of them had been able to find good positions in other industries in the Southern California area. However, as things got tighter, even the senior, highly qualified engineers had to be laid off, and by then most of the available positions in the area were already taken up. The general economic recession and the high level of unemployment didn't help. Besides, he had heard that many companies were giving preferential hiring to women and minorities in order to meet equal employment opportunity requirements. What chance did a white, middle-aged, obsolete engineer have? Cliff often thought that it would have been better if he had been laid off some 3 or 4 years earlier when other good jobs were available.

Cliff began quietly looking around for other employment opportunities. Because of the highly specialized nature of his work, there really weren't many demands for his skills. All the aircraft companies were laying off rather than hiring. One of his former engineering coworkers, now employed by a large engineering firm, had come up with a spot for Cliff. He would have to take a fairly substantial cut from his current salary and the work would not be directly in his line or as interesting. But at least it was a job. Cliff was in a dilemma. He had always enjoyed his work with Advanced and was very loyal to the company. But, was it loyal to him? Over the past several years he had seen many excellent and dedicated workers laid off by the company. He kept thinking about Alfie Wilson who lived just down the street. Alfie had worked for the company for 25 years, but the project he was on had been canceled and he was laid off with a small pension. His wife had gone back to work and Alfie seemed to spend his time doing housework and puttering around the yard. Was this to be Cliff's future? He had often thought about retirement and how he would play more golf, fish, and enjoy his leisure. But, forced retirement at 48 with little income—no thanks! Besides, he needed to see the kids through college and that would cost a bundle.

He tried to talk the situation over with his supervisors at Advanced. They assured him that he really was needed on the project and that they would do everything possible to keep him on. But, there were no guarantees. In fact, Cliff felt that they were very much concerned about their own jobs. And he continued to hear rumors that the entire project would be canceled and that there would be another round of layoffs.

On October 31, 1975, Cliff resigned his job at Advanced and went to work for the engineering firm. "What the hell. It's a job and I can't bank on Advanced to take care of me. It would be too tough to be a has-been at 48. At least this job will put bread on the table."

SUMMARY AND CONCEPTUALIZATION

You have read and analyzed a number of cases or incidents depicting individual, group, and organizational behavior in work situations. It is likely that you were exposed to a variety of perceptions and interpretations of why people acted the way they did. First, there was a process of inferring motivation from the behavior described in the specific situations. In each case, a number of factors or forces were involved, with varying degrees of importance for explaining behavior. Second, interpretation and inference are heavily dependent on the eye of the beholder. If the class members have diverse backgrounds and experience, they are likely to perceive and interpret the same situation in significantly different ways.

The challenge is to understand the complexity of the motivation-behavior relationship. Simplifying assumptions, such as "everyone wants more money," or "all people are power-oriented," or "managers function best under pressure," seem to make understanding and predicting easier. However, such an approach may provide a false sense of security. The various needs or goals that help explain motivation and behavior are probably distributed differentially in the general population. Thus, for some people the need for social esteem is extremely important; for others it is almost insignificant. Moreover, for one individual the same motivational force may vary significantly over several situations.

For the manager, the task is one of developing enough understanding to provide guidelines for motivating people to "perform" in work situations. This responsibility involves recognizing the forces within people and the factors in the environment that cause people to behave in certain ways. Because of the complexity involved, it is important to develop a contingency approach that is flexible, multifaceted, and based on astute diagnosis of the situation. For some people, the work itself is paramount in motivating good performance. In such cases, job enrichment can facilitate self-actualization. Key elements of enriched jobs are meaningfulness of work, responsibility, and knowledge of results (feedback).

For individuals or groups that emphasize achievement and self-actualization, a management-by-objectives-and-results approach can be effective. Challenging goals that are accepted by participants can be a powerful motivating force. Making sure accomplishments are recognized and rewarded is an intuitively obvious approach that is often neglected. Positive reinforcement can shape behavior in appropriate directions. In a sense, we are all behavior modifiers because we provide feedback implicitly if not explicitly. Positive and negative feedback can be inadvertent and haphazard, or it can be planned in a way that causes or motivates desired behavior.

Managers should be alert to the dangers of not differentiating between good and bad performance. If the rewards (feedback) are not significantly different for desirable and undesirable performance, there is no reason to expect improvement and satisfaction. Therefore, it is important to determine desired behavior, know ahead of time how to measure performance, and design reward systems that are appropriate.

All potential motivating forces should be considered in designing overall systems of motivating behavior. For some people, participation in a group or team effort may be extremely important. For others, individual autonomy is essential. In short, there is no one best way to motivate people. We need to be aware of situational complexity, understand general tendencies as identified in the body of knowledge based on research and conceptualization, and recognize individual differences when considering the issue of motivation.

Exercise 13
Influence Systems in Organizations: Leadership Styles

LEARNING OBJECTIVES
1. To understand and distinguish between leadership and management.
2. To increase our understanding of influence systems and leadership styles.
3. To identify your own leadership style and compare it with others in the class.
4. To develop situational prescriptions for leadership effectiveness.

ADVANCE PREPARATION
Read the Overview.

OVERVIEW
An adage says, "Leaders are born, not made." This fatalistic view suggests certain inherent abilities and/ or personality traits. Also, greatness has been considered a function of being in the right place at the right time. Apparently these views have not been widely accepted, because leadership has been one of the most extensively researched subjects in behavioral science during the twentieth century. It may well be the most written about and discussed aspect of organization and management.

We have emphasized the managerial role of planning, coordinating, and controlling organizational activities in the interest of objective accomplishment. The role includes attention to organization-environment relationships, task-technology considerations, structural arrangements, goals and values, and the psychosocial system. Managers are charged with maintaining and, if possible, improving overall organizational effectiveness, efficiency, and participant satisfaction. Management involves the coordination of both human and material resources toward objective accomplishment; it is more than leadership.

Leadership is an essential part of management with particular emphasis on the human aspects, the psychosocial system. The concept of leadership implies followership; hence, it involves relationships among people. More specifically, leadership suggests differential influence among people in social, particularly organizational, relationships. Leadership is "interpersonal influence, exercised in situations and directed, through the communication process, toward the attainment of a specified goal or goals. Leadership always involves attempts on the part of a leader (influencer) to affect (influence) the behavior of a follower (influencee) or followers in situations."[1] Differential influence is a process that is apparent in informal social relationships and in formal organizations. Typically, designated leaders, such as supervisors, chairpersons, or directors, do have a positive balance of official power in the influence system. However, this power may not always result in effective leadership. The positional authority of a so-called leader may not be enough to persuade subordinates to engage in appropriate activities; influence attempts fail, and leadership is ineffective. Informal patterns of influence often develop because of personal expertise, knowledge, or persuasiveness. Thus, the phenomenon of leadership-followership is always present in groups, but the specific patterns depend greatly on the particular situation.

Much of the effort in leadership research has been devoted to understanding the traits and behaviors of good leaders—with "good" being related to the performance of the group. One goal of such endeavors is to be able to predict who would be good leaders so that they can be selected for positions of responsibility. So far, the results are not clear enough to provide easy answers. A number of forces are involved in every situation, including environmental constraints, organizational climate, group dynamics, follower characteristics, and leadership behavior. "In view of the complexity of the factors that determine the relationships between leader behavior and group performance, it is apparent that no simple recipe for leader effectiveness will be applicable in more than a small proportion of situations encountered."[2] This conclusion suggests that there is no "one set of ideal leader traits" nor "one best way" to lead.

On the other hand, the situation is far from hopeless. We do have a body of knowledge evolving from behavioral science research on the leadership process. It suggests a contingency view with guidelines for leader behavior depending on the interaction of a number of situational variables. We will consider some of these factors in more detail as we proceed through this exercise. Before continuing, however, it will be important for you to identify your own leadership approach more explicitly. Then you will have an opportunity to compare your style with others in the class and with prescriptions for effective leader behavior.

PROCEDURE

STEP 1
Fill out the Leadership Questionnaire on page 181.

[1]Robert Tannenbaum and Fred Massarik, "Leadership: A Frame of Reference," *Management Science*, October 1957, p. 3.
[2]Ralph M. Stogdill, "Historical Trends in Leadership Theory and Research," *Journal of Contemporary Business*, Autumn 1974, p. 10.

Leadership Questionnaire

The following items describe aspects of leadership behavior. Respond to each item in terms of actual past experience; your past experience is the best estimate of the way you would be most likely to act if you were the leader of a work group. Circle the letter symbolizing the way in which you would be likely to behave:

(A) Almost Always   (F) Frequently   (S) Sometimes   (I) Infrequently   (R) Rarely

If I were the leader of a work group . . .

A	F	S	I	R	1.	I would trust the members to exercise good judgment in the interest of the organization.
A	F	S	I	R	2.	I would encourage close interpersonal relationships between myself and my subordinates and among group members.
A	F	S	I	R	3.	I would stress being ahead of competing groups.
A	F	S	I	R	4.	I would provide definite guidelines for work procedures, and expect members to follow them.
A	F	S	I	R	5.	I would give members feedback on their performance, both positive and negative.
A	F	S	I	R	6.	I would stress the use of group meetings to plan and critique our work.
A	F	S	I	R	7.	I would push the group members to work harder.
A	F	S	I	R	8.	I would press for acceptance of my expertise and ideas regarding the technical aspects of task performance.
A	F	S	I	R	9.	I would seek members' ideas and opinions, including criticism.
A	F	S	I	R	10.	I would encourage members to interact in goal setting and planning without my direct involvement.
A	F	S	I	R	11.	I would establish definite standards of performance and stress meeting them.
A	F	S	I	R	12.	I would assign members to particular tasks based on my perception of their special knowledge and/or skills.
A	F	S	I	R	13.	I would be concerned about the personal problems of group members.
A	F	S	I	R	14.	I would consider improving "the way we work together" to be as important as improving task accomplishment.
A	F	S	I	R	15.	I would urge the group to beat its previous record.
A	F	S	I	R	16.	I would assume prime responsibility for coordinating the work of group members.
A	F	S	I	R	17.	I would value differences of opinion and try to achieve consensus in problem solving.
A	F	S	I	R	18.	I would consider it my responsibility to facilitate resolution of interpersonal conflicts.
A	F	S	I	R	19.	I would modify subordinates' objectives in light of organization goals.
A	F	S	I	R	20.	I would develop overall plans and schedules and use them to control the group's activities.

STEP 2

Score the questionnaire as follows and write the score in the blank space provided in front of each question:

5	(A)	Almost Always
4	(F)	Frequently
3	(S)	Sometimes
2	(I)	Infrequently
1	(R)	Rarely

Add up the scores for the following groups of questions and write the total in the space provided.

1, 5, 9, 13, 17	_____	Support
2, 6, 10, 14, 18	_____	Interaction Facilitation
3, 7, 11, 15, 19	_____	Goal Emphasis
4, 8, 12, 16, 20	_____	Work Facilitation

STEP 3

Place an X on each of the corresponding lines below (and connect the X's) in order to get a profile of your degree of emphasis on four key dimensions of leadership behavior.[3]

Support: Behavior that enhances someone else's feeling of personal worth and importance.

5   15   25

Interaction Facilitation: Behavior that encourages members of the group to develop close, mutually satisfying relationships.

5   15   25

Goal Emphasis: Behavior that stimulates an enthusiasm for meeting the group's goal or achieving excellent performance.

5   15   25

Work Facilitation: Behavior that helps achieve goal attainment by such activities as scheduling, coordinating, planning, and by providing resources such as tools, materials, and technical knowledge.

5   15   25

Based on your general self-insight, does the profile reflect your behavior on these dimensions reasonably accurately? Specifically, is there an element of "how I wish I would behave" and/or "how leaders are supposed to behave" mixed in with "how I actually behave"?

[3] David G. Bowers and Stanley E. Seashore, "Predicting Organizational Effectiveness with a Four-Factor Theory of Leadership," *Administrative Science Quarterly*, September 1966, p. 247.

STEP 4

Meet in groups of 4 to 6 to compare profiles and responses to individual questions.

a. Compare similarities and differences. Where differences occur, explore the correlation between responses and past experience.

b. Invite feedback from peers in regard to their perception, based on experience in class to date, of your leadership behavior.

STEP 5

Your discussion has probably included assertions that appropriate leadership behavior depends on the particular situation. In this phase of the exercise we will pursue this concept in more detail. For example, read (without discussing) the following pairs of brief position descriptions and try to visualize the situational differences from the leader's perspective:

A Marine basic training drill sergeant	. . .	The Chairperson of the National Security Council
A chief surgeon in an operating room	. . .	The director of an outpatient psychiatric clinic
The captain of a commercial airline	. . .	The V.P. of advertising for a commercial airline
The "head" of a commune	. . .	The mother superior in a convent
The chief of the campus police	. . .	The chairperson of the sociology department
A director of personnel	. . .	A chief engineer
A foreman on an assembly line	. . .	The coordinator of a regional planning task force

Now, using the same subgroup as in Step 4, generate a list of factors or forces that might affect leadership styles. The following categories should be helpful in your analysis:

Forces or factors in the leader:

Forces or factors in the follower(s):

Forces or factors in the situation:

STEP 6

Engage in total class discussion.

  a. Are the dimensions emphasized in the four-factor model (Step 3) mutually exclusive? That is, does emphasis on goals and work facilitation preclude concern for people and relationships? Does emphasis on support and interaction facilitation preclude effective and efficient performance of the task?

  b. What would you prescribe as the ideal profile for a leader?

  c. How can situational analysis help in determining appropriate leadership behavior?

SUMMARY AND CONCEPTUALIZATION

You have had an opportunity to obtain feedback concerning your leadership style via a questionnaire and from peers based on experience in class to date. Additional feedback could be obtained by checking with others outside of class concerning their perception of your behavior in task-oriented situations. This could be based on experience in a variety of organizations—work, recreation, living group, or clubs. For example, if you have assumed a leadership role in any of the above activities, you might ask people whose opinion you respect for their perception of your behavior. This could be done in terms of overall impressions or related to the individual items on the Leadership Questionnaire.

In reviewing the research and writing on leadership, Bowers and Seashore concluded that in spite of the variety of terms used, there is a great deal of common conceptual content. They distilled the four dimensions of effectiveness used in this exercise:

  1. *Support.* Behavior that enhances someone else's feeling of personal worth and importance.
  2. *Interaction Facilitation.* Behavior that encourages members of a group to develop close, mutually satisfying relationships.
  3. *Goal Emphasis.* Behavior that stimulates an enthusiasm for meeting the group's goal or achieving excellent performance.
  4. *Work Facilitation.* Behavior that helps achieve goal attainment by such activities as scheduling, coordinating, planning, and by providing resources such as tools, materials, and technical knowledge.[4]

Support and interaction facilitation are obviously "people" concerns. Emphasizing these dimensions recognizes the need to encourage continued support of individuals in organizational endeavor and the need to maintain and improve interpersonal relationships and group processes such as teamwork. Goal emphasis and work facilitation relate to task concerns and to the path-goal theory of leadership.[5] Good leaders are typically seen as helpful in both setting goals and in structuring or designing means of achieving them. This approach builds on the concept of achievement motivation, and if goals are achieved there is an increase in satisfaction. Performance leads to satisfaction and increased motivation in the future.

In using the above model for prescribing leader behavior we suggest that all four factors are important and should be emphasized *as much as possible depending on the constraints of the situation.* But it is

---

[4] Ibid.
[5] Robert J. House and Terence R. Mitchell, "Path-Goal Theory of Leadership," *Journal of Contemporary Business,* Autumn 1974, pp. 81–97.

unrealistic to expect simultaneous attention to all the dimensions of leadership effectiveness. Some tradeoffs are necessary and bound to occur. Goal emphasis may be paramount in initiating a program of management by objectives. Interaction facilitation may actually need to be decreased in an organization that seems to spend nearly all its time in meetings (leaving little time to work on the task). An appropriate balance should be maintained according to the particular situation.

We looked at situational factors affecting leadership (in Step 5) by considering forces in (1) the leader, (2) the follower(s), and (3) the situation. An example of this approach is provided by Tannenbaum and Schmidt in considering the degree of participation that might be appropriate in decision making:[6]

Leader:
Own value system
Confidence in his/her subordinates
Own leadership inclinations
Feelings of security in an uncertain situation
Follower(s):
Independence-dependence needs
Willingness to assume responsibility for decision making
Tolerance for ambiguity
Degree of interest in participating
Degree of identification with organization goals
Knowledge and experience (or growth potential)
Expectations concerning participation
Situation:
Values and traditions in the organization
Group effectiveness
Nature of the problem
Pressure of time

A key to effective leadership is clarification of expectations between leaders and followers in order to reach a mutual understanding which sets the tone for the entire relationship. This situational approach to leadership effectiveness certainly involves contingency views. If the leader is a good diagnostician, he/she can ascertain the most appropriate leadership style to employ according to the circumstances. An autocratic style might be most appropriate if organizational participants expect it; for example, in times of crisis. In a military combat situation, subordinates typically rely on the decision making of their group leader. The crew of a ship hit by a torpedo would not be inclined to discuss the alternatives and then vote. If the captain announces, "Abandon ship," the order would be carried out immediately.

On the other hand, in situations where time permits, a democratic approach which includes subordinates in the decision-making process may be extremely useful. In still other situations, a bureaucratic approach may be most effective and efficient. For relatively routine decisions, standard operating procedures might be entirely appropriate. But referring to the rules when in fact there is an extraordinary set of circumstances might be dysfunctional for the organization. The manager should be as flexible as possible, gearing his/her style to the specific situation and the individuals involved.

Leaders can influence the behavior of others in a number of ways—suggesting, persuading, or forcing compliance. According to the Chinese philosopher Lao Tse, "When the best leaders' work is done, the people say, 'We did it ourselves.'" This suggests that the more subordinates are involved in the process, the more likely they will be committed to decisions and will implement them. However, there are tradeoffs in terms of time and cost. Autocratic, coercive approaches have appeal in terms of tidiness and speed of response.

Figure 13-1 illustrates a contingency approach to leadership; appropriate behavior is suggested for polar situations on several key variables—external and internal environment plus subordinates' personality predispositions. Prescriptions for "how to succeed as a leader" are rather straightforward in the extreme cases. Directive, boss-centered, task-oriented behavior is appropriate when the external environment is

[6] Robert Tannenbaum and Warren H. Schmidt, "How to Choose a Leadership Pattern," *Harvard Business Review*, May–June 1973, pp. 173–179.

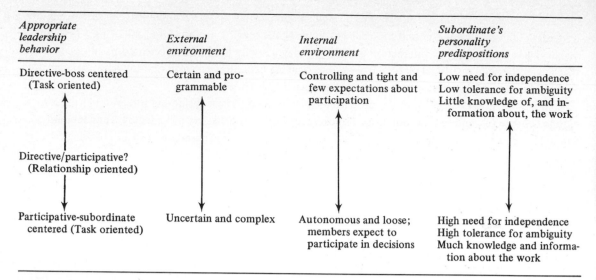

Appropriate leadership behavior	External environment	Internal environment	Subordinate's personality predispositions
Directive-boss centered (Task oriented)	Certain and programmable	Controlling and tight and few expectations about participation	Low need for independence Low tolerance for ambiguity Little knowledge of, and information about, the work
Directive/participative? (Relationship oriented)			
Participative-subordinate centered (Task oriented)	Uncertain and complex	Autonomous and loose; members expect to participate in decisions	High need for independence High tolerance for ambiguity Much knowledge and information about the work

FIGURE 13-1   A contingency approach to leadership. Source: Jay Lorsch and John J. Morse, *Organizations and Their Members: A Contingency Approach*, Harper & Row, Publishers, New York, 1974, p. 131.

certain, the internal environment is tightly controlled, and people don't expect to participate (low need for independence and/or little knowledge about the work, e.g.). Participative, subordinate-centered, task-oriented behavior is appropriate when the external environment is uncertain, the internal environment is loosely structured and autonomous, and people expect to participate (high need for independence and/or much knowledge about the work, e.g.). Effective leaders and organizations, by and large, tend to have good matches of styles and situations.

But the issue is not absolutely clear; the middle area or mixed situation can be confounding for the leader. How should we behave when the environment is semiprogrammable, procedures are moderately tight, and subordinates have some knowledge and/or sometimes expect to participate in decision making? Moreover, the three dimensions don't necessarily vary in unison. What if people expect to participate (having just completed an in-company training program) and yet the internal environment is tightly controlled? In essence, leaders need a contingency view that requires situational diagnosis as a foundation, followed by astute matching of behavior and situation. Note that adjustments may take place in leaders and/or followers and/or situations.

As indicated above, the issue of degree of participation in decision making has been discussed at length in the organization and management literature. In most cases a participative style is advocated. Such an approach may or may not be possible; moreover, it may not even be appropriate. Based on research with a number of practicing managers responding to case situations, Vroom and Yetton concluded that most managers would be more effective if they were *both* more autocratic and more participative.[7] They developed a normative model or prescription for leadership and decision making based on situational diagnosis. They found that managers tended to shy away from an autocratic approach even when it was most appropriate according to the model. And, they tended to be less participative than called for by the model in other situations. This suggests that to be more effective, managers need increased flexibility. A leader must be a good diagnostician and match the situation with an appropriate style—sometimes relatively autocratic and sometimes quite participative.

On balance, it is important for leaders to recognize the complexity of human motivation, group dynamics, and organizational climate. The best leaders seem to have a tolerance for ambiguity and the conceptual ability to cope with multidimensional situations. They emphasize both people and production rather than one or the other; they emphasize support and interaction facilitation as well as goal emphasis and work facilitation; and they are both autocratic and democratic-participative depending on the situation.

[7]Victor H. Vroom and Philip W. Yetton, *Leadership and Decision-Making*, Pittsburgh, Penna., University of Pittsburgh Press, 1973.

Exercise 14
Individual and Group
Decision Making:
The Mountain Survival Problem[1]

LEARNING OBJECTIVES

1. To increase our understanding of individual and group decision making.
2. To compare the effectiveness of individual and group methods for solving a specific, complex problem.
3. To identify some of the factors that influence effectiveness and efficiency in group problem solving.

ADVANCE PREPARATION

Read the Overview. Do not proceed further until the class meets. It is important that everyone begin the exercise simultaneously.

OVERVIEW

Decision making is a pervasive individual, group, and organizational activity. Indeed, management is often considered as synonymous with decision making. We can understand the managerial role by considering decisions made in planning, organizing, coordinating, and controlling organizational activity. The study of leadership can be approached through the degree of participation in decision making.

[1] Designed by Margaret Fenn and James Rosenzweig in consultation with David Kneeland, Director of the Institute for Survival Education, Seattle, Washington. A number of similar exercises have all been patterned after Jay Hall's "Lost on the Moon" (NASA) exercise. This specific exercise has been adapted from "The Desert Survival Problem," which is one of several available from Experiential Learning Methods (ELM), 39819 Plymouth Road, Plymouth, Mich., 48170.

The issue of participation brings up the age-old argument of whether individuals or groups make better decisions. Often, groups (committees) are avoided, primarily because we have all had considerable experience in ineffective committee meetings. It is unlikely, however, that group decision making will fade away. On the contrary, there is considerable evidence that we consider groups to be extremely important in some decision making—for example, the Supreme Court, boards of directors, regulatory commissions, and juries. The adage "Two heads are better than one" represents the rationale underlying the use of groups for problem solving and decision making.

For complex issues, it is important to marshal diverse resources in the form of information and expertise. The pertinent issue is that ineffective groups are likely to make poor decisions. Thus, the challenge is to enhance the effectiveness of groups in the problem-solving/decision-making process.

The primary criterion of effectiveness is decision quality. Do the results move the individual, group, or organization toward an established goal? If so, the decision is considered effective and rational. But rationality is in the eye of the beholder. What seems appropriate for one person or group may be deemed quite inappropriate from the point of view of another person or group. Values (our view of what is good and desirable) play a major role in such determinations. It is often easier to get agreement on what is a rational process than what is a rational choice. If the decision maker (individual, group, or organization) follows a systematic, careful, exhaustive process of defining and diagnosing before choosing, we are likely to consider it rational. On the other hand, a highly intuitive, seat-of-the-pants approach is not likely to be considered rational. Regardless of the process, our opinion that the ultimate choice is or is not rational depends on our own general values and specific views concerning the particular problem.

Another criterion of decision effectiveness is the degree of acceptance and commitment by those involved in carrying out its action implications. There are obvious trade-offs here. High-quality decisions that are not accepted go for naught. Similarly, acceptable decisions of very low quality are not particularly useful. The emphasis on participation is an obvious attempt to balance these two dimensions. If people are involved in the decision-making process, the probability increases that they will accept the choice and be committed to its implementation. If key resource people (in terms of knowledge and ideas) are involved and if the group is able to utilize them effectively, the probability of a high-quality decision increases.

Another aspect of decision making is the time element or efficiency criterion. A systematic, logical, participative process may improve decision effectiveness, but it may be time-consuming and therefore expensive. Therefore, we need to be aware of the cost/benefit ratio in order to determine the efficiency of problem-solving methods. If the quality and acceptance of decisions are not important, we could proceed swiftly and unilaterally—perhaps by flipping a coin. On the other hand, if quality and acceptance are crucial, a more analytical, participative approach will be worth the extra time and effort.

Assuming that we can identify problem-solving/decision-making situations where groups are most appropriate, the next issue becomes one of making the process as effective as possible. The dimensions involved range from simple physical arrangements to complex personal and interpersonal aspects. For example, seating arrangements can have a significant impact on the level and nature of participation.[2] For maximum opportunity to participate, the seating configuration should be as nearly round as possible. For interacting groups, the most appropriate number of participants seems to be in the range of five to seven; however, the number will vary with the type of problem and the participants.

As groups become larger, more attention needs to be paid to relatively formal approaches for facilitating interaction and problem solving. Some examples of effective and ineffective behavior in groups are shown in Figure 14-1. It is important to recognize the two levels of task and maintenance activities, both of which are essential for long-run effectiveness. This is particularly necessary for groups that expect to have a continuing existence and to engage in a sequence of problem-solving efforts. Over-

[2] L. L. Cummings, George P. Huber, and Eugene Arendt, "Effects of Size and Spatial Arrangements on Decision Making," *Academy of Management Journal*, September 1974, pp. 460–475.

emphasis on the task (solving the specific problem at hand) without regard for maintaining and improving the group's ability to solve problems is rather short-sighted. So, some explicit attention should be paid to "how we work" by encouraging helpful behavior and discouraging behavior that is dysfunctional. This approach is easier to state than to do. We find that groups seldom address the issue of how we work; rather, they are almost completely task-oriented, except for the swearing that goes on later concerning how bad the meeting was. If some time can be spent trying to understand why it was bad and in making improvements, it would be an investment that should pay off in the future.

Effective Behavior in Groups		Ineffective Behavior in Groups
Work or task* behaviors	*Group maintenance* behaviors*	
Initiating: Proposing goals or actions; defining problems; suggesting a procedure.	**Harmonizing**: Attempting to reconcile disagreements; reducing tension; getting people to explore differences.	**Displays of aggression**: Deflating others' status; attacking the group or its values; joking in a barbed or semiconcealed way.
Information giving: Offering facts; giving an opinion.	**Gate keeping**: Helping to keep communication channels open; facilitating the participation of others; suggesting procedures that permit sharing ideas.	**Blocking**: Disagreeing and opposing beyond "reason"; resisting stubbornly the group's wish (for personally oriented reasons); using a hidden agenda to thwart the progress of the group.
Checking for meaning: "Is this what you mean?" "Are you implying that . . . ?"		
Clarifying: Interpreting ideas or suggestions; defining terms; clarifying issues before the group.	**Consensus testing**: Checking to see if a group is nearing a decision; sending up a trial balloon to test a possible conclusion.	**Dominating**: Asserting authority or superiority to manipulate the group or certain of its members; interrupting contributions of others; controlling by means of flattery or other forms of patronizing behavior.
Summarizing: Pulling together related ideas; restating suggestions; offering a decision or conclusion for the group to consider.	**Encouraging**: Being friendly, warm, and responsive to others; indicating by facial expression or remark the acceptance of others' contributions.	
Reality testing: Making a critical analysis of an idea; testing an idea against some data to see if the idea would work.	**Compromising**: Offering an alternative that yields status; admitting error; modifying in interest of group cohesion or progress.	**Playboy behavior**: Displaying, in "playboy" fashion, one's lack of involvement; "abandoning" the group while remaining physically with it; seeking recognition in ways not relevant to the group task.
		Avoidance behavior: Pursuing special interests not related to task; staying off the subject to avoid commitment; preventing the group from facing up to controversy.

*The distinction between "task" behavior and group "maintenance" behavior is somewhat arbitrary. Some of these items could be classified in either column.

FIGURE 14-1 Effective and ineffective behavior in groups. *Source:* Adapted from Kenneth D. Benne and Paul Sheats, "Functional Roles of Group Members," *The Journal of Social Issues*, Spring 1948, pp. 41–49.

This exercise provides an opportunity for you to engage in both individual and group decision making. You will be able to compare both the results of the two approaches and the differential effectiveness of several groups. During the exercise, make mental notes about what goes on in your group. You will be asked to fill out a questionnaire concerning your observations and feelings.

PROCEDURE

THE MOUNTAIN SURVIVAL PROBLEM

Your charter flight from Seattle to Banff and Lake Louise (Alberta, Canada) has crash-landed in the North Cascades National Park area somewhere near the United States–Canada border, and then burst into flames. It is approximately 12 noon in mid-January. The twin-engine, 10-passenger plane, containing the bodies of the pilot and one passenger, has completely burned. Only the air-frame remains. None of the rest of you has been seriously injured.

The pilot was unable to notify anyone of your position before the plane crashed in a blinding snowstorm. Just before the crash, you noted that the plane's altimeter registered about 5,000 feet. The crash site is in a rugged and heavily wooded area just below the timberline. You are dressed in medium-weight clothing and each of you has a topcoat.

STEP 1

After the plane landed and before it caught fire, your group was able to salvage the 15 items listed on page 191. Your first task (as an individual) is to rank these items according to their importance to your survival. Write "1" next to the most important item, "2" next to the second most important item, and so on to "15" next to the least important item.

You have 10 minutes to complete this task and record the results on the Scoring Form (page 194).

STEP 2

Divide the class into groups of approximately eight people. This phase of the exercise is concerned with group problem solving. You are to employ the method of group consensus in reaching decisions. This means that the final ranking should be acceptable to each group member. Consensus is difficult to reach. Therefore, not every solution or every part of every solution will meet with everyone's complete approval. Try, as a group, to make each decision one with which all group members can at least partially agree. The Group Decision Form (page 192) is available if you want to use it. Record the results on the Scoring Form (Step 2, page 194).

Guidelines to use in reaching consensus:

1. View differences of opinion as helpful rather than as a hindrance in problem solving.
2. Avoid conflict-reducing techniques such as majority vote, averaging, or trading in reaching decisions.
3. Avoid arguing for your own individual opinions. Approach the task on the basis of information gathering and logical reasoning.
4. Avoid changing your mind *only* in order to reach agreement and avoid conflict. Support only solutions with which you are able to agree somewhat, at least.

When decisions are made by the consensus method, many essential leadership functions (e.g., initiating, regulating, informing, evaluating, coordinating, supporting, encouraging, harmonizing, etc.) should be employed by group members and can, therefore, be experienced and observed. You will have an opportunity to compare the effectiveness of this method with decisions made by individuals, by a controlling minority, and by majority vote.

Individual decision form

_____ Sectional air map of the area

_____ Flashlight (four-battery size)

_____ Four wool blankets

_____ One rifle with ammunition

_____ One pair of skis

_____ Two fifths of liquor

_____ One cosmetic mirror

_____ One jackknife

_____ Four pairs of sunglasses

_____ Three books of matches

_____ One metal coffeepot

_____ First aid kit

_____ One dozen packages of cocktail nuts

_____ One clear plastic tarpaulin (9′ × 12′)

_____ One large, gift-wrapped decorative candle

Group Decision Form

Individual rankings

	1	2	3	4	5	6	7	8	*Group consensus ranking*
Sectional air map of the area									
Flashlight (four-battery size)									
Four wool blankets									
One rifle with ammunition									
One pair of skis									
Two fifths of liquor									
One cosmetic mirror									
One jackknife									
Four pairs of sunglasses									
Three books of matches									
One metal coffeepot									
First aid kit									
One dozen packages of cocktail nuts									
One clear plastic tarpaulin ($9' \times 12'$)									
One large, gift-wrapped decorative candle									

STEP 3

Fill out the questionnaire, Feedback on How We Worked, on page 196. Process the responses as indicated in order to get a frequency distribution for the group. Discuss the various items and issues as long as time permits.

STEP 4

As the instructor/facilitator reads the ranking and rationale for each item (based on a consensus of survival experts), record it under Step 4 on the Scoring Form (page 194).

STEP 5

Record the absolute difference (ignoring plus or minus) between your rank (Step 1) for each item and the experts' rank (Step 4). Add the differences for 15 items to get your *individual score*.

STEP 6

Record the absolute difference (ignoring plus or minus) between the group's rank (Step 2) for each item and the experts' rank (Step 4). Add the differences for 15 items to get the *group score*. Record it on the Comparative Analysis Form (page 195).

STEP 7

Record all the individual scores for your group on the Scoring Form; add them; and divide by the number of people in the group to obtain the Average Individual Score. Record it on the Comparative Analysis Form.

STEP 8

Note the lowest and highest scores in your group in order to determine the *range of scores*. Record on both the Scoring and Comparative Analysis forms.

STEP 9

Note the number of individual scores that are better (lower) than the group score (Step 6) and record it on the Comparative Analysis Form.

STEP 10

Record the gain or loss of the group score over the most accurate individual.

STEP 11

Put the Comparative Analysis Form on a blackboard or flipchart and fill it out according to the input from each group. During a break, have everyone scrutinize the results and begin to speculate on what they mean.

STEP 12

General discussion:

   a. What conclusions can be drawn from the results for all groups as shown by the Comparative Analysis Form?
   b. What effective and ineffective behaviors can be reported by the groups? (Why we did so well or so poorly.)
   c. What guidelines are important for future problem-solving efforts of this type?
   d. Can groups have too much consensus?

Scoring Form   **Group number** _____

	Step 1: Your individual ranking	Step 2:* The group ranking	Step 4: Survival experts' ranking	Step 5: Difference between 1 and 4	Step 6: Difference between 2 and 4
Sectional air map of the area					
Flashlight (four-battery size)					
Four wool blankets					
One rifle with ammunition					
One pair of skis					
Two fifths of liquor					
One cosmetic mirror					
One jackknife					
Four pairs of sunglasses					
Three books of matches					
One metal coffeepot					
First aid kit					
One dozen packages of cocktail nuts					
One clear plastic tarpaulin (9′ × 12′)					
One large, gift-wrapped decorative candle					
Total (The lower the score the better)				Your score	Group score

Step 7: Individual scores:

———— ———— ———— ———— ———— ———— ———— ————

        Add up the group's individual scores and divide by the number in the group to get the average individual score   ☐

Step 8: Lowest (best) score in the group   ☐

        Highest (worst) score in the group   ☐

Step 9: Number of individual scores lower than the group score (Step 6)   ☐

    *Step 3: Complete the questionnaire, Feedback on How We Worked, on page 196.

Comparative Analysis Form

Group number	Before Discussion		After Group Discussion			
	Average error score of group members	Range of individual error scores	Group error score	Gain or loss over average error score	Number of individual error scores lower than the group error score	Gain or loss over the most accurate individual
Overall averages						

Feedback on How We Worked

1. What impact did the physical arrangements of the work place have on:

   a. Effectiveness _____

   b. Efficiency _____

   c. Participant satisfaction _____

2. How much time was spent initially in planning how to approach the task, developing a framework for analysis, etc.? (Check one.)

   _____   _____   _____
   None   Some   Quite a bit

3. How much time was spent in explicitly identifying available resources for the task? (Check one.)

   _____   _____   _____
   None   Some   Quite a bit

4. What was the participation pattern during this meeting? (Check one.)

   _____ Extremely unbalanced; not everyone participated; a few did all the talking.

   _____ Slightly unbalanced; a few talked a bit too much; others didn't talk enough.

   _____ Appropriately balanced; we didn't all talk the same amount, but we each talked about the right amount.

5. Members who did not talk may have been tuned out or attentively involved. How many were attentively involved when they were not talking? (Check one.)

   _____   _____   _____   _____
   All of us   Most of us   A few of us   None of us

6. How many occasionally "checked for meaning" to make sure that remarks were understood as they were intended? (Check one.)

   _____   _____   _____   _____
   All of us   Most of us   A few of us   None of us

7. How many occasionally summarized; e.g., what we had accomplished, what we agreed on, what we disagreed on? (Check one.)

   _____   _____   _____   _____
   All of us   Most of us   A few of us   None of us

8. How many helped keep the discussion "on track"; e.g., by orienting us to our task, by bringing back members who digressed? (Check one.)

   _____   _____   _____   _____
   All of us   Most of us   A few of us   None of us

9. How many facilitated a climate of "warmth and support"; e.g., by encouraging the participation of others, by indicating approval of contributions, by trying to reduce tensions? (Check one.)

   _____   _____   _____   _____
   All of us   Most of us   A few of us   None of us

10. Did we openly state our disagreements and discuss them rather than ignore them or pretend there were none? (Check one.)

_____   _____   _____   _____
Almost always   Usually   Sometimes   Almost never

11. When we had trouble making progress, did we openly discuss the signs of the difficulty and try to find the reason for it? (Check one.)

_____   _____   _____   _____
Almost always   Usually   Sometimes   Almost never

12. How were minority positions dealt with? (Check one or more.)

_____ Politely ignored

_____ Minority members "seduced" to go along with group

_____ Listened to politely but group moved on for sake of expediency

_____ Overpowered, out-talked

_____ Listened to and resolved; group moved on only after understanding and truly reaching agreement

13. My own feelings on the following issues are (circle one):

	Poor Low Little	Neutral		Good High Much
a. How good the group's decision is	1	2	3	4
b. How committed I am to the group's decision	1	2	3	4
c. How much attention the group paid to my ideas	1	2	3	4

d. Did I have any feelings of irritation, frustration, or dissatisfaction? If yes, they were:

_____

_____

_____

After each member has completed the questionnaire, tally all members' responses for questions 2 through 13c.

As each member calls out her or his rating for question 2, the others can make tally marks above the ratings called. When all have done this, each member will have a picture of how the whole group responded on question 2. This frequency distribution can be compared with each member's own rating.

Questions 3 through 13c should be done in the same way, one item at a time.

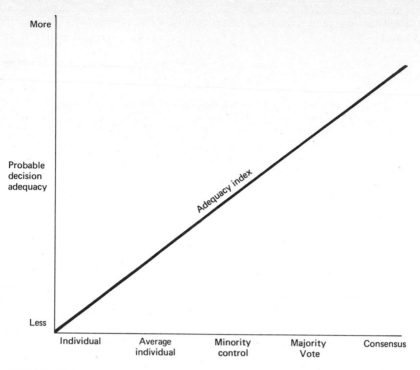

FIGURE 14-2 Relationship between methods of utilizing group resources and probable decision adequacy. Source: Jay Hall and Vincent O'Leary, *The Utilization of Group Resources in Decision Making*, National Training Laboratories, Washington, D.C., 1967, p. 4. (Mimeo)

SUMMARY AND CONCEPTUALIZATION

You have experienced an exercise in individual and group problem solving. The task and the method were specified in order to demonstrate the effectiveness of striving for consensus on complex issues. As Figure 14-2 indicates, the probable decision adequacy increases as one moves from individual decisions to averaging, voting, and consensus. These results have been borne out in a number of similar problem-solving tasks where the quality of the solution can be measured.

Remember, we are considering probable decision adequacy. Some individuals in your group or in the class may have offered solutions superior to that of the group. If we could identify such a person and charge him or her with the responsibility for making the decision, we would have an effective and efficient approach. However, what if we happened to pick someone with a very high (very incorrect) score whom we then charged with a decision that affects our survival? Even if the group score did not improve as dramatically as it typically does in this and similar problems, participation in the decision-making process would normally increase acceptance and commitment to carry out a plan of action. Following through on a moderately good solution may be better than half-hearted support of an optimal solution.

It is important to recognize that consensus is an approach that is appropriate in certain situations—particularly when information and expertise from a variety of sources are desirable. Minority rule or majority voting ensures some interaction but does not push the group to consider all controversial ideas thoroughly. Since unanimity is typically a utopian concept in complex situations, consensus is the most effective approach. It does not ensure success, but it does facilitate thorough exploration of the issues. In rare cases, it may result in "paralysis by analysis," but effective groups are usually able to balance the need for diagnosis and action.

A number of situations call for less participation; perhaps subordinates provide only information or minimal consultation. Some situations require unilateral decisions and autocratic approaches. The key factor for managers and group members is to understand the range of situations and alternative approaches and to have a consistent view with regard to which approach fits which situation. Thus it may be quite appropriate for managers to make a decision unilaterally when they have all the relevant information, when satisfactory decision quality is assured, and when it is likely to be accepted and implemented. When managers need more information, they might request it from others in the group or organization on a one-to-one basis. Then, using the information collected, the manager could make the decision. Another approach would be consultation with an advisory group but with the decision remaining the prerogative of the manager. All these approaches are appropriate, depending on the situation.

Contrary to popular belief, participation is not a panacea. For example, Vroom and Yetton have found that, given their normative model of effective decision making, most managers would improve the quality of their decision making (and implementing their decision) if they became *both* more autocratic and more participative.[3] In short, many managers engage in ineffective, middle-of-the-road participative approaches that don't fit very well with specific situations. The selection of appropriate problem-solving/decision-making processes must be based on astute diagnosis of particular situations.

We have referred to, and you have experienced, some of the factors that lead to effectiveness or ineffectiveness in group activity, particularly problem solving. As you listened to the reports of the class groups and observed the results shown in the Comparative Analysis Form, did you note any correlations? Did effective groups identify their resources and use them in solving the problem? For example, we have had several experiences where one individual had an extremely low score, but the group had a very high score. In one extreme case, the group members reported that the individual who made the wisest decisions did not say one word throughout the group discussion. In another case, the group did not reach a consensus within the time limit because one individual held out for his ranking. It turned out that he had the least effective score in the class and subsequently was quite apologetic. Obviously, the issue is not that everyone should participate equally. Rather, it is that participation should be reasonably balanced with expertise. Over time, the balance may shift according to the particular problem.

Whose responsibility is it to see that group members participate appropriately? The leader's? The individual's? All members? We suggest that all group members are responsible for effective task and maintenance activities. However, most groups seem prone to expect the formal leader to do all the work, including eliminating or toning down the ineffective behavior of dysfunctional members.

Now that you are aware of some of the dimensions of effective and ineffective behavior in problem-solving groups via a structured experience, observe what goes on in real groups of which you are a member. If the situation warrants (that is, if it is not too threatening), try some new behaviors and see what happens. Group activity is pervasive, and there is much room for improvement.

[3] Victor H. Vroom and Philip W. Yetton, *Leadership and Decision-Making*, Pittsburgh, Penna., University of Pittsburgh Press, 1973.

Exercise 15
Evaluating Performance: State University Grading System

LEARNING OBJECTIVES

1. To consider the problems in evaluating individual and organizational performance.
2. To relate these issues to a more specific problem in measuring accomplishment—a university grading system.
3. To develop your own system for evaluating the performance of students in colleges and universities.

ADVANCE PREPARATION

Read the Overview and the case, Changing the Grading System at State University. You may also want to obtain background information on the current grading system in your college and investigate any recent trends, changes, or proposals for changes.

OVERVIEW

One of the most difficult problems confronting organizations is measuring performance. Every organization develops some means of indicating how effectively and efficiently it is accomplishing its functions. An automobile company may look at return on investment, profits, market share, and sales volume. The professional football team's success may be in terms of its win-loss record, whether it went to the Super Bowl, or whether it provided a good return on investment for the owners.

It is difficult to develop appropriate overall measures of the performance for certain organizations. For example, how does the college or university determine its accomplishments—by number of graduates, its rank in prestige among the top schools, or its success in its football conference? How is a hospital evaluated? By the number of patients treated? By the number who can walk out rather than be carried out? By the perceptions of the patients and medical practitioners in the community?

Business organizations do have an ultimate measure of performance. If they are not successful, they go broke and out of existence. In the public sector, there usually is no such overall measure. In recent years, numerous programs have been initiated to relate more specifically goal setting, planning, and performance evaluation in public institutions. The Planning, Programming and Budgeting System (PPBS) was developed initially by the federal government and has been used extensively by numerous states, universities, cities, and other agencies.

Measuring the performance of people in accomplishing their tasks is also a problem. It is not difficult to set standards for routine tasks. For example, we can develop output standards for workers on assembly lines, people sorting mail, and cashiers in a fast-food service operation. However, it is likely that we can determine the volume of output more easily than we can determine the quality of the product or service. We can count the number of customers served by the counterperson at a McDonald's, but it is more difficult to determine whether the service was provided in a friendly, courteous manner. Furthermore, there are other complicating issues in performance evaluation in even routine jobs. How about absenteeism and tardiness and its impact upon the output not only of the individual but of the rest of the work group?

When we move to nonroutine tasks, performance evaluation is even more difficult. How do we appraise the work of higher-level managers, teachers, surgeons, and scientists? The more dynamic and uncertain the task, the greater the problem of establishing criteria for measuring performance.

A recent approach to establishing goals and measures of performance is management by objectives and results (MBO&R). You experienced the first phase of the process in a previous exercise, Goal Setting: Personal and Organizational. Although there are a variety of approaches to MBO&R, these programs typically provide organizational participants with more clearly defined operational objectives against which their accomplishments can be judged. The most successful MBO&R programs involve substantial participation on the part of individual managers or employees in setting their own objectives and means for appraising results.

A college or university has many problems in measuring performance. For example, how do we evaluate the overall accomplishments of the institution in performing its social function? We usually use rather general output measures, such as the number of graduates, the perceived prestige of the institution by outsiders, its number of Nobel Prize winners, and the national recognition of its faculty. We may also use input measurements, such as the quality of the students that it attracts, the funds provided by the legislature, alumni, and donors, or the number of research grants received.

Measuring the performance of individuals, primarily students and professors, within the university is also difficult. How is the effectiveness of the professor to be determined when it comes time for merit increases, promotion, and tenure? Most universities emphasize the three criteria of teaching, scholarly research, and service to the community. Decisions are also influenced by environmental factors, such as the availability of funds from legislatures, student fees, government grants, and endowments. Consideration may also be given to what comparable universities are doing and, in particular, whether the individual faculty member has received competitive offers from other institutions.

One of the key problems is establishing measures for performance evaluation. In the past, it has been easier to appraise professors on their research and publications and community service than on their teaching effectiveness, giving rise to the cry of "publish or perish." However, in recent years most universities and colleges have developed more adequate measurements of teaching effectiveness. Procedures for student evaluation of teachers have become commonplace. Although there still remains a good deal of controversy over such processes, current discussion suggests that more emphasis will be placed on teaching effectiveness.

It is apparent that people in organizations adapt their performance according to the specific factors that are measured more precisely and tend to disregard those performance criteria that are vaguely expressed and incapable of measurement. For example, if you measure only the quantity of production in a factory, quality of output may suffer. If you have fairly precise measurements for research and publication (at least you can see the stack of books and articles on the desk) and no way of determining teaching effectiveness, then even professors are smart enough to recognize what really counts. For all organizational members, performance tends to be strongly influenced by the measures of effectiveness utilized.

At the student level in the university or college, the grading system is one of the key means of performance evaluation. Although we may have strong feelings that "grades aren't everything" and that learning involves a great deal more than just achieving a high grade-point average, the grading system is still the most important, quantifiable criterion of student performance in most colleges and universities. This exercise will focus on changes in the grading system for a state university and the process by which such a change was achieved.

Changing the Grading System at State University

The grading system at State University, which was typical of many other universities and colleges, was as follows:

A — Honor
B — Good
C — Medium
D — Poor
E — Failure, or other than official withdrawal
I — Incomplete

Generally, students are required to maintain a 2.0 grade-point average at the undergraduate level and 3.0 at the graduate level. (The grade-point average is calculated on a basis of A = 4.0, B = 3.0, C = 2.0, D = 1.0, and E = 0.0.) However, individual departments have shown a continuing trend to establish higher grade-point average requirements for students majoring in their areas. In addition, there were special provisions allowing students to take a limited number of courses on a credit/no-credit basis. Grades at State University were all recorded as a full letter grade; no pluses or minuses were recorded. This meant that if the student earned a B— or B+ (as perceived by the instructor), it was still recorded as a B.

This grading system had been in existence for many years without any major modifications except for the addition of credit/no-credit grades for selected courses. In the early 1970s, there was a growing concern among the faculty, administration, and some students about the "grade inflation." In the past, grades had been more evenly distributed throughout the A to E range. However, there had been a gradual upward shift of the grades so that almost no D's and E's and few C's were given. In 1973, over 72 percent of the letter grades awarded in undergraduate classes were A's and B's. This increase in grades was enhanced by a liberal policy on withdrawals from class and on the granting of "incompletes." In most cases, a student doing poorly in a class could escape a low grade by withdrawing from the class or by requesting an incomplete.

The rising level of grades was by no means confined to State University but was a phenomenon occurring throughout the nation. A number of surveys indicated that A's and B's were becoming commonplace and that a B was about equivalent to a C+ 10 years ago. A national magazine reported that 42 percent of all undergraduate grades at Yale University were A's, and 46 percent of the senior class graduated with honors. The *Stanford Observer* reported that its sample survey indicated that the average grade-point average for undergraduate students had risen to 3.55 by 1974. A national survey of 197 institutions, conducted by Arvo E. Juola of Michigan State University and reported in the *Chronicle of Higher Education*, showed an average increase of nearly half a letter grade between 1960 and 1973.

The faculty and administration at State University, aware of these national trends and the situation at their own university, were concerned over the implications. The Faculty Committee on Scholastic Standards was the official body of the University Senate charged with looking at the grading situation and with proposing changes.

This faculty committee was concerned that the grade inflation was leading to a compression of the grading scale which made it difficult to identify the outstanding student. In the committee's words, "The grading system is too crude and imperfect to make a distinction in level of performance." In addition, the liberal withdrawal and incomplete policies meant that students would frequently withdraw from classes or receive incompletes even when they were doing satisfactory work but were afraid of receiving a grade which would lower their grade-point average. Records indicated that combined withdrawals and incompletes increased from 5 percent of all grades awarded in 1967 to 11.1 percent in 1973. It was suggested that many students signed up for more courses than they planned to complete, then selected those that they liked and/or in which they were doing well and dropped the rest. There was concern about the misallocation of resources under this liberal policy. Because of budgetary constraints, there were not sufficient classes, and many students could not attend the classes they wanted. Many professors found it disconcerting to turn away 10 to 15 students who wanted their class and then to find that 10 or more students out of a class of 50 withdrew or took incompletes. The question of fairness and equity for all students was raised. This view can be summarized by the following statement by the committee:

> The current high rate of withdrawals and incompletes and the resulting waste of resources clearly cannot be blamed on students. The fault lies in the system. The system encourages students to register for the largest number of courses they could possibly complete under the most optimistic assumptions of work load and to withdraw later if they find themselves short of time. With this system, it is little wonder the current withdrawal rate is so high, particularly end-of-the-quarter withdrawals.

THE NEW GRADING SYSTEM

The Faculty Committee on Scholastic Standards began its deliberations on the grading system in 1972. The committee reports to, and is directly responsible to, the University Senate, which is an elected, representative body of the faculty. There were nine faculty members on the committee. Two student representatives attended the meetings, but did not have a vote.

The committee held numerous meetings and communicated with a number of groups on campus. It held open meetings to obtain different viewpoints. After several years of deliberation, it finally proposed the following changes in the grading system to the University Senate in the fall of 1975.

DECIMAL GRADING SYSTEM

The committee recommends that the basic grading system now in use be retained, but that faculty record grades directly in grade points on a 0.0 to 4.0 scale to the nearest tenth of a point rather than only "whole" letter grades of A, B, C, D, and E. Under this system, the current reference point of A = 4, B = 3, C = 2, D = 1, and E = 0 would be retained but an instructor could record an intermediate grade point between these reference points, such as 3.2 or 3.3. A student's transcript under this system would indicate only numbers. For example, under the old system, a student with a B− or B+ would receive a recorded grade of B and a grade point for the course of 3.0. Under the decimal system, a B− would be recorded as 2.7 and a B+ as a 3.3. Under the old system, there were only five possible letter grades. Under the new system, there were 40 possible decimal grades.

THE WITHDRAWAL POLICY

Briefly, the new withdrawal policy would permit a free withdrawal during the first 2 weeks of the quarter with no entry on the student's record.

During the third and fourth weeks, the student could withdraw for any reason, but the registrar would record a grade of W on the student's transcript.

From the fifth week on, the general rule would be no withdrawals during this period. There were provisions for granting students a limited number of unrestricted withdrawals during their academic careers and for reasons of illness, etc.

THE INCOMPLETE POLICY

Under the previous grading system, an incomplete was supposed to be made up during the next quarter. If not made up, however, there were no penalties. Under the new provision, an incomplete grade (I) would be automatically converted to an E if not made up by the end of the next quarter. A student could petition the registrar to retain the I grade on the student's record for a maximum of three additional quarters with approval of the instructor.

STUDENT REACTIONS

Substantial negative reactions to the proposed changes were expressed by many students. A campus vote indicated that 60 to 70 percent of the students favored the existing grading system. The *Daily* ran many articles expressing the negative views. In December 1975, 2 days before the scheduled meeting of the University Senate, the *Daily* ran a full-page ad listing the offices and phone numbers of all the 141 faculty members who were on the Senate and urged students to express their opinions concerning the new grading system directly. Many students did call the senators and offered a wide range of suggestions (some not so flattering). It was evident that many students were against the new grading system. The *Daily* ad also urged students to attend the Senate meeting scheduled later in the week to express their opinions.

DECEMBER 1975 SENATE MEETING

At this meeting, the chairman of the Faculty Committee on Scholastic Standards presented the proposal. There was substantial debate among the senators and various amendments were proposed. The president of the Associated Students, the president of the Graduate Students Association, and the student representatives on the Faculty Committee on Scholastic Standards presented arguments against the proposal. There were several hundred students in the audience and a number of them expressed their views—mostly negative—of the proposal.

There were many parliamentary maneuvers with proposals for amendments, tabling, recess, and adjournment—all defeated. Finally, a motion to close debate was passed and the vote on the three proposals was taken. All the proposals passed by a narrow margin.

It was quite evident that many of the students attending the meeting were very upset by the procedure and by the motion to close debate which ended discussion. They walked out of the meeting in mass after the vote was announced. Many felt that they had not been given a full hearing to express their opposition to the program. Some of the typical reactions were reported in the *Daily* over the next several days.

> "What a farce. The faculty sat there with closed minds. The proceedings were rigged so that the students didn't have a chance to express their views."

> "I support effort to maintain the present grading system as it is. Students have, in two elections, already shown their opposition to proposed changes and I feel, since students are the ones directly affected, that their vote should be taken into consideration. It is their future in terms of grades that is on the line. We certainly weren't given a fair hearing at the Senate meeting yesterday."

> "During the December Senate meeting when the new provisions were voted on, students filled the room to capacity to display their dissatisfaction with the proposals. Students went with the hope they would have some impact on the outcome. What they ended up seeing, however, was a bunch of arrogant, anesthetized faculty senators who completely ignored student wishes and adopted the changes anyway. In essence, the faculty senate was telling the audience they really didn't care what students thought. It's easy to see why students would come away disillusioned and apathetic."

Not all students were against the proposal, as indicated by the following:

> "The decimal system sounds good to me. A number of times professors have told me that I was at the top of the B range and should have received a B+. I received the same grade as someone who scraped through with a B−. Under the new system, I would have received a 3.3 and he would have received a 2.7. The new system would have been much better in really indicating the differences in performance."

"I resent the fact that some students take up class space when I couldn't get in and then withdraw towards the end of the quarter. They kept me from getting a class I needed and wasted everybody's time."

"I don't understand the beef. I have only had one withdrawal in my three years here and don't know why anyone would need to have total freedom for withdrawals. The new policy is liberal enough to meet the needs of the students who are really interested in an education and not just scraping through."

Although there were mixed views, it was evident that many students were not happy with the new system. Several expressed the view that it was not so much the new grading system itself which they disliked, but the process by which it had been instituted.

Although the issue was heated at times, there was some humor and a variety of alternative proposals. The "animal system," one of the more inventive of these, is shown in Exhibit 15-1.

SUBSEQUENT EVENTS

Under University Senate rules, if 1 percent of the total faculty objects to a Senate action, the action is resubmitted to the University Senate for consideration. There were sufficient objections, and the three proposals were resubmitted for a full Senate hearing in February 1976. The February meeting was essentially a repeat of the December meeting. Several hundred students attended, and some of them were heard in opposition to the proposals. After further discussion, a vote was taken which reaffirmed the previous action. The vote was much stronger in favor of the proposed changes than at the December meeting. The report showed: "The Senate reaffirmed its approval of changes in the grading system by the following vote: decimal grading— 72 in favor, 28 opposed; incomplete policy—61 in favor, 32 opposed; withdrawal policy—62 in favor, 37 opposed."

Student reaction was even stronger than earlier, as indicated by the following excerpt from the *Daily*.

Faculty Stands on Grade Policy Change: A "Ludicrous Academic Farce"?

Nearly 250 students watched in stunned silence yesterday as the University Senate overwhelmingly reaffirmed three major changes in the University grading system. Hundreds of students joined with the President of the Graduate Students Association and President of the Associated Students in a second futile attempt to block the changes. . . .

After the meeting, students filed out of the hall feeling helpless. "That was the most ludicrous academic farce I've ever seen," said one student. "Democracy at this University died in there today."

But this was not the end of the process. Under the Senate procedures, the action was to become final unless a referendum poll of the entire faculty was requested in writing by 10 percent or more of the voting faculty. And 245 faculty members did sign letters asking for a referendum poll of the entire faculty.

Prior to the vote, activities to influence the faculty reached the highest point. The Faculty Committee on Scholastic Standards circulated information explaining the change—reiterating the arguments stated earlier. The Associated Student Task Force on University Governance, a student group opposed to the change, circulated the statement set forth in Exhibit 15-2. The issue became heated on all sides.

The results of the faculty referendum indicated a large majority in favor of the proposed changes as shown here:

	Yes	No
Decimal grading	1,190 (80%)	292 (20%)
Withdrawal policy	1,260 (85%)	215 (15%)
Incomplete policy	1,247 (84%)	228 (16%)

This vote was the final stage, and the new grading system was to be implemented in the autumn of 1977.

A few of the comments appearing in the *Daily* after passage of the new system suggest the adverse feelings of some students.

Elephant—slow, tedious, boring, good recall but myopic

Kangaroo—skips around, sporadic, inconsistent, argumentative

Tsetse fly—pays to have term papers written

Amoeba—no central point, rambles, indifferent

Armadillo—impenetrable logic

Turtle—lack of expression, shies away from discussion

Giraffe—idealistic, too much extrapolation, pie-in-the-sky attitudes, tendency to copy during exams

Sheep—no goals, takes up space, nicely dressed especially in winter, always in fashion

Martian—no basis for conclusions, possible misunderstood genius

Zebra—schizoid, contradictory, can't read between the lines, always brings notebook paper to class

Duck—talkative, nonsensical

Beaver—diligent, industrious, organized

Lemmings—can't handle it

Pig—hungry for facts, misses central idea, emulates faculty

Cobra—ambitious, wants professor's job

Sasquatch—never comes to class but always gets the assignment in (foreign students receive a Yeti)

Skunk—bad vibes, obnoxious, avoided

Penguin—pensive, scholarly, lonely, despairing, wears tuxedo to class

Peacock—egotist, all show

Prairie dog—overly systematic

Ant—computer jock, always developing contingency plans

Parrot—follows directions well, no mind, always gets a good job because he-she tells good stories

Hyena—math student (restrictive grade) who notices prof make a mistake on blackboard early in a problem but doesn't say anything until he-she is finished

Fruit flies—conformists

Tree sloth—never misses class, does nothing

Chameleon—always subscribes to the taught thesis, good memory, future civic leader

Eagle—pedantic, always making speeches in class, balding

Mustang—gallant, untethered mind, soon extinct

Bat—takes only University Extension courses

Brontosaurus—takes up three chairs, complains for lack of left-handed desks

Ostrich—opposed to the theory of evolution

Tasmanian devil—ROTC (mandatory)

Three-toed sloth—never comes to class sooner than ten minutes late

Whale—always spouting off in class

EXHIBIT 15-1 Here's how you'd be graded under the animal system. *Source:* Howie King and Jack Pfeifer, *Daily*, December 11, 1975.

"It seems like kind of a pain in the butt. What I've seen is that students haven't had much input or they (the faculty) haven't accepted student input. The faculty seems to be saying they're going to set up 'their' system. And it's their system, not a system for the students."

"The emphasis shouldn't be so much on grades. I'm disappointed because I think most students are adults, adult enough to handle what they want to do, what classes they want to take, what classes they want to drop. And I think it's the students' decision."

"The faculty as a whole doesn't seem to be listening to students. Individual faculty members that I have had contact with, they have. But not the majority."

"My feeling was that the faculty really never intended to, nor did they ever, listen to students." (Comment of the president of the Associated Students)

"A sad day for the University." (Response of the president-elect of the Associated Students)

It should be emphasized that these comments represent the views of selected students. Students did have widely different views and it would be impossible to express a single student consensus on the new grading system. The same is true for the faculty—there were widely opposing opinions. However, interviews with several faculty members who were closely involved in the new grading system do suggest certain faculty views. The chairman of the University Senate, in an interview after the vote, was reported to have said:

> "In my personal opinion, it was an overwhelming vote. I am glad the faculty spoke definitively. Time will tell whether it's an improvement in the educational process. . . . The faculty's vote possibly will alienate students. If the training professors have is worth something, then students should do what professors tell them to do to get trained. The grading system is unfortunately part of it. It would be a nice world if nobody got graded; it would be a nice world if everybody had enough to eat; it would be a nice world if everybody lived in peace with his fellows. But we don't. It's a bitterly competitive world. The University is not a place where students play in a sandbox and pretend there is no competition. It's a tough damned world."

EXHIBIT 15-2   Excerpts from "A Student Position on Grading Changes"

We feel that the Faculty Committee on Scholastic Standards and the Senate have become so involved in the question of grade changes that they have failed to determine whether grades, as presently structured, are fulfilling their function—that is, to measure, communicate and enhance the degree of learning which students achieve. A change in grading should be made on the basis of how well it improves the evaluation of student learning. Converting the present system to one that does not improve evaluation is a poor use of time and money.

Decimal grading is not a good solution.

It is a refinement of a poor system of measurement, and does not get at the real question of how to evaluate learning. Although a point system may be useful in some classes, in a large number of classes it would be arbitrary since knowledge is not often clear cut, and few answers are absolutely right or wrong. This makes it difficult to measure learning with the precision that a decimal system implies. . . .

The withdrawal and incomplete proposal is punitive.

We recognize that withdrawals are sometimes administered unfairly (e.g., the arbitrary assigning of PW-EW) and are used by some students to improve poor GPAs.

Withdrawals are used by most students for valid reasons. Students may enroll for a heavier course load than they can reasonably expect to finish if they are not advised of the work they will be required to complete. Without sufficient information, in advance, on course content and requirements, students may register for classes with unrealistic expectations of what the course will cover and what level of preparation or ability is assumed for the course. Another problem is a change in the scope or requirements of a course midway through the quarter, making it necessary for students to drop the class. Students should not be punished for a lack of information or a change in the course over which they have no control.

There seems to be an assumption that students fail to learn if they are not "evaluated" (i.e., graded). We recognize that evaluation is crucial for learning but grading is only one form of evaluation. Students learn all during a quarter; we take something with us from a dropped class regardless of when we withdraw. A punitive withdrawal and incomplete policy can detract from education by locking students into classes they are unable to finish, punishing them for not learning.

Converting incompletes to E's after one quarter may not leave enough time for a student working on the next quarter's classes to complete the I and still carry a full load. Also, it creates a hardship for students who change their academic goals, making the unfinished class inappropriate for their program of studies. . . .

Associated Student Task Force
on University Governance

In an interview with the *Daily*, the chairman of the Faculty Committee on Scholastic Standards was reported to have said:

> "The faculty has a responsibility to the institution. Students have a short-term interest in the institution. The faculty has a much longer-term interest. The students who are the most vocal about it don't look at it in the same perspective that the faculty does. The faculty has a responsibility to persons other than the immediate group of students. As I've mentioned before, we cannot justify to the taxpayers of this state why we allow students to remain in the University who are doing failing work and who conceal this by withdrawing from a class every time they see they're headed for a poor grade. . . . I don't think the system (grading) stifles creativity and imagination. There is a competitive system, but the competitive system is not here because we have a grading system. The competitive system is imposed on us because we have limited resources. That's typical of the whole world. There are limited resources in many fields of endeavor, and you'll always find there are more people who want these resources than there are available. So we have to find some way of allocating them. And the grading system is one way of allocating these resources."

In response to the question of not listening to the students' voice, he responded:

> "I am not sure whether you are talking about the *Daily*'s reaction and the leaders of the Associated Students or the body of students. I've gotten a lot of favorable reaction from students, but certainly not from the *Daily* or among student leaders. I'm not sure they're representative of the students in this case. I don't think students understand the issues. There has been so much misinformation in the *Daily*, and that's where they have gotten their information. They don't understand the reasons underlying the action; they are not a very well-informed group. The whole matter about there being no student input on this all along is certainly gross misinformation; that simply is not true. . . . I think they were listened to. We have listened to them and we understood them, but we disagreed with them. They certainly participated in the debate and the proposals were changed as a result of their comments."

PROCEDURE

STEP 1
The entire class should meet to discuss the issues raised in the case: Changing the Grading System at State University. You might also discuss the grading system in your own institution. The class should develop a composite list, "Key Issues Involved in the Case," and put it on the blackboard.

STEP 2
The class will then divide into groups of five or six to develop an appropriate grading system for your institution. Use the form, An "Optimal" System for Evaluating Student Performance in Our Institution, on page 210, to record your key ideas.

STEP 3
Next, as a group, consider the process by which such a system might be designed and implemented within your institution. Use the form, A Process for Designing and Implementing an "Optimal" System for Evaluating Student Performance in Our Institution, on page 211, to record your key ideas.

STEP 4
Each group should then meet with another group to compare and discuss their two lists.

A Process for Designing and Implementing an "Optimal" System for Evaluating Student Performance in Our Institution

SUMMARY AND CONCEPTUALIZATION

It is easy to say that organizations and their members should have well-defined goals and means for measuring accomplishments. It is much more difficult to develop goals and measurements that are appropriate and acceptable to everyone.

We have used grading systems to evaluate the performance of students over an extended period, but we recognize that there are many problems. Theoretically, a grading system should measure the individual student's learning of knowledge and/or skills during the course. But, how do we measure the knowledge gained or skills acquired? The issue is made even more of a problem because students come into the classroom with different backgrounds.

Furthermore, in most classes the goals of the learning experience are determined by the instructor rather than by the students. Although there has been some trend toward having students share in setting the learning objectives for classes, this approach is still rare and frequently difficult to organize and manage. Such an approach recognizes that there may be different learning goals among students that require diverse activities and measures of effectiveness. There may be several alternative means to accomplish learning objectives. These disparities create major problems of evaluation for the instructor. This is particularly true where the institution requires that the instructor give single, definitive, quantifiable grades at the end of the class.

Although there are these and many other criticisms of current grading systems, you probably found it difficult to reach a group consensus on the optimal grading system. The group members probably had a variety of ideas.

You also faced the issue of how to develop and implement a new grading system. As illustrated in the case, Changing the Grading System at State University, it may not be just a question of the best grading system but also, and perhaps more important, how *any* change should be planned and implemented. Throughout the case, we noted complaints of "we weren't listened to" and "we didn't have a chance to participate." These are real issues in any organizational change, particularly when it affects the participants directly. The professors favoring the new grading system at State University were right; there were many attempts to obtain student inputs, but many students did not consider them satisfactory. How do we get a "student voice" on issues which affect them directly? Should there be voting on major issues? Should students be members of the University's committees and legislative bodies? Should they have voting rights? How will they be selected?

In other organizations, members have joined together to represent their viewpoint to the administration. Collective bargaining, although frequently an adversary relationship, has become a common means for legitimizing participation in companies, hospitals, schools, and governmental agencies. In other cases, joint problem solving and collaboration have been used.

One of the obvious problems associated with greater participation by students in college affairs is the fact that they are short-term members of the institution. How do they gain the perspectives, knowledge, and background to participate effectively? Furthermore, major policy changes usually take a long time period and students who may have been "listened to" 3 or 4 years ago may not be current members of the institution. How is consensus achieved when there is a continual turnover of one major university group—the students? These issues are apparent in the State University situation.

As an employee in your future work organization, you will face many issues concerning your individual and organizational goals and performance evaluation. There also will be a continual question of how much participation the individual members of the organization should have in setting goals, in developing plans, policies, and procedures for their implementation, and in devising measures of performance. Although the trends are by no means clear-cut, we do see that lower-level participants are having a greater say. Collective bargaining, management by objective programs, democratic-participative leadership styles, and many other changes point in this direction. Power equalization is coming to many organizations, our colleges and universities included. Even though the students may have felt they lost the battle at State University, the long-range trends indicate more student inputs and participation.

PART 6
THE MANAGERIAL SYSTEM
IN ORGANIZATIONS

The managerial system is essential in any organization. Its function is planning and controlling organizational activities toward objective accomplishment and it involves coordinating human, material, and financial resources. As indicated in Figure 2, page 8, the managerial subsystem is primarily responsible for the input-output flow of materials, energy, and information that are required to produce goods or services. The environmental suprasystem and the other subsystems—goals and values, technical, structural, and psychosocial—strongly influence, and in turn are influenced by, the managerial subsystem.

Managers carry out the functions of planning and controlling organizational activity by making decisions. Thus, one approach to understanding management is to study how decisions are made by individuals and groups. Overall perspective can be gained by looking at information-decision systems. This requires the identification of decisions to be made in various parts of the organization, as well as the information that is relevant for the decision-making process. Another approach is to look at goal setting—including general missions or purposes and specific objectives. Once goals are set, the managerial task becomes one of planning and coordinating the activity necessary to achieve them.

The managerial subsystem can be related to several typical levels in organizations. At the strategic level, top management is involved in relating the organization to its environment—identifying a niche that it must fill in order to survive and grow. Strategy formulation also involves designing comprehensive systems and plans. At the strategic level, there is typically a long-run time perspective, and decision making is highly judgmental because of the inherent uncertainties in forecasting future external and internal conditions.

At the operating level, the primary task is accomplishing stated objectives effectively and efficiently. It is here that the organization "does its thing"—producing bicycles or toothpaste, providing health care or fire protection, or selling and servicing automobiles. Management in the operating subsystem typically involves a short-run perspective and rather standard operating procedures that may be highly mechanized or automated.

In the coordinative subsystem—ranging between the strategic and operating activities—the primary concern is integrating internal activities that have been specialized by function and/or level. Middle management is involved in translating comprehensive plans into operational plans and procedures, in interpreting the results of the operating system, and in focusing existing resources in appropriate directions. Middle management facilitates coordination of several functions or projects within an overall organization. A pragmatic point of view is essential in integrating short- and long-run considerations. Compromise is often necessary in decision making in the coordinative subsystem in order to achieve workable solutions to problems.

In most organizations, management faces many situations that are dynamic, inherently uncertain, and frequently ambiguous. Managers are not in full control of all the factors affecting outcomes. They are often constrained by many environmental and internal (technological, structural, and psychosocial) forces. Local, state, and federal regulations have an important impact on organizational activities. Pollution control, truth in advertising, and affirmative action are just a few examples. Changing value systems of consumers and employees have a significant impact. Blue- and white-collar unionism—collective bargaining—is another significant factor. In spite of the increasing complexity of a dynamic, evolving environment, managers typically seek regularity and predictability in organizational activities. Indeed, technology, structure, and interpersonal relationships must be stable enough to allow the organization to achieve its objectives. At the same time, adaptation and innovation are essential for long-run success. Thus, managers must develop means to get the job done in the short range but devote enough attention to changing circumstances in order to ensure long-run success.

In the exercises that follow, we will be looking at the managerial subsystem from a number of perspectives but with particular emphasis on decision making. We will be concerned with decision making by individual managers and by groups such as boards of directors. Several exercises focus on decisions about people—selection, promotion, and controlling behavior. These types of decisions tend to be complex and value-laden, but they are a fundamental part of the typical managerial task.

Managerial Decision Making: Sentry Federal Savings and Loan Association is an in-basket exercise that requires decision making and action planning under time pressure. It allows you to compare, with several colleagues, your decisions and plans with regard to a number of issues.

Decision Making in Organizations: The College Book Store provides an opportunity to participate in, or observe, top-level decision making by a board of directors. The exercise also asks you to consider effective and ineffective behavior in group decision making.

Organization Control: Appearance Standards requires you to write explicit policies for dress and hair styles for a variety of organizations. This specific example provides a springboard for consideration of organization control in general.

Evaluation and Selection: MBA Admissions Committee requires you to evaluate a group of applicants for a limited number of positions. This exercise provides an opportunity to compare selections by different evaluators using various criteria.

Managerial Effectiveness: Assessing Individual Potential asks you to work individually and in small groups to compile a list of skills and attributes that are important for managerial effectiveness and success. The exercise provides an opportunity for each of you to complete a self-rating of managerial potential, using the dimensions you have developed.

Exercise 16
Managerial Decision Making: Sentry Federal Savings and Loan Association

LEARNING OBJECTIVES

1. To experience an actual managerial situation that requires decision making and action planning.
2. To compare your decisions and plans, including the reasons behind them, with peers in small group discussions.
3. To relate the specific issues, decisions, and actions to the general problem of allocating managerial time.

ADVANCE PREPARATION

Read the Overview and the description of Sentry Federal Savings and Loan Association. Do not read the Procedure or the in-basket items.

OVERVIEW

A key aspect of management is decision making for planning and controlling organizational activities. Although the scope of decision making may vary according to the level (strategic, coordinative, and operating) and time horizon (long-, medium-, and short-range), the basic process is the same. It involves problem finding, diagnosis/analysis, alternative generation and evaluation, choice, implementation, and follow-up. Operating decisions can often be made rather quickly by reference to policies, procedures, rules, and past experience. Strategic decisions are usually less programmable; they are often ill-structured, novel, one-time issues that require considerable reflection and judgment. Coordinative decisions lie somewhere in between and require a mixture of standard operating procedures and managerial wisdom based on experience.

A number of factors affect the decision-making process in organizations—the environment, goals and values, technology, structure, and psychosocial aspects. General societal conditions and trends (legal, political, and economic) obviously have an impact. The established goals provide a framework for planning and controlling. Cultural, organizational, and personal values all are general guidelines concerning what is good and desirable. Technology and structure also have an impact. Managers make decisions concerning methods and equipment to be used in the operating system. Once established, systems and procedures (for example, computerized information systems) dictate the process used in making decisions. Similarly, the organization structure indicates authority relationships—who has the right to make decisions and who is affected by them. The psychosocial system is involved in numerous ways. People are the focal point in hiring, evaluating, promoting, and firing decisions. Human relationships are major factors in decisions regarding equitable compensation, conflict resolution, and coordination among individuals, groups, and departments. In addition, people are typically responsible for implementing decisions; thus, acceptance should be a primary concern.

Acceptance is usually facilitated if people are involved in the decision-making process. However, participation is not a cure-all and may be inappropriate in some circumstances. Managers need to diagnose each situation to determine the best approach. If the manager has all the relevant information at hand, if the outcomes of the alternatives seem clearly equal, and if the choice will be implemented readily, the manager can make a decision unilaterally. However, if more information is needed, if the various alternatives will have significantly different consequences, and if support of other organizational members is essential for implementation, then a participatory approach is more appropriate. The degree of participation should vary according to the specific problem.

Managerial effectiveness is a direct result of making good decisions—considering both quality and acceptance. Furthermore, managerial effectiveness is a function of allocating time appropriately. Most managers are faced with a number of constraints or impositions that decrease the amount of discretion they have in allocating their time. These constraints are imposed by the system, bosses, peers, and subordinates.[1] The goal is to have as much discretionary time as possible to devote to critical tasks and decisions that determine individual and organizational success. Effective managers are able to eliminate nonessential activities, delegate tasks and decisions that are more relevant for others in the organization, and concentrate their time and energy on high priority issues.

Our experience, and that of a number of other observers, indicate that effective managers (and organizations) are astute diagnosticians (aware of relevant issues). They are able to assign priorities to problems in terms of their degree of impact on organizational performance; they can concentrate their time and energy on high priority items; and they are diligent in following up to see that decisions are implemented and that the results are checked against established measures of performance.

In this exercise we will have an opportunity to consider some issues that are brought to the attention of an upper-middle manager. You are asked to play a role and respond to a number of items that show up in the manager's in-basket. In the initial phase of the exercise, you are required to work under what might appear to be unrealistic constraints—an extremely tight time schedule, no access to related material in the files, and no access to or help from others in the organization (subordinates, peers, and superiors). However, these constraints are designed to force you to make explicit decisions, including those of delegation or no action. The following background information is provided to set the stage for the exercise that follows.

[1]See William Oncken, Jr., and Donald L. Wess, "Management Time: Who's Got the Monkey?" *Harvard Business Review*, November–December 1974, pp. 75–80; and Peter Drucker, *The Effective Executive*, New York, Harper & Row, 1967.

Sentry Federal Savings and Loan Association

The first savings and loan association in the United States was organized by 37 thrifty pioneers in 1831 in Frankfurt, Pennsylvania. The organizers were familiar with the contribution that English building societies had made to the promotion of systematic savings. Each original member of this first savings and loan association agreed to save a specific amount of money each week. When the combined amount of these savings was large enough to enable one member to buy a home, the right to borrow that money was offered to the highest bidder from within the group. As the savings and loan idea spread, however, associations opened their membership to people who were interested only in saving or borrowing money and thus were able to serve the special needs of many more people.

As is typical of all savings and loan associations today, Sentry Federal accepts the savings of individuals and organizations and uses these funds to make long- and short-term loans, mostly within the local community, for the purpose of purchase, construction, or repair of homes. In addition, Sentry Federal makes mobile-home loans, invests in government bonds, and operates a subsidiary corporation engaged in mobile-home parks and other real estate development. From the interest collected on its investments, the association covers its operating expenses, pays earnings to savers for the use of their funds, and sets aside reserves for protection against possible future losses. According to Sentry's president,

> It has never been our goal to be the biggest savings and loan association. In fact, our basic philosophy has always been to simply make Sentry Federal the best place for people to save and borrow. We have an idea about people—about how to treat them right and to serve them well. We have found that customers respond positively to kind, thoughtful treatment from congenial, well-trained employees who make a sincere effort to look after their interest. That's what this business is all about—people serving people. When we do our job well, we will be rewarded with the positive benefits enjoyed by a viable, growing institution.

Sentry Savings and Loan Association began in 1925 in Seattle. In 1936, Sentry was granted a federal charter under the Home Owner's Loan Act of 1933, and became a participant in the Federal Savings and Loan Insurance Corporation program for the insurance of savings accounts. Over the years, the association's office has been moved several times to accommodate growth and expansion. However, throughout its history it has remained as essentially a suburban organization. In the late 1960s, a branch expansion program was undertaken. One other small suburban association was acquired and converted to a branch of Sentry. Three other branches have been opened and two others are contemplated within the next year or two.

Sentry is a medium-sized association with $103.5 million in assets, 25,000 savings accounts, and 3,300 loans. Its current passbook savings interest rate is 5¼ percent, with higher rates paid on certificates of deposit depending on the amount and time to maturity. Sentry has experienced significant growth since 1970, more than doubling, and has performed above the average for all associations, in terms of operating ratios published by the Federal Home Loan Bank Board.

Sentry employs approximately 60 people in the headquarters and five branches. The largest or main branch has 18 people; the others are considerably smaller satellite operations. Figure 16-1 shows the organization structure with functional descriptions. Figure 16-2 provides a list of the key personnel in headquarters and all personnel in the Westgate branch.

For purposes of this exercise, you are to consider yourself Robert Allen, who has just recently been promoted to Westgate branch manager. You have a degree in business administration with a major in finance. You are 39 years old and have been in the savings and loan industry for 12 years. You came to Sentry when it acquired your association 5 years ago. You have worked in all phases of the business and were executive vice president of that organization. You have always assumed that you would eventually find a place in the top management of Sentry and have been satisfied with your job as Dogwood branch manager.

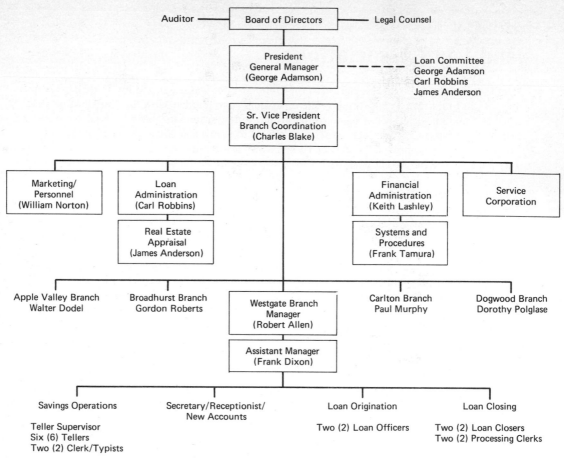

FIGURE 16-1 Sentry Federal Savings and Loan Association.

Your recent promotion came quite suddenly upon the death of Phil Curtis who was killed in a plane crash while on a fishing trip in Northern British Columbia. The president, George Adamson, called you on Wednesday in Chicago (where you were visiting your wife's parents) to inform you of Phil's death and your selection to replace him. Your appointment was announced to employees and the media on Thursday.

You were not able to return to Seattle until Saturday, and are scheduled to leave Sunday morning for a 3-day conference in San Francisco. You have discussed the situation briefly with the president but have not had a chance to talk with Charles Blake, the branch coordinator. However, you feel you have a reasonably good perspective because of your experience in the Dogwood branch plus exposure to overall problems in the weekly branch manager meetings.

During the years since the merger, you have found the president, George Adamson, to be friendly and supportive, although a bit old-fashioned. A number of your ideas, based on experience in your former association, have not been accepted. You feel the organization is more conservative than it should be. In your view, Charles Blake is a competent administrator and fair in his dealings with the branches. However, you feel that he has put too much emphasis on making all the branches "identical." You believe in consistency but have argued for more leeway in individualizing the branches. You are a little concerned in moving to the Westgate branch because it is in the same building with headquarters personnel and the close proximity may "cramp your style." In general, you like and respect the people in the headquarters office. On the other hand, you feel the loan committee has been too conservative in turning down a number of your deals and that Jim Anderson, the appraiser, is a bit unrealistic at times.

The other branch managers seem competent, and owing to your interactions with Frank Dixon, you feel he will be a good assistant for you. You wonder whether or not he had his eye on the manager's job.

Title	Function	Name
President	General Manager	George Adamson
Senior Vice President	Branch Coordination	Charles Blake
Vice President/Controller	Financial Administration	Keith Lashley
Assistant Vice President	Systems and Procedures	Frank Tamura
Vice President	Loan Administration	Carl Robbins
Assistant Vice President	Real Estate Appraisal	James Anderson
Assistant Vice President	Marketing and Personnel	William Norton
Vice President	Branch Manager (Westgate)	Robert Allen
Assistant Vice President	Assistant Branch Manager	Frank Dixon
Stenographer	Secretarial/Receptionist/New Accounts	Beth Woodley
Loan Officer	Loan Origination	David Cooper
Loan Officer	Loan Origination	Michael Holmes
Loan Closer	Loan Closing	Mary Swartz
Loan Closer	Loan Closing	Sheryl Berg
Clerk/Typist	Loan Processing	Sue Campbell
Clerk/Typist	Loan Processing	Arlyne Lobush
Teller Supervisor	Teller Supervisor	Ruth Kolar
Teller	Customer Service	Carol Rogers
Teller	Customer Service	John Porter
Teller	Customer Service	Sally Satasut
Teller	Customer Service	Martha Pounds
Teller	Customer Service	Mary Lopez
Teller	Customer Service	Amy Tanaka
Clerk/Typist	Record Keeping	Shirley Gill
Clerk/Typist	Record Keeping	Phyllis Manley

FIGURE 16-2 Sentry Federal Savings and Loan Association personnel.

As a result of some informal discussions with the late manager, Phil Curtis, you feel comfortable that the staff at the Westgate branch is doing a good job and will continue to do so. He did indicate, just recently, that there was some unrest (more complaints than usual) among the tellers and clerks.

PROCEDURE

Assume that you are Robert Allen, the new manager of the Westgate branch of Sentry Federal Savings and Loan Association. Background information has been provided in the case just described. You have an organization chart and a list of personnel to help provide some perspective for the material that follows. Tear them out and keep them handy for ready reference.

You have been on vacation for the past week. It is Sunday morning, September 7, and you have only one hour before you must leave for the airport. You have dropped by your new office in the Westgate branch to look over any items that may need your attention before you leave. No one else is around, nor can anyone be reached by telephone. Moreover, you cannot take any work-related materials to the conference.

STEP 1

The following pages contain an assortment of items that have accumulated in your new in-basket during the past week. They include letters, reports, memoranda, telephone messages, etc. You will have one hour to work with the material. Indicate on each item the action you will take and briefly explain why. Make memos to yourself about things you will want to do when you get back in the office. Write drafts of letters or memos that you will have your secretary complete. Make notes to yourself concerning what your intentions will be in future face-to-face or telephone conversations. Outline plans and/or agendas for meetings you may want to arrange. Sign papers if appropriate. In summary, briefly record all decisions and plans in writing. This will be important for your input to later steps in the exercise.

STEP 2

Meet in groups of three or four in order to discuss the decisions and plans made by each individual. Compare notes; have the group members individually describe their approaches to each item and then discuss their actions.

STEP 3

The combined groups discuss the exercise. Check with the groups to see how much consensus developed on ways of handling the various items. Do any overall patterns emerge? For example, is there substantial agreement on items to (1) ignore, (2) delegate, (3) postpone, (4) postpone but initiate action, and (5) complete before leaving? What guidelines were used in making such decisions? Did people finish each item in order of appearance? Or, did they run through all the material quickly to determine order of importance and then begin working? In the latter event, were important items dealt with first or saved until last, after the decks were cleared of trivia?

- 1 -

September 5, 1975

To: Robert Allen

Due to the unrest among the women employees of the Westgate branch of Sentry Federal Savings, we would like to have a joint meeting with management. We feel it is important to discuss this with you at the beginning of your new job.

We want to discuss our salaries, which we feel are far below the open job market. Several of our former employees have moved to similar jobs in the community at considerably higher salaries. We would like to be compensated fairly for our efforts and not penalized for being loyal to Sentry.

Please advise us of a time which would be convenient for all of us to meet with you to discuss these issues.

cc: Frank Dixon

Sue Campbell   Martha Reando
Mary Lopez   Agnes Lobush
Margie Berg   Phylis Menley
Carol Rogers   Shirley Hill

- 2 -

William G. Scott
1800 Park Place Building
Seattle, Washington

August 29, 1975

Mr. Philip Curtis
Sentry Federal Savings and
  Loan Association
Seattle, Washington

Dear Phil:

As I mentioned on the telephone, we would like your organization to sponsor a Seattle Junior Soccer Team this coming year.

The $200 sponsor fee purchases jackets, balls, and league fees on behalf of the team. The players will be entered under the name of Sentry Federal Savings and Loan or other appropriate name as you may wish and will wear jackets with a team identification.

The team which you will be sponsoring is an 11-year-old team.

Since we are buying equipment at this time, we would like very much to have your payment by September 15. Your support will be very much appreciated.

Sincerely,

William G. Scott

William G. Scott

Managerial Decision Making: Sentry Federal Savings and Loan Association   221

- 3 -

MEMORANDUM

DATE: August 15, 1975

TO:　Branch Managers

FROM:　William Norton

As you will recall, we have discussed the possibility of using polygraph (lie-detector) tests to aid discovery and elimination of dishonesty among our employees. This service can be provided by professional testing firms such as Fidelity Testers, Inc. I would like to know your personal views regarding this matter and who you think should be subjected to the test. Could you have your reactions and ideas to me by September 10, please.

- 4 -

MEMORANDUM

DATE: September 3, 1975

TO:　All Branch Managers

FROM:　William Norton

SUBJECT: Alternative Promotion Plans

One of the agenda items for next week's meeting is the advertising and promotion plan for 1976. We are committed to perpetuating an appropriate image for Sentry Federal.

As you know, Samaritan Federal has acquired property and has begun construction of a branch that will compete directly for our customers.

What should be the relative emphasis on advertising versus promotion? With regard to the latter, what is your feeling concerning incentives such as merchandise, vouchers redeemable at Jafco, or a lottery for cash prizes?

MEMORANDUM

TO: Bob Allen

FROM: Frank Dixon

DATE: September 5, 1975

This might be a good time to reemphasize the importance of neatness in work habits and appropriate personal appearance. Ruth has indicated a concern that some of her people are not as meticulous as they ought to be. She has mentioned the problem to the worst offenders but feels that a word from you at a meeting of all branch employees would be helpful.

A related issue is that some of the women have expressed resentment over having to wear uniforms at work. They would like to be more individualistic and receive the uniform allowance in cash. A couple of the men have suggested that they should have a suit allowance as a comparable fringe benefit to the women's uniform allowance.

Sentry Federal Savings
Seattle, Washington

Dear Sir:

Enclosed is payment on my loan plus $16 to be added to my savings. However, my passbook is not enclosed. It fell victim to one German shepherd who believes that anything small enough to pick up may be eaten.

I would appreciate a new savings book with a record of deposits, if possible. I'm sorry, but I don't know my account number.

Yours truly,
Donald B. Cadwell
7206 8th N.W.
Seattle, Washington

2237 Cypress Rd. N.W.
Seattle, Washington
August 28, 1975

Manager, Sentry Federal Savings
and Loan
Seattle, Washington

Dear Sir:

I would like to commend one of your employees, Cheryl Berg.

Miss Berg was most helpful in setting up our payment terms. She conducted her business with us in a laudatory and complimentary manner and was most helpful with any questions that we might have had. Miss Berg demonstrated to us the high quality and standards of a valuable employee.

We hope to open a savings account with you at some point in the future for repayment of the assistance given to us.

Sincerely,

Mr. & Mrs. Matthew Edwards

STATE UNIVERSITY

August 15, 1975

Mr. George Adamson, President
Sentry Federal Savings and Loan
Seattle, Washington

Dear Mr. Adamson:

This letter is to confirm the field trip we discussed over the telephone concerning a visitation of 36 Japanese bankers to your organization on Monday, September 8, 1975.

As you suggested, we will meet in the lobby of the Westgate Branch where you indicated you would provide a brief orientation before dividing the group into smaller sections. A roster of the participants in the program, Banking and Society in America, is attached. Please call me if you have any questions or if there is anything further we should do in preparation for this trip.

Sincerely,

Gordon C. Carlton

Gordon C. Carlton
Director of Business
Administration Seminars

GCC/cp

- 10 -

MEMORANDUM

DATE: August 28, 1975

TO: Phil Curtis

FROM: Charles Blake

SUBJECT: Failure to Promptly Complete Loan Files and Return to
          Headquarters

    The loan files for loans closed at Westgate have not been completed
and turned in promptly. Some of these files date back to November of
1974. Please have these loan files completed by September 30, 1975, and
return to headquarters for final check.

cc: G. Adamson

- 9 -

D R A F T

DATE: September 8, 1975

TO: Charles Blake

FROM: Bob Allen

    On August 20, 1975, you sent a memo to Phil Curtis expressing
your concern over the fact that Westgate's subsidiary savings account
records were not in balance. Frank has indicated to me today that the
savings subsidiary records are balanced through August 29, 1975, the
date of the last computer printout which we have received. We are
making every effort here at the Westgate office to keep our subsidiary
ledgers balanced. However, I am concerned that with the approach
of another quarterly interest period we may again fall behind unless
the computer printouts are delivered to us in a more timely manner.

cc: G. Adamson

[handwritten note:]
Bob,
If this reply is
O.K. with you, SPB
have Betty type it.
Frank

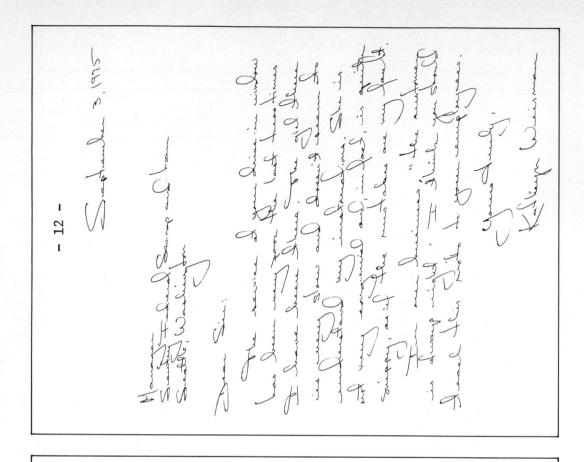

- 11 -

WASHINGTON STATE BAR ASSOCIATION

September 3, 1975

Mr. Robert L. Allen
Sentry Federal Savings and
    Loan Association
Seattle, Washington

Dear Mr. Allen:

We are in the process of investigating a complaint by Mr. Ralph R. Nettles. Mr. Nettles filed an objection to a property settlement agreement that was filed in a divorce action. The property settlement agreement bears your signature as a notary. I would appreciate it if you could advise us of the circumstances surrounding the execution of the property settlement agreement. In particular, we are inquiring whether Mr. Nettles executed the property settlement voluntarily without threat or duress from a third person. It is also presumed that you placed Mr. Nettles under oath prior to having him sign the property settlement agreement.

Your prompt reply will be appreciated. Please correspond directly with the committee member assigned to the investigation:

    Mr. Walter T. Roberts
    Suite 233
    Professional Building
    Bellevue, Washington

Very truly yours,

Walter T. Roberts

WTR:dq

- 14 -

CYPRESS SAVINGS AND LOAN ASSOCIATION

September 2, 1975

Mr. Robert Allen
Sentry Federal Savings and
Loan Association
Seattle, Washington

Dear Bob:

As I am sure you are aware, our application for a branch in the Clearwood Shopping Center has been approved, and we anticipate opening by the first of the year.

We are considering Mr. James M. Weldon for the position of branch manager. He has given your name as a reference. We would appreciate your candid comments concerning his strong and weak points. Your opinion of his managerial ability and integrity, and other relevant factors in this very important decision, will be very much appreciated. Naturally, your comments will be confidential and I would be grateful to you for an early response.

Very truly yours,

Owen F. Marshall
Executive Vice President

OFM/lu

- 13 -   September 2, 1975

Mrs. Phillip Curtis
Sentry Federal Savings
Seattle, Washington

Dear Mrs. Curtis:

I received your letter thanking me for my account (#03-08679-4). I was most unhappy to note that the envelope was addressed to Mrs. Gilbert. I hope this was an honest mistake and not an assumption that anyone with $10,000 to deposit must be a man.

Sincerely,

(Mrs.) Jean Gilbert

- 16 -

MEMORANDUM

DATE: September 4, 1975

TO: Frank Dixon

FROM: Ruth Kolar

Amy Tanaka has requested three weeks extra vacation in order to accompany her husband on a job interviewing trip to the East Coast.

Should I let her go?

*Bob - do you think?
What to advise?
Thanks, Frank*

- 15 -

MEMORANDUM

DATE: 9/5/75

TO: Bob Allen

FROM: Frank Dixon

Mrs. William Kane was in the office and claimed that her husband had cleaned out their joint savings account ($5,000) and gone to San Francisco with his girl friend. She withdrew slip apparently had Mrs. Kane's signature and may forgery and she remembers Mrs. Kane making the withdrawal. Mrs. Kane contends that she did not make a withdrawal and that it must have been someone impersonating her and forging her signature.

What is we do now?

- 18 -

MEMORANDUM

TO: Branch Managers   DATE: September 2, 1975
FROM: Charles Blake

This is a reminder of the commitments to call on businessmen in your areas to sell the "Cash Flow" plan which enables them to utilize their excess cash in checking accounts by placing it in a savings account with us. Let's get off to a good start and complete the quota of calls for September.

- 17 -

MEMORANDUM

TO: Bob Allen   DATE: September 4, 1975
FROM: Dorothy Roberts

Congratulations on your promotion to the main branch. It is well deserved. Given your new "power position," how about pushing our request for company cars for branch managers? There's no time like the present!

- 20 -

MEMORANDUM

TO: Phil Curtis   DATE: August 20, 1975

FROM: Charles Blake

It has come to my attention that the savings control for your branch has not been balanced since July 1. This is an extremely serious matter which exposes Sentry Federal to possible losses of a very large magnitude. You are directed immediately to take steps to bring the balancing of your savings up to date. If this involves overtime work, it is authorized. If it means additional personal work on your behalf, then you should undertake this work. I cannot over-emphasize the seriousness of letting the savings be out of balance for an extended period of time. The ability of your office to keep the branch subsidiary records in balance is a direct reflection of your capability to manage that office and should be attended to accordingly.

cc: G. Adamson

- 19 -

MEMORANDUM

TO: Bob Allen   DATE: 9/9/75

FROM: George Adamson

I know you are busy "getting settled" in your new assignment, and that you will be away from the office for a few hours. I'd like to discuss with you some ideas for facilitating a smooth transition from Bill's leadership to yours. Before you leave, how about setting down a list of steps you plan to take when you return. We can discuss them at that time.

Incidentally, Frank seemed to be quite disappointed that he was not promoted to branch manager. I assume he will "come around" in due course and give you his best effort.

– 21 –

Dear Mr. Curtis:

One of your employees (Mr. Holmes) is carrying on with
a divorcee who lives in my apartment building. This kind
of behavior shouldn't be tolerated by a respectable business.

A Good Customer

– 22 –

MEMORANDUM

TO: Mr. Allen   DATE: 9/5/75

FROM: Beth

SUBJECT: Abuse of the Copy Machine

   Before he left, Mr. Curtis asked me to draft a memo to all
employees regarding abuse of the copy machine. It had become apparent
that employees were using it for personal matters such as income tax
forms, church programs, kid's term papers, etc. I suggest the
following:

TO: All Employees

   Effective immediately, the use of the copy machine for matters
not directly involved with association business is strictly prohibited.

   The cost of unauthorized use of the copy machine and related
supplies has made this action necessary. Failure to adhere to this
policy will henceforth be grounds for dismissal.

                                    _____
                                          (signed)
                                       Branch Manager

SUMMARY AND CONCEPTUALIZATION

You have had an opportunity to consider a number of items in a typical manager's in-basket and have been forced to make some decisions and to plan specific action steps. After you have compared your approach with several others in detail, and with the entire class in general, what patterns have emerged? Were you able to assign priorities to the various issues involved, to ignore some of them, and to delegate others? Or, did you feel compelled to keep control by handling all or most items yourself? Did you develop an overall plan for following up the issues? Did you make any plans for reducing the amount of material in your in-basket in the future?

This exercise illustrates the need for managers to allocate their time appropriately by ranking the issues that come to their attention by priority, delegating where appropriate, working on high-priority items, and following up to ensure implementation and desired results. The direct impact of better time management on individual or organizational performance is unclear; there are no research results that prove that it works. The impetus for increased attention to this facet of management comes from personal testimonials and a *feeling* that "if an executive can be cajoled or maneuvered into honing his/her workload down to the essentials, his/her effectiveness can soar."[2]

Research results are available with regard to typical time-allocation patterns for middle and top managers. For example, one survey indicates that "most executives enjoy the luxury of one hour or less in uninterrupted work time per week."[3] This finding is particularly interesting because most time-management consultants stress the importance of relatively large blocks of discretionary time for problem solving and planning.

Some suggestions for improving the allocation of managerial time are included in the following article; more detailed discussions can be found in the other sources cited in this exercise. The learning can be extended beyond the organization to your personal situation and can facilitate increased effectiveness in managing your own activities.

TEACHING MANAGERS TO DO MORE IN LESS TIME*

At 5 or 6 a.m., when W. Price Laughlin, chairman of Saga Corp., arrives at his Menlo Park (Calif.) office, he reads philosophy—sometimes *The Prophet*—for 15 minutes. Then he ponders "the key issues for the whole year—the five or six things that require change or improvement." Next, Laughlin jots his weekly chores on a yellow pad for discussion later with his secretary over coffee. The topics range from a needed haircut to Saga's liquidity. Laughlin, in short, is organized. To time-management consultants, he is a model executive who gets the maximum mileage from his time.

Most managers, unfortunately, are far from the ideal. But increasing numbers of them are turning to a breed of consultants called time-management specialists for help in organizing—and hopefully trimming—their work loads. Companies as diverse as IBM, Bank of America, Kimberly-Clark, and 3M have sent managers through time-management courses, and the consultants' business is booming.

The economic crunch, with its widespread management layoffs, is prompting companies to try to make better use of executives who are still on the payroll. Frederick H. Pryor, whose consulting firm of Schmidt, Pryor & Co., in Kansas City, saw a 10% increase in business last year, attributes it to layoffs of corporate managers. And Barre L. Rorabaugh, a production superintendent at 3M Co.'s New Ulm (Minn.) plant and one of 30 company managers who attended a time-management seminar last fall, says his plant saved time equal to that of three jobs because of "time" training, although that hardly made up for the nearly 100 people laid off at his plant.

Too much work. What the time-management consultants teach managers is really "common sense wrapped up in a neat package," says San Francisco consultant Alan Lakein, who began

[2] "Teaching Managers to Do More in Less Time," *Business Week*, March 3, 1975, p. 69.
[3] Paul L. Rice, "Making Minutes Count," *Business Horizons,* December 1973, p. 18.
Business Week, March 3, 1975, pp. 68–69.

full-time consulting seven years ago, charging clients $100 per session. A few basic rules about making the most of available time can, once they are understood, make for a more effective, efficient manager. Today, with 400 group sessions and a best-selling time-management book behind him, Lakein says that his fees now run up to $2,000. Dallas consultant William Oncken, who recently added time management to his specialties, says that business jumped 25% last year.

Most executives say that the reason they seek help in managing their time is that they simply have too much work. Saga's Laughlin, who sat in on an Oncken course with 80 of his managers, says that he had his time well under control before the session but still learned something new: how to fend off time-consuming requests from his managers. "Ordinarily," he says, "it's so easy to say, 'I'll take a second look at that.'"

Time-management advice is aimed mainly at middle managers, but many top executives think they can benefit too. If an executive can be cajoled or maneuvered into honing his workload down to the essentials, his effectiveness can soar. Marshall McDonald, president and chief executive officer of Florida Power & Light Co., says that he has not only saved time because of what he learned at an Oncken seminar but also reduced employee resentment by learning how to delegate authority more effectively. Another senior official at Florida Power who had "felt he had to do everything himself," says McDonald, learned to focus on his real duties after attending a seminar with 30 other company executives.

Selwin Belofsky, president of Drawing Board, Inc., of Dallas, a business-forms company, says he has increased his discretionary time on the job to 50%, from 5% before he learned the art of delegation. And Jack Linkletter, son of TV personality Art Linkletter and president of Linkletter Enterprises, of Irvine, Calif., says he learned to free one-third of his time for managing by having his secretary write letters and by organizing his time with a daily list of things to do.

Minutes count. Still, it is middle managers who are filling the time-management seminars. Like Rorabaugh of 3M, many turn to time management "to get out of all the paperwork." Because of a seminar with Pasadena consultant Robert Rutherford, says Rorabaugh, he has saved two hours a day that used to be spent in nonproductive meetings, emptied three filing cabinets, eliminated 10 company reports, and cut the time spent on take-home work from five hours a week to one.

Rorabaugh, who oversees about 300 employees, has cut his paperwork in half by having his secretary screen all his mail. She posts dates of scheduled meetings, then throws the letter away. And anything that requires immediate attention goes right to Rorabaugh. The remaining mail goes into one of the folders Rorabaugh has on his desk: one for each of the four supervisors who report to him, plus his own future file. Only when the folders are full does Rorabaugh discuss the contents with each subordinate. He estimates that he has saved 15 minutes a day for each man, a full hour a day for himself.

Every two weeks, Rorabaugh plunges into his future file, responding to the mail that has piled up or throwing it away. The result is three fewer file cabinets in his office and 50% less time spent by his secretary in filing.

Some executives who use time-management principles think they can do very well without the consultants. "The people who report to me don't dump their problems on me," says Harry P. Letton, Jr., president of Southern California Gas Co., who feels he has already learned how to delegate. And some executives think the consultants' spoon-feeding techniques are designed for managers who are too lazy to get themselves organized. Robert McElroy, vice-president for personnel at Bank of California, says that managing time "requires discipline—if you lack it, you pay for it." McElroy acknowledges that he bought a film version of Lakein's seminar as a training aid but explains: "These guys are making money primarily because people are not exercising self-discipline."

The major problem with time management, however, is the difficulty of obtaining statistical proof that it works. According to a Hewlett-Packard Co. personnel manager, results are "based 99% on faith." At Hewlett-Packard, where 500 top managers took the Oncken course, says the personnel man, "We have to let people go at their own pace. The value only can be judged by the joy it seems to bring the managers."

Keeping track. Companies that want hard results, though, can now go one step further. Extensor Corp., a year-old Minneapolis-based marketing company, leases a small, desk-top device developed in Sweden that records a manager's activities up to 30 times a day. At the sound of randomly spaced beeps, the manager punches a code that represents his activity at the moment. He may, for example, hit buttons on a keyboard indicating that he is on the phone, discussing the budget with someone within the company. Or he might honestly report that he had been daydreaming.

For several hundred dollars more, the unit can be set up so that the executive can report his emotions at the time of his phone call, to probe the most stressful and most enjoyable activities of his job. A five-week experiment, costing $200 to $800 per executive can show an executive just how he or she spends time—in hours and minutes or in percentages.

"The mere fact that you report what you do," says Extensor President Tor Dahl, "makes you stop and think about what you are doing. It's a conditioning machine: You can't help changing yourself."

So far most Extensor users in this country have been university and hospital managers. A group of 13 University of Minnesota administrators underwent the program. "Like most organizations, we felt we had been wasting time," says Darrell R. Lewis, associate dean of education. Lewis discovered that he was spending two-thirds of his time in meetings, many devoted to community rather than university affairs. His administrative assistant now goes to many of these community-oriented sessions so that Lewis can catch up on reading and budgets. Another lesson: "Ninety-five percent of the stuff on my desk was problems that others hadn't solved."

Samuel Davis, executive president at Mt. Sinai Hospital in Minneapolis, found that his most unpleasant tasks were also the ones he was worst at. He eliminated from his schedule negotiating sessions with government and universities, a task he does not like, and concentrated on what he likes best—planning. He also delegated letter-writing and meeting-scheduling. As a result, Davis and his staff were able to cut their work week from 60 to 48 hours.

Many companies are pushing ahead with time-management programs even without proof that they work. Bank of America is preparing an in-house time-management course for 5,000 employees and a film to be distributed to branch offices. American Microsystems, Inc., in Santa Clara, Calif., has already printed a brochure for managers, listing time-saving tips and techniques. And Florida Power's McDonald says he is going to boost this year's time-management budget. "The lessons stick better," he says, "when the facts are sugarcoated."

TIME-SAVING TRICKS THAT MANAGERS FOLLOW
Teaching time management is mostly common sense. But obvious as some of the lessons are, most executives can profit by putting them into practice. Here are a few ideas that have worked:

Don't work on petty chores with the idea of working up to bigger projects. Start with the most important activity of the day and work your way down. Patrick J. Frawley, Jr., chairman of the executive committee at Schick, Inc., sets daily priorities. He uses "A" for the most important things he has to do, "B" for the next, and so on down the list. If there is time at the end of the day, he looks at the "Cs." Invariably, says Frawley, "you wipe out a lot of Cs altogether."

Block out big chunks of time to see you through a tough problem. This may mean shutting your door to keep interruptions to a minimum. Harry P. Letton, Jr., president of Southern California Gas Co., does that about twice a month just to catch up on reading. But too many closed-door sessions may irritate fellow employees. Time spent waiting for you is likely to be wasted time.

Give more of your own work to your secretary. Letton's secretary monitors trade journals for him, showing him only the few stories he most needs to see. Consider promoting your secretary to a position where she can help you even more. Joyce E. Cannon, formerly an executive secretary at American Microsystems, Inc., now serves her boss as administrative assistant with new duties as a researcher and information gatherer. One drawback is that you may then have to hire a new secretary.

Write less. A phone call will often be just as effective as a letter, and when you must write, use memos. Selwin Belofsky, president of Drawing Board, Inc., which manufactures business forms, came out of a time-management course with ideas for an action request form. It gives the person who will do the job a description of the task, a deadline, and who to report to.

Cut back on meetings. Barre L. Rorabaugh, 3M Co. production superintendent, used to hold a two-hour monthly meeting with 10 department heads to decide what to do with scrap. Invariably it was decided to throw the scrap out. Rorabaugh simply eliminated the meeting altogether.

Make lists ahead of time to organize your work. During the last five minutes of his day, Jack Linkletter, president of Linkletter Enterprises, jots down phone calls to be made, meetings to attend, and work to be done to give himself a head start on the next day. The biggest dividend: He no longer is working from 7 to 7. Bank of America Vice-President William Terry advises breaking up a list of complex tasks into "do-able pieces" right at the start.

Analyze how you spend your time to see how much of it you are wasting. One way is to record your activities for a week, breaking them into 15-minute blocks, and then determine what need not have been done at all. A time-evaluation analysis showed University of Minnesota Associate Dean Darrell R. Lewis that two-thirds of his time was spent on meetings. Now he often sends an assistant in his place.

Cut down on needless reports. At one division of Saga Corp., says President James W. Morrell, managers now post progress reports on a bulletin board. Those who must see the reports can, others are not obliged to waste time on marginal material.

Cut the flow to your in-basket. Saga has a new rule against mass copying and routing of magazine articles. Now if a story is routed, the sender underlines the key points so that those receiving it can skim it quickly. Executives no longer feel they have to read everything that comes along.

Learn to use otherwise idle time. Letton of Southern California Gas has a driver take him to and from his office so he can work along the way. It gives him an extra hour in the summer and 30 minutes in the winter (when it is too dark to read on the way home). Saga's Morrell saves bulky reports and statistical surveys for airplane trips, where they can be digested, he says, with the help of a martini.

Exercise 17
Decision Making in Organizations: The College Bookstore

LEARNING OBJECTIVES

1. To increase our understanding of organizational decision making at the top management level.
2. To identify effective and ineffective behavior in group decision making.
3. To develop guidelines for making meetings more effective.

ADVANCE PREPARATION

Read the Overview. Visit your local university or college bookstore to observe its operation.

OVERVIEW

Managerial decision making involves determining the goals of the organization, as well as planning and controlling the activities required to achieve them. Strategic decisions are made by top management. The overall strategy provides a framework within which planning and decision making take place at various levels and in the various subdivisions of an organization. In the case of a college bookstore, for example, strategic decisions are made with regard to issues such as product line and location. Should the store open a branch on the campus? Should it concentrate on textbooks and student supplies, or get involved in gifts and sporting goods? Such decisions lead to others of a more operational nature. For example, if it is decided to include gifts, plans must be developed to operate the store over Christmas vacation in a different manner. Policies and procedures must be developed for buying and selling merchandise, allocating space, and acquiring appropriate personnel.

When an organization is small, the planning and doing activities may be the function of one person or of several people—a proprietorship or partnership, for example. As organizations grow larger and more complex, the planning and doing activities may become separated, particularly strategic planning and day-to-day operations. In addition, the work may be divided by functions (production or marketing), by location (southwest or northeast), or by product (kitchen appliances or radio and TV). When such division of activity occurs either horizontally or vertically, it calls for some means of coordination. The more complex the organizational activity, the more need there is for appropriate means of planning and controlling activities. Therefore, organizations devote considerable effort to coordinating decisions over time by integrating long-range and short-range plans.

We have been discussing organizational decision making in terms of goal setting, planning, coordinating, and controlling. It is important to recognize how decisions are made. Routine operating decisions are typically made by individuals who are guided by policies, procedures, and rules. For more complex issues, particularly strategic planning, decisions frequently are made by groups. For example, the president or general manager will often have an executive committee to consider problems that involve several or all departments or divisions in the organization. And for issues that require outside input, the board of directors becomes a relevant decision-making body.

The general trend today is increased representation of various groups affected by organizational decisions—employees and customers, for example. In the past, particularly for small and medium-sized companies, managers have merely tolerated a board of directors because its existence is a legal requirement in most states. More astute managers have recognized the value of outside expertise and have included knowledgeable people in the decision-making process. Typically, there is a balance of directors from both inside and outside the organization.

The board of directors of the College Bookstore (today's case) was designed to represent the major groups of people affected by its operations. It includes two students, two faculty members, and one administrator. Two top managers usually attend the meetings to provide relevant information for the board's deliberations. This approach has potential advantages and disadvantages. It provides for a variety of views on relevant issues. However, if the views held by the members are too diverse, it makes decision making more difficult. It may be impossible to reach a consensus—a decision in which all members are satisfied that the issue has been fully explored and that they can support the conclusion even though they may have some reservations. While consensus is always the goal, there may be situations where voting is necessary to reach a decision.

This exercise is a simulation of managerial decision making at the strategic level. The focus is on the board of directors of a typical college bookstore. The kinds of problems identified are essentially strategic in nature, involving a long-run time perspective, nonprogrammable decision processes, and considerable judgment on the part of the participants. Some facts are available, as is the technical expertise of operating managers and experienced directors. However, the decision-making process is typically affected by the values and opinions of the various participants.

Another issue is that of group effectiveness in decision making. While groups—committees, commissions, task forces, councils, and boards—have received much bad publicity concerning effectiveness ("A camel is a horse put together by a committee"), they play an increasing role in organizational activity. The "one-person show" is a decreasing phenomenon in our society. People are becoming more involved at all levels, and managers are recognizing the merits of more participatory approaches to organizational problem solving. Given these trends, the issue is not that groups are bad per se; rather, that ineffective groups are bad. Thus, the critical issue is how to make groups more effective.

In this exercise we will be able to experience or observe a typical top-level decision-making group in action. By coupling this experience with concepts of group effectiveness, we will be able to develop some guidelines for group problem solving and for meetings in general.

The College Bookstore

In 1975 the College Bookstore celebrated its seventy-fifth anniversary. It began in the supply room of the college president's office in 1900. For many years it was a cooperative venture of students and faculty. In the 1920s the store was moved off campus because of lack of space. For the past 50 years, it has operated in the same location, which is approximately one block off campus in a suburban business district of a large metropolitan area. The store has expanded its space approximately tenfold during the last 50 years. In the 1930s, the store was incorporated but remained connected to the college with ultimate control vested in the Student Board of Control and the College Board of Regents.

In the early 1960s the president of the college appointed a committee to review the corporate structure of the bookstore. Numerous legal and tax questions had evolved and it was deemed important to explore all alternative approaches. The committee included three faculty members from the areas of marketing, accounting, and law. The student members were the president of the college student body and the president of the Associated Women Students. Ex-officio members included an assistant attorney general, the vice president for business and finance of the college, and the manager of the College Bookstore.

The basic assumptions on which the committee predicated its thinking were:

1. The primary function of the Bookstore is to maximize its service to students, faculty, and staff.
2. Ownership should be retained by students, faculty, and staff.
3. Policy control should remain with students, faculty, and staff.
4. The store is a business organization; it must earn and sustain sufficient income to finance its operation.
5. Available information suggests that modification of the present legal organization structure will permit the Bookstore to maximize its service to the college family.

The problem was to recommend a corporate structure for the Bookstore that would clarify its legal relationship to the student body and the college, and would attain and perpetuate the following set of seven objectives:

1. To have a store that will provide maximum service to students, faculty, and staff at a saving when possible.
2. To maintain the store as a business organization to meet the needs of the anticipated increase in student enrollment.
3. To perpetuate the store's benefits for future college generations.
4. To guarantee continuing student representation on the Bookstore's board of trustees equal to that of the faculty.
5. To make certain that, in event of the dissolution of the store, the residual assets will be utilized solely for the welfare of the college's students.
6. To continue to provide part-time employment for students.
7. And to maintain maximum goodwill in all areas consistent with these objectives.

The committee considered several alternatives and unanimously recommended that a trust agreement be established. This was logical in light of the legal conclusion that the store had operated under an implied trust from the beginning. The essential provisions of the trust agreement follow:

> The Student board of control agreed to transfer the 1,000 shares of Bookstore capital stock to a board of trustees which shall hold it in trust.
> Two students, two members of the faculty, and one member of the college administration shall constitute the College Bookstore board of trustees.
> At least one student trustee must be present at any meeting of the Bookstore board of trustees to constitute a legal quorum.
> Student members of the board are appointed by the president of the student body with the approval of the Student Board of Control. Faculty and administration members are appointed by the president of the college—with no recommendations from student leaders.
> Students and faculty members are appointed for staggered terms. The objective is to ensure substantial continuity of board membership. The faculty members and the administration member may be reappointed without limitation; this provision tends to ensure long-range board continuity.

The chairperson of the board of trustees must report annually to the Student Board of Control and to the College Board of Regents.

The board of trustees is charged, among other powers, with selecting the manager and establishing general operating policies. It is prohibited from buying, selling, or leasing real estate; disposing of any principal assets; opening stores in new locations; or voting to dissolve, reorganize, or merge the store without the consent of the Student Board of Control and the College Board of Regents.

The Bookstore board of trustees holds the store's capital stock in trust and passes the active control of the corporation over to the Bookstore board of directors. The trustees annually elect the members of the board of directors; it is intended, but not required, that trustees and directors generally be identical personnel.

The College Bookstore differs from many, perhaps most, similar stores in five respects:

1. It is incorporated.
2. It pays all forms of taxes—federal income tax included—that other private corporations pay.
3. It is located off campus.
4. It pays an annual patronage refund to eligible students, faculty, and staff.
5. It sells a wide variety of merchandise in addition to textbooks, trade books, and student supplies.

An organization chart for the College Bookstore is shown in Exhibit 17-1. It includes the major functions of the key managers. The product line has been broadened extensively over the history of the Bookstore to include general merchandise (gifts, etc.), photography and office equipment, sports equipment, men's apparel, and women's apparel. However, books and student supplies typically provide more than two-thirds of the total sales. An interesting aspect of merchandising in the past 2 years has been in electronic calculators. The Bookstore had a headstart in selling scientific calculators to the campus community, and in 1973–1974 sales in this category topped $1 million, out of a total of over $9 million (see Exhibit 17-2).

The Bookstore employs an average of 200 people: 130 full-time and 70 part-time. Most of the part-time employees are students.

Some relevant financial data are provided in Exhibits 17-3 and 17-4. Because of increases in costs of sales and operating expenses, operating income has declined over the past several years. This has been a particular concern of the store managers because they find that, for the first time in the store's recent history, they may have to recommend deleting the patronage refund for next year. Some of the issues involved are indicated in Exhibit 17-5. Other issues currently of concern to top management and the board of directors include physical expansion to increase selling space, purchase of property for a parking lot, and addition of a music department (records, tapes, and hi-fi equipment) to the product line. The physical expansion issue revolves around lack of adequate space for existing store operations. Whether or not additional merchandise lines are added, there is evidence of overcrowding in the existing facilities.

There is an opportunity for the Bookstore to buy property which it is now leasing and using as a parking lot across the alley from the existing store. The purchase would have obvious advantages in retaining and expanding the clientele that would otherwise be walk-in traffic. On-street parking is quite limited.

A number of these issues have been under consideration previously. The most urgent item is the proposal to eliminate the patronage refund for the following year. In order to be a legitimate expense for tax purposes, the refund rate must be established in advance of the fiscal year. Therefore, the board will have to make a decision at its next meeting (June) in order to be effective for the fiscal year beginning July 1.

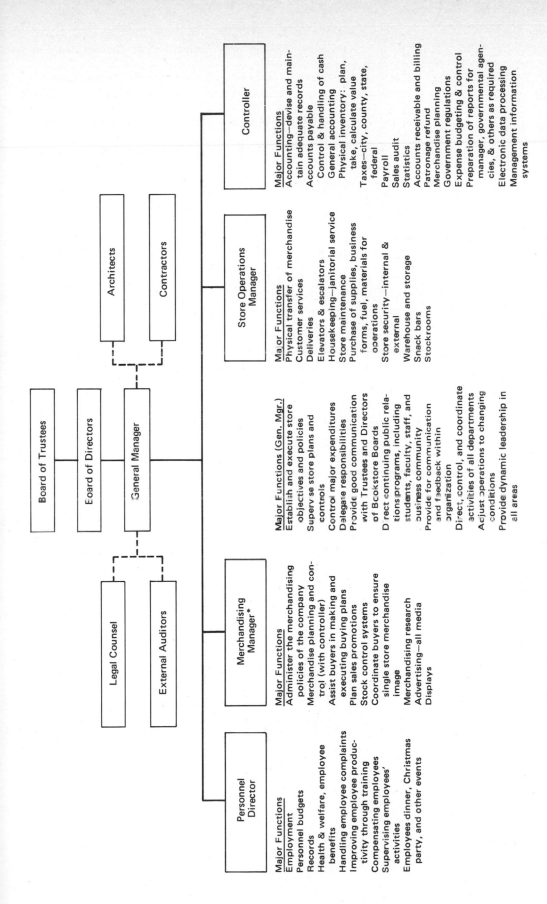

Board of Trustees

Board of Directors

General Manager

Legal Counsel

External Auditors

Architects

Contractors

Personnel Director

Major Functions
Employment
Personnel budgets
Records
Health & welfare, employee benefits
Handling employee complaints
Improving employee productivity through training
Compensating employees
Supervising employees' activities
Employees dinner, Christmas party, and other events

Merchandising Manager*

Major Functions
Administer the merchandising policies of the company
Merchandise planning and control (with controller)
Assist buyers in making and executing buying plans
Plan sales promotions
Stock control systems
Coordinate buyers to ensure single store merchandise image
Merchandising research
Advertising—all media
Displays

General Manager

Major Functions (Gen. Mgr.)
Establish and execute store objectives and policies
Supervise store plans and controls
Control major expenditures
Delegate responsibilities
Provide good communication with Trustees and Directors of Bookstore Boards
Direct continuing public relations programs, including students, faculty, staff, and business community
Provide for communication and feedback within organization
Direct, control, and coordinate activities of all departments
Adjust operations to changing conditions
Provide dynamic leadership in all areas

Store Operations Manager

Major Functions
Physical transfer of merchandise
Customer services
Deliveries
Elevators & escalators
Housekeeping—janitorial service
Store maintenance
Purchase of supplies, business forms, fuel, materials for operations
Store security—internal & external
Warehouse and storage
Snack bars
Stockrooms

Controller

Major Functions
Accounting—devise and maintain adequate records
Accounts payable
Control & handling of cash
General accounting
Physical inventory: plan, take, calculate value
Taxes—city, county, state, federal
Payroll
Sales audit
Statistics
Accounts receivable and billing
Patronage refund
Merchandise planning
Government regulations
Expense budgeting & control
Preparation of reports for manager, governmental agencies, & others as required
Electronic data processing
Management information systems

* Departments include Textbooks, Trade Books, Student Supplies, Sports, Photography and Office Equipment, Men's Apparel, Women's Apparel, and General Merchandise.

Exhibit 17-1 College bookstore organization and functions.

	Textbooks	Trade books	Student supplies	Sports	Photography & office equip.	Men's apparel	Women's apparel	General merchandise	Store total
Gross Margin (%)	23.21	35.60	46.03	31.78	23.63	39.85	40.47	38.92	30.59
Sales/Sq. Ft. of Selling Area	$473.29	$282.57	$208.61	$202.18	$1,173.30*	$196.92	$160.42	$192.77	$343.51

*Unusual performance in this department this year is a result of pocket calculator impact.

EXHIBIT 17-2 Gross margin and sales per square foot of selling area by department, 1973–1974.

	Percent
Net sales	100.00
Cost of sales	69.30
Gross margin	30.70
Operating expenses	23.70
Operating income	7.00
Operating expenses	
Payroll	14.13
Fringe benefits	.27
Pensions	.35
Payroll taxes	1.13
Total personnel	15.88
Other taxes	1.25
Supplies	1.27
Services purchased	.55
Unclassified	.59
Travel	.06
Communications	.44
Advertising	.67
Insurance	.51
Depreciation	.86
Professional services	.40
Donations	.08
Bad debts	.12
Equipment costs	.15
Real property rental	.87
Total operating expenses	23.70
Percent of total sales	
Textbooks	42.0
All books	62.7
Other merchandise	37.3

EXHIBIT 17-3 Income and expenses, 1973–1974.

Assets

CURRENT ASSETS:

	1974
Cash	$ 481,343
Certificate of deposit	120,000
Accounts receivable:	
Customers	198,462
Employees	5,201
Other	8,921
Allowance for doubtful accounts	(7,000)
Claims for receivable from vendors	84,711
Merchandise inventory	1,197,785
Prepaid expenses	8,363
Total current assets	2,097,786

INVESTMENT:

Business District Parking Associates, Inc., capital stock (at cost)	7,500

PROPERTY (at cost):

Land	470,378
Buildings	979,120
Furniture, fixtures, and equipment	336,731
Total	1,786,229
Less accumulated depreciation	1,007,907
Property, net	778,322
Total	**$2,883,608**

Liabilities

CURRENT LIABILITIES:

	1974
Accounts payable	$ 201,244
Accrued patronage refund	80,000
Accrued salaries and wages	39,644
Federal income tax	104,601
Other accrued and withheld taxes	123,231
Current portion of long-term liabilities	41,000
Total current liabilities	589,720

LONG-TERM LIABILITIES:

Bank note, payable $3,417 monthly plus interest at the prime interest rate plus 1/4 of 1% but between the limits of 5 and 6 1/2%	
Total	136,640
Less portion due within one year	41,000
Long-term liabilities, net	95,640

STOCKHOLDERS' EQUITY:

Capital stock - amount allocated to 1,000 shares of no-par-value stock authorized and outstanding	100,000
Capital in excess of amount allocated to no-par-value shares	117,223
Retained earnings	1,981,025
Stockholders' equity	2,198,248
Total	**$2,883,608**

EXHIBIT 17-4   Balance sheet, June 30, 1974.

How Is the Bookstore's Income Distributed?

First, let's define income, for the purpose of this question, as gross operating income before payment of patronage refund and federal income taxes. Gross operating income is defined as total sales less the cost to the store of the goods it sold, less all expenses to make those sales.

This income is distributed in three ways:

    (1)   Patronage refund to students, faculty, and staff.
    (2)   Federal income taxes.
    (3)   Funds retained by the Bookstore for operations.

To get a comparative relationship of these three distributions let's look at the 10-year period ending with June 1974. If the total sales for the 10-year period were $1.00, then:

Cost of the goods sold would have been	$ .69
Total expenses to sell those goods would have been	$ .24
Gross operating income would have been	$ .07

That $.07 income was distributed as follows:

Patronage refund paid was	$.031
Federal income taxes were	$.018
Funds retained were	$.021

This means that during this 10-year period, the Bookstore retained for operations only 2 cents out of every one dollar in sales, while it paid back to its eligible customers 3 cents out of every dollar. This amounted to over $1 million. During the last 2 years, the Bookstore has retained less than 2 cents out of every dollar in sales. Rarely could you find a business that returned so much of its earnings to its customers and retained so little for its operation.

Why Should the Bookstore Make a Profit?

Every business, including cooperatives, must have income in excess of its expenses, or be subsidized. Call that excess income "profit," "retained earnings," "surplus," or what you will, it *must* exist for every nonsubsidized business.

No one — not students, faculty, or the college administration — has *ever* been willing to subsidize the Bookstore. It has bought its property, built and remodeled its plant, and increased its inventory entirely out of its own earnings. It has done this while returning over $1,700,000 to students, faculty, and staff, and putting well over $75,000 into student and campus activities. Few if any college stores can match that record.

Contrary to other business organizations that can raise money through the sale of stock or debentures, the Bookstore can provide capital only by borrowing. No bank would loan money to a business without a demonstrated ability to repay the loan. So far the Bookstore, through sound business practices, has been able to do that.

Another point worth repeating — *No one* except the college's students, faculty, and staff have ever received *any* of the store's profit. *Every penny* not needed for the store's operation has been returned in the form of patronage refunds.

What Is the Patronage Refund?

The patronage refund, or rebate, is, by definition of the College Bookstore trust agreement, "the distribution, where possible, of earnings *except* those funds reasonably required for the efficient operation, growth, and expansion of the store." This point should be emphasized. Where there are no sufficient earnings to operate the store satisfactorily, there can be no patronage refund. This may be the case in 1975–1976.

The decision whether or not to pay a rebate, and the rate of the rebate, must be determined by the College Bookstore board of directors prior to the beginning of the fiscal year for

*Advertisement appearing in the *College Clarion* newspaper, Oct. 1, 1974.

EXHIBIT 17-5   Profits and patronage refunds.*   (Cont.)

which it is to be effective. The board is solely responsible for this decision and must make it on the basis of the projected capability of the store to pay such a refund.

As presently instituted, eligible students, faculty, and staff return their sales receipts for the fiscal year, July through June, to the store by the end of June. The following October they are paid in cash a refund at the rate previously declared by the board of directors.

The College Bookstore has, since 1930, returned to students, faculty, and staff, more than $1,700,000 in this manner.

Why Not a Cash Discount Instead of Patronage Refund?

This question has come up again and again. Each time, it has been resolved that a patronage refund as presently instituted is the "best" way to return savings to students, faculty, and staff. Let's look at some of the disadvantages of a cash discount system.

(1)   In order to return savings to students, faculty, and staff only, it would be necessary to check identification with every purchase.

(2)   The computation of a discount on each sale would slow down the check-out process and create havoc at rush periods.

(3)   The rate of a cash discount the Bookstore could afford to allow, during the years when it paid an 8 percent patronage refund, would have been only about 3 percent. This is simply because not every eligible customer chooses to participate in the patronage refund.

(4)   The bookstore would not enjoy the good standing it has now in the business district if it turned itself into a discount store.

(5)   Several lines of merchandise could not be carried by the store were they to be discounted.

Remember, much of the income to provide a patronage refund is provided through the sale of merchandise that carries a higher markup than books to noncampus customers who cannot participate in the refund.

PROCEDURE

The setting is the boardroom of the College Bookstore. The monthly meeting of the board of directors is about to begin. The members in attendance include two students, two faculty members, and one college administrator. One of the faculty members is currently chairperson of the board. As usual, the general manager and the controller are also in attendance.

STEP 1

The class should select an individual to serve as chairperson of the board. The chairperson can select two additional people to serve as advisors in planning the meeting. Although the advisors will not participate in the meeting proper, the chairperson may confer with them at any time and will caucus with them during the break in the meeting. The meeting will run for approximately 1 hour with a 15-minute break at some point.

STEP 2

Divide the remaining members of the class into six equal groups and assign them to the following roles:

Student no. 1
Student no. 2
Faculty member no. 2

University administrator
General manager
Controller

STEP 3
Each subgroup will meet for 20 minutes to develop the rationale for their role in the board meeting. Each group should refer to the instructions for its particular role and use them as a base for their position or point of view. Ideas and opinions can be added to the basic instructions. The only constraint is that they should be reasonably consistent with the role as defined.

STEP 4
Each group should select an individual to play their assigned role in the meeting of the board of directors.

STEP 5
The chairperson should call the meeting to order and proceed with the business at hand. Those people not involved in the meeting should make notes on the form entitled Observing Group Dynamics (page 251.

STEP 6
After 20 or 30 minutes, take a 15-minute break, during which time each of the subgroups should meet with their representative and the chairperson should meet with the two advisors. During this meeting the observers should report on what they see occurring in the meeting and make any suggestions for improvements.

STEP 7
The chairperson should reconvene the meeting and proceed with consideration of the various items on the agenda.

STEP 8
After 1 hour, stop the meeting and debrief the exercise. This discussion should involve the entire class.

   a. Ask the participants for their reactions to the simulated board of directors' meeting. What were their feelings during the course of the meeting? Were they satisfied with the results of the meeting? What did they think of the process of the meeting — good aspects and bad aspects?

   b. Open the discussion to the observers for their comments. What are their overall impressions of the effectiveness of the meeting? Have the observers report specific behaviors that either helped or hindered the group's effectiveness. List the items on a flipchart or blackboard.

   c. Develop guidelines for future meetings. If we were to have another meeting, what would we do differently?

INSTRUCTIONS FOR CHAIRPERSON'S ROLE
You are responsible for running the meeting, which will begin in 20 minutes. You and your two advisors should use the time to develop a plan for the meeting and to do whatever else you feel is necessary to get prepared. One item that must be considered is the patronage refund for the next fiscal year; the rest of the agenda is open. The meeting should last for 1 hour with a 15-minute break somewhere during that period.

   You are a professor of marketing, and are now in the second year of a 2-year term on the board. You believe that the Bookstore should be institutionally oriented, serving the educational needs of students and faculty with required books and supplies. However, you know from experience that stores which confine their activities to required books and supplies have seldom, if ever, been self-sufficient—they have required institutional subsidies. As chairperson, however, you plan to remain as neutral as possible during the early part of the discussion. You tend to be a little impatient with the "far out" ideas of some of your colleagues and with the inexperience of some student members of the board of directors.

FACULTY MEMBER NO. 2

You are a professor of English and are serving your first year on the board of directors. You are just beginning to understand the operation of a bookstore and are still concerned about some of the current policies. You would like the College Bookstore to be a genuine cultural center — its architecture distinguished, its walls covered with shifting displays of paintings, its interior offering pleasant rooms for reading, listening to music, reflection, and conversation. The product line should include articles worthy of a college — books, art and art materials, music, theater and travel tickets. They should be sold at the minimum price necessary to maintain only that commercial activity of the store. The employees should have the pay and status of fully integrated members of the college family. You don't see any reason for selling "ceramic squirrels." If the Bookstore runs a deficit, it should be assumed by the administration as a continuing cost of running a first-rate college. You don't understand why it takes 3 months' lead time for ordering textbooks, or why last-minute changes are resisted by the textbook manager. After all, it is important to have up-to-date, relevant material. Recently, you were upset because the textbook manager would not buy your sample copy of a book (sent gratis by the publisher) for the full retail price. You are convinced that operating expenses, particularly personnel costs, can be reduced significantly.

STUDENT NO. 1

This is your second year on the board of directors and you are beginning to understand the problems involved in operating a complex enterprise such as a college bookstore. In the past you have been concerned about the product-line policy and have leaned toward concentration on books and supplies. However, you have seen how the store's other departments have contributed to profitable operations and to the patronage refund. You are convinced that the refund must be continued at all costs in order to maintain the students' favor. You are convinced that top management is doing a good job, and are generally willing to support it in its proposals for change. Several students have been "bugging" you to get the textbooks out of the basement and up to the main floor.

STUDENT NO. 2

You have been on the board of directors for only 2 months, having replaced another student who had to resign because of ill health (mononucleosis). You are interested in expanding the product line with the addition of a music department. You are currently working part-time in a record store across the street from the College Bookstore. In fact, you are in favor of a "full service" store catering to nearly all the needs of students. For example, you would like to see the addition of diapers and baby clothes in the apparel department. You have been wondering whether it would be feasible for the Bookstore to operate a day-care center. (The proposal to provide one on the campus has been rejected by the college administration.) You are not sure you understand the financial aspects but would be reluctant to reduce or cancel the patronage refund because of its negative public relations impact. Last semester you were quite angry when you could not sell one of your texts back because a new edition had been published.

UNIVERSITY ADMINISTRATOR

You have been employed by the college for over 20 years and have been on the College Bookstore board of directors for the past 12 years. You are currently vice president for business and finance. You have supported efforts to make the Bookstore as separate and distinct as possible from the college financial picture. Therefore, you have encouraged the development of a multiline retail operation with emphasis on the generation of profits for survival and growth. You see a continuing need for more space because of extremely crowded conditions over the past 10 years. You have been pushing the board of directors to purchase the parking lot which it has leased from the college for several years. You see the parking lot as a distinct asset for the Bookstore and would hate to see the site purchased by some developer as a building site. Because the college is in financial trouble, such a sale is imminent.

CONTROLLER

You have been in your position as controller for 7 years and regularly attend the board of directors meeting to provide relevant financial information covering historical trends and projections for the future. Currently, your main concern is that costs of goods sold and operating expenses have risen faster than revenues, and that operating income has decreased significantly over the past year. Your current projection is that it may be less than 3 percent for the next fiscal year. In recent years, rebates to customers (students, faculty, and staff only) have been 8 percent of their total expenditures, as indicated by their accumulated receipts. You plan to bring the following information (Exhibit 17-6) to the board's attention at today's meeting.

Fiscal year / Percent of sales	Sales	Cost of sales	Operating expenses	Operating income	Patronage refund	Federal inc. tax	Retained earnings
1965-1966	100.0	69.4	24.7	5.9	2.5	1.4	2.0
1966-1967	100.0	69.7	24.9	5.4	2.4	1.3	1.7
1967-1968	100.0	68.4	24.2	7.4	2.7	2.2	2.3
1968-1969	100.0	68.3	23.2	8.5	3.2	2.5	2.8
1969-1970	100.0	69.0	23.2	7.8	3.0	2.0	2.8
1970-1971	100.0	70.3	23.1	6.6	3.2	1.5	1.9
1971-1972	100.0	67.5	23.6	8.9	3.0	2.5	3.4
1972-1973	100.0	68.9	23.5	7.6	3.0	2.0	2.6
1973-1974	100.0	69.3	23.7	7.0	2.9	1.9	2.2
1974-1975 (est.)	100.0	70.3	25.9	3.8	2.7	0.5	0.6
1975-1976 (projected)	100.0	70.0	27.5	2.5	0	1.2	1.3

EXHIBIT 17-6 Income distribution (actual and projected), 1965–1966 through 1975–1976.

Your proposal to the general manager and to the board of directors is to cut out the patronage refund entirely for fiscal 1975-1976 in order to provide some financial "breathing room." A patronage refund of any magnitude would very likely leave no net profit and hence no resources for modernization, product-line increase, or physical expansion (either in store space or the parking lot). Although the bank is willing to lend funds for such projects, it wants assurances that the Bookstore can meet its payments out of operating income.

GENERAL MANAGER

You have been general manager for 17 years and have seen considerable growth and development in the College Bookstore. You are a respected member of the business community, a past president of the Kiwanis, and are currently serving as president of the College Bookstore Association. You have mixed emotions about the controller's proposal for cutting or deleting the patronage refund; you recognize the need for operating capital but have always been concerned about public relations with students, faculty, and staff. You are interested in expansion of store space because of the crowded conditions, and are particularly supportive of the proposal to purchase the parking lot. A recent fire inspection has resulted in a negative report because of crowded conditions during rush periods and because of hazardous conditions in the basement and in the store's storage facilities. You feel necessary changes to existing facilities would be more expensive in the long run than expansion to additional footage on Main Street. You have just yesterday become aware of the opportunity to lease an adjacent building with an option to purchase within a 5-year period. The adjacent space has 60-foot frontage and is a two-story building in reasonably good repair. Acquisition of such space would also provide an opportunity to add additional product lines — a music department, for example.

Observing Group Dynamics

A number of factors can either (1) facilitate or (2) inhibit, deflect, or stop group progress toward the accomplishment of task goals, the maintenance of effective work relationships, and the satisfaction of individual needs. Some common blocks to effectiveness are spatial problems (physical arrangements), communication difficulties, interpersonal conflict, wide status differentials, rigid positions on issues, and hidden agendas (e.g., trying to make another member "look bad" for purely personal reasons, regardless of the actual agenda item under discussion). Keep these issues in mind as you observe the meeting. Note your observations in the appropriate space below.

Dimension	Observations (specific behaviors)*	Impact on individuals or groups
Communication pattern		
Decision-making process		
Task behavior		
Maintenance behavior		
Self-oriented behavior		
Interpersonal conflict		
Other		

*When giving another person feedback (sharing observations), it is extremely important that you be able to point to specific behaviors, both verbal and nonverbal, rather than to stereotype, to assume motives, etc.

SUMMARY AND CONCEPTUALIZATION

You have experienced or observed organizational decision making at the top management level. The issues and roles were taken from an actual situation. Were you able to empathize with the role and point of view assigned? Or, did you find your own values taking over? The ability to empathize is helpful in understanding attitudes and behavior different from our own.

How much conflict came to light in discussing the various issues? Was it resolved? If not, why not? If so, how was its resolution accomplished? For example, was the board of directors able to reach consensus on major issues, or was it necessary to decide by voting?

As you reflect on your experience during the meeting (playing a role or observing), what factors seemed to help or hinder the progress of the group? Did the physical arrangement of the participants facilitate or inhibit communication? Was the communication pattern reasonably balanced? Was participation differentiated appropriately in terms of information and expertise that individuals could contribute in resolving the various issues? Was the group able to concentrate its attention on one issue at a time or did the conversation wander from item to item depending on personal interests? For example, was an agenda developed fairly early and then followed during the meeting? Were the items discussed differentiated in terms of those needing immediate action and those requiring exploration only?

Refer back to our earlier exercise on group decision making and our identification of effective and ineffective behavior. Were you able to discern effective task behavior, such as initiating, giving information, checking for meaning, or summarizing? Could you identify effective group-maintenance behavior such as harmonizing, gate-keeping, encouraging, compromising, or consensus testing? Were you able to identify ineffective behavior such as avoidance, blocking, or dominating? Each group activity that we engage in provides an opportunity to increase our skills in observing what goes on and in practicing effective behavior.

Most groups tend to rely on designated leaders (chairpersons) for ensuring effectiveness. However, in reality this is a responsibility of all group members. Increased skill will come only with practice—either in simulated situations in class or in actual, everyday organizational endeavors.

Several fundamental factors should be kept in mind when trying to make meetings more effective. First, make sure that the appropriate people attend—those who are interested and have something to contribute. Set the agenda early and encourage participation in the agenda-setting process. This approach will increase the probability that the people attending will be interested in the subject matter of the meeting.

Segregate the agenda into categories such as information sharing, exploration only, and decision making. This step facilitates realistic expectations. Sometimes people become frustrated if decisions aren't made. However, if an issue is clearly labeled as "exploratory," a final decision should not be anticipated.

A key factor in meeting effectiveness is a sense of accomplishment. Therefore, it is important to develop and disseminate a written record that recaps decisions made, along with at least tentative action steps for implementation. Responsible individuals should be identified and explicit dates established for completion. Also, there should be a clear indication of how we will follow up to ensure implementation and ultimate success.

Exercise 18
Organizational Control: Appearance Standards

LEARNING OBJECTIVES

1. To increase our understanding of the concept of organizational control
2. To identify formal and informal means of control in organizations.
3. To write and compare explicit personal appearance standards for a variety of organizations.

ADVANCE PREPARATION

Read the Overview. Think about your own experience in organizations—family, school, clubs, athletics, work, etc.—to date. What policies, regulations, or rules (written or implied) were used to control your behavior? Have the so-called rules changed significantly in recent years? Are there significant differences between organizations? Between departments in the same organization? Think about any specific problems you have experienced or witnessed with respect to appearance standards, e.g., dress or hair style.

OVERVIEW

Managing includes planning, coordinating, and controlling organizational endeavor. The control function is necessary to coordinate and regulate activities. For example, checkstands at the supermarket coordinate the interaction of customers and cashiers; and traffic signals regulate the movement of vehicles and pedestrians at intersections. In organizations, control serves an important function in determining (1) whether the desired results (plans) have been achieved, and/or (2) whether appropriate means (policies and procedures) are being used. The basic elements of control include (1) a measurable and controllable characteristic for which standards are known; (2) a means (sensory device) of measuring the characteristic; (3) a means of comparing actual results to standards and evaluating differences; and (4) a means of effecting changes in the system in order to adjust the pertinent characteristic.

During Jack Andrews's ill-fated skiing expedition, he would typically plan to reach the bottom of the slope on each run. His perception of physical location would serve to monitor the process so that once he reached the bottom he would stop. "Controlling" his means of descent could be more difficult. He might be satisfied just to get to the bottom—with or without skis. Or, he might adjust his style on the next run if he had not been able to apply the appropriate technique(s) to his own satisfaction. Of course, the skiing instructor might also compare his performance with a standard and suggest improvement.

The same elements or processes are central to all control systems, formal and informal. Production processes include standards regarding number of units of output as well as specifications with regard to quality. Each aspect is checked at regular intervals to ensure satisfactory performance. Budgets provide financial plans that are reviewed periodically to see if adjustments need to be made in areas such as sales volume, expenses, and cash flow. Merit rating of employees is often formalized via review procedures that are designed to evaluate and control the behavior of individuals. Similarly, the testing and grading of students in educational systems can be viewed as a control process—measuring knowledge and comparing the results to standards (absolute or relative to peers) with the implicit assumption that adjustments in teaching and/or learning may be required.

The control function can be defined as that phase of the managerial process which maintains organization activity within allowable limits as measured from expectations. These expectations may be implicit, or explicitly stated in terms of objectives, plans, procedures, or rules and regulations. Just as there is a hierarchy of plans on a continuum of comprehensiveness, there are comparable control procedures appropriate in different parts of the organization and/or in different circumstances.

Informal controls play a major part in organizations. Norms come to be understood by participants even though they are never written down. Employees are "conditioned" to certain behavior patterns through screening at the point of hiring, formal and informal orientation, and on-the-job experience.

Feedback is an essential ingredient in any control process. In relatively closed systems, feedback leads to automatic adjustments in the system. In relatively open systems, information is received by human beings who process it and decide on appropriate action. Many kinds of feedback systems can be designed to facilitate control. Managers may desire a continual flow of information to monitor the system. Or, they may assume that "no news is good news" and hence require information on only the exceptional situations.

The time dimension is important to the control function in several ways. Organizations develop precontrol by means of standing plans comprised of policies, procedures, and rules or regulations. The development of relatively uniform value systems among organization members provides valuable precontrol. Emphasis is on preventing the system from deviating too far from preconceived norms. Considerable organizational effort goes into maintaining the system within designated limits—preventing undesirable occurrences. Education of the citizenry with regard to traffic laws and the consequences of breaking them is an attempt at precontrol of driving behavior.

However, it is apparent that precontrol is often not sufficient to maintain systems within desirable limits. Therefore, considerable effort must also be devoted to postcontrol—ascertaining the results of behavior, evaluating it, and taking action which is designed to correct or adjust behavior in future situations. For example, a flashing red light, a siren, and a $30 fine are a form of postcontrol designed to "persuade" a person to drive within the posted speed limit. In such a case, the precontrol effort of education and a set of rules did not prove effective. Therefore, postcontrol in the form of punitive action is invoked.

There is considerable disagreement concerning the relative weight which should be placed on pre- and postcontrol. The most extreme position suggests that if enough effort is given to precontrol, there will be no need for postcontrol. That is, if group value systems were internalized completely, all individual and organization actions would fall within desirable limits and the system would be self-regulating. So far, however, this concept appears to be utopian, and considerable attention continues to be devoted to postcontrol. Many examples of postcontrol in organizations could be cited: reviewing profit performance as related to established goals; checking the reject or scrap rate at the end of the year; or checking a sales agent's expense account at the end of the month. In each case the difference between actual and expected would be ascertained, and a decision would be made concerning the appropriate corrective action which, if successful, would lead toward improved performance in the future.

Throughout this discussion on organizational control, we have referred to both ends and means. Clearly, an organization must continually monitor its progress toward stated goals. Concern about means used in achieving those goals is somewhat more fuzzy. Obviously, long-run considerations are important—an organization cannot focus on short-term goals without concern for maintenance of physical and human resources. The process used to produce goods and services is an area of much concern and it should be continually improved if possible.

Within these general constraints, organizations are often concerned with details (that may or may not be relevant) regarding the means used to achieve objectives. This interest in means is typically highlighted when organizations are embarking on such programs as management by objectives and *results*. It is difficult for managers at any level to concentrate on results only. They typically want to know *how* an objective is to be achieved. This may or may not be appropriate, depending on how crucial the particular dimension is for organizational success.

Most organizations cannot accept the existential view that "anything goes." The actions of a branch manager, department head, or supervisor must be legal and ethical. An executive cannot squander physical or human resources to achieve short-run objectives. But concern about "how" can be overdone. For example, is it appropriate for a manager to state, "I'm interested only in results," and then question a subordinate about the amount of time spent on a job or about when the normal amount of working time is put in during the week. Can the same results be obtained by working from 6 AM to 2 PM, or from 10 AM to 6 PM—both approaches apparently "violating" the traditional 8 to 5 work day? Such concerns bring up the question of what to do with the maverick, the person who is "far out." Given the organization's legitimate need for stability and continuity, can extreme individualism be accepted? By definition, organization means cooperation and, hence, the sacrifice of individualism to some extent. But how much? George Bernard Shaw once said, "The reasonable man conforms to the world. The unreasonable man expects the world to conform to him. Therefore, all progress depends on the unreasonable man." Unquestionably, managing participants with widely diverse value systems is more difficult than coordinating a group of people selected in the manager's own image. And we may be surprised to see a process of mutual accommodation as participants recognize the need to submerge individual values and goals to a degree in order to facilitate the accomplishment of organizational objectives.

A significant issue in controlling means and dealing with differences is the decision on what is substantive for organizational performance and what is superficial. Obviously, managers with different values will disagree on this question. One example is the approach used by two football coaches in the 1975 Super Bowl game. Bud Grant, of the Vikings, ruled that the players would live together (sans wives) for the several days immediately preceding the game. Chuck Noll, of the Steelers, ruled that the players would continue to live with their wives immediately before the game, on the assumption that this was normal behavior. Here, two managers have different opinions on how much control to place on the *means* of obtaining the same result—winning the Super Bowl football game.

Athletics provide another example that has received much publicity in our society recently. How important is it for members' appearance (including dress and hair styles) to be "appropriate" for organizational purposes? Less than 5 years ago, a number of players were disciplined or suspended for wearing their hair too long or growing beards. Many coaches felt that long hair and beards were dysfunctional—if not in terms of actual physical performance, at least in terms of an example of the discipline needed for team effectiveness. What a difference 5 years make! The world champion Oakland Athletics (baseball) nearly all sport handle-bar mustaches. Many of the Pittsburgh Steelers had full beards on January 12, 1975. Many coaches (managers) have apparently succumbed to societal pressure and are much less restrictive than previously. The same problems were evident at all levels—professional, college, high school, and Little League.

Similar issues have been much in evidence in organizations in general. Dress codes and hair styles are often the focus of much attention even now. (See Figure 18-1.) Military and paramilitary organizations (police, fire, etc.) have rather restrictive policies. One large, nationwide insurance company requires all male employees to wear plain white shirts. A state-owned ferryboat deckhand was suspended for sporting a beard (although at the time the governor of the state also wore a full beard). In many organizations, women have been admonished for wearing very short skirts while at the same time (and often in the same organization) they were not allowed to wear pants.

Obviously, some standards are probably appropriate. The real question is, "How detailed should the policies or rules and regulations be?" Should they be absolute or merely recommended? Should they cover everyone in the organization or only some employees? This exercise focuses on giving you experience in writing appropriate policies or rules and regulations with regard to appearance.

PROCEDURE

STEP 1

Divide the class into groups of approximately five people. Randomly assign each of the groups to one of the following types of organization:

a. Bank
b. Police department
c. Retail store
d. Restaurant
e. Military
   (1) Regular unit
   (2) Reserve unit

f. Athletic team
g. National computer manufacturer
h. University
i. Hospital

STEP 2

Each group is responsible for writing a recommended policy and regulations with regard to employee appearance; "appearance" refers to (1) dress, and (2) hair styles (including mustaches and beards). Use the form headed Appearance Standards (page 259) for your final draft.

STEP 3

Each group should select an individual to report the recommendations to the total class. A minority report (dissent or suggested modification) may also be presented.

STEP 4

After each report and some discussion, the entire class will vote on acceptance or rejection of the recommendations. Record the results of the voting on the summary form (page 260) and also on the blackboard or a flipchart.

STEP 5

Entire class discussion.

   a. How much agreement is there on the various recommendations? Can we expect unanimity? Why or why not?

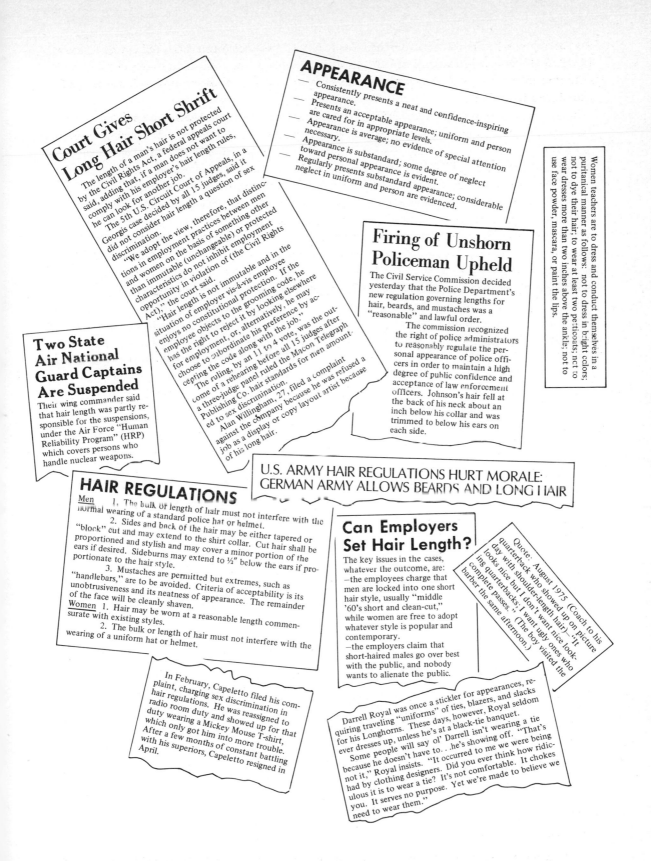

FIGURE 18-1 Examples of control of appearance in organizations.

b. Should the standards vary within organizations; e.g., by departments, by regions in the United States, by country (multinational firms)?

c. What factors (key criteria) should be considered in establishing policies regarding appearance?

d. Should work organizations lead or follow in setting societal appearance standards? Why?

e. As a manager, how would you deal with employees who are out of line in appearance?

SUMMARY AND CONCEPTUALIZATION

A basic connotation of the word "control" is "maintaining the system within allowable limits." The limits can refer to expected results and/or appropriate means of achieving them. For quantifiable characteristics such as number of units, physical dimensions, or financial data, the control process is relatively straightforward and often routine. For other characteristics, such as employee morale, managerial skill, and socially responsible behavior, the control process is often ill-defined and hence much more complex.

Appearance standards can fall in both categories, depending on the particular type of organization and/or managerial tolerance for ambiguity. In some cases, management may publish precise codes for dress and hair style, complete with pictures and specifications. In other cases, there are no written rules; instead, there is a general "understanding" that employees will be neat and well-groomed. Of course, this approach invites diverse interpretations. Is an open sportshirt "neat" enough, or is a tie required? Is a dress neater than a pants suit? Is a man with shoulder-length hair well-groomed? How about mustaches and beards?

What are the consequences of detailed regulations? What are the consequences of no regulations at all? Is there a middle ground that is appropriate for all organizations, or should our approach vary among organizations and among parts of organizations? What criteria should be used in deciding how explicit dress and hair-style regulations should be?

You have experienced the development of explicit regulations for several organizations. It is likely that there were differences of opinion based on the background and experience of class members. Note that a college or university class is likely to be relatively homogeneous when compared with the population as a whole or with all employees in a fairly large, complex organization.

Most of us will be subject to rules and regulations established by other people who are typically considerably older and often conditioned to past practices. If we disagree with the standards as set, how should we behave? In the future, we may be in the position of deciding what the regulations should be. How should we behave in that case? In other words, how should we go about designing dress and hair-style regulations that are functional for the organization and yet cognizant of personal preferences?

Our approach to the specific issue of appearance standards can be broadened to include the design of control processes for a wide range of individual and group behavior in organizations. You may want to think about your own approach to developing organizationally appropriate guidelines to which employees are personally committed. Such an approach decreases the need for spending valuable managerial time on checking compliance with standards, particularly for dimensions that are not actually relevant for individual, group, or organizational success.

Appearance Standards

Organization: _____

A. *Dress* (75 words or less)

B. *Hair style* (75 words or less)

Summary of Action on Appearance Standards

Name of organization	Action recommendations	
	Number accepting	*Number rejecting*
_____		
A. Dress	_____	_____
B. Hair style	_____	_____
_____		
A. Dress	_____	_____
B. Hair style	_____	_____
_____		
A. Dress	_____	_____
B. Hair style	_____	_____
_____		
A. Dress	_____	_____
B. Hair style	_____	_____
_____		
A. Dress	_____	_____
B. Hair style	_____	_____
_____		
A. Dress	_____	_____
B. Hair style	_____	_____
_____		
A. Dress	_____	_____
B. Hair style	_____	_____

Exercise 19
Evaluation and Selection:
MBA Admissions Committee

LEARNING OBJECTIVES

1. To understand how different values and goals influence decisions in organizations.
2. To be able to participate effectively in a decision-making process where there may be different points of view.
3. To be able to confront and resolve differences in order to reach a consensus decision.

ADVANCE PREPARATION

Read the Overview and complete Step 1 of the Procedure. Be prepared to discuss your individual ranking of the applicants with a group of your colleagues. *Do not read* the Summary and Conceptualization at this time.

OVERVIEW

Organization members frequently have to make decisions that are constrained by environmental factors, resource limitations, and internal forces. These decisions are also affected by the overall goals and values of the organization. Conversely, decisions on specific issues can create changes that have a vital impact on the future of the organization. For example, the rebate program of the American automobile firms during the winter of 1975 was in response to a decline in the demand for automobiles stemming from the energy shortage and the general economic recession of the time. Chrysler started the rebate plan and other companies were forced to follow for competitive reasons. Was this a good decision? Nobody really knows, even now. It is estimated that the companies suffered a loss of several hundred dollars on each car sold under the rebate program, with the total losses ranging in the hundreds of millions of dollars. The forced sales during the rebate period adversely affected sales volume for the rest of the year.

But what were the alternatives? The automobile companies had huge inventories of unsold cars. Dealers had no customers and many went out of business. Many workers were laid off. It was impossible to change the product lines quickly in response to the customers' demands for smaller, less energy-consuming vehicles. The complex technological system set up to mass-produce automobiles could not be adapted rapidly. Changes would take hundreds of millions of dollars and several years.

Environmental, competitive, and technological constraints severely limited the alternatives for the companies. Was the decision to offer rebates an optimal decision? The companies had a great deal of cost and other statistical data that helped in their decision making. However, there were many uncertainties; judgmental and intuitive processes were important. Decision making is more than feeding in data and cranking out results. The process is strongly influenced by the goals and values (often implicit) of the decision makers involved.

The Midwest Graduate School of Business is part of a large state university that has a total enrollment of over 30,000. It has a large undergraduate program in business administration, 500 students in the master of business administration (MBA) program, and 100 students in the Ph.D. program. It is faced with a situation similar to that described in the *Business Week* article, "The Job Market Starts a B-School Stampede" (see pages 263-265). It has an increasing number of applicants for a limited number of places in its graduate programs.

The graduate school plans to admit 250 first-year MBA students for the coming academic year. There are more than 1,000 qualified applicants. To be considered for admission, an applicant must have a bachelor's level degree from a recognized college or university, must take the Graduate Management Admission Test (GMAT), and must complete an application to the graduate school of the university and to the business school. An undergraduate grade-point average of 3.0 (B) or better in the last 2 years of academic work and a GMAT score in the top quartile are considered positive indicators, but personal factors such as motivation, demonstrated managerial talent, leadership, and organizational experience are also weighed in reviewing the total application. Students have the option of having letters of recommendation sent in to their files. Where possible, it is desirable for them to arrange for a personal interview with the director of the MBA program.

The GMAT is given nationally and is used by most graduate schools of business as one index of potential performance. The test is an "aptitude" type and is not based on business knowledge. The national average for the test is 500 with a standard deviation of 100. The *average* test score for last year's admitted students at Midwest was 550. The *average* grade-point average for admitted students was 3.32. However, the school emphasizes that admission is not based solely on quantitative data; each applicant is judged on ability to complete the program, possible contribution to the school, and desire for, and potential in, a management career.

The Midwest Graduate School of Business has an Advisory Committee on Admissions that provides advice to the director of the MBA program on the selection of qualified candidates. This committee is composed of one faculty member from each of the four academic departments and two second-year MBA students, elected by their colleagues. The director of the MBA program chairs the committee and provides all the staff support. The committee has already made its selection of 250 entering students earlier in the year. However, in early July two of the admitted students have notified the committee that they will not be able to enter the program in the fall. Therefore, two positions are open.

Initial screening of candidates on the alternate list and of those who applied after the earlier selection indicates that seven applicants merit serious consideration. All seven have assured the director of the MBA program that they will enroll in the program if admitted.

The Advisory Committee on Admissions will convene to consider these seven applicants and select the *two* who will be admitted. It is impossible to take more than two.

A summary of the information from the application form and file is provided for each of the seven candidates. The application forms may not be complete because some of the items are optional. Under the heading *Other Information* are brief notations based upon letters of recommendation, personal interviews, and other sources.

PROCEDURE

STEP 1

Before class, read the article, "The Job Market Starts a B-School Stampede." Individually, read the information on the seven applicants and rank them on the form, Ranking of Candidates for Selection to MBA Program (page 273). Briefly, give reasons for your ranking.

STEP 2

Meet in groups of five to seven as the Advisory Committee on Admissions and develop a group consensus ranking of the candidates. Indicate this ranking on the form on page 273.

STEP 3

Each group should write its ranking of the candidates on newsprint or the blackboard and indicate the two it selected for admission. A spokesperson should give the rationale for the group's selection.

STEP 4

The entire class discusses the case.

THE JOB MARKET STARTS A B-SCHOOL STAMPEDE*

After several years of disrepute, the country's business schools are back in favor with students, mostly because MBAs are finding jobs in the current recession when almost no one else can. At Dartmouth's Amos Tuck School, for example, all but six of this year's crop of 127 MDAs have already been placed, and at Wharton Graduate School only 20 of 345 graduating MBSs are still looking for a job.

This lesson is not lost on thousands of men and women unable to find work this spring—including graduating seniors, new lawyers, even some PhDs—and who are applying to business schools for the fall term. A *Business Week* survey of 11 major B-schools indicates that applications for next fall's class are up 24% from last year's, and 69% over 1972, when student esteem for B-schools was at its low point.

Specifically, applications are up 44% at Amos Tuck, 37% at both Columbia University and the University of California at Los Angeles, and 33% at Stanford University. Officials at Harvard B-school say the increase is 15% over last year. "With the state of the economy and the job market for undergraduates so bad, many feel that they should get an MBA to make them more competitive two years from now," says George Ridenour, director of admissions at Cornell University's business school. At Massachusetts Institute of Technology's Sloan School of Management, there has been an increase recently in the number of applicants with advanced science and engineering degrees because, "they feel a management degree will be a boost in their job searches," says Miriam Sherburne, program director of the management program.

What is more, as in the past few years, the number of women applying to business schools increased sharply. They were up 58% at Columbia, 31% at Harvard, and 25% at both Amos Tuck and Cornell.

Indeed, an MBA or management degree does seem to give a job hunter a leg up. For while the job market is not as brisk as it was for the past two years, with fewer companies searching, most graduating MBAs are still landing jobs—and at slightly higher average salaries than last year. "MBAs are not having the trouble finding jobs that other graduates are having," explains J. Fredric Way, assistant dean at Columbia's Graduate School of Business. "They are working

Business Week: June 2, 1975, pp. 50–51.

harder and taking more time this year, but they are finding jobs." And the average starting salary for Columbia grads this spring has increased 5%, to about $17,000, which Way attributes mostly to inflation. At Harvard the median salary this year is up 8%, to $19,000.

Fewer recruiters. The leading recruiters this year, as last, are the money-center banks, public accounting firms, and oil companies. One New York bank, for example, sent 20 recruiters to Harvard, where they interviewed one-third of a graduating class of 800. "Chase Manhattan and First National City Bank were pushing hard," says the placement director at another B-school. "They seem to be in direct competition for people, too." Citibank recruited a total of 261 from colleges last year, 155 of whom were MBAs, and plans to hire a similar number this year. Chase hired 43 MBAs in 1974 and has already signed up 52 this year—with still some offers outstanding. What is more, Peat, Marwick, Mitchell & Co., the largest of the Big Eight accounting firms, has hired 320 MBAs this year, against 260 in 1974—out of a total each year of 1,500 new employees. "We were able to hire the additional MBAs this year because the competition was less keen," says James Morgan, Peat, Marwick's partner in charge of personnel.

The competition is less keen because over-all there have been slightly fewer companies recruiting this year at most B-schools. At Wharton Graduate, for example, 580 companies recruited this year, compared with 622 in 1974. At Cornell, 125 companies recruited, down 5% from last year. Harvard Business School had 306 companies this year, vs. 307, while Amos Tuck ended up with 134 for both years.

Most conspicuous by their absence on campus this year were the automobile companies. According to Arthur Letcher, placement director at Wharton Graduate, the car makers "stopped hiring altogether." Says a spokesman for Ford Motor Co.: "We feel we have a responsibility to call back our laid-off employees first."

But the automobile companies aren't the only ones to curtail recruiting. Many advertising agencies and brokerage firms stayed away this spring, too. And International Telephone & Telegraph Corp., pulled in its horns this year and hired about five MBAs, down from 20 several years ago. ITT cut back its management by laying off 120 persons last fall, and its needs for new MBAs may be less.

Fewer offers. Even the companies that are recruiting are being more selective and are making fewer offers. "The firms are not willing to take people on and call them trainees," says Letcher. "They want them to perform." More graduates, in turn, are snapping up the first job offer they get. "In the past," continues Letcher, "companies would offer three people the same job, anticipating that two of them would go elsewhere. Now, because of the high rate of acceptance, they

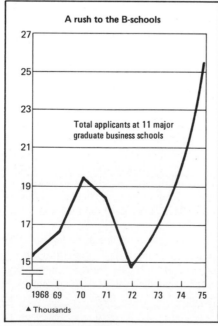

Data: Marlo DeVincentis—BW

are extending only one job offer." Indeed, the average number of offers that a Wharton MBA receives is down to 2.5 this year, compared with 3.8 a year ago. For an Amos Tuck MBA, offers are down to three from four last year.

The hottest groups with recruiters in recent years, women and blacks, are still wooed by corporations, but nowadays the candidate has to make economic sense. "Women and minorities are still heavily in demand," says Ben Greco, director of career services for the B-school at the University of Southern California, "but only if they offer the needed skills. Nobody is putting them in windows any more."

With banks and accounting firms among the big recruiters, it is not surprising that finance and accounting majors are among those in the highest demand. "Finance is generally a 'hot area,'" explains Rod Hodgins, director of placement at Harvard. "Finance jobs can challenge MBAs, but some of those jobs are really short-term analytical positions that don't lead up to the next job. I'd like to see more line jobs available than staff jobs," he says.

Marketing jobs, while available, are less abundant than in past years, and this has forced many marketing majors to settle for their second or third choice. "There aren't many jobs in marketing this year," says a woman MBA at New York University, who had interviews at Clairol and Avon, among consumer package goods concerns, and settled for a job in market research. "Practically no one is looking for product managers. Even General Foods didn't hire any from us this year; they took a couple for finance." Adds USC's Greco: "Our people who wanted to enter the consumer goods business are very disappointed."

Nevertheless, most MBAs are getting jobs, when holders of other advanced degrees and law school graduates are not. The University of Chicago Business School has a dozen applications from PhDs in everything from chemistry to English, who could not find jobs in their fields. At NYU law school, most of the graduates in the top half of the class have found jobs, but the rest are struggling. At least partly because of this, NYU law school has had a minuscule decrease in applications this year, after several consecutive years of 10% increases.

Business schools seem to be picking up some of the slack and holding their own. "Students are finding management careers as an alternative," says Charles Grantham, director of admissions at Wharton. "People who in the past saw a law degree as a way of qualifying them for any type of job are waking up to the fact that there are too many law school applicants, and many of those borderline between careers in law or in management are opting for B-school."

Another reason students are opting for B-school is that there has been a substantial improvement in the past five years in their attitude toward business. Karin Paulson, assistant dean at Columbia, attributes this partly to a trend toward "career orientation."

Indeed, most MBAs are practical. "This whole MBA thing is terrific," crows the woman MBA at NYU, who had worked for three years before going to business school. "I've increased my salary 50% since my last job. I was a fool not to have done it sooner."

SUMMARY INFORMATION ON APPLICANTS FOR MBA PROGRAM

Name: *Beaverton, William Essex*

Age: *26*   Sex: *M*   Marital Status: *S*

Dominant Ethnic Origin: *Cauc.*   Citizenship: Instate
U.S.
(International)

Admissions Test Score: *636*

Previous Academic Record:

School	Major	Degree	Years	GPA
Univer. of London	*Economics*	*Bach*	*1973*	*None Graduated with First Class Honors*

Work Experience:

Organization	Title, Duties	Started	Duration
British Foreign Office	*Foreign Investment Analyst*	*Sept. 1974*	*present*

Other Information:

NO PERSONAL INTERVIEW BUT SEVERAL VERY IMPRESSIVE LETTERS FROM FORMER PROFESSORS AND SENIOR OFFICIALS IN BRITISH FOREIGN OFFICE.

HE IS A SECOND COUSIN OF THE PROVOST OF MIDWEST UNIVERSITY.

SUMMARY INFORMATION ON APPLICANTS FOR MBA PROGRAM

Name: Anderson, Phyllis

Age: 28   Sex: F.   Marital Status: separated, supporting 2 children

Dominant Ethnic Origin: Afro American   Citizenship: (Instate) U.S. International

Admissions Test Score: 490

Previous Academic Record:

School	Major	Degree	Years	GPA
California State Coll.	Ethnic Studies	No degree	1970-71	2.49
City University	Sociology	Bach	1972-75	3.02

Work Experience:

Organization	Title, Duties	Started	Duration
Acme Groceries	cashier	1969	1969-1971 Full & part-time while in school
Telephone Co.	operator	1971	1972
Modern Dept. Store	clerk & promoted to assistant buyer	1972	present, part-time while in school

Other Information:

GOOD LETTERS OF RECOMMENDATION. VERY IMPRESSIVE IN INTERVIEW; STRONG CAREER GOALS. HAS BEEN ACTIVE IN CIVIL RIGHTS AND NATIONAL ORGANIZATION OF WOMEN.

Name: *ARROWSMITH, LESLIE*

Age: *25*   Sex: Marital Status: *S*

Dominant Ethnic Origin: Citizenship: *Instate*
                                           U.S.
                                           International

Admissions Test Score: *579*

Previous Academic Record:

School	Major	Degree	Years	GPA
MIDWEST UNIVERSITY	*PHILOSOPHY*	*BA*	*1976*	*3.85*
				PHI BETA KAPPA

Work Experience:

Organization	Title, Duties	Started	Duration
SUNNYSIDE BEACH COUNTRY CLUB	*LIFEGUARD*		*SUMMERS*

Other Information:

VERY GOOD LETTERS OF RECOMMENDATION FROM SEVERAL FACULTY MEMBERS PRAISING EXCELLENT ACADEMIC PERFORMANCE.

HAS BEEN ACTIVE IN STUDENT AFFAIRS AS AN UNDERGRADUATE.

SUMMARY INFORMATION ON APPLICANTS FOR MBA PROGRAM

Name: Gonzales, Joseph

Age: 28   Sex: M   Marital Status: M

Dominant Ethnic Origin: Chicano   Citizenship: Instate
(U.S.)
International

Admissions Test Score: 560

Previous Academic Record:

School	Major	Degree	Years	GPA
Southwestern University	Accounting	Bach.	1973	3.00

Work Experience:

Organization	Title, Duties	Started	Duration
AFL-CIO	Accountant for first 9 months. Currently a traveling representative to assist groups in holding NLRB Elections	June 73	current

Other Information:

NO PERSONAL INTERVIEW BUT GOOD LETTERS OF RECOMMENDATION FROM SOUTHWESTERN UNIVERSITY PROFESSORS AND AFL-CIO OFFICIALS.

SEVERAL CHICANO GRADUATE STUDENTS AT MIDWEST HAVE RECOMMENDED HIM HIGHLY.

SUMMARY INFORMATION ON APPLICANTS FOR MBA PROGRAM

Name: Robinson, Mrs Mary Jean

Age: 43 Sex: F. Marital Status: M.

Dominant Ethnic Origin:

White / American

Citizenship: (Instate)
U.S.
International

Admissions Test Score:

550

Previous Academic Record:

School	Major	Degree	Years	GPA
Cloverdale College	Psychology	Bach of Arts	1956	3.55
Eastern University	Education	M. Ed	1958	3.60

Work Experience:

Organization	Title, Duties	Started	Duration
Cloverdale High School	Taught Social Studies	Sept 1958	2 years

Other Information:

IMPRESSIVE IN INTERVIEW. HUSBAND IS LOCAL PHYSICIAN AND HAS TWO CHILDREN ENROLLED IN COLLEGE. DESIRES TO RETURN TO WORK IN A NEW CAREER.

STRONG INTEREST IN CLINICS AND OTHER MEDICAL ORGANIZATIONS, BUT SEES NEED FOR ACADEMIC TRAINING IN BUSINESS.

SUMMARY INFORMATION ON APPLICANTS FOR MBA PROGRAM

Name: Goodman, Ralph

Age: 27   Sex: M   Marital Status: S

Dominant Ethnic Origin: _____   Citizenship: (Instate)
                                                 U.S.
                                                 International

Admissions Test Score: 560

Previous Academic Record:

School	Major	Degree	Years	GPA
City community College	Machine technology	Associate of Arts	1971	2.10
Midwest Univ. Under Education release programs	Bus. Adm.	Bach.	1976	3.12

Work Experience:

Organization	Title, Duties	Started	Duration
Longhaul Trucking	Maintenance Mechanic	1972	1974

Other Information:

HE WAS SENTENCED TO FOUR YEARS IN STATE REFORMATORY FOR SECOND OFFENSE OF POSSESSION OF MARIJUANA AND OTHER DRUGS IN 1974. HE HAS BEEN ON AN EDUCATIONAL RELEASE PROGRAM WHERE HE COMPLETED HIS DEGREE IN BUSINESS ADMINISTRATION. PROFESSORS THOMPSON AND HESS HAVE COMMENTED FAVORABLY ABOUT MR. GOODMAN. THEY FEEL HE HAS DONE WELL AS A STUDENT, HAS MADE EXCELLENT PROGRESS TOWARD REHABILITATION AND DESERVES THE OPPORTUNITY TO WORK FOR HIS MBA.

Name: Wellington, Marshall

Age: 42   Sex: M   Marital Status: M

Dominant Ethnic Origin: Citizenship: Instate
                                                           (U.S.)
   White Amer.   International

Admissions Test Score: 510

Previous Academic Record:

School	Major	Degree	Years	GPA
Military Academy	Military Science	B. of Engr.	1956	3.06

Work Experience:

Organization	Title, Duties	Started	Duration
U. S. Army	Various assignments U.S. and abroad. Currently Lt. Colonel requesting retirement after 20 years	June 56	Current

Other Information:

VERY GOOD PERSONAL APPEARANCE. EVIDENCES
EXCELLENT LEADERSHIP CAPABILITIES. MILITARY
PERFORMANCE REPORTS CONSISTENTLY RANKED
IN UPPER 10%. STRONG LETTERS OF RECOMMENDATION.

Ranking of Candidates for Selection to MBA Program

Individual ranking   *Group ranking*

1st _____   1st _____

    Reasons:

2d _____   2d _____

    Reasons:

3d _____   3d _____

    Reasons:

4th _____   4th _____

    Reasons:

5th _____   5th _____

    Reasons:

6th _____   6th _____

    Reasons:

7th _____   7th _____

    Reasons:

SUMMARY AND CONCEPTUALIZATION

Was there general agreement within your group and in the entire class on the two candidates who should be selected for admission to the Midwest Graduate School of Business? What criteria did you use in the selection? Were you most influenced by past accomplishments in terms of grades and test scores? How much weight did you give to other-than-academic experience? Did you feel that the student who probably came from an affluent family and achieved a high grade-point average should be preferred to the student who had to work throughout college and had achieved a satisfactory but not outstanding record? How much were you influenced by a desire to create a balance of MBA students in terms of sex and ethnic factors? How much of an impact did age have in your decision? How did you evaluate students on the basis of whether they were from within the state, from other states, or from other nations? Were there other social or cultural issues which influenced your decisions?

The problems you faced in trying to reach a consensus decision are not unlike those faced by most graduate schools of business and other graduate or professional schools. They also have multiple criteria for selection and must make difficult decisions because there are often conflicts among these criteria. Even assuming that you were trying to select the best-qualified applicant with the highest future potential, what do we mean by "best-qualified" and how do we measure "future potential"? As the following article, "The Unsettled DeFunis Case," indicates, even the United States Supreme Court has difficulty reaching final solutions. The justices skirted the issue of whether so-called academic credentials should be the absolute criterion for admission to a law school. If academic credentials alone were used as the criterion, it is likely that the selection process would favor certain racial and ethnic groups who have had the advantage of greater affluence, a home environment conducive to professional training, and more pertinent (in terms of current testing procedures) educational experiences. Such a criterion would tend to perpetuate the power and influence of the favored groups as compared with other, less-advantaged groups. Throughout the history of our society, one of the main means for upward mobility has been to achieve higher income and status through formal education. Various immigrant groups recognized this process. Many families made great sacrifices to ensure that their sons and daughters went to college and entered the professions.

Obviously, the selection processes of colleges and universities can have an important impact upon the quality of the graduates and the reputation of the institutions. They also can have a major social influence. But the same type of problem is faced by other organizations. What are the criteria for selection and promotion in a business organization? Should educational background, past performance, seniority, future potential, or other factors be the main criteria?

There has been a movement toward creating greater "equality of opportunity" in our organizations. But, is this enough? What happens if certain groups have an inherent advantage over others in seizing opportunities? Are there issues of social equity in which certain people or groups should be given the opportunities for education, promotion, etc., because they have lacked advantages in the past? In our view, it is important for organizations to develop affirmative action programs which will ensure that all groups have an opportunity to achieve higher positions in the social structure.

THE UNSETTLED DeFUNIS CASE*

C. ROBERT ZELNICK

The Supreme Court of the United States dismissed the case of Marco DeFunis against the University of Washington law school because he was in law school and about to graduate. He

---

Christian Science Monitor, May 16, 1974. Reprinted by permission from the Christian Science Monitor. Copyright © 1974 The Christian Science Publishing Society. All rights reserved.

claimed he was rejected for the year beginning September, 1971, because arbitrary quotas established for racial minority students had used up all available places in his class.

The university was instructed to admit DeFunis by three separate courts in order that he suffer no irreparable injury while his case was pending. Those orders, in effect, permitted the Supreme Court to avoid determining DeFunis' case on its merits. But both the court majority and the dissenters agreed that the matter is certain not to remain dormant for very long.

To appreciate fully the complexity of the case it is necessary to examine the dissenting opinion of Associate Justice William O. Douglas. For while Justice Douglas alone purported to reach a decision on the core issue—voluntary racial quotas at state universities—he dodged it every bit as certainly as his brethren who made no similar pretense.

Justice Douglas began with a restatement of the undisputed facts: Thirty-eight blacks, Filipinos, Chicanos, and American Indians were accepted to the class from which DeFunis was rejected. Of these, 37 had lower academic credentials than he. Moreover, the applications of minority candidates were referred either to a black law student or an assistant dean and judged by a variety of standards. White applicants were, for the most part, subjected to a rather rigid mathematical process that combined their last two years of college grades with scores on the standard law school admissions test.

Clearly, as Justice Douglas noted, "the school did not use one set of criteria but two, and then determined which to apply to a given applicant on the basis of his race."

True enough. Not even the University of Washington asserted its law school admissions policies were "racially neutral." State policies that create distinctions on the basis of race, creed, or national origin, while not illegal on their face, are viewed with deep suspicion by the courts. They must be justified by a compelling state interest, one that cannot adequately be served by a more narrowly targeted approach. And not since the Korematsu case of 1944, when the court approved resettlement and curfews for Japanese Americans, has the nation's highest tribunal found any interest compelling enough to sanction racial or ethnic discrimination.

So one would have expected Justice Douglas to condemn out of hand Washington's law school admissions procedures. Instead he recommended that the matter be remanded for a new trial to determine whether law school admissions tests "should be eliminated so far as racial minorities are concerned."

But the question is not whether such tests are relevant to the cultural experience of minority candidates but whether they are helpful indicators as to whether a particular candidate for law school will do well in his studies. If they are, then eliminating them for minority applicants simply to increase minority enrollment at law schools runs afoul of the very constitutional principles Justice Douglas explains in his dissent:

> The equal protection clause commands the elimination of racial barriers, not their creation in order to satisfy our theory as to how society ought to be organized. The purpose of the University of Washington cannot be to produce black lawyers for blacks, Polish lawyers for Poles, Jewish lawyers for Jews. It should be to produce good lawyers for Americans and not place First Amendment barriers against anyone.

Justice Douglas' dissent then was no more satisfying than the holding of the majority. Still one detected an almost audible sigh of relief from the nation's academic community that this issue was not decided on this set of facts. Racial quota systems simply cannot pass judicial muster. Yet the law school door can and ought to remain open to minority candidates, even those who may do less well in law school than certain of their white classmates.

The answer may well be for admissions offices simply to recognize that academic excellence is only one measure of an attorney's value to both the legal and lay communities. The demands upon a practicing attorney often run more to his character than his intellect.

Strength of character, then, is at least equally important. So is a commitment to decent causes, or a devotion to one's fellow man, or an unflinching sense of honor and integrity.

Unlike an ability to do well on multiple choice examinations or master a particular discipline or course of study, these attributes are never the monopoly of a single race or culture. They reside in varying degrees within each member of the family of man. And they must be discovered, nurtured, and rewarded by those in whom custody of our institutions is reposed, including our institutions of higher learning.

Exercise 20
Managerial Effectiveness:
Assessing Individual Potential

LEARNING OBJECTIVES

1. To identify some critical dimensions of managerial effectiveness and success.
2. To understand the concept and operation of assessment centers in organizations.
3. To compare the assessment center approach with other means of identifying and selecting potential managers.

ADVANCE PREPARATION

Read the Overview. Using your own reading and experience, make a list (page 282) of dimensions (skills, attributes, etc.) that you think are important for managerial effectiveness and success. That is, if you were to be responsible for evaluating and selecting potential managers, what criteria would you want to measure?

OVERVIEW

A key factor in the effectiveness of the managerial subsystem, and ultimately in overall organizational success, is the ability to identify and select appropriate individuals for managerial positions. In some cases this process begins with initial hiring decisions; that is, an organization may hire only people who seem to have qualifications for moving upward in the managerial hierarchy. On the other hand, many organizations must hire people with particular technical skills necessary to carry out the operations that are required to produce goods and services. In any case, within the population of organizational members there is undoubtedly a distribution of skills or attributes that can be labeled managerial potential.

How are managers typically selected? In many organizations those with the longest period of service often automatically move into managerial positions. This practice assumes that their experience on the

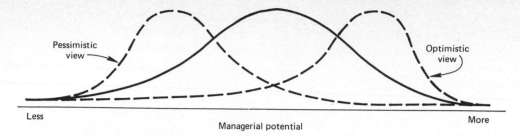

Pessimistic view

Optimistic view

Less — Managerial potential — More

job best suits them for a promotion to a higher level. Another approach is to move those with the highest degree of technical skill into managerial roles. As examples, the best sales person is made the sales manager or the most technically qualified engineer is promoted to engineering supervisor. Should the best accountant become the controller? Should the best teacher become the department head?

If the organization (the existing managers and staff personnel) recognizes that managerial potential may involve more than technical skill and/or experience, what approaches are used to identify and select people? The typical way, of course, is to rely on a supervisor's appraisal of the past performance and future potential of subordinates. For example, if a division manager is being promoted to headquarters, the manager's successor is likely to be picked from among those working directly for that person. Past performance will be important, and the odds are heavily in favor of the individual who most closely mirrors the boss in terms of values, temperament, skills, and overall approach to managing. We all tend to hire and promote in our own image.

If a more formal approach is used in the selection process, there will probably be reference to the file of historical information on each individual that is available in the personnel office. The file may include the results of paper-and-pencil tests taken at the hiring stage — including results on aptitudes, interests, psychological profile, mental ability, creativity, and similar dimensions. Another approach is to administer such tests at the time an important selection is to be made. In this way, current information is available to go along with whatever historical information is in the file. Historical information may also include education, previous experience, and letters of reference. Another step is to interview candidates for open positions in order to gather additional information. An interview allows the evaluator(s) an opportunity to ask questions concerning future behavior, that is, how the candidates may react in certain situations and what their individual approaches to management may be in general.

Another approach that has been receiving increasing attention in many organizations is the assessment center. The "center" is not necessarily a physical entity, but it is a centralized process of measuring managerial potential in an organized and detailed manner. The basic approach is to have employees go through a series of exercises or simulations as a group. Their behavior in these exercises is observed by trained assessors who typically are higher-level line managers. This approach allows the assessors to observe behavior in situations that are designed to be organizationally realistic. The candidates may discuss cases or critical incidents that demonstrate their analytical and communication skills. They may engage in simulation exercises that call for a variety of skills including overall leadership ability. They may be asked to respond to a typical in-basket of memos, letters, reports, etc., in a meaningful way in a limited time. (See Exercise 16, *Managerial Decision Making: Sentry Federal Savings and Loan Association.*) All the exercises are designed to provide insight into a candidate's behavior and potential in a concentrated period (1 or 2 days, usually). Emphasis is placed on those dimensions that will lead to effectiveness and success in the future.

> Assessment centers are most popular and seem to be most valid when the position for which the individuals are being considered is quite different from their current positions, for instance, the promotion of salesmen or technicians into management or from direct supervision to middle management where he or she must manage through others. Because the new job requires different skills or abilities than the present job, it is difficult for managers to assess the candidates' managerial aptitude prior to promotion. Thus, many failures result. By simulating, in an assessment center, the problems and challenges of the level of management for which the individual

is being considered, it is possible for management to determine the potential of the individual for the higher-level position.[1]

The objectives of an assessment center approach may be summarized as follows:

1. To select, from current employee populations, candidates with potential for either first-level or higher-level management
2. To identify management development needs
3. To stimulate self-development through self-insight
4. To train and develop both assessors and assessees

In order to maximize the benefits from an assessment center, considerable attention should be given to training assessors. The benefits to be gained from such training and from participation as an assessor include:

1. Improvement in interviewing skills
2. Broadening of observations skills
3. Increased appreciation of group dynamics and leadership styles
4. New insights into behavior
5. Strengthening of management skills through repeated working with in-basket case problems and other simulations
6. Broadening the repertoire of responses to problems
7. Establishment of normative standards by which to evaluate performance
8. Development of a more precise vocabulary with which to describe behavior[2]

Obviously, the more people that can be involved as assessors in the center approach to identifying managerial potential, the greater the benefit to the organization as a whole. Staff people (professional trainers in the personnel department, for example) or outside consultants may be used as assessors. However, it seems more appropriate, based on the benefits cited above, to use line managers. It is a learning experience for them and also enhances the probability that the results of this approach will be accepted and implemented. Evaluations only by staff and/or outside professionals would very likely be viewed with some suspicion and thus discounted in favor of overall impressions based on past experience with potential managers.

Figure 20-1 shows the typical steps in starting an assessment center, and Figure 20-2 shows potential exercises that might be used.

The following outline represents the principal steps in establishing an assessment center:

---

1. Determine objectives of program
2. Determine dimensions to be assessed
3. Select exercises that will bring out the dimensions
4. Design assessor training and assessment center program
5. Announce program, inform participants and assessors, handle administrative detail
6. Train assessors
7. Conduct center
8. Write summary reports on participants
9. Feedback to participants a summary of performance at center
10. Evaluate center
11. Set up procedures to validate center against a criterion of job success

While the task of starting a center may appear large and extremely time-consuming, it need not be. Numerous organizations have started operating centers less than one month after management gave the go ahead. Like most techniques that have considerable rational appeal to management, there usually is great pressure to get the program going after it is approved.

FIGURE 20-1   Steps in starting an assessment center. *Source:* William C. Byham, "The Training Center as an Aid in Management Development," *Training and Development Journal,* December 1971, p. 18.

---

[1]William C. Byham, "The Assessment Center as an Aid in Management Development," *Training and Development Journal,* December 1971, p. 11.

[2]Ibid., p. 12.

Depending upon the job requirements and the intent of the center, various combinations of these exercise categories can be employed. Many centers are designed to include more than one example of a given category; few centers are designed to include all examples.

1. *Background Interview*—Actual past behavior is appraised as if it were generated from an assessment exercise. The structure and use of the data collected in this type of interview make it completely different from the "typical" evaluation interview model.*

2. *Business Game*—A group of participants must organize and work cooperatively in order to solve a common problem. Typically the group is assigned the operation of a hypothetical business whose goal is to maximize profits.

3. *In-basket*—Each participant must handle the accumulated letters, notes, requests, etc., found in the in-basket of a job to which he or she has just been appointed. The participant must make decisions; delegate responsibility; write letters and reports; assign work; and plan, organize, and schedule his or her activities and those of his or her subordinates.

4. *Leaderless Group Discussion* (nonassigned roles)—A group of participants must organize in a functioning cooperative group to recommend solutions to one or more difficult management (or other) problem(s).

5. *Leaderless Group Discussion* (assigned roles)—A group of participants works together in a competitive setting to solve a problem where the solution must be acceptable to all.

6. *Analysis (Presentation and/or Group Discussion)*—The participant analyzes a considerable amount of data to recommend a solution to a complex problem. This solution is either presented formally to an assessor or to a group of participants who, after all presentations have been made, must decide on the best solution offered.

7. *Fact Finding and Decision Making*—The participant interviews an assessor (the "resource person") to determine facts relevant to making a decision about a hypothetical situation. The assessor then questions the participant who must defend his or her decision.

8. *Interview Simulation*—The participant plays the role of supervisor handling a difficult situation with a subordinate, customer, peer, etc., in a face-to-face encounter.

9. *Written Presentation*—The participant prepares a written report, writes letters to customers or other important individuals, etc.

10. *Oral Presentation*—The participant prepares and delivers a talk to a group of participants and assessors.

FIGURE 20-2 Potential categories of exercises that can be included in an assessment center. *Source:* Development Dimensions, Inc., Suite 149, 250 Mt. Lebanon Boulevard, Pittsburgh, Penna. 15234.

PROCEDURE

STEP 1
Meet in groups of five or six to share your individual lists of important managerial skills and attributes. Develop a composite list of the 15 most important items and record it on the form provided on page 282.

STEP 2
Transfer the items from your group composite list to the form on page 283, Self-Rating of Managerial Potential.

STEP 3

Fill in the form, rating yourself on the 15 dimensions. Use your past experience, including experience so far in this class, as a basis for your analysis.[3]

STEP 4

Share your self-ratings with the members of your group and invite feedback. Note areas of agreement and disagreement.

STEP 5

With the help of your group members, develop action plans for improving yourself on at least one of the dimensions on the self-rating form. Write out your plan in the space provided.

[3]"Even without special feedback opportunities built in, there is a great deal of evidence that most participants gain in self-insight from participating in assessment exercises and that this insight is fairly accurate. The evidence comes from comparing participant responses on self-evaluation questionnaires given after exercises with assessor evaluations. Correlations of .6 and higher based on large samples from several organizations have been found." Ibid., p. 12.

Important Managerial Skills and Attributes *(Criteria for Evaluating and Selecting Potential Managers)*

Individual list

1. _____
2. _____
3. _____
4. _____
5. _____
6. _____
7. _____
8. _____
9. _____
10. _____
11. _____
12. _____
13. _____
14. _____
15. _____

Group composite list

1. _____
2. _____
3. _____
4. _____
5. _____
6. _____
7. _____
8. _____
9. _____
10. _____
11. _____
12. _____
13. _____
14. _____
15. _____

Self-Rating of Managerial Potential

		Self-rating (check one)		
Dimension	*Poor*	*Fair*	*Good*	*Excellent*
1. _____	_____	_____	_____	_____
2. _____	_____	_____	_____	_____
3. _____	_____	_____	_____	_____
4. _____	_____	_____	_____	_____
5. _____	_____	_____	_____	_____
6. _____	_____	_____	_____	_____
7. _____	_____	_____	_____	_____
8. _____	_____	_____	_____	_____
9. _____	_____	_____	_____	_____
10. _____	_____	_____	_____	_____
11. _____	_____	_____	_____	_____
12. _____	_____	_____	_____	_____
13. _____	_____	_____	_____	_____
14. _____	_____	_____	_____	_____
15. _____	_____	_____	_____	_____
Overall potential	_____	_____	_____	_____

Action plan(s) for improvement:

SUMMARY AND CONCEPTUALIZATION

You have experienced part of the process of designing an assessment center—determining important dimensions for predicting managerial effectiveness. If your self-rating was based partially on your experience in exercises in this course, you have approximated another aspect of the assessment center approach to evaluation. The key element is evaluation of performance in activities that are as similar as possible to future managerial roles. Feedback from others and action planning are also important elements of the overall process. Increased self-awareness, plus feedback from peers and assessors, can be extremely useful in designing personal programs of education and experience in order to increase knowledge and skill.

A number of the exercises in this course could be used in assessing managerial potential. Think back over your experience so far and try to determine who in the class, in your opinion, would be the best managers. Do you think that the information you gained from observing their behavior would improve the selection process, when compared with more traditional methods, such as performance on the job, letters of recommendation, or personal interviews? The answer for most people seems to be yes but they are not entirely sure why. These and other questions about assessment centers are covered in detail in an article by Ann Howard. The following material is summarized from that article.[4]

One of the primary questions is why the assessment center approach works at all when most of the procedures used to predict future job success have not proved very effective, by themselves, in the past. For example, projective tests, interviews, and personality tests have dubious reliability and validity. Situational tests are still in an embryonic stage and have not always been successful in predicting performance. And there is some evidence that prediction may get less, rather than more, successful when more than a few variables are included. In spite of all these potential drawbacks, there is increasing evidence that assessment centers work.

The key elements are determining relevant dimensions to test, designing multiple methods of assessing those dimensions (including realistic situational tests), and using multiple assessors in the evaluation process. In reviewing assessment centers in a number of organizations, the following managerial dimensions seem to be important: (1) leadership, (2) organizing and planning skills, (3) decision making, (4) oral and written communication skills, (5) initiative, (6) energy, (7) analytical ability, (8) resistance to stress, (9) use of delegation, (10) behavior flexibility, (11) human relations competence, (12) originality, (13) controlling ability, (14) self-direction, and (15) overall potential. A variety of tests and exercises designed to measure these dimensions is shown in Figure 20-2. Assessment centers emphasize situational tests because they simulate the type of work that the candidate will be exposed to and they allow performance to be observed under somewhat realistic conditions. Actual samples of behavior are used in the assessment process rather than inferences from less realistic tests.

An important question is how the people are picked to participate in assessment centers. If they are nominated by their supervisors, there is at least a slight contradiction because a major purpose of the whole concept is to find a better way of assessing managerial potential than that of relying on the supervisor's judgment. Other approaches to selection include self-nomination, peer nomination, or routine identification of all people at certain levels in organizations. Formalized programs of inventorying people's skills and attributes should help prevent individuals from "getting lost" in the system.

Preliminary evidence seems to indicate substantial reliability and validity for assessment center evaluations. It appears that there is typically substantial agreement among raters on the best candidates. Based on long-range research in several organizations, reasonably good evidence also indicates that future managerial success can be predicted. Therefore, it seems appropriate to continue the development of the assessment center approach. It seems that situational tests contribute substantially to the validity of this method of prediction. Also, the comprehensive assessment procedure, based on a number of items, is clearly superior to the use of any one specific component. However, much work needs to be done on

[4]Ann Howard, "An Assessment of Assessment Centers," *Academy of Management Journal*, March 1974, pp. 115–134.

developing a variety of assessment center components and integrating them in a meaningful way.

The assessment center approach includes some potential problems that should be considered explicitly. For example, people who do well in an assessment center may become "crown princes or princesses," and future managerial success may be a self-fulfilling prophecy. Once an individual is identified as "outstanding," there may be no way to lose. On the other hand, poor performance in an assessment center may be a kiss of death; such candidates may find it impossible to get back in the mainstream in the future. The concentrated attention in an assessment center may be too stressful for some people, even though resistance to stress is one of the dimensions of managerial effectiveness. Some contend that the assessment center approach will result in conformity in organizations and will eliminate the unusual and potentially imaginative managers. The research evidence does not seem to support this contention; at least one study showed assessments correlated negatively with conformity. However, conformity may be more a function of nominating "appropriate" people than of the assessment process.

A formalized assessment center approach to identifying managerial potential can be costly. Therefore, for smaller organizations a joint venture may be a useful way to spread the design/development costs enough to make it feasible.

One important caution is that predicting individual success is risky at best. Unrealistic expectations will lead to disappointment. The careful, comprehensive, systematic approach of assessment centers seems to increase the probability of success in prediction. It is an improvement over other, more traditional methods, but it is not foolproof; some mistakes are inevitable.

Basing her findings on a thorough analysis of experience and research to date, Howard concludes that, although there may be some unanswered questions, the assessment center approach does offer considerable improvement over traditional selection processes. It has a great deal of face validity because it is based on assessment of behavior in activities that are quite similar to actual job requirements. It measures managerial potential based on criteria that are directly relevant to actual jobs in the organization. By including many or all managers in the assessing process, it can have a number of benefits in addition to that of selecting the most appropriate managerial candidates. All in all, it appears that this approach will see increasing use in the future.

This exercise had one additional major purpose. It is hoped that, through the process of developing your own list of important managerial skills and attributes, you have increased your own understanding of what it takes to be an effective manager. Furthermore, the exercise provided you with at least one action plan for improving your own effectiveness. We recommend that you look back at your own listing and action plans to see how well you are doing throughout your academic career. After all, you, more than your instructor or anyone else, will be the prime determinant of how you personally will do when you face an assessment center in your future career.

PART 7
COMPARATIVE ANALYSIS AND CONTINGENCY VIEWS

Throughout this book we have used exercises and cases that deal with various types of organizations—businesses, hospitals, universities, public schools, unions, governmental agencies, etc. In your daily life, you have the opportunity to analyze different organizational types. We are all continually involved in simplified comparative analyses of organizations. When selecting a college or university to attend, students will frequently investigate several institutions. They are likely to look at a limited number of dimensions upon which to compare schools: distance from home, tuition costs, academic reputation, where friends are going, and similar criteria. As consumers, we are continually making comparisons among organizations. Why do we select one automobile repair shop over another? Because it is closer, cheaper, or more reliable? Why does the homemaker shop at A&P, Safeway, or an independent grocer? Prospective employees compare a number of organizations for employment opportunities. Many will look only at the short-term rewards, such as salary and fringe benefits. Other, more sophisticated analysts, will scrutinize and compare organizations on many dimensions.

These are rather simple examples of comparative analysis of organizations. They are typically limited to only a few dimensions, usually those most directly pertinent to the observer's role as prospective student, customer, or employee.

For organization theorists and practicing managers, comparative analysis is much more comprehensive—all relevant dimensions should be considered in order to describe, analyze, or design effective organizations. The systems approach, as discussed in the Introduction (pages 7–9), provides an appropriate framework for comparative analysis. Organizations can be compared on the basis of their environmental suprasystems—the general societal milieu or culture—as well as their more specific task environments. Similarly, organizations can be compared in terms of the various subsystems that are part of any organization—goals and values, technology, structure, psychosocial, and managerial. In order to be meaningful for comparative analysis, more detailed dimensions or characteristics for each of these subsystems need to be identified. For example, in studying the psychosocial subsystem, we need to understand such things as the factors which motivate the people, group dynamics, status and role relationships, and leadership styles.

Contingency views are a natural outgrowth of comparative analysis based on the systems approach. These views recognize that each organization is in some ways unique and that managerial practices must be adapted to particular situations. They seek to understand the interrelationships within and among subsystems as well as between the organization and its environment and to define patterns of relationships or configurations of variables. Contingency views are a means of determining organizational design and managerial actions most appropriate for specific situations. For example, geographic dispersion and critical local knowledge suggest decentralization of decision making.

As Figure 1 indicates, organization and management theory has evolved continually. And, as in biological evolution, no radical transformation has ever eliminated the old and substituted the new. Rather, the resulting theories at each stage have been mutations of the old, retaining many of the more enduring concepts.[1] Contingency views are the most recent stage in this evolutionary process.

The exercises in this section require sophisticated analysis. However, your experience in previous exercises and the conceptual knowledge gained from texts and other sources should prepare you for this step. The exercises use the systems approach to help you understand and analyze total organizations, including their environmental suprasystems and various subsystems. Even more importantly, they are designed to help you develop your own understanding about the pattern of relationships among the various subsystems and to develop a contingency or situational view of managerial action. We will use two exercises to help us with this process.

Comparative Organizational Analysis: Hard Rock Prison and Sweet Joint Correctional Center asks you to use a systems approach in the comparative analysis of different types of correctional institutions.

Comparative Analysis and Contingency Views: Study of Specific Organizations provides you the opportunity to investigate an organization of your choice and to analyze it in terms of systems concepts and contingency views. Class members will study a number of other organizations, and therefore you will have substantial information to share for your comparative analysis.

[1] For a more complete discussion, see Fremont E. Kast and James E. Rosenzweig, *Organization and Management: A Systems Approach*, 2d ed., New York, McGraw-Hill, 1974, Chap. 19, "Comparative Analysis and Contingency Views," pp. 496–519.

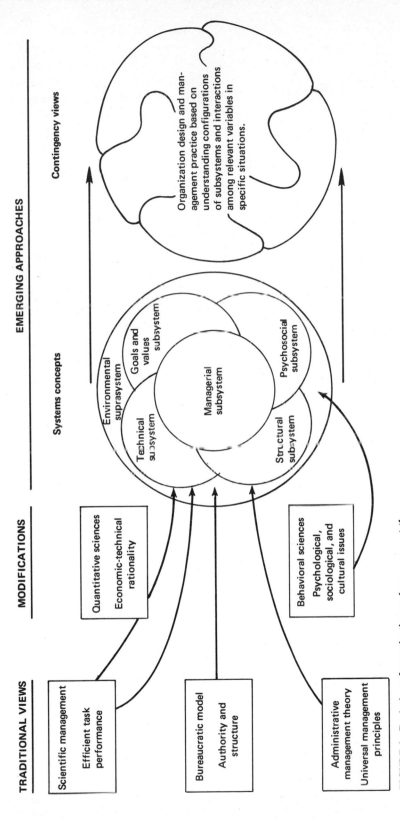

FIGURE 1 Evolution of organization and management theory.

Exercise 21
Comparative Organizational Analysis: Hard Rock Prison and Sweet Joint Correctional Center

LEARNING OBJECTIVES
1. To improve our ability to use a systems approach in the comparative analysis of organizations.
2. To increase our understanding of organizations in the correctional field, including the major problems they face.
3. To develop and refine your own conceptual model for studying different types of organizations in our society.

ADVANCE PREPARATION
Read the Overview and the Procedure. Then complete the forms entitled: My Analysis of Hard Rock Prison (page 304) and My Analysis of Sweet Joint Correctional Center (page 305). You may also want to do some outside reading to help you in your analysis. If so, you will find a great deal of discussion of correctional institutions in current newspapers, popular periodicals, and paperbacks.

OVERVIEW
To the outsider, all jails, prisons, and correctional institutions might be assumed to be the same. To the insider and to professionals in the field, there are significant differences. A vast array of correctional organizations comes under the direction of federal, state, and local authorities. They may be differentiated in terms of types of inmates and seriousness of crimes committed and vary according to maximum, medium, and minimum security. They range in size from the massive prison confining thousands of inmates to the small half-way houses with only 30 or 40 members.

In this exercise we will look at two representative types—Hard Rock Prison and Sweet Joint Correctional Center—but we should recognize that they represent only two types among many. But before we make this comparision, it will be helpful to review the historical development of correctional institutions, to look at some current data on the cost of maintaining the system, and to consider the role of prisons in society.

Historical development of correctional institutions. In earlier times, prisons were used to confine the accused. If found guilty, they were punished immediately—beheaded or hanged. For lesser crimes, they might be flogged, whipped, maimed, subjected to the stock and public ridicule, or banished. Punishment was direct and immediate in the form of death or pain, and those who survived were set free.

In the latter part of the eighteenth century there were reform movements, particularly among the Quakers in Pennsylvania, that substituted imprisonment for capital and physical punishment. This idea was the foundation for the development of the concept of imprisonment as punishment and led to the creation of the massive prisons in the United States and many other countries. The Quaker reformers met in the home of Benjamin Franklin to listen to a paper, presented by Benjamin Rush, which outlined the new program for the treatment of prisoners. Although humanitarian in its proposals, it did lead to rather harsh treatment of prisoners.

> It was Quaker belief that a man who had done wrong, and had been convicted of it, must be brought to realize that he had done wrong, and desire to do better; he must become penitent before he could be helped. To accomplish this the Quakers established solitary cells in the Walnut Street Jail of Philadelphia (1790) where the evildoers were confined alone to meditate over their sins and wrongdoings. This jail has been called the "birthplace" of the prison system, in its present meaning, not only in the United States but throughout the world.[1]

The very word "penitentiary" reflects this view of doing penance for the crime committed. Rehabilitation came through solitary meditation and seeking forgiveness and salvation from God.

In the early part of the nineteenth century, this concept of solitary confinement gradually gave way to the congregate system, first adopted at Auburn State Prison and Sing Sing in New York, where prisoners were allowed to work and eat together during the day but were confined to solitary cells at night. They were generally forbidden to converse with fellow inmates while working and eating. This system became the standard approach for most prisons and existed without substantial modification for the next 150 years. The high walls, rows of cell blocks, work areas, and other physical manifestations of this system remain in many prisons today.

During the nineteenth and twentiety centuries there have been trends toward more humane treatment of prisoners. In the earlier period, physical punishment was by no means lacking. Walking the treadmill, being flogged, carrying chains and cannonballs, and other inducements of physical pain were used. Gradually, punishments within the prison became less physical and more psychological. The threat of solitary confinement in a black hole with only bread and water was ever present for deviants. Even though there were reform movements for more humane treatment, the system remained basically the same with the emphasis on confinement and punishment.

There has been a gradual trend toward the establishment of differentiated institutions; maximum security prisons for hardened criminals who commit major crimes, minimum security prisons and work farms for lesser criminals, and juvenile correctional centers. Correctional systems have become much more complex, with a wide diversity of types. Slowly, emphasis has shifted from pure confinement and punishment toward treatment and rehabilitation of inmates.

Current data on corrections. Correctional institutions (ranging from prisons through half-way houses to probation and parole activities) are a part of the criminal justice system that is substantially hidden from public view. It rarely gets much publicity unless we have an Attica type of riot. Many of the major

---

[1] Karl Menninger, *The Crime of Punishment*, Viking, New York, 1968, p. 222.

prisons are located in remote rural areas out of sight. "Its invisibility belies the system's size, complexity, and crucial importance to the control of crime. Corrections consists of scores of different kinds of institutions and programs of utmost diversity in approach, facilities, and quality."[2]

Approximately 1.5 million persons are under correctional authority in the United States. Of this one-third, or 500,000, are in institutions—federal and state prisons, jails, juvenile training centers, etc., and the other million are supervised in the community on probation or parole. Approximately 2 percent of our male population is under some form of correctional authority. In the course of a year, our correctional system handles 2.5 million admissions and involves expenditures of $3 billion. But these expenditures are not evenly distributed between those in institutions and those in the community. Some 80 percent of the total expenditure is related to the one-third of the offenders who are incarcerated in institutions, while only 20 percent is expended in dealing with those who are on probation or parole. Society's costs of warehousing prisoners in institutions is very high indeed! It costs about one-tenth as much to supervise a person under probation or parole as it does to confine that person to an institution. Of the more than 120,000 people employed in corrections, only 24,000 have any connection with rehabilitation. The other 80 percent are involved with guard duty and custodial care of the 500,000 prisoners.

Responsibility for the administration of correction is very diffused in the United States. The federal government, all 50 states, the District of Columbia, and almost all cities engage in correctional activities. Typically, each level of government acts independently of the others. The federal government has no overall control over state corrections agencies. Although the states generally have responsibility for prisons and parole programs, probation is most frequently tied to court administration as a county or city operation. Counties generally do not have jurisdiction over the jails operated by cities and towns. Thus, the whole system of corrections is made up of relatively autonomous units that are not very well integrated. This lack of integration creates major problems of organization and administration.

The prison and society. Donald R. Cressey suggests that "the variety of organizational patterns characterizing modern prisons has grown out of changing conceptions, in the society as a whole, of what ought to be done to, with, and for criminals. . . . In contemporary American society, there are at least four distinguishable attitudes toward the control of crime, and each of them incorporates a program of action for correctional agencies and institutions."[3]

First there is the desire for *retribution*. Taking individual revenge is usually illegal, but we can act collectively to make the criminal suffer. It is hoped that such treatment will reinforce anticriminal values.

Second, society desires that the suffering imposed on criminals act as a *deterrent* to potential criminals. Swift and sure punishment will arouse in noncriminals a fear of transgression.

Third, there is the obvious desire for *protection* against the lawbreaker. The criminal must be physically isolated from the rest of the community for its own safety.

Finally, there is the social desire to reduce crime rates through *rehabilitation* or changing the antisocial behavior of criminals.

We can see these broad social values represented in our contemporary society, and they serve as primary determinants of the actual design and administration of our correctional institutions.

Two types of prison systems. Now that you have some historical background on the development of correctional institutions and a broader theoretical framework for looking at prison systems, we can turn to a more specific consideration of two alternative types for comparative purposes:

[2] *The Challenge of Crime in a Free Society*, A Report by the President's Commission on Law Enforcement and Administration of Justice, Washington, D.C., Government Printing Office, 1967, p. 159.

[3] Donald R. Cressey, "Prison Organizations" in James G. March (ed.), *Handbook of Organizations*, Chicago, Rand McNally, 1965, p. 1025.

The *punitive-custodial* type characterized by the maximum security prison that emphasizes the goals of punishment and confinement. We will identify this type as Hard Rock Prison.

The *rehabilitative-treatment* type characterized by the community correctional center which places minimal emphasis upon security and punishment and more emphasis on rehabilitation. We will identify this type as Sweet Joint Correctional Center.

In order to provide you with a general view of the nature of the organizational climate of these two types, we have provided some excerpts from current literature which describe their specific characteristics.

Hard Rock Prison

This is the traditional correctional institution characterized by thick walls, locked doors, and guards with machine guns in the towers. Such institutions, typically located in remote rural areas, emphasize confinement, custodial care, and security against escape. You have probably seen movies that depict this type of institution.

The following two excerpts provide some insights about these institutions.

LIFE IN THE JOINT IS THE LAST STOP*

"YOU TURN YOUR BRAIN OFF IN HERE"

Walla Walla—Jack Smith was 22 when he pulled his first burglary, got caught and was "busted" to the State Reformatory at Monroe. Now he's 35 and one of the long time clients of the Washington State Penitentiary at Walla Walla, an armed robber, escapee and stick-up artist.

He's been inside the "joint" so long that he refers to his brief releases in the free world as experiences which put him "outside my comfort zone."

Smith sat in the deserted office of a penitentiary guard just before lockup one night recently and tried to tell a reporter what it's like inside the state's last-stop prison.

He looked back over his 13 years of incarceration and concluded, "Trust and love is lost in here. Living in this kind of environment makes a cold-blooded person out of you.

"If they'd have sprung me six weeks after they put me in here the first time, I'd have gone out and never stolen another dime—that's how much the place scared me.

"From '62 until now I've been in the system and this system just destroys people.

"You have to become a little harder in order to live in a negative, violent society like this one. You get hurt over and over and you build a wall between you and feeling.

"My mother committed suicide while I was in here. After I got over the shock and loss, I wouldn't let myself care about it. I knew where she had been. I had been there myself about two years ago. I cut both wrists and my throat. I tried it three times in a couple of days. You get to where nothing can hurt you anymore.

"You turn your brain off when you come in here and you don't turn it on again until you leave. Your normal reactions are suppressed. You see a guy hang himself or get cut up and you suppress your feelings.

"You're living in a totally negative environment all the time. An unhappy one. You're living around violence.

*Hilda Bryant, *Seattle Post-Intelligencer*, May 4, 1975.

"I've packed a knife a lot of times but I never had to use it. But I've used my fists a lot. I was dumb and ornery. But now there's a lot of cutting and less using fists.

"It's a drug problem in here now more than crime. It used to be a small booze problem that led to fist fights but now it's a lot more serious—drugs lead to knife fights."

Fear walks with you daily in the penitentiary, he said. Fear of what the state will do with you and fear that you will be killed in a knife fight—maybe over a pack of smokes or a pittance of money you borrowed and you can't pay back. And fear that maybe you will have to kill somebody.

He talked of his wife from whom he is divorced. "If you're married and you are sent up you quit growing together. When you're in here and your wife's out on the street you start living differently. You become like your environment. You pick up traits and characteristics pretty quick.

"There's no solitude in here, no privacy. No way to get away from eyes but to fantasize. There is noise all the time. Doors are banging, guys are hollering or acting out or playing radios.

"You go a whole year without getting tagged and you go up before the parole board and they say you're conwise, you just got slick.

"You hate and become hostile. You hate them and plan little ways to kill them in your fantasies and all the time it is you, but you still hate the 'bulls' and the administration. But it is really that you hate the system."

"I think you lose your normal drives in here to achieve. Five years in and you're a long way down hill. This is a school of crime.

"You lose all your work habits. You become the best procrastinators in the world. You become a cold-blooded liar.

"You learn to live in this place by its values and norms and then you have to unlearn it all to make it back outside.

"There have been a few programs that got me to thinking about how programmed I am. I didn't know it had happened until it was too late. It's probably the last thing in the world a person wants to admit to themselves—that they're institutionalized."

He had been disillusioned by so-called rehabilitation programs in prison. He tried occupational training a decade ago when he was a first offender back in Monroe Reformatory.

"I went to an 18-month course in auto mechanics but when I got out I found out it was obsolete. I thought I had learned something. God, I was stupid!"

When he was in Shelton Diagnostic Center he said he called forth his best powers of appeal to "make them send me to Monroe instead of Walla Walla because Monroe is closer to civilization."

But he was sent to the state penitentiary in 1967. At first he could remember what it was like outside. "You remember some of the old places, the way you used to live. You dream about it. It's the only thing that keeps you going for a while.

"But in time it fades and you build fantasies to live on."

And finally, inevitably, you become institutionalized.

He said thoughtfully, "You sentenced me to the wrong place. I know how to live in an institution. It is out there that I can't make it."

REPORT ON ATTICA*

Forty-three citizens of New York State died at Attica Correctional Facility between September 9 and 13, 1971. Thirty-nine of that number were killed and more than 80 others were wounded by gunfire during the 15 minutes it took the State Police to retake the prison on September 13. With the exception of Indian massacres in the late 19th century, the State Police assault which ended the four-day prison uprising was the bloodiest one-day encounter between Americans since the Civil War.

The New York State Special Commission on Attica was asked to reconstruct the events of those September days and to determine why they happened. . . .

On the day the Attica uprising began, with smoke still pouring from parts of the prison

---

*Attica, The Official Report of the New York State Special Commission on Attica, New York, Bantam Books, Inc., 1972, pp. xi, 2–5.

destroyed by inmates, Vincent Mancusi, then the superintendent of the correctional facility in western New York State, shook his head in disbelief and asked: "Why are they destroying their home?"

Their home was a complex of barred cells 6 feet wide, 9 feet long, and 7 feet high, in buildings hidden from public view by a solid gray stone wall 30 feet high and 2 feet thick, not very different from, and certainly no worse than, New York State's five other maximum security prisons. But it did not have to be better or worse than the others for it to explode, as it did, in September 1971. For the Atticas of this country have become lethal crucibles in which the most explosive social forces of our society are mixed with the pettiness and degradation of prison life, under intense pressure of maintaining "security."

The titles "correctional facility," "superintendent," "correction officer," and "inmate," which the Legislature bestowed on the prisons, wardens, guards, and prisoners in 1970 were new. But these euphemisms expressed goals that dated back to the founding of the modern prison system in the early 19th century by men who believed that prisons should serve the purpose of turning prisoners into industrious and well-behaved members of society. Prison administrators throughout the country have continued pledging their dedication to the concept of rehabilitation while continuing to run prisons constructed in the style and operated in the manner of the 19th-century walled fortresses. "Security" has continued to be the dominant theme: the fantasy of reform legitimitized prisons but the functionalism of custody has perpetuated them.

The rhetoric about rehabilitation could not, however, deceive the men brought together inside the walls; the inmates, 54 percent black, 37 percent white and 8.7 percent Spanish-speaking, almost 80 percent from the cities' ghettos, and the correction officers, all white and drawn from the rural areas in which we build our prisons.

For inmates, "correction" meant daily degradation and humiliation: being locked in a cell for 14 to 16 hours a day; working for wages that averaged 30 cents a day in jobs with little or no vocational value; having to abide by hundreds of petty rules for which they could see no justification. It meant that all their activities were regulated, standardized, and monitored for them by prison authorities and that their opportunity to exercise free choice was practically nonexistent: their incoming and outgoing mail was read, their radio programs were screened in advance, their reading material was restricted, their movements outside their cells were regulated, they were told when to turn lights out and when to wake up, and even essential toilet needs had to be taken care of in view of patrolling officers. Visits from family and friends took place through a mesh screen and were preceded and followed by strip searches probing every orifice of the inmate's body.

In prison, inmates found the same deprivation that they had encountered on the street: meals were unappetizing and not up to nutritional standards. Clothing was old, ill-fitting, and inadequate. Most inmates could take showers only once a week. State-issued clothing, toilet articles, and other personal items had to be supplemented by purchases at a commissary where prices did not reflect the meager wages inmates were given to spend. To get along in the prison's economy, inmates resorted to "hustling," just as they had in trying to cope with the economic system outside the walls.

The sources of inmate frustration and discontent did not end there: medical care, while adequate to meet acute health needs, was dispensed in a callous, indifferent manner by doctors who feared and despised most of the inmates they treated; inmates were not protected from unwelcome homosexual advances; even the ticket to freedom for most inmates—parole—was burdened with inequities or at least the appearance of inequity.

For officers, "correction" meant a steady but monotonous 40-hour-a-week job, with a pension after 25 years' service. It meant maintaining custody and control over an inmate population which had increasing numbers of young men, blacks, and Puerto Ricans from the urban ghettos, unwilling to conform to the restrictions of prison life and ready to provoke confrontation, men whom the officers could not understand and were not trained to deal with. It meant keeping the inmates in line, seeing that everything ran smoothly, enforcing the rules. It did not mean, for most officers, helping inmates to solve their problems or to become citizens capable of returning to society. For the correction officers, who were always outnumbered by inmates, there was a legitimate concern about security; but that concern was not served by policies which created frustration and tension far more dangerous than the security risks they were intended to avert.

Above all, for both inmates and officers, "correction" meant an atmosphere charged with racism. Racism was manifested in job assignments, discipline, self-segregation in the inmate mess halls, and in the daily interaction of inmate and officer and among the inmates themselves. There was no escape within the walls from the growing mistrust between white middle America and the residents of urban ghettos. Indeed, at Attica, racial polarity and mistrust were magnified by the constant reminder that the keepers were white and the kept were largely black and Spanish-speaking. The young black inmate tended to see the white officer as the symbol of a racist, oppressive system which put him behind bars. The officer, his perspective shaped by his experience on the job, knew blacks only as belligerent unrepentant criminals. The result was a mutual lack of respect which made communication all but impossible.

In the end, the promise of rehabilitation had become a cruel joke. If anyone was rehabilitated, it was in spite of Attica, not because of it. Statistics show that three-quarters of the men who entered prison in New York State in the sixties had been exposed to the "rehabilitative" experience in prison before. If Attica was a true model, then prisons served no one. Not the inmates, who left them more embittered than before. Not the correction officers, who were locked into the same confinement and asked to perform an undefined job made impossible by the environment. Not the prison officials, who became accomplices in maintaining the fiction that maximum security prisons serve a useful purpose. And not the public, which requires penal institutions that serve a useful role in the reduction of crime. . . .

The only bright spots at Attica were two experimental programs available to less than 4 percent of the inmates—the Division of Vocational Rehabilitation (DVR) and work release. These programs showed that when inmates were given responsibility and the opportunity to engage in meaningful activity, rehabilitation was possible. . . .

Most of the inmates now at Attica will be returned to the streets, and every risk that the prisons have declined to take in affording these men the freedom and opportunity to develop a sense of self-control will be passed to the public. There is no rebuttal to the testimony of one inmate shortly after his release from Attica:

> The taxpayers paid thousands of dollars per year to keep me incarcerated. They didn't get anything for their money. It was a waste.

Sweet Joint Correctional Center

There is increasing sentiment for moving away from large prisons located in remote rural areas toward much smaller community-based correctional centers. The following excerpts suggest this trend. The first is the summary recommendations of the President's Commission on Law Enforcement and Administration of Justice. It is followed by several other excerpts describing the organizational climate in such institutions.

A MODEL FOR INSTITUTIONS*
The Commission's national survey of corrections and other studies showed it how far many jurisdictions still were from optimal uses of institutions. It was disturbed to find that much planning for institutional construction, and the attitudes of many officials concerned, indicated that these conditions were not likely to be radically changed in the future.

The Commission believes that there is, therefore, value in setting forth, in the form of a "model," the changes that it sees as necessary for most correctional institutions. There will, of course, continue to be special offender problems that must be dealt with in other kinds of institutions. But in general new institutions should be of the sort represented by the model, and old institutions should as far as possible be modified to incorporate its concepts.

The model institution would be relatively small, and located as close as possible to the areas from which it draws its inmates, probably in or near a city rather than in a remote location.

*The Challenge of Crime in a Free Society, A Report by the President's Commission on Law Enforcement and Administration of Justice, Washington, D.C., Government Printing Office, 1967, pp. 172–174, 297.

While it might have a few high-security units for short-term detention under unusual circumstances, difficult and dangerous inmates would be sent to other institutions for longer confinement.

Architecturally, the model institution would resemble as much as possible a normal residential setting. Rooms, for example, would have doors rather than bars. Inmates would eat at small tables in an informal atmosphere. There would be classrooms, recreation facilities, dayrooms, and perhaps a shop and library.

In the main, however, education, vocational training, and other such activities would be carried on in the community, or would draw into the institution community-based resources. In this sense the model would operate much like such programs as the Highfields and Essexfields projects. Its staff, like probation and parole officers, would be active in arranging for participation by offenders in community activities and in guiding and counseling them.

Some offenders might be released after an initial period of detention for diagnosis and intensive treatment. The model institution would permit correctional officials to invoke short-term detention—overnight or for a few days—as a sanction or discipline, or to head off an offender from prospective trouble. Even if initial screening and classification indicated that long-term incarceration was called for, and an offender was, therefore, confined in another facility, the community-based institution could serve as a halfway house or prerelease center to ease his transition to community life. It could indeed serve as the base for a network of separate group homes and residential centers to be used for some offenders as a final step before complete release.

The prototype proposed here, if followed widely, would help shift the focus of correctional efforts from temporary banishment of offenders to a carefully devised combination of control and treatment. If supported by sufficiently flexible laws and policies, it would permit institutional restraint to be used only for as long as necessary, and in carefully graduated degree rather than as a relatively blind and inflexible process.

A final advantage of the concept suggested here is that institutions that are small, close to metropolitan areas, and highly diversified in their programs provide excellent settings for research and experimentation and can serve as proving grounds for needed innovations. Not only are they accessible to university and other research centers, but their size and freedom from restrictions foster a climate friendly to inquiry and to the implementation of changes suggested by it.

Federal and state governments should finance establishment of model, small unit correctional institutions for flexible, community-oriented treatment.

Even in institutions committed to longer term custody, many steps can be taken of this model to improve capacity to contribute to the reintegration of offenders. The most fundamental of these changes may be summed up as the establishment of a collaborative regime in which staff and inmates work together toward rehabilitative goals, and unnecessary conflict between the two groups is avoided.

Institutional communities in which persons are kept against their will tend to generate tension and conflict between the inmates and the staff. The task of preparing the inmate for reintegration into the community becomes lost in elaborate forms of competition, in covert and corrupting reciprocities between guards and inmate leaders, and in forced maintenance of passivity on the part of inmates. This encourages anger toward—and yet complete dependence on—institutional authority.

The collaborative approach seeks to reverse this too common pattern. The custodial staff, for example, is recognized as having great potential for counseling functions, both informally with individual inmates and in organized group discussions. Administrators and business staff likewise have been brought into the role of counselors and assigned rehabilitative functions in some programs. This collaborative style of management is more readily achieved if the institution staff is augmented by persons from the free community with whom inmates can identify. This involves recruiting outsiders who can help the inmate to develop motivation for needed vocational, avocational, and other self-improvement goals. Volunteers and subprofessional aides can be as useful in institutions as in community-based corrections.

Another important dimension of the collaborative concept is the involvement of offenders themselves in treatment functions. Group counseling sessions, for example, provide opportunities for inmates to help each other, through hard and insistent demands for honesty in self-examination, demands that cannot be made with equal force and insight by staff, whose members have not had personal experience in the world of criminal activity. The loosening of inmate-to-staff and of inmate-to-inmate communication tends to reduce the inmate politician's power. Moreover, the "rat" complex, which brings great social stigma and physical danger to an inmate who cooperates with staff in traditional institutions, is greatly diminished.

A delicate balance is involved between giving inmates a meaningful role to play in the life of the institution, and allowing them to usurp authority that should only be carried by staff. The line is still being fashioned in most institutions today, and more experience will be required to decide where it lies in specific areas such as assignment of inmates to job, work, and living units and decisions involving discipline and security.

All institutions should be run to the greatest possible extent with rehabilitation a joint responsibility of staff and inmates. Training of correctional managers and staff should reflect this mode of operation. The wholesale strengthening of community treatment of offenders and much rehabilitation are the main lines where action is needed to make correctional treatment more effective in reducing recidivism. Correctional programs of the future should be built around small centers, located in the communities they serve. These would be better suited than present facilities for flexible treatment, combining the short-term commitment sufficient for most offenders with a variety of partial release or community corrections programs in which job training, educational, and counseling services would be provided or coordinated by the center's staff. Careful screening and classification of offenders is essential so that handling can be individualized to suit the needs in each case. So, too, is greater emphasis on evaluation of the effect of programs on different offenders.

Much can be done to advance corrections toward such goals with existing facilities, but large increases in skilled diagnostic, rehabilitation, and research personnel are needed immediately. A new regime should be inaugurated in institutions to involve all staff, and encourage inmates to collaborate as much as possible, in rehabilitation. Prison industries must give more meaningful work experience. Counseling, education, and vocational training programs for inmates must be strengthened. Greater use should be made of release for work and education, of halfway houses, and of similar programs to ease the offender's reintegration in society.

HALFWAY HOUSES GIVE CONVICTS A CHANCE TO WORK IT OUT*

The big, old house is airy rather than spacious, informal rather than cozy, comfortable in an austere way.

It's less scabby than the two that flank it on the corner of 11th Avenue and Spruce Street. Together, the three are known as Pioneer Fellowship House.

Thirty-three convicts live there. They all have jobs and pay their own way although they are still doing time. It's called work-release. It's community-based corrections.

Tommy Curtis, 34, has live there since January, 1974. Before that, he lived in the Washington State Penitentiary and the Monroe Reformatory for a total of 15 years.

An armed robber and consummate conman, no one gave him more than two weeks "outside."

Fifteen months later Curtis is married, buying a home, has an eight-year-old daughter and is head chef in one of Seattle's good restaurants.

Curtis tilted back in his chair at Pioneer House, a private institution, and "flashed back" to that day he entered the halfway house, nervous and acutely aware that he was viewed by the staff and other residents as a poor risk.

"When I first came out I was like a kid. All I'd ever done was capering. It kind of freaks you out to come to a place where they want you to think for yourself instead of them doing the thinking for you.

"So they don't let you go out for the first week. They try to get you to relax instead of throwing you right outside and telling you to 'go get it.'

"This is a good program. They put me back where I should have been.

"If they had put me back out on the streets from the pen I seriously think I'd be packin' a gun again.

"It helped me get back into the community without my being paranoid like I always was before."

---

*Hilda Bryant, *Seattle Post-Intelligencer,* May 4, 1975.

Curtis has been paroled twice directly to the streets. The first time he was "busted" after five months, the second time, inside of a year. Of those times, he said, "It took me four months just to get over that weird feeling that everybody was looking at me and as soon as I got over that I was capering again."

His eyes ranged around the bright, clean office of Pioneer House supervisor Harry Bauermeister. "This place is like a refuge if you need it to be. It helped me break back into society and that's hard. Probably one guy in four doesn't make it because of the initial shock.

"I almost ran once. That was my normal pattern. I really don't know why I didn't—unless it was because I had a friend I'd been able to rap with. And I was just tired of doing time. And there were friends at work who cared that I stay straight.

"It's like night and day—being here and being inside. But I've stopped relating to the penitentiary now. That's something thousands are never able to accomplish.

"Maybe that's why I'm still out here."

Curtis said he had never worked more than four months at a stretch in his entire life before he came to the halfway house. But you can't stay in the halfway house without a job. Each resident pays $5.50 a day for board and room.

When Curtis was in the State Reformatory he cost the taxpayers $6,200 a year. When he was in the penitentiary it cost taxpayers $7,000 a year to support him. Work release, state prison officials say, costs the taxpayers about half the cost of warehousing adult offenders.

Curtis said, "We all pay $165 a month to stay here but in comparison to inside the joint most dudes would pay $300 a month to stay here.

"If a guy can make it out here for five weeks he's free. Because that's when you move up into phase five and you have more social outing time.

"When you've been here three months you move up into unlimited social outing hours—that's phase seven. In phase seven you can apply for early parole hearing.

"It's like graduating. Now I'm as far as I can go. I went from a dishwasher to head chef at a nice restaurant. I was kind of like a 17-year-old because I'd never gone straight and I had to learn the system. A lot of ordinary things were sort of perplexing.

"In a way this is a bummer because we're supposed to be perfect and not make mistakes. But we have the same problems everybody else out here does. For example a speeding ticket can put us back in jail. For the normal man on the street it would just be a ticket.

"We're supposed to be super. It only takes one person to break the program."

But the pressure for the offender to live straighter when he is on the "outside" than a free person is required to is clearly worth it to Curtis. He said, "All a prison is is a warehouse, a jungle. It's a sad way for a human to have to live. In a penitentiary you are part of a mass. Out here you become an individual again."

MODERN PRISON IS A BETTER PLACE TO LIVE*

Arlington, Snohomish County—Three men work in a lush, organic garden where pea vines are 4 feet high.

Another threesome tosses a football on the spacious green lawn circled by tall, cool evergreens.

One man vacuums a car in the warm sunshine.

A couple more shoot pool in a well-equipped gymnasium.

Another reads in the lounge with its handsome beamed ceiling.

Some do kitchen work and grounds maintenance.

These are some of the 60 convicted felons serving "time" at the Indian Ridge Treatment Center near here.

There are no fences, walls or guard towers.

"We don't always lock the doors," said Donald Look, the superintendent.

A few miles away in the woods, a crew works for the State Department of Natural Resources. Sprinkled throughout the nearby communities of Everett, Marysville, Lake Stevens and this town are 10 men on fulltime work-release jobs. They all have weekends off.

One man working swing shift drives his own car to his job. He makes $4.40 an hour. Most of it will go to pay his family back for lawyer fees.

*Marjorie Jones, *The Seattle Times*, July 1, 1974.

Eight are attending classes at Everett Community College.

Some are in the small classroom in the complex of buildings that make up this institution, the most modern prison in the state—perhaps in the country.

The Indian Ridge program operates on a concept of incarceration and treatment similar to that of the juvenile youth camp, which it was prior to its transition to an adult facility.

Look said the Indian Ridge program may become a model for community-based corrections of the future.

"We've made a good start," he said.

Look, largely responsible for the switch to an adult corrections facility with full backing from Olympia, said the center will have been in operation a year on July 9.

There has not been an escape.

"We're way overdue," said the realistic Look, an experienced corrections professional.

Why they don't run may be attributed to a combination of factors, Look believes.

Some men are genuinely concerned that the program continue to be available to them and others. Escapes might reduce its effectiveness.

The obvious reason is that if they have to spend "time" they'd "much rather spend it here than any other institution," as one 19-year-old prisoner said.

"I'd say a person would have to be a fool to run," said a Renton man, 20, committed for grand larceny. "He could end up in Walla Walla (the penitentiary)."

But the 19-year-old is not happy. He's been here 8½ months and can't get work or school release. He had a drinking infraction.

"You only get that (work release) if you're perfect," he said.

But he feels the program has done him good. The staff is "tight" however, he said. They are supposed to take a head check every two hours, but they take one every hour, he said.

Another complained that the staff, used to counseling juveniles in the former program, doesn't know how to counsel adults. "They baby-sit us," he said.

The security rooms, of which there are six, have been used fewer than a dozen times during the year. Only one man has had to be transferred to a maximum-security prison. That was for use of marijuana.

The operation of Indian Ridge has been geared to succeed. The clientele has been carefully selected, ranging in age from 18 to 34. Screened out are men who have committed crimes of violence, such as murder, assault and sex offenses. Only those on first commitments are accepted.

Forty-five per cent have drug commitments. Others are for burglary, auto theft, robbery, grand larceny, forgery and second degree assault. Six federal prisoners have been placed here, four on charges related to draft evasion.

All the men at Indian Ridge have spent some time at the State Corrections Center at Shelton.

Before they are accepted at Indian Ridge the men must have been reviewed by the classification staff at Shelton and approved for transfer by the corrections office in Olympia and by Look.

One 25-year-old who worked in the organic garden is a business-administration graduate who had his own business in California. He was convicted of a marijuana charge.

"I feel this program is a step in the right direction," he said. "It puts some humanity into imprisonment."

He has freedom to work in the garden he loves and is getting into yoga.

Another man who works in the garden has a couple of years of college. He also was "busted" for selling marijuana.

Some men resent the fact they can't go out at nights and even Look believes it would be possible with many of the men to go unescorted. But the 25-year-old said he thought that would "make it too easy."

They can't umpire Little League games without staff escort.

Look said there are a large number of men in state prisons who do not need the confinement of a maximum-security institution.

"This may be the solution," he said.

The program is not too different from that of the youth camp. Most of the men are only a few years older, but they are expected to behave as adults. There is a counselor for every five men here, and a program set up for each individual.

The cost of operation is $10,000 a year per resident. At the reformatory the cost per year is $7,785 per year, and there is only one counselor for every 70 residents.

The freedom of Indian Ridge compared to the security of locks, fences, guard towers and uniforms at a maximum-security prison is "quite a transition" for most of the men.

But the 21-year-old committed for marijuana sale said, "You can't see them, but the fences are still there. They're invisible."

It's tougher staying behind the invisible walls, a 22-year-old committed for burglary said. It requires more discipline.

The biggest gripe is "doing time." A lot of the men (Look included) feel that there comes a time in a man's imprisonment when he is "ready" to leave. Further imprisonment will only make adjustment on the outside more difficult.

But release is still dependent upon the State Board of Prison Terms and Parole, which has the authority to override any recommendations by staff.

Another gripe is "crew," that is the work crew in the woods. In cold, wet, winter months, they bend over planting trees all day. Many of the men hate it.

The men get $25 monthly gratuity when they work plus $1 a day incentive. They think they deserve more.

There are two dormitories with 16 men in each. As the men progress they are moved to more privileges and into the single rooms.

When the institution was a juvenile facility there were a couple of incidents in the community, Look said, but there have been no problems with the adults.

He attributes this largely to the staff's job of public relations.

"The community was fearful at first but everything has worked out well," the superintendent said.

Lyle Poolman, vocational-training coordinator, said the community has cooperated beautifully in providing jobs for the men.

"In the past two weeks I've had a half a dozen employers contact me for more of the fellows (prisoners) to work for them," Poolman said.

PROCEDURE

In this exercise you are asked to use a systems approach to compare Hard Rock Prison and Sweet Joint Correctional Center. In order to facilitate comparison and discussion, use the model set forth in this book:

Environmental system
Goals and values subsystem
Technical subsystem
Structural subsystem
Psychosocial subsystem
Managerial subsystem

STEP 1

Read the Overview, including the excerpts. Before class, complete the forms, My Analysis of Hard Rock Prison and My Analysis of Sweet Joint Correctional Center (pages 304 and 305). Use descriptive words and phrases to depict the key characteristics of each organization.

STEP 2

Meet in groups of five or six and develop a group composite of your comparative analysis. Refine your descriptions and record them on the form, Comparative Analysis of Hard Rock Prison and Sweet Joint Correctional Center (page 306).

STEP 3

Select one group to report on its analysis of Hard Rock Prison and another group to report on its analysis of Sweet Joint Correctional Center.

STEP 4

The entire class participates in discussion.

My Analysis of Hard Rock Prison

Environmental system

Goals and values

Technology

Structure

Psychosocial system

Managerial system

My Analysis of Sweet Joint Correctional Center

Environmental system

Goals and values

Technology

Structure

Psychosocial system

Managerial system

Comparative Analysis of Hard Rock Prison and Sweet Joint Correctional Center

	Hard Rock	Sweet Joint
Environment		
Goals and values		
Technology		
Structure		
Psychosocial		
Managerial		

SUMMARY AND CONCEPTUALIZATION

Using a systems approach to compare these two types of correctional institutions should be relatively straightforward. For example, there are many differences in the environment of these two institutions. Hard Rock Prison is generally a closed institution with tight boundaries separating it from society. The philosophy seems to be to isolate inmates as much as possible, "lock them up and throw away the key," and to severely limit interactions with the outside world. In contrast, Sweet Joint Correctional Center has semipermeable boundaries. Although inmates are confined, there is substantial interaction with the environment. They are closer to the communities in which they previously lived; families and friends are closer and are encouraged to continue their contacts with inmates; and work and educational release programs are typical.

These environmental relationships affect, and are manifestations of, the major differences in goals and values. The goals of Hard Rock are confinement and punishment, reflecting the view that criminals have done wrong and must suffer. The goals of Sweet Joint are therapeutic treatment and rehabilitation, reflecting the view that the deviate behavior of the inmates is a product of social conditions as much as their own doing. The goal is to help inmates adjust to the requirements that society will impose on them when they are released. The assumption is that in a more open system, the necessary behavioral and social adjustments can be accomplished more effectively and efficiently.

Perhaps the most difficult area to deal with is the technical subsystem. If we define technology as the application of knowledge to the effective and efficient performance of tasks, we can begin to see the differences. In Hard Rock the technical subsystem is geared to the goals of confinement and punishment. The physical manifestations of the technology are quite evident—high, thick walls, cell blocks, solitary confinement, and armed guards on the watch towers. This is a rather simple, stable, and easily applied technology. It can be uniform for all prisoners. We have excellent hard technology for meeting the goals of confinement and punishment.

In contrast, for Sweet Joint, where the goals are treatment and rehabilitation, the technology is much more complex, diverse, and uncertain in its results. Here we are dealing with behavior change—where methods are ill defined and results are difficult to measure. Rather than all inmates being treated alike, they must be treated individually. This responsibility involves education and reeducation, motivation to adopt more socially acceptable behavior, development of positive reward systems to help modify behavior, and a host of other means of changing behavior. Typical techniques include individual counseling, group processes, and resocialization. It is obvious that Sweet Joint is dealing with a much softer technology than Hard Rock.

Goals, values, and technology have a major impact on the structure of these two organizations. Generally, the structure of Hard Rock fits the more traditional bureaucratic/mechanistic model, whereas Sweet Joint is more flexible, less structured, less hierarchical, and typical of the organic/adaptive type. You probably had little difficulty in describing significant differences in their psychosocial and managerial systems.

After looking at each of these major subsystems, it is important to recognize how they interact to create a total organizational system. Hard Rock Prison is a total system in which the environmental relationships and characteristics of the internal subsystems are interrelated. It would be difficult to change any one of the subsystems without having to make substantial modifications in the others. For example, it is generally acknowledged that the goals cannot possibly be changed from confinement and punishment toward rehabilitation and treatment in traditional Hard Rock Prison. The physical characteristics and other subsystems are typically insurmountable obstacles.

Sweet Joint Correctional Center is also a total system in which the various subsystems must be compatible if the goals of rehabilitation and treatment are to be achieved. In many ways the two types of institution, with totally different systems, are as unlike, in many respects, as a mass-production assembly line producing automobiles is from a laboratory engaged in cancer research.

This disparity points up one of the major dilemmas in the field of corrections. It is difficult, if not impossible, to establish a correctional facility that can effectively accomplish the diverse goals of confinement and punishment *as well as* treatment and rehabilitation. These goals are not compatible within the same institution. Therefore, it is likely that in the future we will move toward even greater diversity among correctional institutions. Hard Rock Prisons will remain as human warehouses to protect society from habitual criminals who have little potential for rehabilitation. Sweet Joint Correctional Center will minimize the emphasis on confinement and will be geared to rehabilitation. Through better understanding of human behavior, we hope we will be able to develop more effective rehabilitation technologies that will greatly reduce the number of people warehoused in Hard Rock and increase the number that can become acceptable members of society.

Exercise 22
Comparative Analysis and Contingency Views: Study of Specific Organizations

LEARNING OBJECTIVES

1. To describe a variety of organizations in terms of basic characteristics.
2. To compare and contrast organizational types in terms of dimensions common to all organizations.
3. To increase our understanding of contingency views of organization design and management practice.

ADVANCE PREPARATION

Read the Overview and the Procedure. Complete Step 1. With a partner, and utilizing your past experience and fieldwork, fill in the form, Analysis of a Specific Organization (page 316), for a specific organization of your choice. It may be helpful for you to do additional research and reading about your selected organizational type.[1]

OVERVIEW

In the previous exercise, Hard Rock Prison and Sweet Joint Correctional Center, you were provided with a substantial amount of information about two organizational types. In this exercise, you are asked to use a similar approach, but you and your partner will develop the background information yourselves. You will have the opportunity to select a specific organization of your choice and to use the systems approach as a basis for your analysis. You will then share your findings with a subgroup and the entire class.

[1]For example, a systems approach to comparative analysis of two organizational types can be found in Fremont E. Kast and James E. Rosenzweig, *Organization and Management: A Systems Approach,* 2d ed., New York, McGraw-Hill, 1974: chap. 20, "Comparative Organizational Analysis: The Hospital," and chap. 21, "Comparative Organizational Analysis: The University."

You will likely find a number of similarities among the various organizations that you analyze as well as differences. It is hoped that you will find the systems approach a useful conceptual scheme for looking at all types of organization. You will also become more aware of the importance of contingency and situational views. Each organization type will be operating in a different environmental suprasystem and will have varying characteristics in its goals and values and in its technological, structural, psychosocial, and managerial subsystems. Most important, you should develop some understanding of the unique interrelationships among these subsystems. The essence of the contingency view is the understanding of these patterns of relationships and of ways in which organizations can be designed and managed most effectively under varying conditions.

Figure 22-1 provides a conceptual model of contingency views which you may find useful in the analysis of your specific organization. It sets forth the typical characteristics of two quite disparate organizational types: the closed/stable/mechanistic one and the open/adaptive/organic one. It should be emphasized that we would not expect to find real-world organizations with the exact characteristics of these two types. They are primarily conceptual models for purposes of illustration. But many real-world organizations (or parts thereof) come close to fitting these descriptions. For example, a mass-production assembly line or a fast-food service outlet has most of the characteristics of the closed/stable/mechanistic type, whereas a research and development laboratory, a consulting firm, and a university graduate program will have most of the characteristics of the open/adaptive/organic type. On reflection, you can see that Hard Rock Prison fits the mechanistic pattern, whereas Sweet Joint Correctional Center fits the adaptive type.

You may also find changes over time for the same organization. For example, the "traditional" school system may fit closer to the mechanistic type, whereas the "open" school may be more the adaptive type. When you investigate your specific organization, you should look for trends toward one type or the other.

Furthermore, you may find that departments within the same organization have differing characteristics. Sales departments tend to be more open and adaptive than production departments. Research departments are often more adaptive than others. Look for these differences in the individual departments of the organization that you investigate.

The contingency view also suggests that, in various organizational types, management approaches and leadership styles should be adjusted in order to be most effective. For example, in the mechanistic organization, strong authority of position, tight controls, and more directive leadership styles are generally most effective. In the adaptive organization, shared authority, more general controls, and more participative leadership styles work best. In the analysis of your organization, you should try to ascertain what managerial approaches and leadership styles seem to be used most. One method is to ask managers directly for their views. Another method is to ask people about their observations of others (peers, subordinates, and superiors). Try to determine in your own mind whether their managerial practices seem to fit; i.e., do they lead to organizational effectiveness, efficiency, and participant satisfaction? This exercise provides an opportunity to engage in comparative analysis of a range of organizations. Obviously, our time constraints (for both fieldwork and discussion) will not permit detailed analysis. However, we can get the "flavor" of comparative analysis and begin to develop some contingency views with regard to managerial practice.

PROCEDURE

STEP 1
Form into pairs of students for the first part of this exercise. Each pair should pick a specific organization (by name, if possible) and analyze it in terms of the characteristics indicated on the form entitled

Systems and their key dimensions	Characteristics of organizational systems	
	Closed/stable/mechanistic	Open/adaptive/organic
Environmental suprasystem:		
General nature	Placid	Turbulent
Predictability	Certain, determinate	Uncertain, indeterminate
Boundary relationships	Relatively closed. Limited to few participants (sales, purchasing, etc.). Fixed and well defined.	Relatively open. Many participants have external relationships. Varied and not clearly defined.
Overall organizational system:		
Goal structure	Organization as a single-goal maximizer	Organization as a searching, adapting, learning system which continually adjusts its multiple goals and aspirations
Decision-making processes	Programmable, computational	Nonprogrammable, judgmental
Organization emphasis	On performance	On problem solving
Goals and values:		
Organizational goals in general	Efficient performance, stability, maintenance	Effective problem solving, innovation, growth
Pervasive values	Efficiency, predictability, security, risk aversion	Effectiveness, adaptability, responsiveness, Risk taking
Goal set	Single, clear-cut	Multiple, determined by necessity to satisfy a variety of constraints
Involvement in goal-setting process	Managerial hierarchy primarily (top down)	Widespread participation (bottom up as well as top down)
Technical system:		
General nature of tasks	Repetitive, routine	Varied, nonroutine
Input to transformation process	Homogeneous	Heterogeneous
Output of transformation process	Standardized, fixed	Nonstandardized, variable
Methods	Programmed, algorithmic	Nonprogrammed, heuristic
Structural system:		
Organizational formalization	High	Low
Procedures and rules	Many and specific. Usually formal and written.	Few and general. Usually informal and unwritten.
Authority structure	Concentrated, hierarchic	Dispersed, network
Psychosocial system:		
Status structure	Clearly delineated by formal hierarchy	More diffuse. Based upon expertise and professional norms.
Role definitions	Specific and fixed	General and dynamic. Change with tasks.
Motivational factors	Emphasis on extrinsic rewards, security, and lower-level need satisfaction. Theory X view.	Emphasis on intrinsic rewards, esteem, and self-actualization. Theory Y view.
Leadership style	Autocratic, task-oriented, desire for certainty	Democratic, relationship-oriented, tolerance for ambiguity
Power system	Power concentration	Power equalization
Managerial system:		
General nature	Hierarchical structure of control, authority, and communications; combination of independent static components	A network structure of control, authority, and communications; coalignment of interdependent, dynamic components
Decision-making techniques	Autocratic, programmed, computational	Participative, nonprogrammed, judgmental
Planning process	Repetitive, fixed, and specific	Changing, flexible, and general
Control structure	Hierarchic, specific, short-term. External control of participants	Reciprocal, general, long-term. Self-control of participants
Means of conflict resolution	Resolved by superior (refer to "book") Compromise and smoothing Keep below the surface	Resolved by group ("situational ethics") Confrontation Bring out in open

FIGURE 22-1 A conceptual model of contingency views.

Organizations   *Analysts*

Manufacturing

_____   _____

_____   _____

_____   _____

Farming

_____   _____

_____   _____

_____   _____

Retailing

_____   _____

_____   _____

_____   _____

Banking and finance

_____   _____

_____   _____

_____   _____

Organizations   *Analysts*

Church

_____   _____

_____   _____

_____   _____

Recreation/amusement/sports

_____   _____

_____   _____

_____   _____

Federal agencies

_____   _____

_____   _____

_____   _____

Volunteer

_____   _____

_____   _____

_____   _____

Schools

———————————————————   ———————————————————

———————————————————   ———————————————————

———————————————————   ———————————————————

Correctional institutions

———————————————————   ———————————————————

———————————————————   ———————————————————

———————————————————   ———————————————————

Military

———————————————————   ———————————————————

———————————————————   ———————————————————

———————————————————   ———————————————————

Police, fire, etc.

———————————————————   ———————————————————

———————————————————   ———————————————————

———————————————————   ———————————————————

Organizations   *Analysts*

City, county, or state government

_____   _____

_____   _____

_____   _____

Unions

_____   _____

_____   _____

_____   _____

Other

_____   _____

_____   _____

_____   _____

_____   _____

_____   _____

Organization: _____

Record, in the space below, your description of a specific organization. Illustrate relevant characteristics with actual examples.

Task environment	
Goals and values	
Technology	
Structure	
Psychosocial	
Managerial	
Other _____	
Other _____	

Analysis of a Specific Organization (page 316). Coordinate the selection of organizations in order to get as wide a variety as possible for the entire class. Use the list on page 312 to record organizations and analysts.

Each pair should analyze its specific organization, basing its study on past experience and/or a field trip to the site. The trip might involve talking with managers in that organization. An obvious approach would be to pick an organization in which one or both students are now working or have worked in the past. Describe the characteristics for the organization in as specific terms as possible. Describe the situation as you understand it. Use examples.

STEP 2

Basing your judgment on your own evaluation, do the existing managerial practices and leadership styles foster overall effectiveness, efficiency, and participant satisfaction?

STEP 3

Join with two other pairs and share your analyses. Try to get a variety of organizational types in this phase of the exercise. Develop a summary of the three organizations' characteristics on the form Comparative Organizational Analysis (page 318). Discuss the results. Is it difficult to characterize and classify an entire organization? Is it possible to focus on subparts of organizations for comparative analysis?

STEP 4

Using the form called Similarities and Differences among Organizations (page 319), note some overall similarities and differences among the organizations you have analyzed. What are some common threads? What are the major differences?

STEP 5

After the small groups have discussed the results of their analyses, all the class comes together to share insights from the subgroups and to summarize and develop conclusions.

   a. Of what benefit is comparative analysis of organizations?

   b. Did you find that different management practices and leadership styles were appropriate for different organizations?

   c. Can comparative analysis be extended across cultures as well as institutions? Would you expect to find organizational designs and managerial practices similar in different cultures?

Comparative Organizational Analysis

Dimension	Organization 1.	2.	3.
Task environment			
Goals and values			
Technology			
Structure			
Psychosocial			
Managerial			
Other			

Similarities and Differences among Organizations

Similarities among organizations	Differences among organizations

SUMMARY AND CONCEPTUALIZATIONS

This exercise was probably difficult for you. It is frequently hard to take our conceptual models from the classroom to the real world. They get severely tested and frequently battered. Models don't exactly fit any organization because all organizations are different just as all people are different. But, people do have some common characteristics, and so do organizations. The behavioral sciences are built on the premise that there are some similarities and that human behavior is at least somewhat predictable. Behavior is not totally individualized, random, and unpredictable. The same is true for organizational science.

Although we recognize that each organization is different, our own experiences suggest that there are some overall approaches that help us understand all organizations. The systems approach is such an overview. Our observations also suggest that many issues are common to all organizations—we hear about them frequently from managers in a wide span of organizational types. For example, when talking for a few minutes with a business leader, hospital administrator, chief of police, or school superintendent, we are very likely to touch on such issues as:

Problems of goal setting
Environmental relationships
Problems of structure
Appropriate leadership styles
Development of effective control systems
The ever-present "people" problems
Etc.

The frequent appearance of such issues indicates that there are certain typical problems facing all organizations. Although organizations do have similar characteristics and common problems, there are no universal solutions. This is where modern organization and management theory differs from traditional views.

Traditional management theory emphasized the development of principles that were appropriate and applicable to all organizations and all managerial tasks. These universal principles were quite prescriptive—there was an appropriate way to design and manage organizations. Although the quantitative and behavioral sciences have introduced new concepts to the study of organizations, they, too, have tended toward prescribing the "one best way."

Once we accept systems and contingency views, it becomes apparent that we cannot possibly prescribe principles that are appropriate to all organizations, or even to all parts of a single large, complex organization. There are so many relevant variables that it is impossible for a simplistic model to depict reality. Such a view is appropriate only when the system under consideration is stable, mechanistic, and effectively closed to intervening external variables. Once we begin to consider organizations as open systems with interactive components, we can no longer think in simplistic, unidimensional terms.

Within a general societal environment, there are a number of specific variables that must be considered in order for the manager to understand the situation. For example, cultural values are often an overriding consideration in determining appropriate managerial action. Differences across continents and national boundaries are obvious. Similarly, it is easy to discern differences between the public and private sectors, where such distinctions exist. Industry and institutional differences should also be taken into account; the "culture" in a steel firm is not the same as in an insurance organization, or a military unit, or a school. Moreover, the "culture" can vary significantly within organizations; significant differences are often evident across departments or levels—production vis-à-vis marketing or operating level vis-à-vis middle and top levels.

Noting the multivariate nature of the organizational setting, it is no wonder that managers often respond by saying, "The theory may be appropriate in general, but our organization is different." The thrust of contingency views of management practice is to offset such claims by providing appropriate guidelines for action. The general flavor of systems and contingency views is somewhere between simplistic, universal principles and complex, vague notions ("it all depends"). It is a mid-range concept which recognizes the complexity involved in managing organizations and uses patterns of relationships and/or configurations of subsystems in order to facilitate improved practice. The art of management depends on a reasonable success rate for actions in a probabilistic environment.

Do systems concepts and contingency views provide a panacea for solving problems in organizations? The answer is an emphatic *no;* this approach does not provide "10 easy steps" to success in management. Such cookbook approaches, while seemingly applicable and easy to grasp, are usually short-sighted, narrow in perspective, and superficial—in short, unrealistic. Fundamental ideas, such as systems concepts and contingency views, are more difficult to comprehend. However, they facilitate more thorough understanding of complex situations and increase the likelihood of appropriate actions. This approach requires a considerable amount of conceptual skill on the manager's part.

Conceptual skill distinguishes really effective managers at all levels and particularly those who progress to the top. It involves the ability to comprehend complex systems, to discern key interrelationships, and to attach degrees of importance to the various factors bearing on a problem. The manager must be flexible in order to cope with a variety of situations. This approach is obviously more difficult than that of reliance on general principles and rules.

As we consider systems and contingency views in diagnosis and action, it is important to recognize that many managers have, and will continue to use, such an approach implicitly. They have an intuitive "sense of the situation," are flexible diagnosticians, and adjust plans and actions accordingly. Thus, systems concepts and contingency views are not new. However, if this approach to organizational diagnosis and managerial action can be made more explicit, we can facilitate better management and more effective and efficient organizations.

PART 8
ORGANIZATIONAL CHANGE
AND THE FUTURE

Well, our old friend Jack Andrews made it through Winter Quarter in spite of his broken leg. Things went pretty well, considering the inconvenience of a full-length cast and crutches for several weeks. Oh yes, there was one problem; he had to have the walking cast changed after he cracked it when he inadvertently tried to run to catch a bus.

At the end of the quarter, he headed straight for the bookstore's buy-back department in order to sell his texts for half the original price. What a shock! Phyllis, the woman behind the counter, told him that two of his texts were worth only 25 cents apiece because new editions had been published in January. "My God," thought Jack, "why do they have to keep changing things?"

Jack's experience is familiar to us all. New automobile models every year cause the value of the old ones to dip precipitously. We are bombarded with messages about "new" toothpaste, deodorant, soap, etc., and we're sure that all that has been changed is the package. Skirts go up and down; pants go from pegged to flaired; lapels go from narrow to wide; and shoe styles vary incongruously. In short, change is inevitable and the pace seems to be accelerating.

Technological change in our time is nothing short of amazing. It is said that half the people who have ever lived are now alive, and that 90 percent of the scientists in our world history are now alive. Our store of knowledge doubles in less than 15 years. Technological and sociological changes are an important part of the organizational environment. Organizations must adapt to changing conditions. At the same time, there must be enough stability and continuity to get the work done on a day-to-day basis.

Although it seems that we should be used to change, resistance is commonplace, particularly when it threatens the security or status of individuals, groups, or organizations.

An important factor in overcoming resistance to change is the incorporation of a process of planned change as an integral part of the managerial task. If organizations routinely look at themselves and engage in a process of problem sensing, diagnosing, action planning, and following up, they will tend to do the right things and do them well. Appropriate participation of organization members in the planning process will increase the probability of smooth implementation of changes. Various strategies can be employed to encourage such implementation. Coercion may be necessary at times, but suggestion and persuasion may be more effective and lasting.

What of the future for organizations and their management? It seems inevitable that both the external environment and the internal subsystems will be more complex as we go along. Will Jack Andrews find organizations unmanageable by the time he is ready for a top executive role? Remember, he finally took a job with a large metropolitan hospital—one of the most complex organizations in existence. Although we aren't so pessimistic as to term future organizations as unmanageable, their management ain't gonna get any easier! Here are some predictions:

1. Organizations will be operating in a turbulent environment which requires continual change and adjustment.

2. They will have to adapt to an increasing diversity of cultural values in the social environment.

3. Greater emphasis will be placed on technological and social forecasting.

4. Organizations will continue to expand their boundaries and domains. They will increase in size and complexity.

5. Organizations will continue to differentiate their activities, causing increased problems of integration and coordination.

6. Organizations will continue to have major problems in the accumulation and utilization of knowledge. Intellectual activities will be stressed.

7. Greater emphasis will be focused on suggestion and persuasion rather than coercion based on authoritarian power as the means for coordinating the activities of the participants and functions within the organization.

8. Participants at all levels in organizations will have more influence. Organizations of the future will adopt a power-equalization rather than power-differentiation model.

9. There will be greater diversity in values and life styles among people and groups in organizations. A mosaic psychosocial system will be normal.

10. Problems of interface between organizations will increase. New means for effective interorganizational coordination will be developed.

11. Computerized information-decision systems will have an increasing impact upon organizations.

12. The number of professionals and scientists and their influence within organizations will increase. There will also be a decline in the proportion of independent professionals with many more salaried professionals.

13. Goals of complex organizations will diversify. Emphasis will be upon satisficing a number of goals rather than maximizing any one.

14. Evaluation of organizational performance will be difficult. Many new administrative techniques will be developed for evaluation of performance in all spheres of activity.

15. Processes of planned change, with widespread involvement of organizational participants, will receive increasing managerial attention.

In general, we see a trend away from bureaucratic-mechanistic toward adaptive-organic organizations. However, we see some of both and are convinced that both approaches are appropriate and will continue to be so. Effective managers will be flexible enough to survive in both types of systems. They will be astute diagnosticians who can tailor their approaches to specific situations. An open-minded contingency view of organization and management will be increasingly important in order to cope with the dynamic complexity of our changing world.

The exercises in Part 8 provide an opportunity to explore changing values with regard to women in management, to test various strategies of overcoming resistance to change, and to plan a specific change.

Exercise 23, *Changing Values and Roles: Women in Management,* allows you to explore a number of critical issues with regard to women in society. You will have an opportunity to experience sex-role stereotyping via a role-playing exercise.

Exercise 24, *Organizational Change: Municipal Light*, is a case situation that asks you to play the role of either a striking employee or of top management. You will be able to experience several approaches to conflict resolution and action planning.

Exercise 25, *Problem Solving and Action Planning: Force Field Analysis*, provides an opportunity to work on a specific problem defined as the difference between a current condition and a desired condition. You will be asked to carry out a programmed process of force field analysis.

Exercise 23
Changing Values and Roles: Women in Management

LEARNING OBJECTIVES

1. To increase our understanding of factors that affect women in organizations.
2. To examine our beliefs and assumptions concerning women as managers.
3. To consider strategies for organizational change that facilitate the development and utilization of women as managers.

ADVANCE PREPARATION

Read the Overview.

OVERVIEW

When your baby girl is fretful, you go to the good book:
It says, "Turn him over on his back, change his diaper, and take a look."

Then your daughter is old enough to go to school,
And the instructions read at the top of every test:
"Everyone take his assigned place and do his best."

At the PTA meeting the chairman is Mrs. Rule.

The minister exhorts, "Act as a brother
Unto one another."

The college catalogue lists courses on
"Man and Society,"
"Man and Survival,"
"Man: Is He Godhead's New Rival?"

You graduate as a Bachelor of Science or a BA,
and with a fellowship your master's degree is underway

Until one day

You wind up calling a psychiatrist and his advice is
"I can't understand why you should be feeling an identity
crisis."

Eve Merriam, 1970

In discussing the subject of women in management, one issue is, "Where are they?" While women make up 40 percent of the labor force, only 3 percent are "managers and administrators," according to the 1970 census. In 1973, *Fortune* magazine surveyed 1,300 companies—the 1,000 largest industrial companies and the 50 largest in each of six nonindustrial categories—and found that of approximately 6,500 officers and directors, only 11 were women.[1] "With only two exceptions (they) were helped along by a family connection, by marriage, or by the fact that they helped create the organizations they now preside over. In short, most of them did not have to deal with at least two problems that have over the years held back even the most able and qualified women: they did not start out in their companies in jobs with limited futures; they did not have to work their way through a corporate hierarchy that discriminated against them."[2]

Additional perspective can be obtained from the following 1973 data concerning white-collar employees in the federal government.[3]

GS level	Percentage, women
Above 18	2.6
13–18	4.5
7–12	23.4
1–6	46.6

These examples are illustrative of most organizations in our society. Although women make up a large portion of the work force, they are extremely underrepresented in middle and top management. What accounts for this phenomenon? In our view it is a reflection of societal, organizational, and personal attitudes that are translated into behavior. Attitudes and behavior are changing—slowly or rapidly, depending on your point of view. Before we look at some of the changes and consequences, it will be useful to understand some of the underlying causes that have led to the current condition of women in our society.

In a recent article Barbara Polk outlines four major approaches to understanding the contemporary condition of women: analysis in terms of sex roles, differences between feminine and masculine culture, male-female power relationships, and economic relationships (socialism versus capitalism).[4] While we may or may not agree with any or all of these conceptualizations, they provide food for thought. According to Polk, the main components of sex-role socialization are:

> 1. Each society *arbitrarily* views a wide variety of personality characteristics, interests, and behaviors as the virtually exclusive domain of one sex or the other. The fact that societies vary in their definition of feminine and masculine roles is proof that sex roles are based on social rather than on biological factors.

[1] Wyndham Robertson, "The Ten Highest-Ranking Women in Big Business," *Fortune*, April 1973, pp. 81–89.
[2] Ibid., p. 83.
[3] *Study of Employment of Women in the Federal Government: 1973*, U.S. Civil Service Commission, Manpower Statistics Division, Washington, D.C., 20402.
[4] Barbara Bovee Polk, "Male Power and the Women's Movement," *The Journal of Applied Behavioral Science,* vol. 10, no. 3, 1974, pp. 415–431.

2. The parceling up of human characteristics into "feminine" and "masculine" deprives all of full humanness.

3. Sex roles are systematically inculcated in individuals, beginning at birth, by parents, the educational system, peers, the media, and religious institutions, and are supported by the social sciences and the economic, political, and legal structures of society. Individuals learn appropriate roles through role models and differential reinforcement.

4. Sex roles form the core of an individual's identity. Because self-evaluation is closely linked to sex ("That's a good girl/boy") and to adequacy of sex-role performance, the propriety of the role to which one was socialized becomes difficult to dislodge in adulthood, even when it is seen as dysfunctional. In addition, individuals often link concepts of their adequacy in sex *roles* to their adequacy in *sexual* interactions and vice versa. Thus, a threat to one's role definition is perceived as a threat to one's sexual identity. Such threats are a major mechanism for psychologically locking people into traditional roles.

5. Sex roles are basic roles and thus modify expectations in virtually all other roles. Differential expectations by sex in other roles leads to differential perception of the same behavior in a woman and a man (a businessman is strong-willed; a business woman, rigid). Differential expectations and selective perception limit the extent to which individuals can step outside their sex roles and are major mechanisms for the maintenance of sex roles.

6. Female and male roles form a role system in which the expectations for and behaviors of each sex have implications for the definitions of and behaviors of the other sex. (A man can't be a "gentleman" if a woman will not let him hold the door for her.)

7. The male role has higher status. This status is directly rewarding and provides access to other highly valued statuses and rewards; however, male status also places heavy pressures on men to maintain that status.

8. Males have power over females because of role definitions. "Being powerful" is itself a part of the masculine role definition. In addition, the "rationality" assigned to the male role gives men access to positions of expertise as well as credibility, even when they are not experts.

Regardless of the reason for our current condition, there is ample evidence of sex discrimination in organizations. The data cited previously concerning the incidence of women in middle and top management can hardly be explained otherwise, unless one assumes women are inherently less qualified to be managers. A number of lawsuits have been filed on behalf of women claiming that organizations have paid them less than men doing essentially the same work. American Telephone & Telegraph Company and Safeco Insurance Company, among many others, have agreed to pay substantial amounts of back salaries and damages to past and present women employees who claim they were discriminated against on the basis of sex.

In many occupational categories, women were systematically excluded until recently. They are now employed as telephone installers, and we sometimes hear a male voice say, "Number please?" We have a few female jockeys and fire fighters. (Most of the protest against women fire fighters has come from the wives of male fire fighters.) Women are now attending military service academies and some are actually serving aboard ship—until recently an absolute male domain. More women have become certified public accountants, overcoming the taboo of mixed sexes working and traveling together while performing auditing functions.

Changes are occurring; progress is being made; but equal treatment and equal opportunity are a long way from realization. Deep-seated prejudices have been witnessed for a long time and are not likely to disappear overnight. Our general societal approach is evidenced by the second verse and the chorus of Kris Kristofferson's song, "Jesus Was a Capricorn."

> Eggheads cussing rednecks cussing hippies for their hair
> Others laugh at straights who laugh at freaks who laugh at squares
> Some folks hate the whites who hate the blacks who hate the Klan
> Most of us hate anything we don't understand
>
> 'Cause everybody's gotta have somebody to look down on
> Who they can feel better than at anytime they please

> Someone doing something dirty decent folks can frown on
> If you can't find nobody else then help yourself to me

Women and other minorities (different groups over the years) have been in large measure excluded from the executive hierarchy. This is particularly true of the secretarial "class," a significant factor in most organizations. Women have often performed executive types of activities in the helping role of "assistant to." "In order to survive, a dominant hierarchy must create and maintain a parahierarchy composed of members of a subordinate class."[5] This suggests that not only do organizations have someone to look down on, but the subordinate classes or parahierarchies or paraprofessionals contribute significantly to their survival and success. Thus we can understand the reluctance of organizations to change a system that has worked so well for the in-group. Yet, regardless of the consequences, the system will change, not so much because attitudes will change as that behavior is being changed by law.

Most organizations, unless very small (four or fewer employees), come under federal or state laws against discrimination based on sex. The following is a summary of some of the practices typically covered by sex discrimination provisions of the law:

1. Any action, based upon sex, with respect to the hiring process, promotion, lay-off or discharge (unless sex is established as a bona fide occupational qualification for that particular position) is prohibited.

2. Any action, based upon sex, with respect to compensation, hours of work, or other terms and conditions of employment (unless sex is established as a bona fide occupational qualification) is prohibited.

3. Any action, based upon sex, which limits opportunity for overtime work, or which classifies employees by sex for purposes of establishing seniority, which will in turn affect promotions or lay-offs (unless based upon a bona fide occupational qualification) is prohibited.

4. Any action to classify job opportunities by sex, either in advertisements or otherwise (unless such classification is based upon a bona fide occupational qualification), is prohibited.

5. As a rule, all jobs must be open to both men and women unless the employer can establish that sex is a "bona fide occupational qualification." The burden of proof is on the employer in establishing the need for such a qualification, but some general guidelines are:

   a. Jobs may be restricted to employees of one sex for reasons of authenticity in the fields of acting, modeling, etc.

   b. Jobs may be restricted to employees of one sex because of community standards of morality or propriety, such as restroom or locker room attendant, sales clerk for certain items of clothing, etc.

On the other hand, many of the assumptions and preferences which have heretofore resulted in hiring individuals of one sex only will not be considered bona fide occupational qualifications. Among these are:

   a. The assumption that individuals of one sex are unwilling to apply for certain types of work traditionally done by persons of the other sex;

   b. The assumption that coworkers, clients, or customers prefer employees of one sex, not the other;

   c. The fact that certain positions have traditionally been filled by one sex, not the other;

   d. The fact that the job involves travel with members of the opposite sex;

   e. The fact that physical facilities are not now available on the job for both sexes;

   f. The assumption that individuals of one sex, not the other, have certain personality characteristics which are desirable for a certain position.

Provisions in the law, such as the above, have led to changes in hiring practices so that women are not automatically excluded from certain occupations. However, it is not evident that progress in the managerial hierarchy has kept pace. Here again, legal constraints may force behavior changes before any genuine attitude change occurs. For example:

[5]Lane Tracy, "Postscript to the Peter Principle," *Harvard Business Review,* July–August, 1972, p. 69.

The Bank of California, the thirty-ninth largest in the nation, is now operating under a consent decree that establishes one of the most far-reaching standards ever set for employment of minorities and women. The terms pledge the Bank of California to fill at least 60 percent of future promotions to management levels with women and members of minority groups. As a result, by 1982 the bank's managerial ranks must include at least 9 percent blacks, 14 percent Hispanic, 37 percent women. These goals were established in a decree approved by U.S. District Court Judge Robert Peckham as the outcome of a suit brought by civil rights organizations and women's groups.[6]

The consequences of this approach remain to be seen. Our experience suggests that organizations typically have three general approaches to "differences" in participants: (1) disallow and mold (submerge); (2) accept and tolerate; and (3) understand and value. Some organizations have moved toward the third approach; understanding and valuing differences is an important step in keeping the organization tuned to current conditions. However, it is easy to see a spectrum of all approaches in modern organizations. Some organizations still maintain rigid codes of dress and hair styles, consider the term "woman executive" a paradox, and avoid employees who are racially and ethnically different from existing managers. Many organizations will change reluctantly in the face of legal and economic sanctions. However, they may discover that an initial approach to "accept and tolerate" will gradually change to "understand and value."

Of particular concern in the issue of women in management is whether women must become more like men in order to succeed. Must women become more competitive, aggressive, and independent, as well as less compassionate, supportive, and nurturing? Would organizations be better places if men displayed more female characteristics? Would we all be better off if we not only tolerated but also valued a wider range of humanness in all managers—male or female? What are the substantive dimensions of managerial effectiveness? These are some of the issues we want to explore in this exercise.

PROCEDURE

ROLE CONSTRAINTS

STEP 1

Share the results of your sentence completion exercise (provided by your instructor) in groups of two to six. If possible, each group should have a mix of men and women in order to ensure exposure to their respective points of view.

ROLE PLAYING

STEP 2

Divide the class into trios and have each person select one of the three roles in the Happy Home Insurance Company interview (page 332): Applicant; Receptionist; and Interviewer.

STEP 3

Act out the interview process by reading the parts as written. Empathize with the roles involved.

STEP 4

Debrief the exercise in the entire class.

a. How did Myra "feel" during the interview? (Ask for volunteers to share their feelings and to indicate what their actions will be.)

b. Were any laws broken during the interview? Give examples.

[6]*Business and Society Review/Innovation,* Winter 1973–1974, p. 86.

c. Is discrimination and/or prejudice evident in this incident? Be specific and indicate whether it is overt, covert, or inadvertent.

HAPPY HOME INSURANCE COMPANY*
Characters: Applicant (A), Receptionist (R), Interviewer (I)

R: Good morning. Can I help you?

A: I hope so. I am looking for a job.

R: All of our available positions are posted on the board over there. The clerical jobs are on the right. There's a schedule there, too, for the typing test.

A: Aren't there any other kinds of jobs?

R: What do you mean?

A: Well – something professional, where I can apply what I learned in college and Vista.

R: Everything we have is posted. You'll have to look them over yourself.

A: Can you tell me something more about the supervisor's job in Accident Records? I think I would be interested in that.

R: I'll make an appointment for you with one of our interviewers. I don't know anything about the jobs. Did you sign up for the typing test?

A: Well, no. . .I –

R: Typing is required for all our jobs.

A: But I haven't even filled out an application form yet.

R: The results of your tests – there's dictaphone and shorthand after the typing – are a very important part of your application. Without the scores your application form cannot even be considered.

A: Oh! Well. I guess I'd better sign up then.

R: Here's an application form. You can see Ms. Belton at 10:30. She does all our office and clerical interviewing.

A: Thank you.

I. Myra Beckenroot. Ah! Good morning, Myra, I'm Ms. Belton.

A: Good morning, Ms. Belton.

I: Do you have your form filled out? Are all your test scores attached? We can sit in here where it is a little quieter. I see you've attached a resumé to your application. Most of the girls don't have resumés.

A: I didn't think the normal application form told enough about me. I was hoping to find a job where I could use my college education and Vista experience.

I: Well, let's see, you did extremely well on your tests—only four mistakes on the dictaphone. Which job was it that you were interested in?

A: Well, I was looking for something professional, and I thought the supervisor's job in Accident Records might be a good start and still let me apply some experience.

I: I see. Let's look at your background. You have two children?

A: Yes.

I: Um hum. I'm not trying to pry, but I'm afraid I'll have to ask you about your day-care arrangements. I see you're divorced.

A: Yes, I am divorced. I have made adequate plans to see that my children are cared for.

I: Could you tell me what these plans are?

A: My 4-year-old is enrolled in the Up and Out Child Care Center, and I take my daughter—she's 18 months—to a neighbor's. She looks after four children in her home.

I: Will someone take care of your children when they are sick? We expect our employees to be at work every day unless there is a serious emergency.

A: I plan to be at work every day.

I: You're not planning to have any more children, are you?

A: Why—uh—no. You see, I'm divorced.

*This case was prepared by Ernesta Barnes as the basis for a group discussion. It is not intended to illustrate either effective or ineffective handling of an administrative situation. It is based on interviews with 25 recent college graduates looking for their first permanent jobs.

I: Yes, I know, but a girl your age could easily remarry.

A: I don't have any plans to remarry.

I: Good. I'll just make a note of that. Now, where were we? Oh yes, your college education. Your resumé is very impressive. You seem to have been very active in college.

A: Yes, I was. It was a small school with no professional athletic staff. I was Varsity Football Manager my senior year. I made most of the purchases and arranged travel schedules and accommodations. I had three assistants and a $50,000 budget.

I: My, that's quite impressive for a girl. You must be very proud.

A: Well—yes, I am.

I: Can you tell me something about your decision to major in business administration, Myra? That's somewhat unusual, isn't it?

A: Well, no, actually, there were 180 economics majors in my senior year.

I: Oh, I meant unusual for a girl. We don't see many girls with degrees in business administration.

A: I got interested in business administration in my freshman year when I had a staff job on the college newspaper. A lot of my assignments were on budget and planning problems in the administration. I was Business Manager—handling advertising and supplies in my junior year.

I: What did you hope to do with your business administration when you graduated?

A: I hoped to get a job where my education would be useful—something in business management.

I: But of course you haven't had much experience, Myra. Let's see—just 6 months' actual work experience in the Reserves as a WAC. I'm afraid you'll need more than that to qualify for the supervisor's job.

A: But I thought my college degree might make me eligible for some sort of management training program.

I: With only 6 months' clerical experience, I'm afraid our Personnel Director would hesitate to invest training time in you. We expect girls to have at least 2 years of professional experience before they are eligible for our training jobs. Also, the salary for our training positions is a bit high for your background. We usually start the women at $650. You'd have to give a better indication of your abilities as a supervisor before we could make an exception for you.

A: Could I find a job here that would give me a chance to do that? I mean, demonstrate my supervisory abilities?

I: Perhaps. But then there's the problem of making a girl supervisor over men. Generally, we try not to do that because it makes the men nervous and reduces their productivity. I think you'd be better off looking for something clerical. After all, you have very little relevant experience even in that area.

A: Isn't there any substitute for clerical experience? How about my year in Vista?

I: Oh, of course we recognize the value of a year like that—the challenge of working in areas of such extreme poverty—but we really can't apply that experience to our clerical requirements. We can substitute a year of your college work. We feel a year of college gives you a good sense for organization and communication skills.

A: What about the other 3 years of college?

I: I'm sorry, we only will allow substitution of 1 year of college.

A: Is 5 years the minimum requirement for the supervisor's job?

I: Yes.

A: Then I'm 3½ years short?

I: I'm afraid so.

A: Do you have any other jobs?

I: Well, we have a nice opening in a clerical position in Salesmen Service. It's a clerk-typist job with lots of telephone work. The salary is $450, which is realistic for someone of your age and experience. Most girls start there and move up when there's an opening.

SUMMARY AND CONCEPTUALIZATION

We have explored the general issue of sex-role stereotypes for men and women in our society. In order that you may compare your attitudes and those of your classmates with a larger sample, we include the summary and conclusions from an article based on a number of studies over a period of years.

> Our research demonstrates the contemporary existence of clearly defined sex-role stereotypes for men and women contrary to the phenomenon of "unisex" currently touted in the media. Women are perceived as relatively less competent, less independent, less objective, and less logical than men; men are perceived as lacking interpersonal sensitivity, warmth, and expressiveness in comparison to women. Moreover, stereotypically masculine traits are more often perceived to be desirable than are stereotypically feminine characteristics. Most importantly, both men and women incorporate both the positive and negative traits of the appropriate stereotype into their self-concepts. Since more feminine traits are negatively valued than are masculine traits, women tend to have more negative self-concepts than do men. The tendency for women to denigrate themselves in this manner can be seen as evidence of the powerful social pressures to conform to the sex-role standards of the society.
>
> The stereotypic differences between men and women described above appear to be accepted by a large segment of our society. Thus college students portray the ideal woman as less competent than the ideal man, and mental health professionals tend to see mature healthy women as more submissive, less independent, etc., than either mature healthy men, or adults, sex unspecified. To the extent that these results reflect societal standards of sex-role behavior, women are clearly put in a double bind by the fact that different standards exist for women than for adults. If women adopt the behaviors specified as desirable for adults, they risk censure for their failure to be appropriately feminine; but if they adopt the behaviors that are designated as feminine, they are necessarily deficient with respect to the general standards for adult behavior.
>
> While many individuals are aware of the prejudicial effects of sex-role stereotypes both from personal experience and hear-say, evidence from systematic empirical studies gives added weight to this fact. The finding that sex-role stereotypes continue to be held by large and relatively varied samples of the population and furthermore are incorporated into the self-concepts of both men and women indicates how deeply ingrained these attitudes are in our society. The magnitude of the phenomenon with which individuals striving for change must cope is well delineated.[7]

With reference to women in management, we can identify a number of more specific *stereotypes or myths,* such as the following:

Women are temperamentally unfit for management responsibility.

Women won't work for a woman manager.

Men won't work for a woman manager.

Women are unable to deal with problems on a logical, rational basis.

Women work only for pin-money.

Women work only until married, or until they start a family.

Women are not ambitious.

Women are too emotional.

Women take more sick leave than men.

Women put family requirements ahead of job responsibilities.

Etc.

Thus we have a two-step process of clarifying and/or changing our views of women in general and women managers in particular. Because masculine characteristics tend to be highly correlated with our concepts of "mature adult" and "effective manager," significant attitudinal changes must take place before women are welcomed into the managerial hierarchy. Women in work organizations tend to be caught in a double bind. An aggressive woman is often described as "pushy, ruthless, and domineering."

[7]Inge K. Broverman, et al., "Sex-Role Stereotypes: A Current Appraisal," *Journal of Social Issues,* vol. 28, no. 2, 1972, pp. 75–76.

But an aggressive man, behaving in essentially the same way, is called a "go-getter" or a "take-charge guy." If a woman behaves in a typically more feminine manner, she is likely to be considered over-cautious and incapable of decisive action.

It is our view that adjustments can and should be made in several directions simultaneously. We need to determine the personal characteristics and behavior that result in effective management in a variety of situations. Overall competence involves a number of characteristics in appropriate amounts. One may be too aggressive or not aggressive enough; one may be too emotional or may lack sensitivity; one may be too dependent or too independent, etc. Once we define ranges of appropriate behavior, individuals can decide what adjustments they need and *want to make* in order to enhance their progress in the managerial hierarchy. Individuals, men or women, may decide that success in a particular job and/or organization requires behavior that is beyond their ability and desire. Such a situation may exclude some people from the managerial hierarchy, but there is an element of choice; no one is excluded on the basis of sex and preconceived notions about who might be appropriate.

Exercise 24

Organizational Change: Municipal Light

LEARNING OBJECTIVES

1. To increase our understanding of change in organizations.
2. To identify a variety of forces for and against individual and organizational change.
3. To compare and contrast several change strategies in a particular situation.
4. To design appropriate and workable processes of planned change.

ADVANCE PREPARATION

Read the Overview and the case, Municipal Light.

OVERVIEW

"They would often change who would become constant in happiness or wisdom."

Confucius

In modern society, it seems that the only thing constant is change. Change has become a way of life and the most obvious changes are technological. This is dramatized by equating human history to a 1-hour period.

> If man's time on earth is taken as 240 thousand years, he spent 55 minutes of that time in paleolithic (old stone) culture. Five minutes ago, he embarked on neolithic culture—the cultivation of plants, the domestication of animals, the making of pottery, weaving, and the use of the bow and arrow; 3½ minutes ago he began the working of copper; 2½ minutes ago he began to mold bronze; 2 minutes ago he learned to smelt iron; ¼ of a minute ago he learned printing; 5 seconds ago the industrial revolution began; 3⅓ seconds ago he learned to apply electricity;

and the time he has had the automobile is less than the interval between the ticks of a watch, i.e., less than one second.[1]

And the automobile has been with us for over 75 years. Think of the technological changes that have occurred in the twentieth century. Thus, it is fairly obvious that we are involved in an accelerating pace of change and that people have, by and large, come to accept such changes. On the other hand, there is evidence of human desires to slow or stop technological changes that are deemed detrimental to the quality of life—pollution of air and water, atomic testing, atomic generating plants, supersonic airplanes, etc. Even simple technological changes are resisted by some. For example, credit cards have resulted in individual behavior changes for most of us—allowing us to carry less cash and to approach buying with a different psychological point of view. However, some people have declined to use credit cards at all.

Although technological change is obviously the most dramatic in our society, we have become particularly concerned with sociological change—individual, group, and organization. While recognizing the desirability of adaptation and innovation, it is also important to recognize the need for stability and continuity. For both individuals and organizations, stability *and* adaptation are essential to survival and growth. Change may occur slowly or rapidly, but, in either case, the individual or organization must be able to function on a day-to-day basis.

Changes may occur in either goals or the means of attaining them. In organizations, management is charged with the responsibility for maintaining a dynamic equilibrium by diagnosing situations and designing adjustments that are most appropriate for coping with current conditions. A dynamic equilibrium for an organization would include the following dimensions.

1. Enough stability to facilitate achievement of current goals
2. Enough continuity to ensure orderly change in either ends or means
3. Enough adaptability to react appropriately to external opportunities and demands as well as changing internal conditions
4. Enough innovativeness to allow the organization to be proactive (initiate changes) when conditions warrant

This process is obviously a delicate balancing act which gets more difficult with the accelerating nature of change.

The impetus for change comes from many sources, both internal and external to the organization. For example, the actions of one firm in an industry usually lead to changes in other firms in the industry. They scramble to meet a product innovation; raise or lower prices to remain competitive; and adjust advertising campaigns accordingly. When CBS develops a successful television program, both NBC and ABC are quick to follow with similar offerings. When one airline provides movies on transcontinental flights, others soon follow suit.

The government—local, state, and federal—is another obvious impetus for change. Pollution control and affirmative action in hiring and staffing are good examples.

Internal sources of change include new technological advances, structural realignments, improved managerial techniques for planning and controlling activities, better information systems, and feedback from employees who suggest, request, or demand that something be done differently.

The focus of change efforts can be the products or services delivered as well as the human and technical processes used. A change effort may be directed toward an individual with the desire to get that person to behave differently—to do more or less of something, to quit or start doing something. Similarly, the focus could be a group of people—a committee, task force, work team, or department. Larger-scale change efforts might focus on the relationships between two or more departments or on the organization as a whole. Changes in goals, policies, or procedures typically affect everyone in the organization.

[1]Wilson D. Wallis, as cited in Charles R. Walker, *Modern Technology and Civilization,* New York, McGraw-Hill, 1962, p. 10.

Although many people seem to welcome variety and change in their lives, there is often considerable resistance to change in organizations. A certain amount of resistance is healthy because it preserves enough stability and continuity to get the job done. However, in many cases it hinders organizational progress which may be needed for satisfactory performance or even survival. Why do people resist changes that (according to management) are in their own best interests? One obvious reason is vested interests. When people put much time and effort into learning certain skills and performances, they feel threatened when such skills or procedures become obsolete. In 1974, when the National Football League moved the goalposts from the goal line to the back of the end zone, the place kickers were not enthusiastic. Arguments to the effect that it would improve the overall game by decreasing the number of field goals fell on deaf ears. If a sales representative has built up considerable rapport with customers, a shuffling of sales territories which requires the agent essentially to start over will not be particularly palatable.

Lack of information, particularly if it leads to misunderstanding, is another powerful source of resistance to change. People need to be aware of possible changes in the early stages. It is natural to resist the unknown; therefore, it is important to know exactly what the change proposal is, why it is being proposed, and what the possible consequences are likely to be.

A change in power structure is also likely to foster resistance—particularly if someone's sphere of influence is to be decreased. Diversity of values is also a common source of resistance to change. Widely diverse views of a particular matter make it extremely difficult to get enough consensus to move in the direction of a proposed change.

While there are no panaceas in overcoming resistance to change, there are several guidelines which might be kept in mind.

1. Define the problem explicitly (including current and desired conditions).
2. Provide information in detail (including reasons for, mechanics of, and likely effects).
3. Encourage participation at all stages.
4. Anticipate the feelings of participants.
5. Work with acknowledged informal leaders.
6. Positively reinforce changees.

A number of the issues discussed earlier are illustrated in the case described in this unit Municipal Light. It involves an organization with a long history and much tradition. It has been quite successful as measured by a number of dimensions. However, the mayor and the city council believed that some changes were necessary and their decision was communicated to a new superintendent. An outside consulting firm wrote a report which served as additional impetus for change. Management's approach was resisted and the issue resulted in accusations, counteraccusations, much bitterness, and, eventually, an unauthorized strike. The purpose of the exercise is to diagnose the case, understand as much as possible, and develop an approach for management to cope with the situation as it currently exists.

The lessons to be learned in this unit revolve around designing workable processes of planned change. Recognizing the need for stability and continuity, how can organizations build into their day-to-day managerial processes the means by which they can adapt and innovate when necessary? The goal is for problem sensing, problem solving, and action planning to be an integral part of the managerial task rather than an ad hoc response to crisis.

Municipal Light

In 1902 the citizens of Hamilton passed a proposal to develop a source of hydroelectric power for street lights and other public purposes. Up until that time all power had been supplied by private companies. During the first half of the twentieth century, a number of dams and steam-generating plants were developed in order to supply a large portion of Hamilton's power needs. The existence of Municipal Light also served as a rate regulator for electric power purchased from private companies. Since its beginning in 1902, Municipal Light has developed into one of America's most efficient electric utilities, powered almost entirely by nonpolluting hydroelectric generating facilities. This self-supporting, tax-paying utility maintains rates that are among the nation's lowest (less than half the national average), with but two rate increases in 66 years. In addition to low rates, Municipal Light provides a spectrum of consumer services: electric range, electric water heater, and electric heating system repair service at no charge—except for parts; advice on heating and air conditioning; free estimates on electric heating costs; advice on use and care of electric appliances; recipes and other household hints; advice on adequate wiring; 24-hour emergency light trouble service; and water-heater rental as low as $1.25 monthly. As a consequence, Municipal Light has built up a good image in the minds of consumers for low rates and free services.

Municipal Light employs approximately 1,800 women and men for the Hamilton service area and the hydroelectric projects. Employees have considerable pride in their organization and enjoy the company's good image with customers. Many jobs have been passed from father to son, and in a number of instances three generations are represented on the Municipal Light payroll. In many cases, several members of the same family are currently working in the organization. Obviously, many traditions and norms have evolved over time with respect to employee relations—among peers as well as among superiors and subordinates. Approximately 700 of the 1,800 employees are represented by the International Brotherhood of Electrical Workers.

In 1972 Charles Newman was appointed superintendent of Municipal Light. He was a retired Air Force brigadier general with a distinguished military career and experience in managing large-scale weapon procurement programs. The appointment was controversial because many Municipal Light workers, as well as some members of the city council, contended that the superintendent should have had experience in an electrical utility. The mayor and a majority of the council, however, felt that managerial skills were transferable and that Mr. Newman was the right person for the job at that particular time. They were concerned that Municipal Light was entering a new era in which the emphasis would have to be placed on cost savings in order that rates could be held down to the current very attractive levels. In this context, the new superintendent accepted a mandate which emphasized public responsiveness and implemented programs designed to develop a greater sensitivity to the needs of Municipal Light's customers and owners, and to provide them with more effective, efficient service.

An outside consulting firm—Donner, Blitzen, and Associates—was hired to conduct a comprehensive study of the organization—the first in its 70-year history. A year later, the study conclusions pointed the way toward an annual saving of over $2 million for the utility's rate payers, plus substantial increases in the speed and efficiency of customer service. An automated customer information system (CIS) was designed to provide near-instantaneous customer data from a control computer. By eliminating duplicate filing systems and reducing incidents of error, CIS would save an estimated $1 million annually. A proposed management reporting system involved a broad range of coordinated reports to assist Municipal Light managers in evaluating performance and analyzing work procedures on a regular systematized basis. Another recommendation involved a work management system to establish a project priority and scheduling procedure together with more precise work control and documentation in the engineering and operations area of the utility. A proposed organization and systems planning and coordination report would provide the necessary research capability and control to coordinate the new and ongoing utility programs. It was anticipated that implementation of all the recommendations should take approximately 3 years.

Municipal Light receives over 18,000 telephone calls a day for service and information, plus several hundred of an administrative nature. In April 1974, an automated centrex telephone system replaced equipment that had been installed in 1935. The new electronic switching means faster, more efficient service for Municipal Light customers.

Automation, plus implementation of the Donner, Blitzen, and Associates study, has resulted in certain personnel changes, reductions in some areas, and additional hiring in others. When the automation program was first started in 1970, the utility made a firm commitment to all personnel that there would be no layoffs or reductions in salary—a commitment that Municipal Light has stood by during the past years. To retain personnel for certain jobs in the utility, a skill redistribution program was created as an ongoing effort. To complement the skill redistribution program as well as to provide opportunities for all personnel to upgrade performance in various disciplines, Municipal Light established a training division in June 1973. The newly formed section was authorized to ascertain training needs in the utility and to develop appropriate courses to augment the already established tuition reimbursement and other education programs. Courses have been conducted in office and technical skills as well as in the management area.

Municipal Light has a firm commitment to Hamilton's Affirmative Action Program. The target for reaching minority parity within the service area is 1975, while 1978 is the goal set for equal representation of women. In 1974, women were admitted to training programs in the electrical trades, an area from which they had been historically excluded. This program was coordinated with the International Brotherhood of Electrical Workers, the Civil Service Commission, and the Hamilton personnel department.

In 1972, Superintendent Newman established a Citizens Policy Advisory Committee, consisting of 14 members who represented a wide spectrum of the community. Their recommendations have been included in policy deliberations on matters such as rates, generation and research, street lighting, underground policy, energy marketing, finances, and environmental impact.

On Wednesday, November 22, 1972, the following story appeared in the Hamilton *Harbinger*.

NEWMAN SUSPENDS 16 AT MUNICIPAL LIGHT

PRIVATE DETECTIVES TURN UP "ABUSES"

City Light Superintendent Charles Newman disclosed yesterday he has suspended 16 field employees and reprimanded 2 for abusing coffee break periods.

Newman said he hired a private detective firm to shadow Municipal Light crews for one week after getting complaints from citizens that some men were taking extended coffee breaks at their Hamilton cafés.

The investigation also turned up possible abuses of coffee break times by "15 to 18" employees of the Hamilton Engineering Department, according to George Everest, principal assistant city engineer for operations.

However, Everest said he cannot say if there are any actual violations in his department until he has had each reported case checked out. This is being done now.

The three cafés involved, Everest said, are near 2d Avenue and Barstow Street, 7th Avenue N.E. and Interlake Way, and N. 34th Street and Stevens Way N.

Newman said two Municipal Light employees were suspended for 10 days without pay, five were suspended for 2 days and nine for one day. Two others received letters of reprimand.

The superintendent said at least one of the disciplined employees also was disciplined in a similar investigation three years ago, for the same thing.

Everest said his department also has to discipline employees from time to time for coffee break time abuses.

The private detective agency placed the three locations under surveillance during the work week of October 30 through November 3 and made its reports according to vehicle license numbers.

The private eyes timed the length of time crews spent in the cafés. Normal time allowed for coffee breaks is 15 minutes in the forenoon and afternoon, Everest said.

Newman said: "We talked to our people involved and they admitted the abuses. The severity and frequency of the violations varied."

Newman stressed that the infractions involved only a small minority of Municipal Light workers and "I continue to be amazed at the dedication of 99 percent of our employees."

He said those abusing lunch or coffee break periods not only are gypping the city—"they also are cheating on their fellow employees."

"I will not stand for this."

He said most of the violators "had been around for a while." He said that if any "extenuating circumstances" turn up later, the disciplinary actions will be rectified.

"We're not against coffee breaks—just the abuse of them," Newman declared.

The president of the security agency involved maintained that his agents did not spy upon employees of the utility. Their job was to check only on vehicles and that this task fell within their overall contract of protecting Municipal Light facilities and equipment. Citizen reaction was quick and varied. Some supported management in its efforts to "shape up" employees. Others felt that this goal, however meritorious, was overshadowed by the sneaky tactics used. They emphasized that control and discipline should be handled within the organization via normal managerial procedures.

This episode touched off a series of disputes within the organization, some of which were given publicity in the press. Two of the four city council members who voted against the superintendent at his confirmation hearing in 1972 said publicly that Newman hadn't done badly. One stated, "On balance, I would have to say he's done a good job." Another observed: "I like a number of things he's done, changes that I favored such as reducing personnel and opening up the utilities operations. I also hear about morale problems among the rank-and-file workers. There are pluses and minuses. . . ." The majority of the council who supported Newman in the beginning reaffirmed their position by stating, "Yes, we think he is doing a good job, making the kinds of changes we wanted to see." In December 1973, supervisory personnel—not Newman—suspended six more utility workers for coffee break abuses. This time, supervisory personnel did the surveillance rather than the security firm. Newman stated, "Those who were abusing their privileges were being unfair to their fellow workers. I felt that the previous management had failed to stop such abuses and that I must. Letters from the public supported the disciplinary actions 50 to 1."

During this period, a new discipline code was written, at the request of employees, to make penalties more equitable. According to Newman, union leadership failed to attend drafting sessions. The code was put into effect on March 21, 1974. In early April, two foremen were suspended for 3 days for alleged coffee break abuses. One of the foremen, Arnold Knutson, claimed that his crew had to move its truck out of a customer's driveway at 4 PM. Because it was too late to set up again and get anything accomplished by quitting time, he decided to take the crew back to a substation for a coffee break before quitting at 4:30. He maintained that they had not taken a normal 15-minute break during the afternoon. The new rules specified that crews would return to the main dispatching area rather than stop at substations en route. Jack Simmons, the other foreman, did not comment on the specifics of his case, but did say that he wasn't even aware of any new rules covering suspensions, discharges, and other disciplinary measures. Other workers suggested that the new rules were adopted unilaterally by Municipal Light Superintendent Charles Newman without approval of the Civil Service Commission. Newman's comment was, "Municipal Light insists on being able to discipline employees when they fail to put in 8 hours work for 8 hours pay. There are standing work orders, dating back to 1970, explicitly requiring crews to return to headquarters at the close of their last job for the day. Loafing away from headquarters to round out the work day is not acceptable work procedure." He stated that citizens had complained that the two work crews involved were parking their trucks and loafing for 30 minutes or longer at the end of their work day.

The next day, about 700 members of the electrical workers' union walked off the job, refusing to return until the suspensions were rescinded. By the second day, the strike had spread to over 1,000 of the 1,800 employees. An ad hoc committee representing the workers presented the following demands in the form of a memo to Superintendent Newman, the mayor of Hamilton, and the city council. The demands included:

1. Rescinding the suspensions of the two foremen
2. Resignation of Superintendent Newman
3. Suspension of the new work rules until they are approved by the employees, the union, and the Civil Service Commission
4. The development of an employees' bill of rights
5. The suspension of implementation of new programs which appeared to have exceeded the ability of the organization to absorb changes

/signed/

The superintendent responded by saying that he was willing to hold the suspensions in abeyance and meet with the ad hoc committee.

PROCEDURE

STEP 1
The class is divided into subgroups of five or six. Groups are randomly assigned to the roles of (*a*) dissident employees, and (*b*) managers. There should be at least three manager groups.

STEP 2
Meet in groups for 20 minutes to discuss and refine the assigned role. Empathize with the people in the case and try to internalize their points of view. Manager groups should designate three of their members to attend a meeting of employees and managers.

STEP 3
Select one of the employee groups (all members) to meet with one of the manager groups (three members). Those not involved in the meeting should be silent observers. (15 minutes)

STEP 4
Change the manager group and have the new group (three members) meet with the same employee group. (15 minutes)

STEP 5
Change the manager group again and have the new group (three members) meet with the same employee group. (15 minutes)

STEP 6
Debrief the exercise.

a. The employee group should describe its reactions to each of the three manager groups.
b. Each manager group should explain the rationale underlying its approach to the situation.

STEP 7
The entire class discusses the problem, including
a. General observations.
b. Advantages and disadvantages of the various approaches.

SUMMARY AND CONCEPTUALIZATION

You have experienced a particular role in a real organization—Municipal Light. Did you have trouble empathizing with the role assigned, i.e., with employees or managers? Typically, some students ask to be reassigned because they just cannot "live the part." In reading the case, they have sided quite definitely with either management or employees, depending on their particular background, experience, and values. Nevertheless, it is good experience to force ourselves to view situations from perspectives other than our own. Although we may not change our minds, we should be able to increase our understanding of different points of view.

Municipal Light is an old, tradition-bound organization with established norms. The superintendent was not an engineer and had had no previous experience in a utility. This was a major departure from past practice and undoubtedly shocked the system. The use of outside consultants was also a first. This approach resulted in a number of proposed changes that promised to have widespread repercussions. While many benefits, including cost reductions, were expected, none had materialized during the period of the case. Expectations of benefits are typically overstated; therefore, they should be scrutinized in order that any cost/benefit analysis will be realistic.

The numerous changes had a definite impact on the general organizational climate. There was a good deal of resistance to change in general and the suspensions over coffee break abuses seemed to be the straw that broke the camel's back.

The several manager groups approached resolution of the current management-employee conflict in different ways. Did you accept a particular approach as most appropriate? Or were there elements in all three approaches that might be useful? Is there one best way?

A broader issue is that of coping with change in general. If you were advising Mr. Newman, what would you suggest for getting commitment to implement "appropriate" changes as of the end of the case?

Exercise 25
Problem Solving and
Action Planning:
Force Field Analysis

LEARNING OBJECTIVES

1. To increase our general understanding of problem solving and action planning.

2. To develop skill in the use of force field analysis by applying it to both personal and organizational problems.

3. To determine the factors that are most relevant in making the problem-solving and action-planning process effective.

ADVANCE PREPARATION

Read the Overview and complete Part A of the Procedure, Personal Problem Solving and Action Planning, before class. Be prepared to share your analysis and action plans with two colleagues and to use them as a sounding board to help you refine your plans.

OVERVIEW

What is a problem? How do we know when decisions are required? We suggest that a problem is a gap between expected results or conditions and actual results or conditions. Whenever we can identify a gap between current conditions and desired conditions, we have a problem. The process of goal setting leads to such a situation because it results in explicit desired future conditions for individuals or organizations. The problem, then, becomes one of how to achieve the desired condition—a "B" in Business Law 301, a 10 percent increase in sales, or better employee morale. The control process involves continually checking to see whether actual results are in line with expected results. If so, the system is in control and operations can proceed normally. If not, we have a gap between the expected and the actual outcome, and we must engage in a problem-solving process to determine why and to develop action plans for getting back on the track.

The first stage—problem finding—is crucial and yet has not been emphasized as much as analysis and choice. Many high-powered analytical techniques are applicable to well-defined, straightforward problems. In some cases, problems are made to fit the techniques, and the result is sophisticated solutions to the wrong problems. In our earlier exercise on goal setting, we emphasized specific objectives for key high-priority dimensions. This ensures attention to important issues. We pointed out the potential pitfall of focusing on dimensions that are easily quantified and measured and yet not necessarily the most important in determining organizational success.

Problem sensing may occur in a variety of ways, such as reviewing operating results, obtaining feedback from participants, soliciting customer complaints, or receiving a question from the boss. The next step involves refining the problem to make sure that relevant organizational members agree on the definition. It also involves dimensions such as:

Who is involved—an individual, a group or groups, the total organization?
Who is causing it—a few people, a specific department or function, top management?
What kind of problem is it—lack of skills, lack of effort, unclear goals, intergroup conflict?
What is the goal for improvement?
How can we evaluate results?

The last question suggests having an accurate picture of the current condition as well as a clear idea of the desired condition.

An important step in problem solving is the consideration of alternatives. To encourage creativity, it is helpful to separate the generation and the evaluation of ideas. This approach follows the concept of brainstorming, where evaluation is delayed in order to facilitate the generation of as many alternatives (including "far out" suggestions) as possible before beginning to evaluate them. The evaluation process includes identifying tentative action steps, anticipating their possible impact, refining them, and, finally, designing an action plan.

Action steps are followed up at some future time in order to check the actual situation against the plan. The results of this follow-up might be reaffirmation of the action plan or reactivation of the problem-solving process if a discrepancy is identified.

Resistance to change is reduced if those involved in implementation of action steps are also involved in the problem-solving process. Analysts and planners cannot operate in relative isolation and then expect others to implement the action steps automatically. Continuing interaction between managers and specialists during the problem-solving process should lead to mutual understanding and higher probabilities for success of planned change efforts.

Force field analysis, as illustrated in Figure 25-1, is a general-purpose diagnostic and problem-solving technique. In any situation there are forces (driving) that push for change as well as forces (restraining) that hinder change. If the forces offset one another completely, we have equilibrium and status quo. Change can occur by increasing the driving forces or by reducing the restraining forces. The latter approach is often more fruitful because to increase driving forces without attention to restraining forces may raise pressure and tension in the system to the point where creative problem solving becomes impossible. This approach facilitates inclusion of a wide variety of factors—technological, structural, and psychosocial (values and feelings, for example). It is particularly important to anticipate antagonism that is likely to be aroused in the implementation of planned change. Accurate assessment will allow creative leadership to cope with hang-ups at the feeling level.

To illustrate the use of force field analysis, let us pick a common individual and/or organizational problem—lack of time. This is a pervasive problem for harried executives. In order to work on the problem effectively, we need to clarify it and state it in terms of current and desired conditions. For

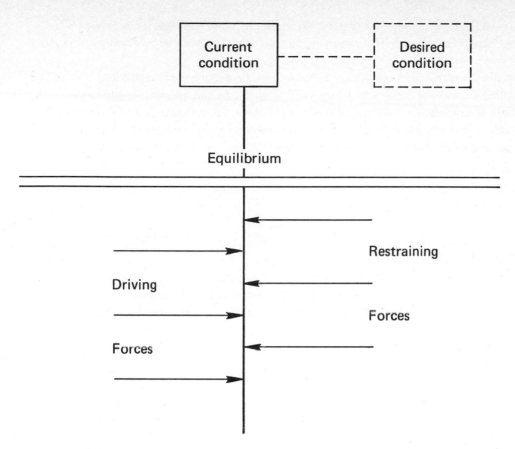

Assumptions:

1. Most problems or situations have multiple causes.

2. Most problems or situations are held in equilibrium between driving and restraining forces.

3. We are more likely to accomplish changes if we identify these forces.

4. It is frequently easier to make changes by reducing restraining forces.

FIGURE 25-1   Force field analysis.

example, the real issue may be lack of time to work on important tasks such as long-range, strategic planning.

Current condition—no time spent on long-range, strategic planning; always reacting to crisis conditions

Desired condition—large blocks of time for critiquing the organization periodically; a creative process of long-range, strategic planning as an integral part of the managerial system

In order to understand the situation in more detail, we can identify those offsetting forces that keep us in equilibrium, with no change from the current condition.

Driving forces (pushing us toward the desired condition)
1. Knowledge of theory that says the desired condition would be "better"
2. Feeling (conviction) that it would be "better"
3. Success stories from current literature (increased effectiveness, e.g.)
4. Success stories from acquaintances in similar organizations

5. Consultants (internal or external) "selling" the virtues of a new approach

Restraining forces (keeping us in the current condition)

1. Programmed, routine activity increases to absorb available time
2. Current deadlines that preclude taking time to analyze the problem of "lack of time"
3. Assumption that we are doing satisfactory work—individually and organizationally (we have survived); no sense of urgency
4. Reluctance of participants to "rock the boat" by analyzing group processes
5. Assumption that there is no slack in time resources, i.e., time is not wasted currently

These lists are obviously not exhaustive; the reader can easily add to or modify them. However, they do illustrate the approach and lead us to the next step, which is picking one or more of the forces (starting with restraining forces) and generating ideas for increasing or decreasing them. After alternatives have been evaluated, action plans can be designed and implemented.

The analysis can be carried out in as much detail as seems warranted by the problem. For complex issues with likely difficulties in implementation, it may be worthwhile to pursue force field analysis in great depth, with widespread participation. In other cases, it may be sufficient merely to outline the problem in the basic framework and move quickly to the tentative solution phase.

This approach to problem solving and action planning can be adapted to many organizational issues. Long-range planning can be addressed by considering goals for 5-year, 10-year, or longer periods. The long range varies according to the particular organizational situation. In any case, the forces can be identified and plans developed to increase driving forces and decrease restraining forces over whatever time span is appropriate. Comprehensive planning can be addressed by considering all the relevant dimensions for success, determining the forces involved, and developing action plans accordingly.

In this exercise, we will illustrate the method by dealing with only one example in each of the situations considered previously in the goal-setting exercise—personal and organizational.

PROCEDURE[1]

The steps involved in the following programmed process cover diagnosis and action planning. The problem-finding phase was initiated in the goal-setting exercise by your selection of specific dimensions to consider. In this exercise, you will need to narrow the process further and select one particular objective for detailed analysis. The control and follow-up phases will depend on the action plans that are developed in the course of completing the exercise, particularly the deadline(s) set with regard to specific results to be accomplished.

[1] Adapted from Saul Eisen, *A Problem-Solving Program,* Washington, D.C., NTL Institute for Applied Behavioral Science, 1969.

A: PERSONAL PROBLEM SOLVING AND ACTION PLANNING

STEP 1
Select one of the specific, relatively short-run objectives that you have listed in the goal-setting exercise (page 104) and write it below.

Objective: _____

STEP 2
Redefine the objective as a problem in terms of (*a*) current condition and (*b*) desired condition. Include as much detail or "flavor" as possible. Remember, a problem well defined is half solved.

a. Current condition:

b. Desired condition:

STEP 3

Using the force field framework, list as many (*a*) driving and (*b*) restraining forces as you can. Brainstorm; don't evaluate at this stage; push for quantity of ideas; we can check for quality later.

a. Driving forces:

b. Restraining forces:

STEP 4

Review the two lists and eliminate (cross out) those forces over which you have little or no control. Rank the others according to priority, noting with an asterisk (*) those factors or forces that are particularly important at this time for this problem. Typically, there will be at least one and maybe as many as three standout items.

STEP 5

For each restraining force that you have noted *, list as many actions as possible that could help to reduce or eliminate its effect. Push for quantity of ideas; don't evaluate at this stage; we will check for quality later.

a. Restraining force: _____

Possible action steps to reduce this force:

b. Restraining force: _____

Possible action steps to reduce this force:

c. Restraining force: _____

Possible action steps to reduce this force:

STEP 6

For each driving force that you have noted *, list as many actions as possible that could help to increase its effect. Push for quantity of ideas; don't evaluate at this stage; we will check for quality later.

a. Driving force: _____

Possible action steps to increase this force:

b. Driving force: _____

Possible action steps to increase this force:

c. Driving force: _____

Possible action steps to increase this force:

STEP 7

Now review all the possible action steps you have generated in Steps 5 and 6. Evaluate them for quality in terms of potential effectiveness and feasibility. Without getting too detailed, you can do a form of cost/benefit analysis for each action step. Note the most promising actions with an asterisk (*).

STEP 8

List each of the most promising action steps below and think about implementing them. In each case, indicate the resources needed—people, money, time, materials, etc. Are they available? If so, mark the action step with a check (√); if not, mark the action step with a dash (–) and note the discrepancy.

Action step   *Resources needed/available*

Action step   *Resources needed/available*

STEP 9

You now have some bits and pieces of a comprehensive, integrated plan for closing the gap between the current and desired conditions. Reflect on the potential action steps. Can resource-availability problems be solved readily? If so, specify how; if not, you may have to eliminate the potential action step, or at least give it a low priority. Do all the actions fit? Eliminate or adjust those that don't fit; add any that are needed to complete a comprehensive plan. Develop a time schedule for the sequence of action steps and establish deadlines for future reference and control.

STEP 10

You now have an action plan for achieving a specific objective (desired condition). How will you know when you've been successful? What measures of performance will you use? How will you follow up during the time period covered by this action plan? Write your answers to these questions in the space below.

STEP 11

Implement your plan and follow up.

B: ORGANIZATIONAL PROBLEM SOLVING AND ACTION PLANNING

This phase of the exercise should relate to an actual or hypothetical organization as defined in Part B of Exercise 7, Goal Setting: Personal and Organizational.

Name of organization: _____

STEP 1
Select one of the specific, relatively short-run objectives that you have identified in the goal-setting exercise (page 110) and write it below.

Objective: _____

STEP 2
Redefine the objective as a problem in terms of (*a*) current condition, and (*b*) desired condition. Include as much detail or "flavor" as possible. Remember, a problem well defined is half solved.

a. Current condition:

b. Desired condition:

STEP 3

Using the force field framework, list as many (*a*) driving and (*b*) restraining forces as you can. Brainstorm; don't evaluate at this stage; push for quantity of ideas; we can check for quality later.

a. Driving forces:

b. Restraining forces:

STEP 4

Review the two lists and eliminate (cross out) those forces over which you have little or no control. Rank the others according to priority, noting with an asterisk (*) those factors or forces that are particularly important at this time for this problem. Typically there will be at least one and maybe as many as three standout items.

STEP 5
For each restraining force that you have noted *, list as many actions as possible that could help to reduce or eliminate its effect. Push for quantity of ideas; don't evaluate at this stage; we will check for quality later.

a. Restraining force: _____
   Possible action steps to reduce this force:

b. Restraining force: _____
   Possible action steps to reduce this force:

c. Restraining force: _____
   Possible action steps to reduce this force:

STEP 6

For each driving force that you have noted *, list as many actions as possible that could help to increase its effect. Push for quantity of ideas; don't evaluate at this stage; we will check for quality later.

a. Driving force: _____

Possible action steps to increase this force:

b. Driving force: _____

Possible action steps to increase this force:

c. Driving force: _____

Possible action steps to increase this force:

STEP 7

Now review all the possible action steps you have generated in Steps 5 and 6. Evaluate them for quality in terms of potential effectiveness and feasibility. Without getting too detailed, you can do a form of cost/benefit analysis for each action step. Note the most promising actions with an asterisk (*).

STEP 8

List each of the most promising action steps below and think about implementing them. In each case, indicate the resources needed—people, money, time, materials, etc. Are they available? If so, mark the action step with a check (√); if not, mark the action step with a dash (−) and note the discrepancy.

Action step   *Resources needed/available*

Action step   *Resources needed/available*

STEP 9

You now have a number of bits and pieces of a comprehensive, integrated plan for closing the gap between the current and desired conditions. Reflect on the potential action steps. Can resource-availability problems be solved readily? If so, specify how; if not, you may have to eliminate the potential action step, or at least give it a low priority. Do all the actions fit? Eliminate or adjust those that don't fit; add any that are needed to complete a comprehensive plan. Develop a time schedule for the sequence of action steps and establish deadlines for future reference and control.

STEP 10

You now have an action plan for achieving a specific objective (desired condition). How will you know when you've been successful? What measures of performance will you use? How will you follow up during the time period covered by this action plan? Write your answers to these questions in the space below.

STEP 11

Implement your plan and follow up.

SUMMARY AND CONCEPTUALIZATION

This exercise, coupled with the earlier one on goal setting, has provided you with an opportunity to plan both personal and organizational activity. The first phase involves goal setting in order to determine the results to be achieved. We have emphasized the concept of a problem as a gap between current and desired conditions or actual and expected results. Recognition of such gaps touches off a problem-solving process that includes diagnosis and action planning. The diagnosis/analysis phase involves generating creative alternatives and evaluating them in order to determine the best course of action. Evaluation of tentative solutions includes anticipating potential consequences, determining the resources required to implement them, and developing an integrated approach that identifies personal or organizational responsibility, recognizes interdependence of individuals and subunits, and prescribes an appropriate sequence of activities.

You have experienced an explicit approach to problem solving and action planning. Force field analysis is a specific technique to facilitate change and improvement. It can be applied to both individual and organizational issues; it can be used in isolated problem-solving efforts or as part of an overall program of management by objectives and results. Obviously, there are numerous ways to solve problems, and many occasions call for simpler techniques. However, for complex issues it is important to use some framework which facilitates sufficient diagnosis prior to taking action.

In our view, one of the keys to success in individual and organizational endeavor is an ability to sense problems, to assign priorities to them, to work on high-priority, substantive issues (without wasting time and effort on minor, less relevant issues), and to follow up by checking actual against expected results. A variety of specific techniques may be used to good advantage when this overall process is the basis of managing.